To Katie and Jim
Who have followed the progress
of this work over many years—
and whose friendship has
meant so much for many more—
With all good wishes
Ken

The Avoidable War

Lord Robert Cecil

VOLUME 1

The Avoidable War

Lord Cecil & the Policy of Principle

1933-1935

J. Kenneth Brody

Transaction Publishers
New Brunswick (U.S.A.) and London (U.K.)

Library of Congress Catalog Number: 98-49011
ISBN: 1-56000-374-X (cloth); 0-7658-0498-0 (paper)
Printed in the United States of America

Library of Congress Cataloging-in-Publication Data

Brody, J. Kenneth.
    The avoidable war / J. Kenneth Brody.
        p. cm.
    Contents: v. 1. Lord Cecil and the policy of principle, 1933–1935
    Includes bibliographical references and index.
    ISBN 1-56000-374-X (v. 1 : cloth : alk. paper). — ISBN
0-7658-0498-0 (v. 1 : pbk. : alk. paper)
        1. Europe—Politics and government—1918–1945. 2. World War,
1939–1945—Causes.   3. World War, 1939–1945—Diplomatic history.
I. Title.
D727.B655   1999
940.5—dc21   98-49011
                                                                   CIP

For Alison

Who Shares My Enthusiasms

"We cannot say 'the past is past'
without surrendering the future."
—Winston S. Churchill

Contents

Acknowledgments   ix
Author's Note   xi

Prologue   1
1. A Noble Idea—A Noble Lord   7
2. A Separate Peace   15
3. Collective Security   27
4. Mussolini   33
5. Anglo-Saxon Attitudes   45
6. Adolf Hitler   61
7. Arms Control—1932   85
8. The German Challenge   99
9. France and the German Challenge   125
10. Britain and the German Challenge   141
11. Voting for Peace   173
12. An Abyssinian Incident   201
13. A Double Challenge   219
14. Stresa   263
15. Arms Control—1935   287
16. The Triumph of the Peace Ballot   317

Notes   345
Bibliography   373
Index   379

Acknowledgments

One of the most rewarding aspects of the creation of this history has been the generosity of eminent scholars who have reviewed the manuscript. Their commentaries, criticism, corrections, and suggestions have embellished and enriched this work and its companion volume. For all this, I extend my gratitude to the following: Professor Henderson Braddick of Lehigh University, Professor Bernard V. Burke of Portland State University, Professor Maurice Cowling of Cambridge University, Professor Gordon A. Craig of Stanford University, Professor George W. Egerton of the University of British Columbia, Professor John F. Naylor of the State University of New York at Buffalo, Professor Alberto Sbacci of Atlantic Union College, Professor Donald E. Shepardson of the University of Northern Iowa, and Professor Gerhard L. Weinberg of the University of North Carolina.

For their help and suggestions in a variety of contexts I am indebted to Professor Donald C. Birn of the State University of New York at Binghampton, Professor Martin Gilbert of Oxford University, Townsend W. Hoopes, and Professor Joachim Remak of the University of California at Santa Barbara.

My nonacademic reviewers were Arthur Levinson, Herbert W. Park, and Alfred H. Stoloff. Each made a signal contribution to the work.

I am deeply grateful to Richard Abel, longtime publisher and bookman, to Ambassador Walter J. P. Curley, and to Comte René de Chambrun, historian and history maker, for their indispensable help in achieving publication of this work.

Natasha Kern of the Natasha Kern Literacy Agency led me by the hand across the convoluted pathways of the publishing world.

Much of the work was done in the excellent facilities and with the help of the staff of the Portland State University Library. I am grateful, too, for the resources and help of the New York Public Library and the Sterling and Seeley Mudd Libraries at Yale.

The original manuscript was prepared by Joanne Castles. The revisions were done by Rebecca L. Peer. Their competence, patience and good humor kept the project on track and a continuing pleasure. The software wizardry and support of Richard E. Crall kept the manuscript apace with technical developments.

Grateful acknowledgment is made to the Public Record Office for permission to use extracts from British Cabinet papers and to H.M. Stationery Office for permission to use materials from Documents on British Foreign Policy, Second Series. Crown copyright, including material in the Public Record Office, is reproduced with the permission of the Controller of Her Majesty's Stationery Office. Extracts from its Survey of International Affairs for the years 1932, 1934, and 1935 and Documents on International Affairs for the years 1933 and 1935 are used by permission of Oxford University Press which is gratefully acknowledged.

The dedication of this volume and its companion record my heartfelt gratitude to my wife and daughter for their loving support and never failing encouragement.

Author's Note

Ethiopia is an African state with a long and colorful history. For much of that history it was known as Abyssinia. In the period covered by this book and its companion volume, both Ethiopia and Abyssinia were used but Abyssinia predominated. For clarity and uniformity, Abyssinia is used throughout this work except as required by direct quotation.

Prologue:
Three Years and Three Months

In January, 1933, the principal concern of the peoples and nations of the world was the great depression which held them in its cruel grip, bringing in its wake unemployment, economic dislocation, hunger, misery, and want. This in turn induced severe strains in all societies. The economic machinery seemed to have run down; why and how were fiercely debated, and whether and how it could be started up again were agonizing questions. The great powers of the world of January, 1933, were Great Britain and France. The British Empire incorporated a quarter of the world. It included continents like Australia and transcontinental nations like Canada. These were self-governing dominions like South Africa and New Zealand. The Indian subcontinent, the second-largest population mass in the world, was popularly referred to as the jewel in a crown which also ruled over vast territories in Africa, in Asia, and lesser possessions scattered across all the seas of the world.

The French Empire was the second largest of the world's empires. It dominated the southern shores of the Mediterranean from Libya to the Atlantic, vast areas of Saharan and Equatorial Africa, rich domains in Southeast Asia and, like the British Empire, islands and colonies that dotted the globe from the Americas to the Pacific.

If they were beset by the economic storms of the time, the citizens of Britain and of France could feel safe from any external threat of attack or aggression. They were the victors of 1918 and they had added to their estates the spoils of that victory, the former German colonies and the mandates and protectorates that had once been provinces of the Ottoman Empire. Having emerged victorious from cataclysmic struggles of the War of 1914–1918, they wrote their own

1

recipes for security into the Treaty of Versailles which presumed to close out the issues the war had raised.

For Britain, which the Kaiser's Germany had challenged for commercial and maritime supremacy, the naval challenge was ended. The High Seas Fleet lay deep under the waters of Scapa Flow, scuttled by its own crews. The Versailles Treaty expressly forbade to Germany the submarines which had nearly brought Britain to its knees in 1917–1918. Aerial attack was a new form of warfare which could overcome Britain's formerly splendid isolation from the continent and put its great cities at the risk of destruction. Germany was therefore forbidden by the Versailles Treaty to build or maintain an air force. The Royal Navy was Europe's largest, matched on the world scene only by an America which had largely isolated itself from international affairs.

For France, where elderly citizens remembered the German invasion of 1870 and all but the very young could remember, indeed could scarcely forget, the onslaught of 1914 and the four years of devastation that had occurred on French soil, Germany would always be a potential source of mortal peril. To address this peril the Versailles Treaty limited the German army to 100,000 long-service soldiers. That army was deprived of heavy artillery, tanks, and aircraft. In contrast France maintained a great army, generally thought to be the world's finest, and as powerful on the land as the Royal Navy was on the seas. To these forces were added the costly and complex defensive works of the Maginot Line.

But the most important protection afforded to France by the Versailles Treaty was the demilitarization of the Rhineland, the west bank of the Rhine which bordered on France and which opened the path to Germany's industrial heart in the Ruhr. Demilitarization meant that Germany could maintain no military force in the Rhineland, forestalling preparations for any attack on France and leaving open wide the door to Germany should Germany threaten a move to the East.

This limitation, which had been imposed by the Versailles Treaty, was voluntarily accepted by Germany in the 1924 Treaty of Locarno by which defeated Germany was again reintegrated into the European political and diplomatic system. Under this treaty both Britain and Italy guaranteed France and Germany against any attack by the other. The possibility of any such attack was drastically reduced by the demilitarization of the Rhineland.

If Germany was militarily impotent, its weaknesses ran far deeper. Its economic distress was as great as any nation's, its unemployment as high. The short-lived governments of Von Papen and Schleicher in late 1932 and early 1933 were incapable of forming a parliamentary majority and ruled by decree under the aged President and sometime Field Marshal, Paul Von Hindenburg. If there was disarray in government, there was riot in the streets, fierce melees among Communists, Socialists, and the storm troopers of Adolf Hitler whose Nazi party was now Germany's largest. These were lamentable conditions, but they contributed to the security of Great Britain and France.

There was in the world of January, 1933, another system of security. This was the League of Nations which had been born at Versailles. The Covenant of the League of Nations created an international organization and a process for dealing with international disputes including acts of aggression. It was believed by many that the League of Nations would replace the balance of power which had failed in 1914 plunging the world into a war few wanted and which might, if left to itself, inevitably lead to another arms race and another war.

The League of Nations was new, but in the years before 1933 it had been a repository of hope. It had successes to its credit even if it had not coped effectively in the matter of the Japanese adventure in Manchuria of 1931–1932.

If the people of Britain and France faced daunting economic, financial, and social challenges, at least they could feel able to address these problems in a world at peace, free from the threat of aggression and war.

Three years and three months later, this system of security was irreparably shattered. More than that, Britain and France had by March, 1936, plunged from the security of January, 1933, to the very brink of disaster. The disaster came in 1940 with the collapse of the Third Republic and German domination of the European continent leaving in the field only a weak Britain that was no match for the victorious Third Reich. It was a disaster from which Britain, France, and the world would ultimately be delivered only by the decision of Adolf Hitler to attack the Soviet Union in June, 1941, and to declare war on the United States in the aftermath of the December 7, 1941 Japanese attack on Pearl Harbor. That delivery would come only at a terrible price.

Three years and three months from military and naval dominance and comfortable security in January, 1933, to the brink of disaster in March, 1936. How could it happen?

In January, 1933, Adolf Hitler became Chancellor of Germany and immediately embarked upon an immense program of rearmament. It was the plainly pronounced goal of this program to unite all Germans in a Greater Germany which would become the dominant world power and would not hesitate to carve out vast new territories in the East, Poland and the Soviet Union, as the economic base for that power. All of this was accompanied by strident and hateful propaganda, racial persecution, and an attack on the humane values which Britain and France cherished and which Adolf Hitler scorned.

Nazi Germany proceeded methodically to violate each and every restraint of the Treaty of Versailles. It built an army based on new ideas and new materiel, the tank-fighter team and the doctrines of speed and penetration. Germany built a mighty air force which could attack its enemies and sow terror among their populations. It built a new navy and especially a submarine fleet which threatened to deny to Britain the means of sustenance which had to come from its overseas territories and friends. Most important, on March 7, 1936, backed by this new army and fledgling air force, German troops marched back into the demilitarized Rhineland and proceeded promptly to erect fortifications that slammed shut what had been an open door to Germany and to accelerate the military build-up which would give Germany the forces and the jumping off point for the 1940 attack on France and Belgium. The reoccupation would also deny to France in the Czech crisis of 1938 and in the war that began in 1939 any practical means of coming to the aid of its Eastern allies.

There was one other vital element of Adolf Hitler's program of aggression and hegemony. Shortly after the reoccupation of the Rhineland Adolf Hitler gained the ally he deemed indispensable, Italy.

This was a fatal reversal because it had been Italy's dictator, Benito Mussolini, who had early recognized the deadly peril of Adolf Hitler and Nazi Germany, who had defended Austrian independence, and who had urgently tried to unite Italy, France, and Britain in an alliance to contain the German threat.

In all of this Britain and France, fully informed of the danger, fully advised and aware of Adolf Hitler's every step in mounting his challenge, failed to respond or meaningfully react to Adolf Hitler's destruction of the military clauses of the Versailles Treaty. Indeed, Britain unilaterally abrogated the naval limitations by its 1935 treaty with Germany. At the most critical moment Britain and France failed to respond or react when Germany remilitarized the Rhineland, destroying what was left of French security.

And most perverse of all, Britain, over French objection, literally propelled an Italy which wished to be its partner and ally, into the waiting and welcoming arms of Adolf Hitler. This became the Rome-Berlin Axis.

Three years and three months. How could it happen that this treasure trove of national security was squandered away?

Britain and France were great nations and great powers. They were free societies, liberally endowed with a free press enhanced by all the modern media of communication. They were possessed of constitutional regimes, responsible and democratic institutions, and long traditions of freedom and human dignity, all of which contrasted sharply to the glaring barbarities and revolting ideologies of Nazi Germany.

Three years and three months. How could it happen?

Was it wickedness or deliberate evil that propelled the fall of empires? Was it ignorance or negligence that allowed these things to come to pass?

Or could it have been that the very virtues that adorned these societies—the love of peace, the hatred of war and aggression, an elevated morality—were heavy debits in this dismal accounting.

Did the fault lay with the leaders of either Great Britain or France, or both? Did they betray the trust and responsibility that their peoples reposed in them?

Or was it the people who failed their leaders or who would not support them in those courses of action which the leaders clearly saw as necessary? And was it on Britain or on France that the ultimate burden of responsibility lay?

In those three years and three months were sown the seeds that ripened into the monstrous harvest of death and destruction, the Holocaust, the human tragedies that were the Second World War and from which Britain and France emerged exhausted and diminished and very different from the great powers they had been in January, 1933.

If ever, Churchill said, there was an avoidable war, it was the Second World War. Why did Britain and France throw away chance after chance to contain the clear and present danger of Adolf Hitler and Nazi Germany and muddle and stumble their way to the brink of the abyss?

A careful study of the critical period from January, 1993 to March, 1936, three years and three months, will illuminate the reasons why.

1

A Noble Idea—A Noble Lord

> *"The truth is, I was never a very good Party man. Probably but for the War of 1914, I should have gone on fairly comfortably as a Conservative official. But those four years burnt into me the insufferable conditions of international relations which made war an acknowledged method—indeed, the only fully authorized method—of settling international disputes. Thenceforth, the effort to abolish war seemed to me, and still seems to me, the only political object worth while."*
>
> —Lord Robert Cecil[1]

A. J. Boorman

Mr. A. J. Boorman hardly intended, in January, 1934, to reverse the course of British foreign policy, or to alter the balance of forces in Europe among the dictatorships and democracies. Much less could he have intended to set into motion a chain of events that would five years later explode into the Second World War.

Mr. Boorman labored in modest obscurity as the editor of the *Ilford Recorder*, a local newspaper in a London suburb. He was a leading spirit in the Ilford branch of the League of Nations Union. Its members believed that collective security through the League of Nations was the only reasonable way to avoid a disaster beside which the Great War of 1914–1918 would pale in comparison and which would, quite literally, extinguish civilization. For them the preceding years had been painful.

Defying the League, Japan had invaded Manchuria in particularly lurid circumstances of sword and flame. It had defied the reprimand of the League of Nations and contemptuously resigned.

The Disarmament Conference, which had after ten years' preparation, convened in 1932 amid the hopes and prayers of all those who saw arms as the ultimate evil, was at a standstill. Germany was in the tightening grip of Adolf Hitler, a dictator whose ideas and actions shocked and repelled the British public. Worse still, in October, 1933, Nazi Germany had withdrawn from both the Disarmament Conference and the League of Nations.

Mr. Boorman wanted the authentic voice of the people to be heard. Surely the ultimate issues of war and peace, life and death, ought not to be left exclusively in the hands of the ministers, the diplomats, and the politicians. At least Ilford would be heard. He gathered together 500 volunteer workers and with his newspaper started the Ilford Poll, open to all residents over sixteen.[2]

These were the questions of the Ilford Poll and these were the responses:

	Yes Answers	No Answers
1. Should Great Britain remain in the League of Nations?	21,532	3,954
2. Should the Disarmament Conference continue?	20,472	4,960
3. Do you agree with the Locarno Treaty which binds Great Britain to go to the help of France or Germany if the one is attacked by the other?	5,898	18,498
4. Should the manufacture of armaments by private enterprise be prohibited?	20,415	4,819[3]

The poll showed overwhelming support for the League, for the Disarmament Conference and for a ban on the private manufacture of arms. The balloters were far from enthusiastic, however, about a treaty commitment to armed intervention on the European continent.

Mr. Boorman's Ilford trial balloon could have quickly faded and been forgotten—a small and rudimentary attempt at a public opinion poll in a suburban backwater. Instead, there took place the union of a man and an idea—the idea that public opinion, expressed in a public opinion poll, could influence and indeed direct national policy. The man was the one man whose whole life and thought had prepared him to seize the idea and carry it with matchless skill and devotion to the whole of Britain and, indeed, to the world. The consequences would be profound.

Lord Cecil

On February 8, 1934 the results of the Ilford ballot were announced at Ilford Town Hall by Lord Robert Cecil, President of Britain's League of Nations Union and British delegate to the Disarmament Conference. In that moment, Lord Cecil found, not his cause—he had discovered that years before—but his vehicle, the public opinion poll.

Lord Cecil's cause was as straightforward as it was grand—the abolition of war. Totally undaunted by the magnitude of the task, he had already achieved immense results. He had first proposed to the British Government those ideas which later became the League of Nations.[4] He had been the British delegate for League of Nations matters to the Peace Conference at Versailles. The intimate colleague of Woodrow Wilson, he was not merely present at the creation of the League of Nations. "Lord Cecil made the League of Nations," said Phillip Noel-Baker, its long time champion.[5] He had since given the League and world peace his entire attention.

What Lord Cecil grasped was the opportunity to reverse the decline of the League of Nations if only the British Government, which he loyally believed had unparalleled influence in world affairs, would champion the League as the dominant force in the conduct of international relations. This, he saw, might be achieved by a dramatic demonstration that this was the policy the British people wanted and indeed demanded.

Lord Cecil's qualifications for the task were formidable. At seventy, his intellect and vigor were undiminished. He was of course, a Cecil, a direct descendant of William Cecil, Baron Burghley (1520–1598), long chief minister to Queen Elizabeth. His father, the third Marquess of Salisbury, had served thrice as Queen Victoria's Prime

Minister. He was succeeded in 1902 by his nephew and Cecil's cousin, Arthur Balfour. The family was as colorful as it was large. James, the eldest son and fourth Marquess held many of the high offices of state over a long career. William was for more than twenty years Bishop of Exeter. Lord Robert Cecil was himself a middle child. His younger brother, Edward, soldiered in Africa, was present at those great Victorian set pieces, the defeat of the Mahdi at Omdurman in 1898 and the siege at Mafeking, journeyed through Abyssinian fastnesses on a diplomatic mission to the Emperor Menelik II, and served for many years as a colonial administrator in the Sudan and Egypt. Hugh became Provost of Eton and was created Baron Quickswood by Churchill in 1940, as Churchill informed him "to sustain aristocratic morale, and to chide the bishops when they err."

Of the sisters, Maud married the Earl of Selborne and Gwendolyn lived out her life at Hatfield House and was her father's industrious biographer.

At Hatfield House, among the stateliest of stately homes, Lord Cecil passed his youth amid memories of Gladstone and Disraeli. When the German Kaiser came to visit, they sat down sixty to dinner, and the Prince and Princess of Wales were relegated to the west wing. The Cecils were aristocratic, but not fashionable. Lady Salisbury advised yellow soap and lots of water for the complexion and entertained the Royal Family in grey woolen stockings and her gardening shoes.

Each day began with prayers. Christianity was a creed to be lived, the undisputed basis of life.[6] The boys were taught mathematics, geology, history, French, Latin, and Greek by private tutors until at twelve they were sent off to Eton.

Oxford, the Bar and Parliament marked Cecil's predestined ascent into public life. With the coming of the World War, he became Minister for Blockade in the Foreign Office. He served as deputy to Balfour, who was then Foreign Secretary, and he often attended the War Cabinet. In 1919 Cecil was Chairman of the Allied Supreme Economic Council.

At the Versailles Peace Conference, Wilson said Cecil had taken the laboring oar in the League of Nations Commission and that it was chiefly due to him that the Covenant emerged in its integrity.[7]

In the 1920s and early 1930s, Cecil was frequently a delegate to the League of Nations and "never enjoyed anything more."[8] He was League of Nations Minister in Stanley Baldwin's first two cabinets. He busied himself with settling a Greek-Italian dispute in Corfu, establishing the border between Mesopotamia and Turkey, investigating slavery in Liberia, and devising improvements to the Covenant and the machinery of the League of Nations.[9]

Deeply religious, he always favored state support of the established churches and the teaching of religion in the schools. In 1938, in the midst of a great international crisis, at the invitation of his lifelong friend, the Archbishop of Canterbury, he became chairman of a commission to study the relationship of church and state.[10] The real basis of peace, he thought, was religion, and Christian doctrine and Christian morality were essential in opposing the appeal to arms. But at the same time, his religion was personal and direct; he saw little need for an intermediary between a Cecil and his God.

His concept of religion called not only for contemplation, but for action. After hearing a sermon at St. Paul's in 1921 on moral responsibility, he mused,"I have a great feeling that I have been 'called' to preach the League spirit in public affairs and there seems so much in the Bible about that sort of thing."[11]

What was remarkable about Cecil was that this product of the British ruling class at its apogee was a natural rebel. He didn't like Eton, where he failed to observe the rules of dress and propriety, hated sports, and wouldn't properly roll his umbrella. "In a word, I was a scug."[12] He tried to reform Oxford and the system of legal education, but there were no signs of success.[13]

As a young man he went to Paris and found it noisy and blatant. He went to Ascot once, decided he didn't like racing and never went again.[14] He hated evening parties.

He found lasting happiness in his marriage to Lady Eleanor Lambton, daughter of the Earl of Durham, though her nine brothers were as hearty and athletic as Cecil was studious. "Their moral position," he complained, "is that of an Eton boy."[15]

Lord Cecil was born a commoner though as a peer's younger son he bore the courtesy title Lord Robert Cecil. He had no great means, earned his living at the bar, and gave a seventh of that to charity. "We live," his wife wrote, "in very middle class professional circles. I feel a fish out of water in the country houses of my relations."[16]

He not only carried on but improved the family tradition of disinterest in dress. "If you cannot dress like a gentleman," the Archbishop of Canterbury, who had a greater feeling for the ceremonial effect of costume, advised him, "I think you might at least try and dress like a Conservative."[17]

A French visitor to the House of Commons was pithier. Spying Lord Cecil, he exclaimed, "Voila! Enfin de vrai ouvrier."[18]

As a barrister, one of his achievements was the Poor Prisoners Defense Act, passed in 1903 on the basis of his proposals. He entered politics as a Tory, but didn't like it.

He was, he said himself, an uncomfortable colleague and, in cabinet office, was perennially on the brink of resignation. He had resigned from the Cabinet in 1918 over disestablishment of the Welsh church, hardly an earthshaking issue.[19] In 1927 he was British delegate to the Washington Naval Conference where, their late enemies having been disarmed, the principal adversaries were Britain and the United States. The Americans thought fifty cruisers sufficient and looking across the Pacific to Japan, opted for heavier calibers of guns. The British Cabinet, to guard Britain's far flung sea-lanes, wanted more cruisers, seventy, with lighter guns. Cecil could not agree. To him, this was "a clear issue between a policy of peace and a policy of prestige in a particularly indefensible form."[20] He resigned, as publicly as possible, and the Conference failed to reach agreement. A resignation is an act of principle, but it leaves the problem to be solved by those who remain.

Cecil nurtured a deep suspicion against all bureaucrats, distrusted the military and harbored the conviction that the politicians and the soldiers were in perennial combination to frustrate the will of the people. They thought war was a normal method of conducting affairs and resented public intrusion into their domains, especially when the public didn't agree with them. Cecil thought that education and communications had changed the world and that the people would no longer allow kings, ministers, and admirals to be the arbiters of their destinies.

Such thoughts did not prevent Lord Cecil, when he wearied of the House of Commons, from seeking a seat in the House of Lords. His great interests lay, not in day-to-day political life, but in the League of Nations. Party and personal considerations had become secondary.[21] He applied for a peerage as other men might apply for membership in a lodge or fraternal order. His brother, the Marquess, intervened on his behalf lest he be made "a mere baron" and in 1923 he was duly created Viscount Cecil of Chelwood, by King George V.[22]

If war were to be abolished, it became clear to Cecil that the matter must be taken out of the hands of the establishment and placed directly in the hands of the people.

From its start in 1918, Cecil cultivated his popular base in the League of Nations Union, which by 1933 had a nominal membership of a million. He knew the value of giving people a part to play and developed and perfected the arts of pressure and persuasion—of lobbying and letter-writing campaigns, pamphlets, questionnaires, mass meetings, and deputations.[23]

For years this tall, stooped septuagenarian who wore the wing collar and cravat of a British statesmen, and who was a true scion of the ruling class, had prepared himself and his allies for the ultimate assault on that class—the transfer of effective and direct power to the people.

The Peace Ballot

At Ilford, the Peace Ballot was born. On March 1, 1934, three weeks after the Ilford results were announced, Lord Cecil proposed to the Executive Committee of the League of Nations Union a national poll on issues of war and peace. He moved as swiftly and effectively as he had in bringing the Covenant of the League of Nations into being. An organizing committee was formed on March 19, 1934, which convened a conference of interested parties on March 27.[24]

Delegates came to the conference from representative national bodies, from the political parties, the churches, peace societies, women's organizations, and cooperative guilds, from all who loved peace and honored principle. A draft of questions was produced, a plan adopted, and an executive committee—the National Declaration Committee—was established. The chairman of this committee was Lord Cecil.[25]

By April 11, 1934, the committee had before it a detailed plan of campaign, submitted by its Chairman, and proceeded to draft the five questions that would be put to the British public. They finally emerged in this form:

1. Should Great Britain remain a member of the League of Nations?
2. Are you in favor of an all-round reduction of armaments by international agreement?
3. Are you in favor of the all-round abolition of national and military aircraft by international agreement?

4. Should the manufacture and sale of armaments for private profit be prohibited by international agreement?
5. Do you consider that, if a nation insists on attacking another, the other nations should combine to compel it to stop by:
    a)   Economic and non-military measures?
    b)   If necessary, military measures?[26]

The questions were framed as broad statements of principle. In this respect, question 5 differed sharply from the specific Ilford question of a commitment to use armed force to repel aggression on the European continent. This was deliberate.[27]

The program, the literature, the lists of cooperating societies were all presented to a meeting of the League of Nations Union Council at Bournemouth in June, 1934. There the decision was taken to go forward.[28]

The organizers thought a half million responses would represent real success. They could hardly have foreseen the fervent appeal of the Peace Ballot to the British public or the avalanche of votes that would pour in before the final results were announced in June, 1935. Much less could they have envisioned the remarkable, indeed the decisive role the Peace Ballot would play in answering the critical question then facing the world: whether Hitler's Germany would be halted in its march to hegemony—and war.

2

A Separate Peace

*"Scratch the surface of any problem at the Con-
ference. . . and you get to French security."*
—Professor Thomas A. Bailey[1]

Peace Aims

Any consideration of how the Second World War started is rooted
in how the First World War ended. On May 1, 1917, when the outcome of the war was far from certain, Lord Cecil addressed the issues
of peace. He proposed that the peace terms should include an international conference to decide disputes between nations, a three months
cooling-off period, and economic sanctions to enforce the terms of
settlement. The conference and cooling-off period reflected the desire
to avoid the powder train of events that had led to war in 1914.
Economic sanctions were rooted in Cecil's experience as Minister of
Blockade.

The British government referred Cecil's proposals to the Phillimore
Committee; its report in March, 1918 included a draft convention for a
League of Nations.[2]

Lloyd George announced Britain's war aims on January 5, 1918.
He wanted to restore the sanctity of treaties and called for an international organization to limit arms. He disclaimed a desire to destroy
Germany or break up Austria-Hungary, but said the peace settlement
should be based upon the self-determination of peoples.[3]

Three days later, President Wilson enunciated his Fourteen Points
as America's program for the peace settlement. There were to be open
covenants, openly arrived at, putting an end to the evil of secret diplo-

macy. Freedom of the seas, disarmament, and an association of nations to keep the peace were fundamental. The territorial settlements should be based upon the principle of national self-determination.[4]

Germany, which had recently not only defeated but dismembered Russia at the Treaty of Brest-Litovsk, was quick to see the advantages of the Fourteen Points in preserving Germany against just such a peace. With its armies rebuffed in the great offensives of March and June, 1918, and grimly retreating to the German border, Germany asked for an armistice and peace negotiations based on the Fourteen Points.[5] Wilson, who had in various pronouncements altered and limited them to some degree, consulted his allies and answered in the affirmative on November 6, 1918.[6]

Clemenceau instinctively perceived the danger the Fourteen Points held for France. Germany would remain incomparably larger and stronger than France, drained by the losses and exertions of victory. He would not ask that more French blood be shed if peace could be had on those terms.[7] But France must be made secure and to France security meant occupation of the left bank of the Rhine. France also demanded reparations for the war damage and losses she had suffered, and a reference to reparations was included in the terms of the Armistice which was signed November 11, 1918.[8] This was only an armistice. It remained to make peace.

The Allies, united in war, had very different agendas for peace. To France, the realities were stark and clear. She had lost two million sons and could never again afford such a bloodletting. Her northern departments, rich in agriculture and industry, had been laid waste both by the operations of war and by the systematic and deliberate destruction of the German retreat.

To America and Britain, the nationality principle was a generous ideal. To France, it was a mortal peril which, in the hour of victory, would turn the balance disastrously in favor of defeated Germany. There were 40 million Frenchmen, 65 million Germans. Germany would no longer be bounded by the once great Russian and Austro-Hungarian Empires. Her neighbors to the East would henceforth be Poland, Czechoslovakia, and Hungary, small, weak states containing large German-speaking minorities, and to the South the German-speaking remnant of Austria. Indeed, the nationality principle that had doomed Austria-Hungary made Germany incomparably the largest population bloc and strongest economic power on the continent.

The French view was blunt, pessimistic, and never wavered. Germany would never accept defeat and would, at the earliest possible moment, fall upon France to reverse the verdict of 1918. The vision of the field—gray hordes marching across the Rhine into martyred France defined the French goal—security against the next war in which France would be doomed.

Marshal Foch, the Allied Supreme Commander and author of victory, defined France's needs on January 10, 1919.[9] The Kaiser had gone, but Germany, he warned, would remain militarist. France must have a secure border and that border was the Rhine. This could be achieved by detaching the Rhineland from Germany and making it an independent entity. Allied possession of the Rhine bridgeheads would leave Germany undefended and would prevent a new German invasion of France. The League of Nations, as yet unborn, must have a military force to protect France; there must be reparations to compensate for the damage done to France; and France must have special accords with Germany's new Eastern neighbors to provide for the common defense. All this sat ill with Woodrow Wilson who objected root and branch to the proposal to detach the Rhineland from Germany as a violation of his principle of self-determination. He thought a League military force would only replace national militarism with international militarism.

Britain felt secure. The surrender and ultimate scuttling of the German High Seas Fleet that had dealt so harshly with the Royal Navy at Jutland, was the crown of British victory. German maritime and colonial threats were simply eliminated. Henceforth, if there were to be a continental rival, it might be victorious France. Far from wishing to dismember Germany, Lloyd George instinctively feared leaving Germans outside Germany's borders, yearning for reunion.

Italy's goal was simple. It was the territorial aggrandizement in the Italian provinces of Austria, on the Adriatic, in the Eastern Mediterranean, and in Africa that she had been promised in the secret treaty of Rome in 1915 which had detached her from the Triple Alliance with Germany and Austria and brought her into the war as an Allied power. Her bitter disappointment at the ultimate dispositions at Versailles caused violent problems at the Peace Conference and poisoned Italy's relations with her former allies thereafter.

The aims of the United States were not so clear and seemed embodied in the character and outlook of Woodrow Wilson. The Fourteen

Points were laudable expressions of an ideal; translating them into a durable peace settlement was quite another thing. Wilson thought that if only these principles were set firmly in place, and if the League of Nations superseded the balance of power as the mechanism of international relations, the practical questions would be worked out by experience. "If it won't work," Wilson grandly said "it must be made to work."[9a]

"There are American principles, American policies," Wilson declared. "We stand for no others. They are the principles of mankind and must prevail."[10] He wanted the League of Nations to be "the organizing moral force of men throughout the world."[11] "A great wind of moral force is moving through the world," he told an audience at the Sorbonne on December 21, 1918 "and every man who opposes himself to that wind will go down in disgrace."[12]

"I am an old Presbyterian," he told Lord Cecil[13]; he was, too, a son of the manse to whom the Covenant was an inspired name for the charter of the League of Nations.

Wilson stood for the destruction of arbitrary power. Power would be wielded by "the opinion of mankind" and he suffered no doubt as to what that opinion might be. He had only to consult himself. It did not occur to him that the nationality principle might be the seedbed of future conflicts. There would be peace as long as all mankind endorsed Wilsonian precepts. His tumultuous welcome as Europe's savior might well have convinced him that they did.

Clemenceau was seventy-eight and his memory was as long as his experience. An independent Poland was not to him a novel idea. "In 1848 at Nantes, I had seen the Poles set off in arms for the conquest of their country."[14] He had witnessed the American Civil War and the debacle of 1870 of which the ruins of the Palace of St. Cloud, smoking at German hands, were a symbol. To him, Wilson was the inspired prophet of a noble ideological venture, armed with insufficient knowledge of European realities, who did his best "in circumstances the origins of which escaped him and whose ulterior developments lay beyond his ken."[15] Of the Wilsonian program he commented: "There are probably few examples of such a misreading and disregarding of political experience in the maelstrom of abstract thought."[16] John Maynard Keynes, who attended the Peace Conference, observed, "Never had a philosopher such weapons wherewith to bind the Princes of the world." To this his colleague Harold Nicholson added, "He did not use these weapons. He was not (the slow realization of this was painful to us), a philosopher. He was only a prophet."[17]

Drafting the Covenant

The early drafts of the Covenant of the League of Nations by Wilson and his intimate advisor, Colonel House, matched closely Cecil's own draft. Cecil and House headed British and American teams that harmonized the two into an Anglo-American draft.[18] The League of Nations Commission considered the Covenant in regular sessions from February 3 to February 14, 1919.

France had a plan very different from the Anglo-American plan. It was a clear and logical embodiment of the French view as Foch had expounded it.[19] It provided the League of Nations with an international tribunal, the judgments of which would be enforced by an international military force under a permanent staff. An international council would be in effect the executive of the League. Security, not debate, was the French goal. But try as they might, with clarity and passion, the French representatives saw their amendments go down to continuing defeat. This was agonizing for Clemenceau, who bitterly described,

> Lord Robert Cecil, a Christian who believes and is fain to live his belief, with a smile like a Chinese dragon and a stubborn mind, banged, bolted and barred against argument.[20]

The Covenant which emerged on February 14, 1919 was essentially the Anglo-American document. It was adopted by the Peace Conference on February 29, 1919, to become an integral part of the Peace Treaty. This was Wilson's wish, to insure, as he thought, adoption by the American Senate.

In presenting the Covenant, Wilson gave vent to his powers of eloquence. "A living thing is born," he proclaimed.[21] It had the deepest of meanings—"The union of wills in a common purpose, a union of wills which cannot be resisted and which, I dare say, no nation will run the risk of attempting to resist."[22] And should the attempt be made, he was confident that it would fail,

> because through this instrument we are depending primarily and chiefly upon one great force, and this is the moral force of the public opinion of

the world—the pleasing and compelling influence of publicity so that the intrigues can no longer have their coverts, so that the design that is sinister can at any time be drawn into the open, so that those things that are destroyed by the light can be promptly destroyed by the overwhelming light of the universal expression of the condemnation of the world.[23]

To Wilson, the principles of the Covenant were what mattered most. France looked beyond the principles to the hard cases of enforcement. Wilson had prevailed. He had his Covenant. It remained to make the peace.

Having secured the adoption of the Covenant, Wilson returned to the United States on February 18, 1919, leaving House with the warning to be on the lookout for French schemes.[24] Other warnings greeted Wilson after his arrival. Thirty-nine senators had signed a round-robin letter declaring the Covenant unacceptable as it then stood. Many thought the Covenant should be set aside till the Peace Treaty had been signed.[25]

Wilson's Democratic allies in the Senate advised him that the necessary votes for the Covenant could be had if amendments addressed these critical issues: control over domestic matters, acknowledgment of the Monroe Doctrine, and a provision for withdrawal from the League.[26] Former President Taft, representing many Republicans, concurred, suggesting similar reservations which might insure acceptance.[27]

What concerned many senators was Article 10 of the Covenant which bound League members "to respect and preserve as against external aggression the territorial integrity and existing political independence of all Members of the League." Did this mean the United States was obligated to go to war at any time in any place at the League's behest contrary to the provisions of the Constitution?[28]

Wilson would have preferred to let the Covenant stand. In meetings on March 17 and March 18, House and Cecil prevailed upon him to accept a series of amendments to meet many of the objections which had been raised. These Wilson adopted, put before the reconvened League of Nations Commission, and loyally promoted. The amended Covenant was adopted on April 29, 1919.[29]

On another point, however, Wilson was adamant:

Gentlemen on this side will find the Covenant not only in it, but so many threads of the treaties tied to the Covenant that you cannot dissect the Covenant from the treaty without destroying the whole vital situation.[30]

The Treaty of Guaranty

During Wilson's absence, the French pressed their view that only a Rhine border could protect France. No principle of self-determination, Clemenceau said, allowed an antagonist to clutch at your throat the first time it was convenient to him.[31] Lloyd George and House understood France's need for security, but Lloyd George was fearful of the effect of an Allied occupation of the west bank of the Rhine and had no desire to commit British troops there. France persisted:

> To ask us to give up occupation, is like asking England and the United States to sink their fleet of battleships. We refuse.[32]

By March 12, Lloyd George had concluded that it would be necessary to offer France meaningful assurance of British support if Germany attacked France.[33]

On Wilson's return to France on March 14, Lloyd George made clear to him the gravity of the situation now at impasse. He explained a guaranty he had proposed in discussions with House. They met Clemenceau the same afternoon.[34] Wilson had a treaty, a League and a Covenant to gain and he did not hesitate:

> There will be neither the establishment of an independent Rhine state on the left bank nor occupation of the line of the Rhine, but America and England will sign with France a treaty by which they will engage themselves to support France with all their forces if Germany makes an unprovoked attack on France.[35]

Stunned, Clemenceau could only ask for time to reflect. In three days of deliberation, the French reviewed positions they had previously prepared, concluding that Germany would evade any disarmament limitations, and that neither the League nor allies could come swiftly enough to its aid in case of attack. These were intangible guarantees. The only guaranty on which France could rely was the tangible guaranty—occupation of the left bank of the Rhine.

"It really is not possible," the French reply of March 17, 1919 said, "for France to give up a certain safeguard for the sake of expectations."

Nonetheless, the French reply offered "possible bases of agreement" for giving up the Rhine border: the date and conditions of the evacuation of the Rhineland after allied military occupation would be set in the Peace Treaty, the Rhineland would be permanently demilitarized under the eyes of a Franco-British-American commission of inspection, and Britain and the United States would agree to consider as an act of aggression any entry or attempted entry by all or any part of the German army into the demilitarized zone.[36]

On March 27, 1919, Britain and the United States agreed and embodied their agreement in a note to Clemenceau on March 28th.[37] But Clemenceau, in the Council of Four once more submitted a formal request for the Rhine border.[38]

This was too much for Woodrow Wilson. In early April he threatened to go home. On April 14, Clemenceau told Wilson that France would accept a fifteen-year occupation of the Rhineland combined with a Treaty of Guaranty.[39] Two Treaties of Guaranty were in fact signed on June 28, 1919—one between France and Britain and one between France and the United States.[40] Wilson thought for political reasons that it would be more difficult to gain Senate ratification of a U.S. guaranty involving Great Britain. On the same day, the Treaty of Versailles was signed. It contained as Articles 42 and 43 provisions giving France the security of a permanently demilitarized Rhineland.[41]

"The Guaranty Pact," said Clemenceau "assumed the position of the keystone of European peace, far above theories."[42] To him, it was more meaningful than the Versailles Treaty.

The Treaty of Guaranty was swiftly and unanimously approved in the House of Commons on July 21, 1919. This was an unusual step; Parliament was not usually consulted on treaties. But Lord Curzon said that "No government would desire to ratify a treaty of this tremendous importance unless they knew it would be approved by Parliament, and the. . . general public opinion.[43]

A Separate Peace

It now remained for Wilson to secure the approval of the two treaties by the United States Senate. On July 10, 1919 he presented the Treaty of Versailles to the Senate. He waited to present the Treaty of Guaranty until July 29, 1919, after the Senate had passed a joint resolution asking that it be placed before them. Wilson felt confident; there was a tide of public opinion in favor of the treaties which might well have resulted in their approval had prompt action been taken. But

Massachusetts Senator Henry Cabot Lodge scheduled a series of hearings that delayed consideration and further embroiled the issues.

When Wilson testified before the Senate on August 19, 1919, he reminded the senators that he had asked for questions in March and had honored the Senate by securing amendments to the Covenant and to the Treaty in the sense they had asked.

The principal issue before the Senate involved the operation of Article 10 of the Covenant and what it meant.

Simply stated, the question was whether the League of Nations could commit the United States to war in defense of the Covenant. Wilson responded that the obligation was moral, not legal; that the League could only advise; that a unanimous League vote was needed; and that the rights of Congress were safeguarded.

Nevertheless, the Treaty was reported to the Senate on September 10, 1919 with forty-five amendments and four reservations. Wilson responded by taking his case directly to the people on a speaking tour of 8,000 miles and thirty-seven speeches in twenty-two days.

His exertions were too great. Wilson collapsed and suffered a stroke on October 2, 1919. The Treaty came before the Senate with fourteen reservations. It is important to review the principal reservations:

In case of withdrawal from the League, the United States would be the sole judge of its international obligations;

There should be no military obligation without the consent of Congress;

The United States should accept no territorial mandate without the consent of Congress;

Congress should reserve the right to determine what were domestic affairs—as, for instance, labor, immigration, tariffs and commerce;

The Monroe Doctrine should stand outside the League of Nations;

There should be no interference with American imports or exports by a Reparations Commission without Congressional assent;

There should be no financial contribution to the League without Congressional consent;

There should be no limitation of armaments without the consent the Congress;

The United States reserved its right to permit nationals of a Covenant-breaking state resident in the United States to continue commercial, financial and personal relationships with nationals of the United States;

The United States should have as many votes as any empire member of the League and its self- governing dominions or colonies;

And finally, there was a resolution of sympathy for the aspirations to self-determination of the Irish people.[44]

The wrongs of Ireland and suspicion of the British Empire were venerable American political credos and tested vote-getters. The other reservations were deeply rooted in the political institution that is the United States Congress. The men who composed the Senate had for the most part been born in the middle of the nineteenth century. They were only a few generations removed from the Founding Fathers, in an age when the separation of the United States from the world was a plain physical as well as spiritual fact. In considering participation in a League of Nations, it was only natural that Congress should seek jealously to preserve its own prerogatives in making war, in the appropriation of funds, and in making domestic law. This was a fundamental position, which time has not altered but often confirmed.

It was not the case that the reservations would have nullified effective American participation in the League. But Wilson did not, would not, or perhaps could not understand a sincere desire both to adhere to the Covenant and to respect the fundamental structure of American government as seen from within by members of the Senate.

Wilson insisted on the Treaty without reservations. On November 19, 1919 it was submitted to Senate vote. Without reservations, it failed to obtain the necessary two-thirds vote. With reservations, it was defeated by the votes of Wilson's own loyal supporters.[45]

Wilson was urged to compromise and to extend the olive branch to Senator Lodge. Let Lodge extend the olive branch was Wilson's reply.[46] He remained adamant. From his sickbed he cried out to Lord Cecil: "We are winning; don't make any concessions."[47]

The final vote on the Treaty, including the reservations, took place on March 19, 1920. Forty-nine senators voted aye and thirty-five nay. Had twenty-three Wilson Democrats, under instructions from the President to vote against the Treaty, voted in favor of it, it would have passed by the necessary two-thirds.[48] Wilson was adamant. Had the Treaty passed with the reservations, he would, he said, have refused to sign it.[49]

The evening of the final vote, Wilson remarked to Admiral Grayson: "Doctor, the devil is a busy man." He sought the consolation of religion and asked Grayson to read to him chapter 4, verses 8 and 9 of Second Corinthians: "We are troubled on every side, yet not distressed; we are perplexed but not in despair; persecuted but not forsaken; cast down but not destroyed."[50]

Curiously, the Treaty of Guaranty never aroused the hostility of the

Senate. Senator Lodge thought that it would help keep Germany in check and that France deserved protection against a repetition of her sufferings. But the Treaty was never presented to the Senate for its action. It languished on a shelf in the State Department until one day in 1935 an archivist sent it back to the Senate.

Wilson declined to sign a separate peace with Germany. That is what President Harding did on August 25, 1921. The Treaty between the United States and Germany accorded to the United States all of the benefits and none of the burdens of the Treaty of Versailles.[51] America had gone to war alongside its Allies, but had signed a separate peace.

Since the American and British Treaties of Guaranty were dependent upon mutual ratification, Great Britain was not reluctant to withdraw its own ratification. All this was a mortal blow to France. She had given up the tangible guaranty of the Rhine border for the intangible guaranty of a treaty. Now that guaranty had been snatched from her grasp.

France had no guaranties. Worse, Germany had its grievances: loss of territory, reparations, disarmament, and war guilt, all as part of a treaty which had been imposed rather than negotiated. These were, in German eyes, grave injustices. But the supreme injustice to Germany was defeat itself.

In Germany, the thesis was industriously propounded that an undefeated Germany had been lured into the armistice by the Fourteen Points only to be subjected to a dictated, punitive peace in which the spirit and the letter of the Fourteen Points were conspicuously lacking.

Clemenceau was haunted by the thought that Germany and Austria would combine on the theory of self-determination, adding to France's disadvantage. "America is far away and protected by the ocean. England could not be reached by Napoleon himself," he had told his colleagues at the Peace Conference. "You are sheltered, both of you; we are not." He was haunted, too, by his vision of Germany "Their idea of justice, I assure you is not ours."[52]

He had said that the Treaty of Guaranty was to be the keystone of European peace, far above theories. To this he added: "Its rejection, for that very reason, amounted to an indirect invitation to the thwarted aggressor to try again."[53]

France judged that Clemenceau had not faithfully guarded its security. His ministry fell on January 20, 1920.

3

Collective Security

*"I do not, therefore, believe that we can imme-
diately and finally destroy all possibility of war;
but I do believe that in practice and as a practical matter, public opinion, properly organized
and properly applied, is strong enough to safeguard the peace of the world and to prevent
international aggression. The League of Nations
is based on that assumption."*
—Lord Cecil[1]

The Meaning of the League of Nations

When the *Official History of the Peace Ballot* was written in 1935,
its objects were stated as follows. First, to demonstrate that the British
people were behind the policy of making the League of Nations a
cardinal point in Great Britain's policy. Second, to influence peace
movements in other countries. Third, an educational purpose: "to place
before the public the real issue—namely, what exactly is involved in
Great Britain being a member of the League of Nations."[2]

What it meant for Great Britain or any other state to be a member of
the League of Nations was far from self-evident when the League first
convened in 1920 and indeed in the years that followed. The task of
translating the Fourteen Points into the practical dispositions of the
Peace Treaty had been difficult enough. The task of translating the
Covenant of the League of Nations into a working system of international relations proved harder still.

At the first Assembly, Canada wished to suppress entirely Article
10, guaranteeing the independence and territorial integrity of member

states and Article 16, providing for sanctions against Covenant breakers. The Scandinavian countries wanted exemption from the automatic application of sanctions.[3]

Italy needed economic growth and access to raw materials. These Italian aspirations were rebuffed; they survived and grew to have a disastrous effect on the fate of the League.

Italy noted that the principle of unanimity would condemn the League to impotence, since it would nullify Article 19 providing for revision of the Peace Treaties as circumstances changed. This had been Wilson's theoretical solution to the practical problems of the future.

In response to discomfort with the rigid and automatic application of sanctions against Covenant breakers, a resolution was adopted in the 1921 Assembly that sanctions should be applied gradually and partially, and that the decision to apply them should be entrusted to the League Council. The resolution did not become legally binding for want of unanimity when France refused to ratify it; but it was accepted as authoritative then and when the time came to apply sanctions.[4]

At the 1923 Assembly a declaration was adopted that although the League could call upon its members to make their armed forces available to halt aggressors, in every case, the final decision must be left with the individual members. Again, a unanimous vote failed; the principle stood.[5]

The League had, of course, no military force as France had wished. Lord Cecil approved. He told the Imperial Conference in 1923 that the League's "method is not . . . .the method of coercive government; it is a method of consent and its executive instrument is not force, but public opinion."[6]

There was never a more ardent supporter of the League than Professor Gilbert Murray. He pointed out one could hardly expect Siam or Canada to mobilize because one Balkan state had attacked another. As to Russian suppression of the independence of Georgia, he was troubled by the thought of an attempt to cure a small evil by engaging in a larger evil, a European war.[7]

France and Great Britain

These were fundamental problems for the fledgling League. Amidst all this, France pursued her unwavering goal of security against the next German attack. If the League could not protect her, she must protect herself. This she proceeded to do by pressing for the rigid enforcement as against a disarmed Germany of the status quo established by the Peace Treaties; by ringing Germany's Eastern borders with allies and client states; and by insisting on the maximum of reparations which would make Germany weaker and France stronger.

Britain, feeling secure, viewed the League as an organ of conciliation rather than coercion. Perhaps out of traditional sympathy for the underdog, Britain adopted a generous policy toward defeated and disarmed Germany. On the issue of reparations, Britain and France quickly found themselves antagonists.

The Peace Treaties had established the principle of reparations, but no fixed sum. This was finally determined by the Reparation Commission on April 27, 1921 over German dissent at $33 billion. From here it was all downhill as Germany, aided by Great Britain, waged a successful struggle to lower the bill. Lloyd George said at the Cannes Conference in January, 1922 that Germany was unable to pay. The Germans naturally agreed. Dispute became more bitter when, on the grounds of German failure to meet certain payments, French troops occupied the Ruhr until they finally found that British opposition and German intransigence made the occupation unprofitable. Germany preferred inflation and financial ruin to paying reparations and when she finally yielded, the whole subject had to be reviewed. Thus came into being the Dawes Commission, presided over by the American General, Charles Gates Dawes. To Clemenceau this was the ultimate in Anglo-Saxon ingratitude and presumption—to find the United States, which had not ratified the Peace Treaty and which had dishonored the hard-bargained-for Treaty of Guaranty, in league with Britain to determine the amount of reparations owed by Germany for damage done to France.[8] Inevitably, the Dawes Commission produced a plan for substantial reduction of German obligations.

Prime Minister Stanley Baldwin thought a stable, disarmed Germany would be a good customer for Britain. As his biographer, G.M. Young noted, "When France was thinking of her debt, Baldwin was thinking of the unemployed."[9] Ramsay MacDonald, Leader of the Labour Party, who alternated with Baldwin as Prime Minister in the 1920s and 1930s, was more critical. France was trying to crush Germany "not for her own security, but in order ultimately to dominate Europe."[10] Inevitably, in British eyes France was becoming the villain and Germany the victim.

The Locarno Formula

The problem of Germany continued to be the crux of the problem of European security. Lord Cecil, ever prolific, drafted a Treaty of Mutual Assistance calling for obligatory armed response to aggression; but this was promptly denounced by the first British Labour Government as too militaristic. The Geneva Protocol, which also had Lord Cecil's blessing, was an attempt to install compulsory arbitration of international disputes likely to lead to war. This was approved by Labour and in its turn disavowed by the Conservative Government which followed.

The parties finally achieved a measure of agreement in the Treaty of Locarno negotiated for Britain by its Foreign Secretary, Sir Austen Chamberlain, whose reward was the Nobel Peace Prize and by Gustav Streseman, the German Foreign Minister. This was a mutual guaranty by Britain and Italy of the French-German-Belgian border against attack whether by Germany against France or vice versa. The guaranty was also extended to the demilitarized zone of the Rhineland. Thus, Germany voluntarily agreed to the demilitarization that had been imposed by Articles 42 and 43 of the Versailles Treaty. Germany was then to join the League of Nations with a permanent seat on the Council.

France had obtained a British guaranty against German attack, but there was a price. No similar arrangement was made for Germany's eastern borders. Sir Austen Chamberlain said that Britain would not risk the bones of a single British grenadier for the Polish corridor. Clemenceau noted contemptuously that France and Germany had renounced war in the Locarno Treaty but not Britain, that the Treaty seemed to say that France and Belgium were as likely to make war as Germany, and that Germany had clearly not given up hope of revising her Eastern frontiers.[11] Lord Cecil naturally opposed the Treaty on the ground that it was a special arrangement which diminished the authority of the League of Nations.[12]

But Locarno seemed at the time to solve the basic problem of Germany's role in postwar Europe and ushered in a period of hope. As Sir Robert Vansittart, later Permanent Undersecretary of the British Foreign Office, remarked in another context, there were those who always felt better when statesmen gathered and signed something.[13]

More Recipes for Peace

There were more documents to sign. The conviction grew that there could be drafted a document which would solve any clash of nations if only the proper words of art could be found. The Kellogg-Briand Pact of 1927 was a solemn renunciation of war by the contracting parties, who in the end numbered almost all of the nations of the globe. "C'est magnifique" was a French reaction "mais ce n'est pas paix." Briand won the Nobel Peace Prize, too.

The General Act for the Pacific Settlement of International Disputes assembled a veritable buffet of formulae for dispute resolution including conciliation, arbitration, and submission to the Permanent Court of International Justice. Like any buffet, it allowed the signatories to take or reject any items on the menu. Ultimately, Belgium, Norway, Denmark, Finland, Holland, and Sweden accepted all or some of the General Settlement; but none of them was likely to threaten world peace.

German Aims and Arms

The proliferation of schemes to enforce peace didn't alter German aims which were as consistent as France's. In negotiating Locarno, one of Streseman's aims had been to keep open the opportunity to revise Germany's eastern border. The army was more precise. In 1926, General Stuelpnagel offered these policy aims to the German Foreign Ministry.

1. The liberation of the Rhineland and the Saar.
2. The abolition of the Polish corridor, regaining Upper Silesia.
3. Anschluss with Austria.
4. Abolition of the demilitarized zone.

Such aims it was noted would mean an inevitable clash with Britain and America, but only after the Franco-German problem had been solved "through either peace or war."[14]

Naturally the Germans envisioned rearmament. They bitterly accused their former enemies of having failed to observe the general disarmament called for in Article 8 of the Covenant. Not that Germany intended to observe that clause. Her programs for training troops and producing arms above Treaty limits, and her expanding military budgets were well known to the Allied Control Commission and its governments.

But treaty observance was gradually relaxed. The Young Commission of 1930 further reduced German reparation obligations, most of which had been paid by American loans. The occupation of the Rhineland, scheduled to last until 1935, was terminated in 1930. That one act, Vansittart observed, permitted Hitler to come to power.[15] None of these steps voluntarily removing the disabilities of the peace settlement evoked much German gratitude. To the contrary, as preparations were underway for the great Disarmament Conference to be held in 1932, Germany had in practice set the agenda—equality of arms for Germany.

The League Spirit

It was easy to overlook, in the buoyant atmosphere of the League in its first decade, that the peace schemes might not prove practical and that Germany remained a problem. The League had produced hope, oratory, formulae for peace, and a great deal of nonpolitical social work that has stood the test of time.

It seemed invidious to question the League spirit and somehow damaging to suggest that the League could not find the solution to any international crisis. After all, as Gilbert Murray said, "The whole enterprise of the League is a great adventure, and an adventure based upon a great Repentance."[16]

Anthony Eden would one day become the League's beau ideal. But in 1926 he worried that human nature could not be changed in a year or two, nor could the passions of nations. "It must take time," he observed, "More harm has been done to the League by people with their heads in the clouds and their brains in their slippers than by the most inveterate enemy the League ever had."[17]

4

Mussolini

> *"Mussolini has the brilliant qualities of the ex-*
> *temporizer and none of the scruples of those*
> *who, convinced of an idea, fear to be false to*
> *it. . . . His mind, given to excessive simplifica-*
> *tion, is bound by no formula; he can pass from*
> *theory to theory, from position to position, rap-*
> *idly, even inconsistently, with neither remorse*
> *nor regret. In this game he has one constant*
> *aim—to lay hold of the elements of imagination*
> *and sentiment that make for success"*
> —A contemporary judgment[1]

Mussolini at Locarno

When the diplomats assembled at Locarno, Switzerland in October, 1925, the most dramatic entrance was made by the Italian Prime Minister, Benito Mussolini. He travelled by special train from Rome to Milan, by racing car to Stresa, and thence across Lake Maggiore to Locarno by speedboat. He expected the tumultuous welcome that would have been organized for him in Italy. But this was Switzerland and the Swiss took a more skeptical view of Fascism and its creator.

Worse still, Mussolini had announced a conference for the day following his arrival at which he would meet the world press. With only two exceptions, the journalists, in a united protest against the violence and brutality of the Fascist regime, boycotted the conference, leaving Mussolini and his large retinue to face an empty conference room. Mussolini's own paper, *Popolo d'Italia*, duly reported on Mussolini's impressive presentation to an enthusiastic audience.[2]

Mussolini had decided only at the last moment to attend the conference and he was present at only one session. He later explained to the
Italian Senate why it had been important for Italy to become a Locarno
guarantor. If she had not, Italy would have no part in an agreement
constituting the basis of relations among the great powers of Europe
and Italy would have lost a chance to put herself on an equal footing
with Great Britain in a memorable event.[3]

Mussolini's motivation at Locarno was not the pursuit of peace
through a Franco-German rapprochement and a Franco-German renunciation of war. Nor was it to advance the cause of conciliation, nor
to enhance the role of the League of Nations of which Germany would
now become a member. Even less was it to confer legitimacy on the
democratic government of Germany.

What concerned Mussolini were power and prestige. Mussolini was
the mirror opposite of Woodrow Wilson. He had literally no program
and was unencumbered by principles. Fascism, he said, was not a
system of beliefs but a path to power.[4] Mussolini denied that there was
any moral basis for policy. Only success counted.

Unlike the statesmen at Geneva who cultivated the League spirit
and who drafted ingenious texts to insure the peaceful settlement of
international disputes, unlike the members of the League of Nations
Union to whom peace was a sacred cause and disarmament its
handmaiden, Mussolini had no dread of war. He rather liked the idea.

He would make Italy a great military power and "create in the
laboratory a new generation of warriors ready at any moment to lay
down their lives." Italians must consider themselves to be "in a permanent state of war." He would fill the sky with airplanes. He detested
"peacemongering." The aim of all this was to create a mighty empire
and to win power and glory, indeed "a century of Italian power."
These were large aims for a country as poor and as undeveloped as
Italy.[5]

Mussolini rejected the democratic and liberal assumptions which
Britain and America thought had triumphed over autocracy in 1918.
He proudly pronounced that fascism was antidemocratic, antiparliamentary and antiliberal: "We have buried the old democratic, liberal,
agnostic and paralytic state—buried with a third-class funeral."[6]

Shortly after the Locarno Conference, Mussolini was given a new
title and a new office. No longer simply Prime Minister, he became
"Head of Government."[7] He could legislate without Parliamentary con-

sent and Parliament could consider a matter only if invited to do so by the Head of State. His grip on Italy was becoming absolute.[8]

Young Mussolini

Mussolini had come to absolute power from humble origins. He was born July 29, 1883 outside the small village of Predappio in the Romagna. His mother was a schoolteacher, his father a blacksmith, an ardent socialist and sometime town counselor. Both his father and grandfather were rebels who had gone to prison for their political beliefs.[9]

Early life was simple. Black bread and soup were the staples of Mussolini's diet; but there were always books in the home. He was a surly and uncooperative student who was expelled from his school at Faenza. After six years, he completed his course at Forlimpopoli and gained a teacher's certificate.

After the academic year 1901–1902 spent as a substitute teacher in Gualtieri, Mussolini went to Switzerland. It may have been a nineteen year old's desire to see the world, to reach out beyond his family, perhaps to evade debts, including his rent at Gualtieri. Certainly he avoided the military draft. He became a casual laborer and at times a tramp. He worked in a chocolate factory, on construction jobs, as a butcher's boy, and for a wine merchant. He disliked regular work. He went hungry, slept under bridges, warmed himself in the public lavatory, was reduced to begging, and was arrested as a vagrant.

At the same time, he pursued his natural interests in self-education and political agitation. He read omnivorously, attended lectures, and studied German and French. He wrote articles for a Socialist newspaper and became secretary of a building laborers' union.

His views were violent. He preached terrorism, mob violence, revolution, the abolition of Parliament, and the expropriation of the ruling class. The Swiss authorities did not take kindly to these distinctly un-Swiss notions. He was arrested as an agitator in Berne and then at Lausanne, expelled from Switzerland in July, 1903, and turned over to the Italian police.

Liable for military training, Mussolini fled back to Switzerland, fraudulently altering his passport to gain entry. He traveled in France, walked to Paris where he lived by telling fortunes, then visited Germany and Austria. In Italy he had been tried in absentia and found guilty of desertion. Meanwhile he was expelled by several Swiss cantons.

In 1905, Mussolini took advantage of an amnesty to return to Italy where he completed eighteen months' military service. He then drifted through a series of teaching posts, his contract never renewed. Home again in Predappio, he went to prison for threatening physical violence in a farm workers' strike.

He remained a radical, but of what persuasion his changeableness made it hard to define. The essence remained the same: no cooperation with existing legal and governmental structures; bloody revolution instead. He learned early and believed late in violence as the basic political tool.

Political Evolution

In 1909, Mussolini was in Austrian Trieste as editor of a Socialist newspaper. In a short stay of seven months he was often arrested, he was imprisoned and his paper was confiscated.[10]

Expelled from Austria, he became a Socialist organizer and editor at Forli. Here he sharpened his skills as a journalist and continued his assault on the Parliamentary system and his dedication to violence as the solution to the problems of society. He was an inveterate anticlerical, so there was no thought of marriage in 1910 when he set up his household with Rachele, daughter of his father's mistress. He wrote pulp novels to support his family.

At the Socialist Party congress in Milan in 1910, Mussolini took the most extreme position, condemning social reform and universal suffrage as inadequate to the necessary changes. He violently opposed the Italian conquest of Libya in 1910 and again went to prison for his attempts to organize an insurrection against the war.

In 1912, he again led the extremist faction at the Socialist party congress where his oratory, fierce as his ideas, won him a respectful hearing. At twenty-nine he became editor of the chief Socialist newspaper, *Avanti*. He now had a broad new public for his uncompromising program of revolutionary Socialism. He found outlets for his abundant energies with his assistant editor, Angelica Balabanoff, an educated, strong-minded, Socialist intellectual and with Margarita Sarfati, his art critic. They were far from being the only other women in Mussolini's life.

When the World War broke out in 1914, Mussolini preached neutrality. Proletarians, he said, should not only refuse to fight in a capitalist war, but should rise up in rebellion if called on to participate.

But Mussolini now had another vision. Neutralism would not regain for Italy the Italian-speaking provinces of Austria. It would not advance the cause of revolutionary Socialism. Great events were afoot and "only blood makes the wheels of history turn."

On October 18, 1914, Mussolini, without consulting his *Avanti* colleagues, wrote that his neutral stance had been wrong and that Italy and his party ought not to stand aside as mere spectators of a world at war.

For this offense, Mussolini was forced to resign his editorship and expelled from the Socialist Party. He promptly founded his own paper, *Popolo d'Italia*. He still claimed to be a hardline Socialist; his claims were compromised by the financial support he received from foreign countries, including England and France, and from Italian industrialists—all of whom had a stake in Italian participation in the war on the Allied side.

He had begun as an antiimperialist who decried colonies as a war aim. But, on the eve of Italy's entrance into the war, he perceived broader vistas—not only Trieste, Fiume, and the Alpine provinces, but now expansion into the Balkans and the Middle East.

He ardently promoted Italian intervention in the war and still counseled insurrection—not against war, but to force the government to join it. When Italy went to war, Mussolini served as a private soldier and then as a noncommissioned officer. Wounded in a grenade explosion during a training exercise, he returned to the editorial chair of *Popolo d'Italia* and the enormous Italian defeat at Caporetto. It was consistent with his antiparliamentary tack to conclude that only a dictator could rally the nation to victory.

Mussolini brought a new word back from the front, "trincerocrazia"—trenchocracy. It was a word awaiting a meaning. To Mussolini it meant the climate of opinion of the fighting forces who would one day return to civilian life. Whether that opinion was left or right, socialist or capitalist, parliamentary or antiparliamentary, mattered little to Mussolini who wanted to capture the support of this mass.

His paper's program promised something to everyone—an eight hour day, land for the peasants, a share in industrial profits for the workers.[11] He went a step further and publicly embraced capitalism.

He justified the change, saying that every intelligent man must change his views; and he found that giving up the pretense of being a Socialist afforded him a sense of genuine relief.

Fascism

When peace came in 1918, Italy was among the victors, but not among the satisfied. In Italian eyes, the promises of external expansion contained in the Treaty of Rome had not been kept, especially the promise to Italy of equitable compensation from the former German colonies. Mussolini saw the League of Nations as an Anglo-Saxon conspiracy thwarting Italian ambitions.[12]

Mussolini was now an experienced, able journalist and a veteran political agitator. If he was no longer a Socialist, two things remained unchanged: his contempt for parliamentary government and his dedication to violence as a political tool.

Chaos and confusion pervaded the Italian government and economy. Mussolini perceived that parliamentary government in Italy was vulnerable to firmness and force.

He founded the Fascist Party in Milan on March 23, 1919.[13] *Popolo d'Italia* launched a broad array of ideas for the new movement: in politics, decentralized government and freedom of speech and ideas, in economics, the eight hour day, a minimum wage, land for peasants, expropriation of factories, and confiscation of war profits and church property.[14] That some of these programs, like decentralization and freedom of speech and thought, were startlingly incompatible with latter-day Fascism caused little problem to Mussolini who later cheerfully admitted that he had no program.[15] His aim instead was to cut across lines of party and class, to appeal to all interests, and to build a mass movement which would carry him to power.

His success came not from ideas but from armed force. He organized the Arditi, restless war veterans with well-developed skills of intimidation and violence. He evened scores with *Avanti* on April 15, 1919 when the Arditi attacked and destroyed its presses and subscriber lists.[16] He learned that his victims were slow and inept in resisting physical force and that the police were not always prompt to intervene.

The hundreds of Arditi he now recruited formed the base of a private army that would soon number hundreds of thousands and place immense power in Mussolini's hands.

The election of November 19, 1919 was disaster for the new party. All of its candidates, who included an unlikely Arturo Toscanini, were defeated.[17] The Socialists became the largest party, thoroughly alarming the propertied classes. In the elections of 1921, Mussolini allied the Fascist Party with the Liberals and the Nationalists. His contribution to the campaign was unprecedented violence by the Fascist squads. His reward was thirty-five seats in Parliament, including one for himself.[18] In Parliament, Fascist violence continued, Fascist deputies brandishing weapons and expelling Socialist deputies with seeming impunity.[19]

Once in Parliament, Mussolini made another turnabout, offering a coalition with the Socialists, which temporarily cost him Fascist party leadership at the hands of his outraged lieutenants.[20] It was then that he explained that Fascism was a "superrelativist" movement with no fixed beliefs, no final principles, ready for any accommodation which would bring it to power.[21]

In the end it was armed force that brought Mussolini and Fascism to power. He continually challenged weak governments with violence and insurrection. When the Socialists proclaimed a general strike in August, 1922, the Fascists destroyed Socialist presses and offices and gained credit by helping to keep public services running. The collapse of the strike was a Fascist victory.[22]

By October, the Fascist leadership felt strong enough to consider a general insurrection against the government. This was postponed[23] but Mussolini was in a position to negotiate with Salandra, the opposition leader, demanding the resignation of Prime Minister Luigi Facta, and five cabinet seats for the Fascists.[24] On October 24, 1922, Mussolini declared that the negotiations had failed. He told a mass meeting in Naples "either we will be allowed to govern or we will seize power by marching on Rome."[25]

On October 27–28, Fascist squads began to occupy telephone exchanges in Government offices in Rome. The Government, which had declined to declare martial law, now advised the King to call out the army to crush the insurrection. He accepted this advice, and the army moved promptly against the Fascists. Th next morning, however the King had a change of heart and mind. Abandoning his constitutional duty, he declined to sign the martial law decree to which he had earlier assented.[26]

The Prime Minister was now forced to resign in favor of Salandra, who invited Mussolini to join his ministry. Mussolini declined. He had armed force behind him; the army and police stood aside. Why should he take a subordinate role? Salandra withdrew and advised the King to call for Mussolini. This time the King accepted the advice. On October 29, 1922, Mussolini became Prime Minister of Italy. He was thirty-nine and only twenty years before he had slept in a packing case and begged for bread in the streets of Lausanne.[27]

As to the famous March on Rome which took place the day after, Mussolini had already been asked to form a ministry, the number of marchers was modest, and the march took place by courtesy of the army. From this scant material, Mussolini created a legend.[28]

The victorious Fascists behaved with their usual violence, administering Fascist medicine—castor oil—to their opponents, pillaging and ransacking their homes and businesses, burning books, settling private scores, and in the end, simply murdering numbers of their foes.[29]

Yet the public seemed pleased. Perhaps anarchy and disorder would be replaced by calm and discipline. Mussolini was moderate at the outset. His first Government contained a minority of Fascist ministers. He himself became Foreign Minister as well as Prime Minister. At the outset he sought not to overthrow the constitution but to work with it.[30]

The next step was to consolidate power.

Mussolini in Power

There was no force in Italian public life to oppose Mussolini. His instinctive recourse was to violence. Three members of Parliament were killed and more than fifty assaulted; the castor oil was now mixed with gasoline.[31] He obtained full powers for a year[32] and in July, 1923 secured passage of a law giving two-thirds of the seats in Parliament to the party which obtained a quarter of the vote.[33] This was not enough for Mussolini. In the election of 1924, opposition journals were destroyed, provincial and town officials dismissed and replaced with compliant Fascists. The Fascists gained an unsurprising 65 percent of the vote.[34]

There was still opposition, led by the deputy Giacomo Matteotti. His murder at Fascist hands was a crisis for the regime and there were those who felt that the end of Fascism was at hand.[35]

Mussolini wavered; he even considered an accommodation with the

Socialists. He was always an opportunist and his Socialist roots ran deep. But in the end, he counterattacked. He dominated Parliament and in his speech of January 3, 1925, he took full responsibility and announced he would put Italy to rights. The opposition collapsed.[36]

Mussolini now declared to the Fascist Party Congress of June, 1925 that liberalism was at an end, that Italy would be wholly Fascist, that Fascist illegality would be legal and that Fascist discipline would prevail. He became Head of Government December 24, 1925 with full powers.[37]

A series of laws in December, 1925 and January, 1926 subordinated all parties, organizations, institutions, and associations to the state, permitted instant dismissal of Government employees, regulated the press, abolished local government and regulated unions.[38]

In 1928 Parliament was dissolved. The new Parliament was to be 100 percent Fascist.[39] All this met with public approval. In the elections of 1929[40] and 1934 the vote for Mussolini was all but unanimous.[41]

Mussolini brought formidable skills to the task of government. As a journalist, he wrote swiftly, easily, and forcefully. He was always an actor playing different roles to different audiences in different seasons. Consistency of principle is not required of an actor, but only to impress and please the audience. In any case, he was convinced that the public was uninterested in ideas. Unable to rule themselves, they wanted only to be ruled and left in peace.

Could a dictator be loved? the German biographer, Emil Ludwig, asked Mussolini. "Yes," Mussolini replied, "provided that the masses fear him at the same time. The crowd loves strong men. The crowd is like a woman."[42]

Like his Roman predecessors, he knew the value of bread and circuses. He cultivated rituals, ceremonies, spectacles. "One must always know how to strike the imagination of the public; that is the real secret of how to govern."[43] His formula was to keep the people interested, not to worry or disillusion them and to keep them in anticipation of a great event.

Once, in his editorial days he had said:

> I put my finger on the pulse of the masses and suddenly discovered in the general mood of disorientation that a public opinion was waiting for me and I first had to make it recognize me through my newspaper.[44]

He was a gambler. He believed in his star.[45] He wanted to be seen as in control of events, but he had a streak of fatalism. Nothing was permanent. "Yesterday was yesterday," he told Margarita Sarfatti. "Today is today."[46] He believed in action, action for action's sake even when it was wrong. Action took the place of policy and principles.

He made an impression on the world. When King George V visited Rome in 1925 he conferred on Mussolini the Order of the Bath.[47] Winston Churchill met Mussolini and was impressed.[48] Nicholas Murray Butler, President of Columbia University, pacifist and winner of a Nobel Peace Prize, visited Mussolini in 1934 and praised his peaceful attitudes and Rome's unrivaled intellectual activity. Indeed, he thought that under Mussolini, Rome might again become the capital of the Western world and unify it in a mutual peace-loving state.[49] By this time the evidence to the contrary was impressive.

Underneath it all was the blacksmith's son whose table etiquette was an embarrassment and whose style of dress reflected peasant dreams of glory. He took up spats and a wing collar and could be seen wearing yellow shoes with evening dress. He gave up bowler hats when he noticed that in American movies, which he adored, only Laurel and Hardy seemed to wear them.[50]

His family stayed in Milan. He lived alone in Rome, first in hotels, then in a bachelor apartment where his meals could be sent up to him. The Duce dined alone in modest restaurants. He was abstemious, little interested in food or drink and said ten minutes a day were as much as anyone should spend in eating. Not unsurprisingly, he suffered from gastric ailments.[51]

In 1925 he finally married Rachele in a religious ceremony. His anticlerical views were overcome by reasons of state.[52] But it was only several years after becoming Prime Minister that Mussolini moved his wife and family, which now numbered five children, to the Villa Torlonia in Rome. There they lived a relatively simple life. When Edda, the eldest daughter, became engaged to Galeazzo Ciano, the prospect of inviting her fiancé and his parents, the Count and Countess Costanzo Ciano, to a simple dinner caused near panic in the Mussolini household.[53]

Mussolini was basically uninterested in money. His passion was to project his image as a universal man, as aviator, racing car driver, equestrian, sportsman, playwright, man of culture, and above all as a decisive, and as time passed, infallible leader. By 1933, after more than ten years of power, he could say that "contradiction only raises doubts in my mind and diverts me from what I know to be the right path whereas my own animal instincts are always right."[54]

Beneath the public facade of supreme ego and self-confidence, there lurked doubt and hesitation and in the end the fatalism, which were to mark his major policy decisions for himself and for Italy.

5

Anglo-Saxon Attitudes

*"Whatever his faults may be the Anglo-Saxon
is without any doubt whatsoever the kindliest
creature in the world. To me, who has lived
abroad as much as I have, this is particularly
apparent."*

—Sir Nevile Henderson[1]

Looking Back

As the 1920s merged into the 1930s, the Great War began to appear
in a new light to the British people. It was no longer quite so clear that
the war had been solely caused by the deliberate will of the German
Kaiser and his fellow Prussian Junkers. The diplomatic archives were
opened and scholars began to see patterns of misunderstanding and
mischance acting and reacting upon the system of treaties and alliances which had divided Europe into two opposing camps. Responsibility seemed less clean-cut, more shared. If there was a real culprit, it
was the balance of power operated by secret diplomacy.

If this were true, then the thesis of German war guilt which had
been written into the Peace Treaty began to look dubious. The Kaiser
now appeared as a mild-looking old gentleman chopping wood at his
estate in Doorn in that most peaceful of countries, Holland. The fiercely
upturned black mustaches had become a trim white beard not unlike
that of his cousin, George V, and the full dress uniform had become a
modest lounge suit. In same age John D. Rockefeller metamorphosed
from a robber baron to an ageless philanthropist.

If Germany was not guilty, then what was to be said about reparations? John Maynard Keynes had taught that they were ruinous and prudent Englishmen accepted this up to the day of the final default.

The territorial dispositions of the Peace Treaty caused uneasiness. In 1919, the Austrians wanted nothing more than to join Germany in a single German state. The Treaty permanently forbade this obvious exercise in self-determination. Czechoslovakia contained more minorities than Czechs and throughout Central and Eastern Europe there were unhappy minorities and irredentist ambitions.

In turn, such feelings distracted from the luster of the Fourteen Points and Keynes argued, as did many other English critics, that Germany had been lured into the Armistice on fraudulent misrepresentations. Naturally, the Germans agreed.

Worse still, it began to be argued that the peace settlement, which had emerged from a cloud of elevated principles was in many respects plainly immoral; and as the argument, rightly or wrongly, gained a hearing in various quarters, the moral authority of the peace settlement suffered precipitously.

George Lansbury, veteran British Labour leader, expressed it this way:

No one thinks of Clemenceau, Lloyd George and Wilson as more wicked than the average. They were all extremely short-sighted and stupid in imagining that it would be possible to secure peace through such muddle-headed proceedings as they engaged in. 'Muddleheaded' because they must have completely lost their heads if they believed it would be possible to secure peace with any nations possessed of self-respect by the imposition of a treaty built upon punishment and vengeance.[2]

All of this resulted in immense sympathy for Germany which crossed party lines. The *London Times* never ceased to plead the German case. The Conservative, Phillip Kerr, later Lord Lothian, and Clifford Allen, Socialist and pacifist, united in bewailing the injustice to Germany.

Underlying the sympathy was a persistent sense of guilt. Whatever might go wrong, there could always be found in Britain a vocal faction that concluded the fault was Britain's. Thus, to George Lansbury, who stood for unilateral disarmament, the responsibility was clear:

It is common knowledge that the first German Republic was destroyed because the victorious allies, drunk with the fear of the consequences which followed the imposition of their imposed penal peace, were afraid to follow up the disarmament of the defeated peoples by disarming themselves, which, according to their pledged word, they were bound to do.[3]

The French suffered from no such sense of guilt. They did not view the Weimar Republic with the enthusiasm of its British admirers. To the French, exchanging spiked helmets for silk hats was not likely to change the hearts and minds of the German leaders.

There were skeptics in Britain too. Sir Robert Vansittart said, "Strong contingents of Britons always praise the country most likely to attack them."[4] On further reflection he added: "Our electors were pro-German, not because they liked Germans, but because they did not know any."[5]

If the balance of power was evil, so was nationalism. Signor Mussolini had his admirers, many of them in England, but his brand of nationalism was noisy and offensive. Racial and ethnic antagonisms still simmered in Central and Eastern Europe; the Germans never took Poland seriously and the Poles responded by ill-treating their minorities. Tariffs and passports hindered British trade and British travelers.

Capitalism was suspect. As depression gripped Europe in the early 1930s, the capitalist system lost credibility and legitimacy. Worse still, it was fundamental Marxist logic that capitalism was itself the prime cause of war and that imperialist war was the last stage of the capitalist collapse. The advent of the Soviet Union removed Marxism from the coffee houses and classrooms to the world of international relations. One did not have to be a Communist to believe, as many respectable Socialists did, that the roots of war lay in the profit motive. This was consistent with the new importance of economics in explaining how the world worked.

More suspect than nationalism and capitalism were arms themselves. Many found in them the ultimate evil. Lord Cecil remarked that to say arms didn't lead to war was like saying alcohol didn't lead to drunkenness.[6] The Covenant of the League of Nations had contained as Article 8 a stricture against the private manufacture of arms thereby linking twin evils—arms and the profit motive.[7]

If arms were evil, then the possessors were suspect. France had arms; Germany didn't. From this one could conclude, and many did, that evil lurked in France and not in Germany. Lloyd George felt this way: "The immense land armaments of France are a glaring and arrogant breach of the undertakings of Versailles."[8]

This did not surprise Vansittart who observed, "Normally the British think no evil of neighbors unless they are allies."[9]

The British people looked cheerlessly at the practical impact of the last war. In the wake of industrial strife that culminated in the General Strike of 1926, and especially as the depression spread across Britain, the numbers of unemployed swelled and business and industry became stagnant, there were many who saw in all these the disastrous consequences of the war.

But to the British public, the searing losses were human. Britain alone lost 702,000 dead and it seemed that no victory could compensate such a sacrifice. If French losses of 1,327,000 and German losses of 2,300,000 were not only absolutely but proportionately far greater, these were hardly arguments to comfort the bereaved. Moreover, in a country whose ruling class was as small and tightly knit as England's, the impact was recognized to be all the more devastating.

Most of the leaders of government and opinion in postwar Britain had suffered personal losses that deeply affected their outlook. Asquith, Prime Minister from 1910 to 1916, lost a son who was widely recognized as among the most promising of his generation. Bonar Law, Prime Minister in 1922–23, lost two of his four sons and Stanley Baldwin and Neville Chamberlain lost cousins to whom they were deeply attached. Arthur Henderson, Foreign Secretary in Labour Governments, lost a son on the Somme; Anthony Eden, Foreign Secretary to be, lost two brothers, one at sixteen at Jutland. The Cecils were childless; of the ten grandchildren of his father, five perished. Vansittart's brother, to whom he dedicated his major poetic work, was killed on the Western Front.

All of the leaders of Britain in the 1920s and 1930s could vividly recall their schoolmates and companions cut down in their youth and their experience was mirrored in homes across the length and breadth of Britain.

When the British public looked back at the war through the war books that began to flow from the presses in the late 1920s and early 1930s, it all looked very different from the war of Old Bill and the First Hundred Thousand. Robert Graves' *Goodbye to All That*, Siegfried Sassoon's *Memoirs of George Sherston,* and R.C. Sheriff's, *Journey's End* presented reality as their authors had lived it and raised the question of what cause could justify the terrors and the indignities they described.

Even more influential was Erich Maria Remarque's *All Quiet on the Western Front* because the idealism and self-sacrifice there portrayed were not those of Prussian militarists but of decent, trusting, loyal

German youths with whom the Anglo-Saxon public could readily identify and deeply sympathize.

To the generation which had lived through the war, and especially
to those who had fought in it, it became increasingly difficult to see
what had been gained to compensate for all that had been lost. Perhaps
Norman Angell had been right: war simply wasn't worth it.

This was the judgment of an eminent authority. Professor Arnold J.
Toynbee, while preparing his monumental comparative analysis of
human civilization which appeared as *A Study of History*, was also
immersed in the contemporary scene. Each year he wrote for the Royal
Institute of International Affairs a copious, brilliant, and readable volume reporting and commenting on the events of the year past.

"The war of 1914–1918," Toynbee declared, "had really demonstrated that war itself has ceased to be a tolerable or practical instrument of change in human affairs."[10]

Looking Ahead

The prospect of another war on the scale and fought with the weapons of 1914–1918 was sobering enough for the British public. It was
when they looked ahead that they perceived an incomparably more
blood-chilling, heart-stopping, mind-shattering spectacle. The next war
would not be like 1914–1918. Aerial bombing and poison gas haunted
the imagination. Neither was limited to the battlefield; both could be
employed indiscriminately against civilian masses. The specter stalked
the public mind of London and Paris destroyed in hours, of the inde-
scribable agonies of chemical warfare, and of war brought home to
every habitation and every living thing.

Winston Churchill was, like Arnold Toynbee, a practicing historian
but his vision, as early as 1929, was more vivid. The ending of the war
in 1918, he said, had hidden but only temporarily, the new weapons of
destruction that awaited their time. Whole populations would take part
in the next war. Governments would use any means at their disposal
and these would include "agencies and processes of destruction, wholesale, unlimited, and, perhaps once launched, uncontrollable." He concluded:

> Mankind has never been in this position before. Without having improved
> appreciably in virtue or enjoying wiser guidance, it has got into its hands

for the first time the tools by which it can unfailingly accomplish its own extermination. That is the point in human destinies to which all the glories and toils of men have at last led them. They would do well to pause and ponder upon their new responsibilities. Death stands at attention, obedient, expectant, ready to shear away the peoples en masse; ready, if called on, to pulverize, without hope of repair, what is left of civilization. He awaits only the word of command. He awaits it from a frail, bewildered being, long his victim, now—for one occasion only—his Master.[11]

Such views met general agreement across lines of political party, class, and nation. Stanley Baldwin told the Classical Association in 1925:

Who in Europe does not know that one more war in the west and the civilization of the ages will fall with as great a shock as that of Rome.[12]

He could offer no comfort that the peril could be avoided. His warning of November, 1932 reverberated down the next decade of English history:

I think it is well for the man in the street to realize that there is no power on earth that can protect him from being bombed. Whatever people may tell them, the bomber will always get through.[13]

Nor was aerial bombing a future horror for all the statesmen of the time. Anthony Eden had experienced it first-hand as a young officer in France in the waning days of the war:

The night was quite silent and there was no shell fire, as was usual at the end of the war, but quite suddenly it began to rain bombs for anything from 10 minutes to a quarter of an hour. I do not know how many bombs fell at that time, but something between thirty and forty I suppose. It seemed to us hundreds. What rests in my mind is not only my own personal terror, which was quite inexpressible, because bombing is more demoralizing in its effects than the worst shell fire, but the comment made when it was over by somebody who said: 'There now you have had your first taste of the next war'
There will be no heroism in a war where the safest place will be the front line if there is one, and the most dangerous the houses of our civilian population.[14]

Mussolini had spoken often of the warlike ambitions of Italy. But he made then, as he did later, a distinction between limited wars for colonial gain and a general European war. "Another General War," he said, "would be an unpardonable crime which would find its retribution in an irretrievable disaster."[15]

George Lansbury was as pacifist as Mussolini was bellicose. He would be leader of the Labour Party when the issue of pacifism passed from the theoretical to the practical. On this point he and Mussolini agreed:

> Surely it must be obvious that once more in the world's history, civilization is at the parting of the ways. If we go forward along the road which inevitably leads to war, then we are all quite sure religion, morals, civilization will all crash into ruins and the world once more collapse into barbarism.[16]

The young journalist, Beverly Nichols, brought all of this to a wide audience in his 1933 book *Cry Havoc*. He prefaced his discussion of the effects of poison gas with this dictum:

> But first we must make up our minds on one very important point, namely that gas *will* be used. Let there be no mistake about that.[17]

His grisly picture of "babies growing black in the face, in quiet English houses, of whole counties being choked by a withering cloud that turns the hedge rose gray" had graphic power. Like all good journalists, he reduced the incomprehensible to the familiar:

> Mustard gas is the most deadly of known gases. In an area, say from Richmond to Barking, and from Finchley to Streatham, an effective lethal dose would be only forty-two tons. In twelve hours every man, woman and child in that area might fail to live.[18]

Estimates varied, but they were all grim. French Professor Lazerin's estimated that one hundred planes, each carrying a ton of gas, could annihilate Paris in an hour. The German, Siegert thought that a few airplanes would be able to reduce the capital of any great state to ashes.[19] Thomas Edison foresaw twenty to fifty planes gassing London's population to death in three hours.[20]

Nichols then proceeded, in highly effective prose, to describe the physical effects of gas and brought the point home with a heartrending picture of his mother slowly expiring in agony:

I fear she will not gasp for long. She will suddenly crumple up and the face you have always loved, that one day you had thought to kiss in its last stillness, would be kissed and crumpled by the mask. And if you tore it off, it will be stained and pock-marked by the encroaching acid as she lies on the floor.[21]

The Basis of Peace

War in these terms came to be seen as plainly immoral. If Greek civilization had flourished after Marathon, and Christian Europe had repelled the Moors at Tours, then in each case civilization, at least to European historians, had been saved. English and French might differ over Waterloo but the Napoleonic era offered a good deal of satisfaction on both sides of the Channel and the victims of the Great War were at first thought to have given their lives in a cause greater than themselves.

What could be said of a war in which there would be no victors and only total ruin? Could such a war be a just war? To the practiced eye of Professor Toynbee, the answer was plain. His analysis recommended itself to lovers of peace and beneficiaries of the status quo:

The truth was that the General War of 1914–1918 had demonstrated in the short span of four years a moral and social truth of vital import for the future of the Western World, which had previously been overlooked or ignored by a society which might have divined it—had it had the necessary sensitiveness and good will—at any time during the preceding fifty years. The truth was that the sin of aggression had become mortal instead of merely venial . . . In the overwhelming experience of 1914–1918, the cumulative result of half a century of historical development had been revealed with a clarity which no adult observer—and certainly no responsible stateman—had any excuse for mistaking.[22]

To Great Britain, which with its Empire dominated a quarter of the globe, these conclusions were as plain as they were satisfying. Professor Toynbee went on bitterly to criticize Mussolini, contemplating his war in Abyssinia for failing, to read and observe "these glaring signs of the times."[23]

Adolf Hitler would have been less affected. One day he would meet Professor Toynbee and it would be the professor who was impressed.

Paths to Peace

To those thinking and caring citizens who understood the ultimate immorality of war, who shunned the balance of power which inevitably brought war when the balance failed, who hated arms and what they did, the creation of a brave new policy was a congenial task.

The nineteenth century in England had been a century of progress and hope based on a series of conclusions that derived from the utilitarian philosophy of Jeremy Bentham. It had taught that the spread of knowledge facilitates reason, that the pursuit of the good is based on right reason, and that who reasons right will act right. This would, of course, operate only in a free society. Now, if only these doctrines could be applied in the international sphere, a series of adjustments might be effected which would eliminate war. Such solutions appealed quite naturally to the idealists, to the intellectuals, and to the internationalists.

They were combined in the Labour foreign policy of the 1920s, tinctured by a deep wash or pacifism,[24] which called for renunciation of war as an act of national policy, disarmament, arbitration of disputes, open diplomacy, and international economic and political cooperation.[25]

In a world where 1918 represented the final triumph of democracy there was something to be said for these policies. But it required careful observation to see if the policies continued to match the realities.

In the face of the apocalypse pacifism seemed to many the only response. Its adherents could argue that the taking of life in any circumstance was a sin. More than that, nonresistance was the more effective tactic and for this the British public had the sometimes infuriating example of the growing power of Mahatma Ghandi.

The ultimate argument was that war was simply not worthwhile and this Beverly Nichols was at pains to demonstrate. What could England lose by defeat? Tribute, he calculated, would be cheaper than what the war had cost. That Britons should labor for the victors? In a day when the gravest social problem was three million unemployed? He could not see that any nation "in its senses" would wish to annex Kent or Suffolk; if France did so, it might result in more sensible drinking hours. As to the colonies, they were virtually free of England. Would the enemy strip the National Gallery of its treasures? Nichols' answer was a question: when was the last time you visited the National Gallery?[26]

If these were as, he confessed "light excursions" they raised real doubts among the uncomfortable.[27] From satire he descended into deadly seriousness. Behind it all, lay the burning memory, the poignant tribute to his brother, Ted, killed on his second day at the front, the day before the Armistice.[28] If he hadn't died to end war, then it had all been in vain.

To the audience that would later respond to *Cry Havoc*, the Peace Letter of December, 1927, was consistent:

> Convinced that all disputes between nations are capable of settlement either by diplomatic negotiation or by some form of international arbitration, we solemnly declare that we shall refuse to support or render war service to any Government which resorts to arms.[29]

To another segment of the British public the answer lay in Socialism. The Labour Party first took office in the early 1920s and again in 1929. It had supplanted the Liberal Party as the second major party. Its Socialist roots included the belief that it was the profit motive that caused war.

Its policy was based on internationalism since Socialism was born international. It was based on principles since Socialism was a body of doctrine before there was a Parliamentary Labour Party. Thus, a Labour Conference could resolve that the Socialist and Labour parties of all countries should oppose any "any war entered into by any government whatever the ostensible object of the war."[30]

The interesting features of such a resolution were, first, that the resolution rested on principle and omitted to consider what the facts of the case might be and, second, that it subordinated to the international principle any question of national interest.

Socialists considered armed forces dangerous; they had often been used against the Socialist cause. They were dangerous, too, to popular liberties and often used to suppress the subject masses in the colonies.

Labour criticized the Treaty of Versailles. It condemned the occupation of the Rhineland as a violation of the principle of self-determination. The French were more concerned with the immediate facts at hand. Labour was concerned over reparations and the exclusion of Germany from the League of Nations and liked to think of Germans as working-class comrades rather than as potential enemies.

Another approach was to resolve the imperfections in the international system and to remedy the injustices which might cause war.

This meant faith in the League. The League was seen as a genuine and welcome alternative to the balance of power, which came to be known by the pejorative label of power politics. Proposed mechanisms to insure peace proliferated: the Geneva Protocol, the Geneva Act, the Optional Clause. A trenchant critic of interwar politics observed, "The metaphysicians at Geneva found it difficult not to believe that an accumulation of ingenious texts prohibiting war was not a barrier against war itself."[31]

Above all, the practical remedy was disarmament and this was exemplified in the Labours of the Commission which was to prepare for the great Disarmament Conference of 1932.

To the British public, nothing was more comforting than the belief that Great Britain exercised a special position of virtue and influence throughout the world. It was in the faith that the British government had "unrivaled influence" in the councils of nations that Lord Cecil founded the Peace Ballot and the Peace Ballot was to be a deliberate exercise of that influence.[32]

Lord Curzon, the British Foreign Secretary had put it eloquently in 1923:

> We have endeavored to exercise a steady and moderating influence in the politics of the world. And I think and hope we have not merely conveyed the impression, but the conviction, that, whatever other countries or governments may do, the British government is never untrue to its word, and is never disloyal to its colleagues or its allies, never does anything underhand or mean; and if this conviction be widespread—as I believe it to be—that is the real basis of the moral authority which the British Empire has long exerted and I believe will long continue to exert in the affairs of mankind.[33]

A simpler expression of this theme was perhaps to be expected from a professor of classics. Gilbert Murray was indignant:

> Even in England, where the old tradition was comparatively innocent, and where League education had been more active and more successful than elsewhere, you hear people in the train making forecasts about the 'next war' and gossiping about supposed 'secret treaties' and secret weapons and the stealing of diplomatic documents, without any consciousness that they are accusing His Majesty's Government of perjury.[34]

These many views combined to result in a series of impressions, by no means uniform, but no less the widespread or appealing: that the issues of foreign policy revolved around the League of Nations and disarmament, not around the ambitions, the goals, the programs, and the power relations of nations, much less British interests.

Great Britain was above the struggle, admired and virtuous. Solutions could be found to all international problems by the exercise of intellectual ingenuity and the application of moral principles. The alternatives did not bear thinking. All this required faith and faith was not lacking. Gilbert Murray wrote:

> 'The pledges are too vague' say the French, 'let us make them absolute and definite.' 'How can we do that' reply the British, 'when we see that you shrink from carrying out the existing pledges. 'Without a firm agreement,' retort the French, 'we will act firmly. We cannot take the risk while you expressly reserve the right to let us down.' On such terms the dispute is insoluble. A little more conscientious loyalty to the Covenant on both sides and the difficulties will dwindle away.[35]

One Man's Crusade

Because he believed that public opinion was the ultimate basis of power, Lord Cecil turned his hand to the practical task of creating a mass movement in support of the League of Nations. Two predecessor organizations were combined on November 9, 1918 to form the League of Nations Union of which Lord Cecil would be the guiding light. A parliamentary LNU group was headed by his brother-in-law, Lord Selborne.

Because its outlook was international and founded on morality and principle, the LNU appealed more readily to Liberals and Labour than to Conservatives. Its members tended to be high-minded, serious, and powerfully affected by the urge to do good. The LNU attracted its share of crusaders and not a few cranks. A 1930 poll of its members painted this self-portrait:

> [T]he middle class are the most favorable to the League. On the whole, clergy, teachers and women . . . are held to be favorable, and businessmen unfavorable. A good many replies suggest that the Free Churches are generally favorable, and there appears to be a consensus of opinion that hostility to the League is to be found largely among comfortable persons retired from the Services.[36]

The LNU found a place for pacifists on the theory that it was an antiwar organization and at the same time appealed to imperialists on the ground that:

> We have a small army and a vast Empire . . . it is immensely important for us to preserve the status quo by the peaceful methods of arbitration and international cooperation rather than by maintenance of arms and navies that a return to the Balance of Power would force upon us.[37]

Disarmament early became the prime goal of the LNU. It established an Arms Limitation Committee as early as 1921 and was concerned with controlling scientific advances in weaponry.[38] In 1926 it called for a halt to increases in armaments and a uniform percentage reduction in expenditures and manpower applied worldwide under Article 8 of the Covenant.[39]

When Cecil resigned from the government in 1927 over his opposition to British demands for more cruisers than the United States at the 1927 Washington Naval Conference, he explained that he had done so, not only on the issue at hand, but "to get full freedom to advocate disarmament."[40] He returned to the 1929 Labour Government as Chairman of the Committee on League of Nations Affairs and spearheaded the LNU's 1929 program for a naval agreement with the United States drastically reducing all classes of warships.

The LNU's position in anticipation of the Disarmament Conference which was to convene in 1932 was twofold: equality of armaments for Germany and a worldwide 25 percent reduction in arms budgets.[41]

What the LNU did not face straightforwardly and what it did not discuss with its membership which included pacifists, unilateral disarmers, and imperialists, was the connection between collective security and disarmament. This anticipated, but did not answer, the avowed object of the Peace Ballot: to educate the public on what it meant for Britain to be a member of the League of Nations.

At its height in the twenties, the LNU claimed a million members and allowed Cecil to observe to Gilbert Murray: "I have no doubt that any Government that really set itself in opposition to the League would be immediately turned out."[42]

The activities of the LNU were vigorous and widespread. Candidates for Parliament were queried on their League positions and indeed, a third were members of the LNU.[43] Local branches were important; Lord Cecil knew how to work the grassroots. Public meetings were numerous and the LNU furnished speakers and Speaker's Notes.

There were pamphlets, press releases, and books cheap enough for all but never, on a shrewd calculation, free. There was the house journal, *Headway*, and a determined effort to work with the press. Posters were effective.[44]

The LNU penetrated deeply in the churches and schools. There was a special corporate membership for churches and the LNU numbered over 2,500 congregations in its membership. The League, it said, was "the one piece of practical Christianity which the war has left us," and it distributed Sunday school lessons pointing out that the League of Nations was a natural extension of the teachings of Jesus. The Archbishop of Canterbury was helpful; the Lambeth Conference of 1930 called on the churches to promote "those ideals of peace, brotherhood, and justice for which the League of Nations stands," and more especially to help by prayer and effort agencies, such as the LNU, which worked to promote good will among nations.[46]

Voluminous curricular materials were supplied to schools to offset the effects of "drum and trumpet" history and the effort extended to extracurricular activities, plays and pageants. Thus, "Banish the Bogie" was "an unusually quaint exposition of the way in which armament manufacturers played one nation off against the others to get orders."[47]

There were junior branches of the LNU which cooperated with the Boy Scouts, Girl Guides, and other youth organizations, and which graduated into Youth Sections and the Universities League of Nations Societies.[48]

All this was serious business; members complained that the meetings were dull and one commented that a dance or Eddie Cantor were far more entertaining. In an effort to make *Headway* more popular, it was suggested that regular news be offered of the Royal Family and the editors, who on principle excluded announcements of the Royal Military Tattoo, agonized over whether to print advertising for birth control.[49]

These were among the forces Lord Cecil could call upon when the LNU launched its climactic effort—the Peace Ballot. It included all those who felt they could make through their membership in the LNU a statement of their ideals, who could thereby contribute their work to the cause of peace, and at the same time discharge their heartfelt debt to the past.

Believers and Skeptics

In 1930, it was still possible for the Labour Government of Ramsay MacDonald to look serenely upon the international scene. He told the British delegation to the 1930 Naval Conference that the international situation had improved because of the League of Nations and the Kellogg-Briand Pact; that the number of cruisers in the British fleet could safely be reduced from seventy to fifty and that French fears simply didn't take into account the improved climate.[50]

Labour wished to see Germany restored with full equality to the community of nations and advocated the complete withdrawal of Allied occupation troops five years ahead of schedule, the settlement of reparations, and Allied disarmament.

Arthur Henderson, Labour's Foreign Secretary, was a member of the remarkable group of men who ascended to power in the Labour Party's first generation. From the humblest background, by perseverance, ability, industry, and character, he came up through the ranks of Labour and municipal government to become in 1903 one of the first four Labour members of Parliament. He was deeply religious and found in trade unionism and in politics, domestic and international, the practical vehicles for his religious ideals.

When MacDonald asked Cecil to act as British representative to the League of Nations, he was installed in a room in the Foreign Office where his father had attended cabinet meetings as Foreign Secretary and as Prime Minister. Henderson, the sometime machinist's apprentice, was amused and delighted to have as his subordinate the son of his predecessor, the Marquess of Salisbury.

Work on the Singapore naval base was postponed. Henderson told the cabinet that the Japanese were pledged to settle issues peacefully and expressed confidence in international peacekeeping machinery and the coming Disarmament Conference of which he was to be the President.[51] Surely," he said, "loyal and effective cooperation in support of the Covenant is what may confidently be expected from every member of the League of Nations. Otherwise their membership is a fraud and a delusion."[52]

Vansittart observed that Henderson was a very good man and a very bad Foreign Secretary.[53] Of the 1930 Naval Treaty he said, "We solved the problem of cruisers by reducing ours to fifty. In diplomacy you can 'solve' anything by giving way."[54]

His general views were no more cheerful:

Historians argued that the war had come about because all nations cherished reprehensible purposes, and that Germany was no more to blame than the rest for having no means of settling such competitions except by arms. We gradually swallowed this mythical equality of sin together with the sister story about the crime that lurks in gold and steel, the culpability of Wall Street, Vickers, Sir Basil Zaharoff, as if such rot would bear a moment's probing. A nation of shopkeepers wanted a tough customer to recover and passed a quick sponge over his debts to others while he took all sympathy as less than his due. We presented to the Germans a case for agitation which they doubled.[55]

German goals had not changed. The dying Streseman told the young Italian diplomat, Dino Grandi, "I am an old man and I am dying but you are young and you will live to see the second Punic War."[56]

The British services worried about their ability, with limited means, not only to carry out the commitments of the Covenant, but to protect British interests.

A few diplomats who studied the European scene were deeply concerned. As early as 1925, Sir James Headlam-Morley posed these questions to the Foreign Secretary:

Has anyone attempted to realize what would happen if there were to be a new partition of Poland, or if the Czechoslovak state were to be so curtailed and dismembered that in fact it disappeared from the map of Europe? The whole of Europe would at once be in chaos. There would no longer be any principle, meaning, or sense in the territorial arrangements of the continent. Imagine, for instance, that under some improbable condition, Austria rejoined Germany; that Germany using the discontented minority in Bohemia, demanded a new frontier far over the mountains, including Carlsbad and Pilsen, and that at the same time, in alliance with Germany, the Hungarians recovered the southern slope of the Carpathians. This would be catastrophic, and, even if we neglected to interfere in time to prevent it, we should afterwards be driven to interfere, probably too late.[57]

To Winston Churchill in 1931 neither the French army nor its arms were inherently evil. They were instead Europe's first line of defense: and "the sudden weakening of that factor of stability . . . might open floodgates of measureless consequences in Europe at the present time, might break the dyke and 'Let the boundless deep/Down upon far off cities while they dance-/or dream.'"[58]

6

Adolf Hitler

*"When the nations on this planet fight for exist-
ence—when the question of destiny, 'to be or
not to be' cries out for a solution—then all considerations of humanitarianism or aesthetics
crumble into nothingness."*

—Adolf Hitler[1]

On October 14, 1918, on the Western Front near Ypres, Corporal
Adolf Hitler was overcome by a new and terrible weapon, Yellow
Cross Gas. Temporarily blinded, he was in a hospital in Pasewalk,
Pomerania on Armistice Day.[2]

Much of the world greeted the Armistice with wild elation. Adolf
Hitler did not rejoice. His eyesight had been recovering. Now all went
black: "I tottered and groped my way back to the dormitory, threw
myself upon my bunk and dug my burning head into my blanket and
pillow."[3] He wept for the first time since his mother's death. The
following days were a time of supreme shock and anguish. Out of
these he resolved to go into politics.[4]

Adolf Hitler's personal response to the war and its aftermath could
not have been more different from the moods and ideas that moved
large masses of the British people. If, by 1930, the British were satisfied with their position in the world, Hitler was bitterly and irrevocably dissatisfied with Germany's. If the British people looked beyond
nationalism to internationalism, Hitler ridiculed internationalism and
preached a flaming nationalism based upon race. After four years on
the Western Front, Hitler neither hated nor feared war, but he had a
supreme contempt of pacifism. The victim of the latest horror weap-

ons, he did not bother his head about the terrors of wars to come. War was the logical and practical way for Germany to gain its ends. The final victory, which in 1918 had been traitorously snatched from German hands, would be worth the price. Morality was totally irrelevant to the conduct of foreign policy. The first step to realizing this program was ruthlessly to suppress all ideas to the contrary.

So thought the man who would become the German Führer.

Young Adolf Hitler

Adolf Hitler was born on April 20, 1889 at Braunau on the River Inn, the border between Austria and Germany. His father, Alois Hitler, was a minor customs official whose third wife, twenty-three years his junior, had been a domestic servant.

Hitler was an indifferent student whose record at the Linz Realschule did not merit promotion. He was sent to board at a school in Steyr, which he left at sixteen in 1905 without a diploma.

He tells us in *Mein Kampf* that he vigorously rejected his father's wish that he become a civil servant and instead declared his intention to become an artist. For two years after leaving school, he lived with his widowed mother in Linz, with no regular job, occupying himself with sketches and architectural drawings. Inspired by visits to Vienna, he tried to enter the Academy of Fine Arts and failed twice. Lacking a secondary school diploma, he could not enter the School of Architecture.[5]

His school years and the five years he now spent in Vienna afford striking parallels to the same years in Mussolini's life. He was a stranger in Vienna, without family, resources, or a job. By his own account, he survived as a day laborer and occasional artist. He slept out in the summers and in the autumn lived in a cheap hotel and then in a men's hostel run by a charitable organization.[6] It was, he said, "the saddest period of my life." But he found compensations. "I owe it to that period that I grew hard and am still capable of being hard."[7]

He pursued self-education with more dedication than a career:

> Hunger was then my faithful bodyguard. He never left me for a moment and partook of all I had, share and share alike. Every book I acquired aroused his interest; a visit to the opera promoted his attentions for days at a time; my life was a continuous struggle with this pitiless friend.[8]

He said he read "enormously and thoroughly" in all of the free time left from work. He immersed himself in social problems and politics. He not only studied the social question in the abstract; he lived it:

> By drawing me within the sphere of suffering, it did not seem to invite me to 'study' but to experience it in my skin. It was none of its doing that the guinea pig came through the operation safe and sound.[9]

Hitler's reading was focused. He claimed the art of sifting out what was useful, instinctively and immediately perceiving the material of permanent value, so that his efforts should furnish tools and building materials for his life's work. The useful parts were like the stones in a mosaic. Lacking such discrimination, he thought, the reader would emerge with a muddle of memorized facts, the conceit of being educated, fitted only for a sanitarium or for a Parliament.[10]

But how to determine what is useful? Hitler gives us a clear picture of the mind that dreamed of world mastery and came so close to achieving it. A man, he told us, "who posseses the art of correct reading" will

> instinctively and immediately perceive everything which in his opinion is worth permanently remembering, either because it is suited to his purpose or generally worth knowing. Once the knowledge he has achieved in this fashion is correctly coordinated within the somehow existing picture of this or that subject created by the imagination, it will function either as a corrective or a complement, thus enhancing either the correctness or the clarity of the picture. Then, if life suddenly sets some question before us for examination or answer, the memory, if this method of reading is observed, will immediately take the existing picture as a norm, and from it will derive all the individual items regarding these questions, assembled in the course of decades, submit them to the mind for examination and reconsideration, until the question is clarified or answered.[12]

In his reading, Hitler searched for a "world picture" and a philosophy. Of his years in Vienna he would later say, "In addition to what I then created, I have had to learn little; and I have had to alter nothing."[12]

Hitler's struggles shaped his ideas but did not broaden his sympathies: "Ultimately, the struggle which is so hard, kills all pity. Our own painful struggle for existence destroys our feeling for the misery of those who have remained behind."[13]

His circumstances improved a little. He no longer had to work as a day-laborer, but described himself as a small draftsman and watercolorist who painted for a living and studied for pleasure. It was in this era that the torrential orator, Adolf Hitler, indulged in a rare exercise in understatement: "I believe that those who knew me in those days took me for an eccentric."[14]

In his years in Vienna, Hitler nurtured and developed his great hatreds, for the Hapsburg Empire, for parliamentary democracy, for Marxism, and for the Jews.[15] All of these hatreds had their root in Hitler's fierce German nationalism.

The Hapsburg Empire was a dynastic, multinational, multicultural state rather than a Germanic state; and Hitler saw its non-Germanic nationalities growing in power and in influence. In Parliament, broad suffrage and the secret ballot eliminated Germanic control. When Hitler's curiosity impelled him to visit Parliament, he was equally repelled by alternating scenes of noisy chaos and drowsy somnolence.[16]

As to the Jews, their basic fault in Hitler's eyes was that they were not Germans but instead were scattered among the nations. They seemed moreover to be identified with the growing forces of Social Democracy, or worse still, with Marxism.[17] All this was incompatible with Hitler's views of the unique historical value of German blood and German nationhood.

In 1913, Hitler moved to Munich, tired of living in the Hapsburg state with its "whole mixture of Czechs, Poles, Hungarians, Ruthenians, Serbs and Croats, and everywhere the eternal mushroom of humanity—Jews and more Jews."[18]

In Germany he wanted, he said, to fulfill the secret longing of his earliest years, to be an architect and to live and work for the reunion of Austria and Germany. What he did not say was that he probably wanted to evade military service for which he had failed to report each year since 1910.[19]

Hitler was as happy in Munich as he had been unhappy in Vienna. Not that his way of life had changed. He read voraciously, he continued his passionate interest in politics and he supported himself precariously by commercial art for ads and posters and by selling sketches to dealers.[20] All this changed with the advent of the World War:

To me, those hours seemed like a release from the painful feelings of my youth. Even today, I am not ashamed to say that overpowered by stormy enthusiasm, I fell down on my knees and thanked Heaven from an over-flowing heart for granting me the good fortune of being permitted to live at this time.[21]

Hitler may have been averse to serving the Hapsburg dynasty. But he promptly addressed a petition to King Ludwig III of Bavaria to be allowed to serve in a Bavarian regiment. To his great satisfaction, his petition was granted; he enlisted in the 1st Company of the 16th Bavarian Reserve Infantry Regiment, known as the List Regiment.[22]

After a brief training period, the List Regiment went into action in October, 1914, in the fifth battle of Ypres. In four days, Hitler reported to his Munich landlord, the regiment was reduced from 3,500 to 600 men.[23] Hitler was wounded on the Somme in October, 1916, and returned to his regiment in March, 1917. This apart, he spent the whole of the war on the Western Front.[24]

Hitler was a regimental runner, responsible for carrying messages between the company and regimental headquarters. He was a dedicated, conscientious soldier who won the Iron Cross, Second Class, in November, 1914 and the much rarer Iron Cross, First Class, in August, 1918. He continued to be lonely, giving the impression of eccentricity, prone to diatribes against Marxists and Jews.[25]

It had been "the greatest and most unforgettable time of my earthly existence."[26] If, as Hitler later said, the war made "the most tremendous impressions" on him of his life,[27] the truly decisive impression was made by Germany's defeat. He resolved to enter politics. But how?

He remained in the army and returned to Munich in November, 1918. After brief service as a guard at a prisoner-of-war camp near the Austrian border, he was again a civilian in Munich in March, 1919.[28] In Bavaria, the abdication of the Wittelsbach dynasty had been followed by a Social Democratic government, a Communist regime, the Social Democrats again, and by March, a right-wing government imposed by the local army commander.[29]

Hitler was called upon to give testimony before an army examining commission concerning revolutionary activity in an infantry regiment. He recalled this as his "first more or less purely political activity."[30]

Ordered by the Army's Political Department, where he worked in the press bureau, to attend a course of political instruction, he met others who shared his views that Germany could never be saved by the parties to the "November Crime," the parties of the center and of the left. At this course occurred two great events. First, Hitler was fascinated by a lecture by Gottfried Feder on loan capital, interest, and international finance.[31] Feder's theme, "breaking interest slavery" fitted a useful economic component into Hitler's racial and nationalist theories. The theme of German economic independence from the influences and controls of international finance and markets naturally appealed to Hitler.

The second event was even more important. One day at the course he asked for the floor. Suddenly he found that all of his years of reading and study, of passionate introspection and reflection had an outlet:

> I started out with the greatest enthusiasm and love . . . and the thing that I had always presumed from pure feeling without knowing it was now corroborated: *I could speak.*[32]

Hitler now received orders to attend a meeting of the German Worker's Party at which Feder was to speak. The meeting in the beer cellar on September 12, 1919, attracted twenty or twenty-five hearers. After Feder's speech, another speaker urged that Bavaria separate from Germany and join Austria. Not surprisingly, Hitler demanded the floor "giving the learned gentlemen my opinion on this point" so that he left the hall, even before Hitler had finished, "like a wet poodle."[33]

On the strength of this performance, Hitler was invited to join the party and express his views at the next meeting. He found it drab and depressing. Following correspondence and some reports, the 7 marks 50 pfennigs in the treasury were enough to justify a vote of confidence in the treasurer. Equally discouraging, Hitler saw no program, leaflet, membership card, and perhaps most dismaying, no rubber stamp, "only obvious good faith and good intentions."[34]

Should he join? Hitler agonized over the decision for two days. In the end he decided that the very smallness and infancy of "this absurd little organization" would offer him opportunities unavailable in the larger parties, and that only a truly new party could create and install a truly new program.

What could he bring to the task? Hitler recognized that he was poor and that the intelligentsia would look down "with limitless condescension" on anyone who "has not been dragged through the obligatory schools and had the necessary knowledge pumped into him."[35]

He did not lack self-confidence. It was, he said, the most decisive resolve of his life. He became Member No. 7 of the German Worker's Party.[36] By his energy, his oratory, and his personality, he soon became its dominant force.

Written invitations to meetings evoked scant response. Newspaper advertisements at last produced a gathering of over 100.[37] Hitler spoke for thirty minutes and again experienced the intoxicating realization "I could speak." Of this there was practical proof; the collection amounted to 300 marks, a very great relief to the penniless party.[38]

Hitler learned another lesson. At the next meeting, the audience grew. There were hecklers and dissenters. Set upon by party adherents, these soon "flew down the stairs with gashed heads."[39]

On February 24, 1920, the party, now called the National Socialist Worker's Party held its first mass meeting. Hitler superintended the preparations. Now there were posters, leaflets, a program. Hitler chose the theme color, red; it was exciting, would provoke and infuriate his adversaries and bring his party to their attention "whether they liked it or not."[40] Where once a dozen, then a hundred had attended the party meeting, now Hitler faced an audience of two thousand: "my heart nearly burst for joy."[41] Again Hitler spoke. Again dissenters were silenced.

Hitler pronounced the party program of twenty-five points. The response was more than affirmative, it was, according to Hitler, joyous and unanimous. Hitler recognized the significance of this meeting:

[I]t was because by it the party burst the narrow bounds of a small club and for the first time exerted a determining influence on the mightiest factor of our time, public opinion.[42]

The party program would have appalled Lord Cecil, but on the importance of public opinion he and Adolf Hitler were in rare accord.

The program which Hitler pronounced incorporated the basic elements of his philosophy. First and foremost came the reunion of all Germans in a Greater Germany. Hard on its heels came the demand for revocation of the Treaty of Versailles. Since only racial comrades could be citizens, Jews were excluded. There must be land to feed the German people and settle its excess population. The duty of the state was to provide a livelihood for its citizens. The corresponding duty of the citizen was to work in the interest of the community. The program's economic appeal was based on the abolition of unearned incomes, the nationalization of trusts and department stores, profit sharing and land reform including expropriation for public purposes. Social programs included improved health care and access to education. Did the provision that the curricula "be bought into line with the requirements of practical life" reflect Hitler's self-education?

There was a ruthless note: criminals, usurers, and profiteers were to be put to death, there was to be strict control of the press and other means of expression:

> Newspapers which violate the general good are to be banned. We demand legal warfare against those tendencies in art and literature which exert an undermining influence on our national life, or violate the moral and ethical feelings of the Germanic race.

Finally, a strong central power should possess unconditional authority over the entire Reich.[43]

This was in large part the program that Hitler was to present in *Mein Kampf* and preach and urge over the length and breadth of Germany until the day came to make the program a reality.

Hitler emphasized the need for sacrifice, the futility of half-measures, the virtues of a totally one-sided but crystal clear propaganda, the racial basis of the movement, and always "the fanaticism, yes the intolerance"[44] with which the Nazi party's adherents would push aside all rivals.

Hitler now threw himself wholly into the new party. Like Mussolini, he quickly learned the importance of violence and terror. Strongarm squads were formed which became the nucleus of the SA. Their function was not only to silence the opposition at Nazi meetings but also to break up the opposition's meetings and intimidate Nazi foes by brute physical force. This was done with the tacit colloboration of the army and especially of Captain Ernst Roehm who later became head of the SA. Hitler found the resources for a weekly newspaper, the *Volkischer Beobachter*.

The party grew, aided by the times. The reparations issue, the French occupation of the Ruhr, and the inflation which affected every class and interest in German society were destabilizing events. Hitler could call out 5,000 storm troopers in a January, 1923 demonstration at Munich[45] and summoned 20,000 to Munich with the deliberate intent of breaking up the Socialist May Day demonstrations of 1923.[46]

Meanwhile, the Weimar Republic struggled to maintain its precarious authority, especially in Bavaria. Bavaria was itself divided between the Bavarian nationalists who wanted independence or a South German state united with Austria and the German nationalists, led by the Nazis, whose eyes turned to Berlin.

In September, the Berlin government called off the campaign of passive resistance to the French in the Ruhr and resumed reparations deliveries. To the nationalists this was a shameful surrender. They stepped up their pressure on the Bavarian governor. The Bavarian government proclaimed a state of emergency and named Gustav von Kahr State Commissioner with dictatorial powers. Nazi provocations led Berlin to impose a ban on the Nazi paper which Kahr refused to honor, nor would he accept the subsequent dismissal by Berlin of his military chief, von Lossow.[47]

Hitler now planned a coup d'etat—the seizure of power in Bavaria to be followed by a march on Berlin. The unique feature was that it was planned not to overpower the forces of the army and the state but at gunpoint to persuade Kahr and Lossow to lead a national revolution.

When Kahr and Lossow announced a meeting on November 8, 1923, in the Burgerbraukellar in Munich, Hitler was ready. He and Hermann Goering burst into the hall during Kahr's speech, backed by storm troopers; Hitler jumped on a table, fired a pistol and shouted: "The National Revolution has begun." He said the hall was occupied by 600 of his heavily armed men and that he had formed a new government replacing the Bavarian and Reich governments.

Kahr, he announced, would head the Bavarian government as regent. As to the National Government, the thirty-four-year-old ex-tramp and ex-corporal proclaimed:

> "The government of the November Criminals and of the Reich President are declared to be removed. A new National Government will be nominated this very day here in Munich. A German National Army will be formed immediately. . . . I propose that, until accounts have been fully settled with the November Criminals, the direction of policy in the National Government be taken over by me. Ludendorff will take over the leadership of the German National Army.[48]

This had not been cleared with Ludendorff, who now appeared. Though angry, he wanted Hitler to succeed. It was all bluff and nerve, but Kahr and Lossow capitulated and announced their adherence to the revolution. This was Hitler's moment of glory. He told the crowd:

> I am going to fulfill the vow I made to myself five years ago when I was a blind cripple in the military hospital; to know no rest nor peace until the November Criminals have been overthrown, until in the ruins of the wretched Germany of today there should have arisen once more a Germany of power and greatness, of freedom and splendor.[49]

The crowd cheered and sang "Deutschland Uber Alles." All, that is, except Kahr and Lossow who slipped out of the hall. Hitler had something to learn about revolutions. They soon reasserted their authority and gathered their forces, backed by Berlin and by the army.

Hitler and Ludendorff knew on the morning of November 9th that their attempt had failed. Ludendorff persuaded Hitler that the Nazis should march on the army headquarters where he was sure the army would not shoot at but obey him. The Nazi column, heavily armed, marched through the city until it reached a police barrier. Firing broke out; Hitler cried "Surrender" and fell to the ground. Only Ludendorff remained erect, imperturbably marching through the police lines. Hitler fled the scene. He was arrested on November 11th and with eight others was tried for high treason.[50]

Hitler now turned the tables. His impassioned defense gained him immense publicity throughout Germany. He proudly accepted full responsibility. Yes, he said, he had wanted to destroy the Republic and he reproached Lossow and Kahr for not joining the effort.

Accused of ambition, he replied:

> The man who was born to be a dictator is not compelled; he wills it. He is not driven forward, but drives himself. . . . The man who feels called upon to govern a people has no right to say, If you want me or summon me I will cooperate. No, it is his duty to step forward.[51]

Hitler was found guilty of high treason and served a term in the Landsberg prison from November 11, 1923 to December 20, 1924. It was here that he dictated *Mein Kampf* to Rudolf Hess and Emil Maurice.

The Ideas of Adolf Hitler

Although he wielded vast power, Adolf Hitler was preeminently a man of ideas. He had no interest in telling a soldier's tale of four years on the Western Front. It was the most stupendous experience of his life, and he had lived it passionately, but he gave it only a few pages of *Mein Kampf.* Hitler wanted to communicate, not his experiences, but the ideas his experience had generated.

Ideas were not enough. It was vital to Hitler to combine ideas into a system which he called a world view. From the start, Hitler insisted on working out an explanation of the nature of things that satisfied him. This was the doctrine he would set forth in *Mein Kampf.* Deeply affected as it is by Hitler's prejudices and predispositions, bearing as it does on every page the stamp of his character, it is nevertheless a tremendous effort by a driven and self-educated man to arrive at a meaning of history, a vision of the future, and, what is more, a program to make that future happen.

Mein Kampf has been described as incomprehensible and unreadable. It is generally vulgar, frequently horrifying, and as often satanic. But it is neither dull nor unreadable. If it were simply the mental and emotional testament of an anonymous German-Austrian, looking back to the collapse of the Hohenzollern and Hapsburg Empires and looking forward to an imagined destiny, it would have ample interest and historical value. What makes *Mein Kampf* truly gripping is the foreshadowing of events to come, the clarity with which the goals are set forth and the methods are laid out to achieve those goals. To read *Mein Kampf* today is like a helpless free-fall to certain death.

Race

Hitler's system rested on the dominant philosophy of race as the foundation of the nation. Old Austria was multicultural and multiracial. Hitler hated that, as he hated Vienna. His loyalty was to his German blood, even if it were necessary to destroy Austria to create a greater Germany.

Hitler announces his racial doctrine and its consequences on page one of *Mein Kampf.* There is no lack of clarity:

German Austria must return to the great German mother country; and not because of any economic considerations. No, and again no: even if such a union were unimportant from an economic point of view; yes, even if it were harmful, it must nevertheless take place. One blood demands one Reich. Never will the German nation possess the moral right to engage in colonial politics until, at least, it embraces its own sons within a single state. Only when the Reich borders include the very last German, but can no longer guarantee his daily bread, will the moral right to acquire foreign soil arise from the distress of our own people. The sword will become our plow, and from the tears of war the daily bread of future generations will grow.[52]

Here in a single paragraph is the essence of *Mein Kampf*: Anschluss, one blood, one nation, land and bread, war and conquest. The rest is commentary.

The function of the state, indeed its highest purpose, is the preservation and development of a race of "physically and psychically homogeneous creatures" who will bestow culture and "create the beauty and dignity of a higher mankind." Blood, not language, is the basis of race; states are founded on nationality, not economics.[55]

There is no equality of races "but along with their differences it (nature) recognizes their higher and lesser value and feels itself obligated, through this knowledge, to promote the victory of the better and the stronger and demand the subordination of the weaker in accordance with the eternal will that dominates the universe."[56]

The enemy of the doctrine of race is Communism which is based instead on class. It is international, not national, and makes enemies of elements of the same race. This was, to Hitler, unforgivable.

The task of the German Reich is therefore to embrace all Germans, assemble and preserve the most valuable racial stock and raise Germany to a dominant position. The results will be dramatic:

We all sense that in the distant future humanity must be faced by problems which only a highest race, become master people and supported by the means and possibility of an entire globe, will be equipped to overcome.[57]

Hitler has no doubt which this race would be. The German people, having guarded the purity of their blood, will one day fulfill "the mission allotted to it by the creator of the universe."[58] For, to Adolf Hitler, this conclusion is supremely logical:

A state which in this age of racial poisoning dedicates itself to the care of the best racial elements must someday become the lord of the earth.[59]

Nature

This all-important doctrine of race was, Hitler thought, founded on the principles of natural selection. The weaker elements would always be more numerous but were subjected by nature to harsh conditions which only the strongest could survive. This was nature's law: "a new and ruthless choice according to strength and health."[60] Hitler called this the aristocratic principle which emphasized the individual. The antithesis was the Marxist doctrine based upon the "mass of numbers and their dead weight."[61]

> A stronger race will drive out the weak, for the vital urge in its ultimate form will, time and again, burst all the absurd fetters of the so-called humanity of individuals, in order to replace it by the humanity of nature which destroys the weak to give place to the strong.[62]
> Those who want to live let them fight, and those who do not want to fight in this world of eternal struggle do not deserve to live.[63]

The social consequences of this doctrine were harsh:

> Just as nature does not concentrate her greatest attention in preserving what exists, but in breeding offspring to carry on the species, likewise in human life, it is less important artificially to alleviate existing evil, which, in view of human nature, is ninety-nine percent impossible, than to insure from the start healthier channels for future development.[64]

Thus, the alleviation of suffering is nothing but "philosophical flim-flam."[65] Hitler prefers "brutal determination in breaking down incurable tumors."[66]

But conscience and guilt stand in the way of these harsh prescriptions. They must be exorcized:

> Only when an epoch ceases to be haunted by the shadow of its own consciousness of its guilt will it achieve the inner calm and outward strength brutally and ruthlessly to prune off the wild shoots and tear out the weeds.[67]

The ultimate accusation against conscience is to Hitler the most telling: "Conscience is a Jewish invention. It is a blemish, like circumcision."[68]

This is metaphor. Hitler is elsewhere more direct. Eliminate the incurables, prevent the defectives from propagating. For Hitler this is "clearest reason" which will spare undeserved suffering and lead to an improvement in public health.[69]

Instead, promote the fertility of the healthiest. Hitler peered into the future. The settlement of newly acquired territories must not be left to chance: "Specially constituted racial commissions must issue settlement certificates to individuals. For this however, definite racial purity must be established."[70]

Hitler now applied his concept of natural law to nations:

> And if a people is defeated in the struggle for human rights, this merely means it has been found too light in the scale of destiny for the happiness of survival on this earth. For when a people is not willing or able to fight for its existence—Providence in its eternal justice has decreed that people's end.[71]
> But it need not be that way:
> Everything on this earth is capable of improvement. Every defeat can become the father of a subsequent victory, every lost war the cause of later resurgence, every hardship the fertilization of human energy, and from every oppression the forces for a new spiritual rebirth can come—so long as the blood is preserved pure.[72]

Hitler saw himself as an artist. In his palmy days, architecture was his diversion and special interest. Perhaps this is the aesthetic vision that stirred him most deeply as recorded in *Mein Kampf*:

> And in general we must clearly acknowledge the fact that the highest ideals always correspond to a deep vital necessity, just as the nobility of the most exulted beauty lies in the last analysis only in what is logically most expedient.[73]

Hitler's Program

Adolf Hitler was not satisfied with ideas unless they were combined into a system. He was not satisfied with the system of ideas—a world view—unless it was molded into a program—a strategy to achieve the society in which his system should reign.

The problem, as Hitler saw it, was how to sustain a healthy increase of a healthy population. What could be done when population outstripped its resource base?

To this, Hitler posed three possible solutions. The first, which he identified with France, was to restrict population. Hitler rejected this as contrary to nature.[74]

The second possibility was a colonial solution. In Hitler's analysis, colonial empires were inherently weak, like pyramids, he said, stood on their heads. In contrast, the United States stood on a firm continental base which gave it immense strength.[75]

In any case, Hitler had in view more glittering prizes than the Cameroons. The solution again rested in nature, in a growing and healthy peasantry, the foundation of the nation, the class least subject to social ills, the balance wheel of industrial and commercial supply and demand—of pure blood, of course.[76]

Clearly the German Empire had been wrong to pursue its maritime, colonial, and commercial policy as England's rival. "For Germany, consequently, the only possibility for carrying out a healthy territorial policy lay in the acquisition of new land in Europe itself."[77]

Step by step by step Hitler marched to his predestined conclusion:

> If land was desired in Europe, it could be obtained by and large only at the expense of Russia and this meant that the new Reich must set itself on the march along the road of the Teutonic Knights of old, to obtain by the German sword sod for the German plow and daily bread for the nation.[78]

After 1918, Germany and Russia shared no common border. The logic of Hitler's program was clear. Anschluss with Austria would unite German blood into one Reich. The destruction of Czechoslovakia and Poland would open the road to the appropriate territorial solution in Russia. Hitler never shrank from the logic of his philosophy.

Hitler now addressed the foreign policy that would make this program a reality. He cannot be accused of obscurity or verbosity when he emphasizes, "land and soil as the goal of our foreign policy."[79] The aim of foreign policy is "to secure for the German people the land and soil to which they are entitled on this earth"[80]:

> But we National Socialists go further. The right to possess soil can become a duty if without extension of its soil a great nation seems doomed to destruction. And most especially when not some little nigger nation or other is involved, but the Germanic mother of life which has given the world its cultural picture. Germany will either be a world power or there will be no Germany.[81]

The exalted beauty of expediency applied to the execution as well as the goals of foreign policy.

The essential, fundamental and guiding principle which we must always bear in mind in judging this question, is that foreign policy is only a means to an end, and that end is solely the promotion of our own nationality. No consideration of foreign policy can proceed from any other criterion than this: *Does it benefit our nationality now or in the future or will it be injurious to it?* This is the sole preconceived opinion permissible in dealing with this question. Partisan, religious, humanitarian, and all other criteria in general are completely irrelevant. (Emphasis added)[82]

Hitler had acquired supreme power when the Peace Ballot was launched. The Peace Ballot asked five questions: Whether Great Britain should remain a member of the League of Nations; Whether arms should be reduced by international agreement; Whether military aircraft and the private manufacture of arms should be abolished; Whether nations should combine to stop aggression by economic or military sanctions.

These were general inquiries. What was never asked was where Britain's interests lay; what policy would advance them; and what policy would in concrete case injure the national interest.

Those who claimed morality as a basis of foreign policy in dealing with Nazi Germany were bound to take into account that Herr Hitler had a decidedly different view.

One of the perennial tasks of foreign policy is the forging of combinations by which a nation may achieve ends beyond its own individual strength and which may overbalance a stronger enemy. Hitler pondered on the alliance opportunities that might come his way, but as to the enemy he never wavered.

The enemy was France, the irrevocable mortal enemy of the Germany people; France which wanted to seize the Rhineland. The great decisive battle would be fought in France; only the destruction of France would enable Germany at long last to embark on her eastward march of conquest.[84]

By way of contrast, the British, whom Hitler delighted to recognize as fellow Teutons, were not a natural enemy but indeed his first choice as an ally. This would be true so long as Germany did not foolishly engage in naval or colonial rivalry with Britain. There was no need of this if Germany followed the correct territorial policy in Europe.[85]

Hitler shrewdly suspected in the 1920s that French hegemony on the continent caused uneasiness in Britain. He noted how the French occupation of the Ruhr in 1923 had alienated the British.[86]

The other prospective ally was Italy. Hitler admired Mussolini. The March on Rome had fired his imagination. Fascism, and the rhetoric of Fascism were very much to his taste and he paid tribute in *Mein Kampf* to Mussolini as one of the great men of the earth.[87]

Italian interests were Mediterranean and colonial. For an alliance with Italy, Hitler was prepared to sacrifice his most sacred principle. He was prepared to abandon to Italian rule the German-speaking natives of South Tyrol whose Austrian province has been awarded to victorious Italy at Versailles.[88]

However brilliantly conceived, however well executed in the national interest a foreign policy alone might be, it could not in every case produce the desired result. Here again, Hitler did not shrink from the logic of his program. As to the territories lost by Germany at Versailles he said:

> We must clearly recognize the fact that the recovery of the lost territories is not through solemn appeals to the Lord or through pious hopes in the League of Nations, but only through force of arms.[89]

But the lost territories were not enough. Again, one blood demands one Reich, to which the 1914 borders of Germany were irrelevant. Once more Hitler looked east to Russia where the German sword would precede the German plow:

> In this case we must not let political boundaries obscure for us the boundaries of eternal justice.[90]

Hitler became increasingly apt to invoke eternal justice which on examination invariably coincided with the interests and programs of Adolf Hitler:

> Nature as such has not reserved this soil for the future possession of any particular nation or race; on the contrary this soil exists for the people which possesses the force to take it and the industry to cultivate it.[91]

All this would be done "in accordance with the laws of the natural order of force, and then it is the peoples of iron will who will conquer."[92] For this policy, there were prerequisites. Germany must gain freedom of action; the lost and oppressed territories could not be freed until Germany regained its independence and mastery at home. It would be necessary to break the servitude of Versailles and to reverse the verdict of 1918. The vital necessity to accomplish this was clear to Hitler. He spoke with utter clarity and simplicity: *Give us arms again.*[93]

Hitler took it as axiomatic that there could be no successful foreign policy except one backed by armed force. Therefore, Germany must rearm. This he never ceased to pronounce; and this is the program he began to carry out almost from the first day of his chancellorship. If Germany were disarmed under the provisions of the Versailles Treaty, this was of small account to Hitler as it had been to his predecessors. It is only that Hitler's goals were more ambitious and his needs stupendously larger.

After rearmament had been achieved, Hitler thought, legal recognition would follow. In this he proved to be an inspired prophet.

Hitler's Methods

These were grandiose goals. The practical problem was how to attain them. Hitler was undaunted by his obscurity, his poverty, and the ridiculously small and despised nucleus of a political movement to whom he spoke. He saw this as a benefit; the aristocratic principle of nature in action:

> What, therefore, may appear as a difficulty today is in reality the premise of our victory. Precisely in the greatness and difficulty of our task lies the probability that only the best fighters will step forward to struggle for it. And in this selection lies the guaranty of success.[94]

That nucleus had to be hard as nails; Hitler wanted no others. And around the toughest and most determined minority the rest would one day cling like filings to a magnet. Supreme persistence was needed and Hitler did not fear the lash of repression. He understood that if repression alternated with forbearance, his doctrine would recover strength and indignation would gain new followers.[95] This nucleus must go straight to the masses. This could only be done with ideas. You cannot combat an idea by force alone—only by other ideas.[96]

There is a grim foreboding in Hitler's statement of the only case in which an idea can be extinguished by force. This can only occur "in the form of the complete extermination of even the very last exponent of the idea and the destruction of the last tradition."[97]

Thus was born the Hitlerian art of propaganda, the complex of ideas that would win the support of the masses. Of this Hitler became the master:

> The art of propaganda lies in understanding the emotional ideas of the great masses and finding, through a psychologically correct form, the way to the intention and thus to the heart of the broad masses.[98]

To this end, Hitler developed the symbols and ceremony that captured attention and allegiance. In the dreariness of defeat and the drabness of the Weimar Republic, Hitler gave the German people massed scarlet banners emblazoned with the swastika. He gave them uniforms—boots, breeches, belts, and brassards; he gave them military caps and chin straps, drums and bugles, parades and torch light. He gave them comrades, mass meetings, and the heartening feeling of no longer being alone but part of a powerful mass. He gave them a good opinion of themselves—undefeated, unequaled, inherently superior. He gave them enemies to hate—Communists and Jews. He gave them outlets for their frustrations and their fears.

He was careful to specify that propaganda must never be directed to the "bright boys."[99] The more modest its intellectual content, the more successful it will be. Truth was irrelevant based upon

> the sound principle that the magnitude of a lie always contains a certain factor of credibility, since the great masses of the people in the very bottom of their hearts tend to be corrupted rather than consciously and purposely evil and that, therefore, in view of the primitive singularity of their minds, they more easily fall a victim to a big lie than a little one since they themselves lie in little things but would be ashamed of lies that were too big. Such a falsehood will never enter their heads and they will not be able to believe in the possibility of such monstrous effronteries and infamous misrepresentations in others.[100]

Hitler was a connoisseur of publicity as well as lies. Again he turned the extremism, even the ludicrous aspects of his ragtag party into an advantage:

> [I]t makes no difference whatever whether they laugh at us or revile us, whether they represent us as clowns and criminals; the main thing is that they mention us, that they concern themselves with us again and again.[101]

There was no hope in parliaments. There parties conciliated and compromised; they courted favor in elections by changes of policy or at least by promises of change. The philosopher that Hitler saw himself to be could never collaborate in a regime he despised or for a moment compromise his granitic program.

The answer, again, lay in the masses, "not in the halls of Parliament but the great public meetings represent the largest direct forum of listeners."[102] The mass meeting was personal, direct and truly effective. Here Adolf Hitler could exert his newfound powers of oratory. The power, he said, which had always launched the greatest religious and political upheavals in history had always been "the magic power of the spoken word."[103] He depicted the great popular orator who "will always let himself be borne by the great masses in such a way that instinctively the very words come to his lips that he needs to speak to the hearts of his audience."[104] The ability to communicate directly, to inspire and to move the masses was one hallmark of the leader, "But the man whose passion fails and whose lips are sealed—he has not been chosen by Heaven to proclaim his will."[105]

What Hitler did not know then was the remarkable portrait he had drawn of the Prime Minister of Great Britain at a critical moment in Hitler's triumphant ascent.

Hitler liked to think that his tactics were "based upon precise calculations of all human weakness" and that they would succeed "with mathematical certainty" unless the opposing side learned to combat poison gas with poison gas. This is precisely what the members of the LNU and the British public at large were not prepared to do.

To oratory, then, was added terror:

> Terror at the place of employment, in the factory, in the meeting hall, and on the occasion of mass demonstrations will always be successful unless opposed by equal terror.[106]

In the streets of Vienna and Munich, in his years in the trenches, in his life among the commonest of the common people, Hitler had formed a vision of their inmost souls:

> The masses love a commander more than a petitioner and feel inwardly more satisfied by a doctrine tolerating no other beside itself.[107]

He arrived at the same assessment of the mass as did Mussolini—the masses are passive, like a woman. They will always submit to force and vitality.[108]

Hitler fastened on another cardinal principle. Choose your enemy and concentrate on him:

> In general the art of all truly great national leaders at all times consists among other things primarily in not dividing the attention of the people but in concentrating it upon a single foe. The more unified the application of the people's will to fight, the greater will be the magnetic attraction of a movement, and the mightier will be the impetus of the thrust.[109]

To achieve power will require boldness, the ability to suffer hard blows. For this, only the sons of the masses will do: "They alone are determined and tough enough to carry through the fight to the bloody end."[110] This was Adolf Hitler's tribute to the rank and file, living and dead, of the Imperial German Army of 1914—1918.

How well Hitler conveyed his message is shown in the testimony of one storm trooper:

> We old National Socialists did not join the storm troops from any rational considerations, or after much contemplation. It was our feelings that led us to Hitler. What we felt, what our hearts compelled us to think, was this— Hitler, you're our man. You talk like a human being who's been at the front, who's been through the same mess we were, and not in some soft berth, but like us as an unknown soldier. You are pleading, with all your being, with all your burning heart, for us, the Germans. You want what is best for Germany not because it will benefit you personally; no, it is because you can do no other, because this is the way you must act out of your most profound convictions as a man of decency and of honor. He who once looked into Hitler's eyes, he who once heard him, will never get away from him again.[111]

This was the follower. Hitler now became the leader:

> Surely, many men may perceive the truth but . . . *one* man must step forward who with apodictic force will form granite principles from the wavering idea-world of the broad masses and take up the struggle for their sole correctness, until from the shifting waves of a free thought world there will arise a brazen cliff of solid unity in faith and will.[112]

This leader will have another distinctive characteristic which Hitler must have had in mind while dictating *Mein Kampf* to Rudolf Hess: The leader will announce himself personally.[113]

The leader will be freely chosen by the people. This is democracy, German democracy, and German tradition as Hitler sees it. For, once chosen, the leader will assume all responsibility. He may have many advisors, but "the decision will be made by one man."[114] The basic principle is terse: "authority of every leader downward and responsibility upward."[115] He will exemplify the "unified collaboration of brutal force with brilliant political will."[116] There is a price the leader must pay for the power of decision; it is the leader who, in another of *Mein Kampf's* eerie forebodings "must answer with his fortune and his life for his choice."[117]

Hitler now completes his portrait of the leader. Shaping ideas is important. The leader must be able to move the masses. Useless to argue which is more important when both are vital:

> However, the combination of a theoretician, organizer and leader in one person is the rarest thing that can be found on this Earth. This combination makes a great man.[118]

These, then, are the basic ideas of Adolf Hitler, reduced to the most summary form. He would not call them a political program; analytic always, he distinguished a philosophy from a political program:

> While the program of a solely political *party* is the formula for a healthy outcome of the next elections, the program of a philosophy is the formulation of a declaration of war against the existing order, against a definite state of affairs, in short, against an existing view of life in general.[119]

Adolf Hitler had declared war against the existing order, a fact that the existing order was slow to understand.

You will look in vain in *Mein Kampf* for tolerance, for kindness, for humanity, for human warmth, for generosity, for magnanimity. This is a spiritual self-portrait of Hitler, the penniless, the rejected, the starveling, the outcast, the homeless vagabond of the Vienna years, the soldier who in four years never a received a letter or a package from home, who kept his distance from his comrades and joined them only for political harangues.

In his immense loneliness, he poured his whole being, intellectual, emotional, and spiritual into his pursuit of ideas that would conform to his own inner vision, and into the construction, not only of a closed system, but of the means of putting it in place.

In the process, the human values slipped and faded away. Hitler steeled himself against any impulses which would corrupt and corrode his system. He took pride in the hardness his hard life had taught. No emotions, no tender impulses would now stand in the way of his demonic quest. To such a mind there was perhaps not only logic but the exalted beauty of expediency in this concept:

> If in the beginning of the War and during the War, 12 or 15 thousand of these Hebrew corrupters of people had been held under poison gas, as happened to thousands and thousands of our best German workers in the field, the sacrifice of millions at the front would not have been in vain. On the contrary 12,000 scoundrels eliminated in time might have saved the lives of a million real Germans, valuable for the future.[120]

Hitler's Ascent

Released from prison, Hitler now resumed the task of party leadership. His putsch had failed. In the future he would pursue power through constitutional means. Means only, for Hitler intended once he had achieved power, to put an end to the constitution.

In the prosperous year of 1928, the Nazis polled 810,000 votes in the Reichstag elections.[121] Now came the terrible years of depression and economic standstill. In the election of 1930, the Nazis polled 6.4 million votes.[122] There were 107 Nazis seated in the Reichstag. The Nazis were a force in the land. They could disrupt Parliament at will. Street demonstrations forced the government to ban showings of *All Quiet on the Western Front*.[123] This was not the image of war the Nazis wanted.

Chancellor Brüning could not organize a parliamentary majority and was compelled to govern by special emergency powers. As unemployment rose to 4.5 million in March, 1931, so did Nazi fortunes.

The term of President Hindenburg now neared expiration. Brüning was ready to retire when the reparations question was settled and a stable political situation attained. It was a tribute to Hitler's rising eminence that on October 10, 1931, that Brüning met Hitler and asked him to support Hindenburg's reelection. Hitler's response was a vocal statement of his program—to rearm, to rid Germany of debts rather than repay them, and to crush France. Neither party was impressed.[124]

Hitler was courted again in January, 1932, and at three meetings Brüning again proposed that Hitler support Hindenburg until reparations were settled and Germany's right to equality in armaments recognized. Brüning would then retire. For Germany and the world were on the eve of the World Disarmament Conference. Hitler's reply was a letter to Hindenburg, bypassing Brüning , and offering to support Hindenburg if he would dismiss Brüning and form a right-wing National Government. This time it was Hindenburg who refused.[125]

But one thing was clear. Adolf Hitler, who could mobilize 100,000 storm troopers for a demonstration and who commanded the allegiance of millions of voters, was now a major power to be reckoned with on the German political scene.

At the same time, he was cultivating his relations with industry and finance. In Dusseldorf, on January 27, 1932, at a meeting arranged by Fritz Thyssen, he spoke to the leaders of the German economy at the Industry Club. His two and a half hour speech swept his audience to its feet. He shrewdly championed private property and vigorously attacked Communism.[126]

What was needed, he said, was a national revival, led by a powerful state. Amid the anarchy of German politics he proclaimed

> that there can be no flourishing economic life which has not before it and behind it a flourishing, powerful state for its protection. . . . There can be no economic life unless behind this economic life there stands the determined political will of the nation absolutely ready to strike and to strike hard. . . . The essential thing is the formation of the political will of the nation.[127]

He did not mince words. The Nazis, he said, were indomitable, aggressive, brutally enforcing their will over the opposition, proud of their intolerance, and inexorably determined to destroy Marxism and build a body politic hard as iron out of the welter of competing interests and associations. For this the Nazis would make any sacrifice.[128] This was a welcome message to his audience, and the financial support which followed was of inestimable aid to Hitler in the political campaigns to follow.

7

Arms Control—1932

"The world wants disarmament. The world needs disarmament. We have it in our power to help to fashion the pattern of future history. Mankind is looking to this Conference with its unrivaled experience and knowledge, its un- challengeable representative authority and power, its massed wisdom and capacity, to be- stow the gift of freedom from the menace to peace and security that the maintenance of huge national armaments must ever be. I refuse to contemplate even the possibility of failure."
—Arthur Henderson[1]

The Disarmament Conference Opens

On the evening of February 2, 1932, a great mass meeting was held in the Albert Hall in London convened by the churches in support of the Disarmament Conference which had begun that day in Geneva.

After a half hour in which the huge audience sang appropriately chosen hymns, the Archbishop of Canterbury asked the throng to join in a silent prayer for the success of the Conference and for divine guidance of the assembled statesmen.

The Archbishop acknowledged the complexity of the issues before the Conference, the greatest international gathering since the Peace Conference of 1919. In the end, the issue before the Conference was, he said, a spiritual one. He added that nothing would or could save civilization save a new obedience to the laws of Christ's Kingdom. He urged that Christendom unite in prayer to the Divine Spirit to move

85

the hearts and minds of the statesmen so that they in turn might not part until they had brought the world nearer the day when the nations would cease to arm themselves and walk together as one body in the ways of justice, reason, and peace. The audience cheered.

The Archbishop of York recognized that Great Britain stood to gain by international cooperation. Such selfish advocacy would avail little when the real test arose. That would be the decisive moment for a distinctively Christian witness. At that moment, loyalty to Christ demanded faith, and the readiness for real risks, real sacrifice.[2]

The Archbishop's taste for risk had been revealed the Sunday before when he had preached a sermon at the St. Pierre Cathedral in Geneva, whither he had carried his ceaseless quest for peace. He had called for the revocation of the clause in the Versailles Treaty assigning war guilt to Germany. "It was the sin of all of us," he said, "that brought forth in those fearful years its flower and its fruit." Adolf Hitler would have embraced the Archbishop's conclusion, if not his theology.[3]

The Reverend W. Chanter Rigott, Chairman of the Congregational Union, said what all believed—that there was today a stronger body of antiwar conviction than at any time in modern history.

The Reverend Leslie Weatherhead of the Brunswick Wesleyan Chapel, Leeds, looked to youth to refuse the call to arms on whatever side. "We young people of today will find another way," he said. It would be impossible to lock up the conscientious objectors of the next war; there would be too many of them. What was needed was not the glamour of military life, but instead, the moral equivalent of war—a great campaign for peace.

The Bishop of Llandaff emphasized the oneness of the human race. That all men were members of the same race, he said, was not a pious platitude, but an undebatable fact.

Well might the Archbishop of Canterbury have taken pride in the assemblage. Their thoughts, their prayers, and their almost passionate hopes, he said, moved from the Albert Hall to Geneva.[4]

Arthur Henderson, President of the Disarmament Conference, opened the proceedings in Geneva an hour later than the scheduled time. This was a small delay after the years of preliminary work that had preceded the Conference. This included the labors of the Temporary Mixed Commission, to which Lord Cecil had been the rapporteur, and which had produced the Draft Treaty of Mutual Assistance. Its rejection had been followed by the Geneva Protocol, which also failed of acceptance. But its principles, in fact, and on a regional basis, were the foundation of the Locarno Treaty of 1925. The Preparatory Commission had been formed in 1925 and in 1930 completed its Draft Convention for the Limitation and Reduction of Armaments. That document was now before the Conference, but wholly without prejudice to any other constructive proposals that might be presented and considered. Needless to say, Lord Cecil had been one of the British representatives to the Preparatory Commission.

Just as the throng had gathered in hymns and prayer at the Albert Hall to witness their passionate devotion to peace, so the President of the Conference opened the meeting to the world's workers for peace prior to the start of formal deliberations. It was important that they should be a part of the Conference to which they had looked forward so long and from which they hoped so much. It was, moreover, an opportunity to impress upon the assembled statesmen the depth and passion of the worldwide yearning for peace. This might perhaps act as a solvent for the residues of world-weary cynicism, and devotion to strictly national interests that were suspected to lurk in the hearts and minds of the diplomats.

Accordingly, it was provided that an extraordinary session should be held on Saturday, February 6th, and that the Conference should hear from representatives of six groups: the churches, the League of Nations Unions, students, women's organizations, Socialists, and trade unions.[5]

The numbers represented were impressive. The President read telegrams from the Cooperative Alliance of Strasbourg representing, it was said, 70 million families in forty-four countries; from the Eastern Council of the Ecumenical Methodist Church representing 50 million; from 190,000 intellectual workers in France; from forty-five PEN Club centers in thirty-four countries; and from 173,000 Japanese men and women. All these stood foursquare for peace.

A touch of drama was lent by Mary Dingman, President of the Disarmament Committee of Women's International Organizations representing a membership of 45 million. As she presented to the President the texts of their petitions, women representing the national groups, each wearing a white sash on which was emblazoned her country's name, came forward carrying the signatures. Britain led with 8 million signatures. They were followed by a similar procession of Roman

Catholic women whose spokesman, Mme. Steenbusch Engeringh, declared that 25 million organized Catholic women stood by actively to collaborate in the cause of peace.

Resolutions and petitions were presented by the Disarmament Committee of the Christian International Organizations. These included the YMCA and the YWCA, the World Student's Christian Federation, the Alliance for Friendship, and the Friends International Service.

Students came forward. The English students presented a petition from the unions, athletic clubs, and other societies of twenty-nine universities. Mr. James Green, representing the United States, thought the times demanded a sterner position. He made it clear that he was presenting, not a petition, but an ultimatum. After considering the events of 1914–1918, his constituents had lost interest in becoming cannon fodder.

Lord Cecil representing the 1.5 million members of the International Federation of League of Nations Societies presented, not simply a resolution, but characteristically a practical plan for the abolition of offensive weapons. Representatives of Labour and Socialist organizations and the International Federation of Trade Unions, representing in all 29 million members, wound up the session.[6]

The strength and depth, the worldwide character of the antiwar movement had been impressively demonstrated.

The World Outside

The hour's delay in the opening of the Disarmament Conference had been occasioned by an emergency meeting of the League of Nations Council. A fierce battle was in progress on the outskirts of Shanghai between the Japanese and the Chinese in full view of the British, French, American and Italian inhabitants of the International Settlements. The battle was a sobering contrast to the hymns, the prayers, and the petitions which had attended the opening of the Conference. Devotion to peace was laudable; but here was a very practical test.

This was not an isolated incident. Japan had signed the Nine Power Treaty at Washington in 1921 by which it pledged to respect the independence and integrity of China. But Japan was united, modern, strong, and expansionist. China, feeble and torn by internal divisions and dissent precluding effective central government, became an irresistible focus of Japanese ambitions. The northeastern Chinese provinces of Manchuria were outside the effective writ of the Chinese government; moreover Japan had since the end of the Russo-Japanese War of 1906 by treaty maintained an army of 15,000 troops in Manchuria, headquartered at Mukden, to protect the railway zone of the South Manchurian Railway.

When on the night of September 18–19, 1931, the Japanese claimed to have discovered Chinese troops attempting to blow up the main line of the railroad, Japan moved promptly and decisively and disarmed 10,000 Chinese troops in Mukden. From here, the Japanese spread steadily across Manchuria, first in the north, then in the south, until on January 4, 1932 they had reached the Great Wall, the traditional frontier between Manchuria and China proper.[7]

Japan, now in de facto control of a vast and potentially rich area, with a population of some 30 million, disclaimed any interest in annexing Manchuria. The actions, Japan said, had been necessary to protect Japanese lives and property from Chinese bandits.[8]

The League of Nations asked Japan to withdraw. Japan declined. The League then resolved to send a commission headed by Lord Lytton to the Far East to investigate and report.[9]

The Japanese action intensified Chinese bitterness and a series of incidents in Shanghai, including a boycott, and attacks upon Japanese monks resulted in the death of one of them. The Japanese naval commander issued an ultimatum to the Chinese Mayor of Shanghai; and even after the Mayor had complied, the Japanese launched an assault, on January 28, 1932, on the densely populated Chinese suburb of Chapei. An incendiary bomb attack soon set much of Chapei ablaze. The Chinese resisted stoutly; the Japanese sent reinforcements and stepped up their activities with attacks on the Woosun Forts, not far from Shanghai.[10]

The flaming ruins of Chapei formed the backdrop against which the Disarmament Conference opened.

The Positions of the Parties

The Conference had not yet begun its formal sessions when France published its disarmament proposals. Veteran observers of the international scene found the themes familiar—French security as the goal and an international force as the means. France proposed that all heavy aircraft and all bombers be placed under the control of the League of

Nations air force, and that heavy artillery and ships carrying eight-inch guns be retained only by powers who had placed them at the disposal of the League.

Such naval provisions were always painful to Great Britain. France also proposed an international police force. France would consider reducing her forces in deference to such an international force but only on the clear understanding that the international force would have as its chief aim enforcing existing treaties and contractual rights. Concerning the structure of the League, France said that the choice must now be made between a League of Nations which had executive authority and a League of Nations paralyzed by the uncompromising principle of national sovereignty.[11]

The demographic and economic balance between France and Germany had not changed. In 1932, eighteen years after 1914, France was entering those years when her annual military contingents would be at their lowest. She believed, with reason, that Germany was rearming. France did not forget that paper pledges, like the Treaty of Guaranty, could not always insure physical security.

Sir John Simon for Great Britain proposed the abolition of gas, bombing, and submarines which, he said, tended to obliterate the distinction between combatants and noncombatants.[12] It is equally true that these were all weapons which could be employed with devastating effect on England's hitherto protected island position.

Sir John's delivery lacked oratorical flourishes and his speech evoked applause only when he paid tribute to the work done by Lord Cecil on the Preparatory Commission.[13]

The United States shared British concerns over submarine and air warfare and offensive weapons. It also proposed extending existing naval limitations and looking to further reductions.[14]

The crux of the Conference was the position of Germany. Germany had been effectively disarmed under the Versailles Treaty, its army limited to a long service contingent of 100,000, its navy miniscule, with absolute prohibitions against submarines, aircraft, tanks, and heavy artillery. Indeed, the basic issue of the Conference was the clash between armed France seeking security and disarmed Germany seeking equality. The demand for equality had been a constant in German political life and thought, without regard to party. Hitler's plea "Give us arms" met a widespread response. One did not have to be a Nazi or a militarist to resent deeply the humiliation imposed on Germany by its being literally at the mercy of an armed and despised Poland. Germany diplomats had made it clear, in their response to the Draft Convention, and in the Conference's preliminaries, that Germany's agenda was equality.[15]

Nor was Germany without a basis for its position. The Peace Treaty had said that German disarmament was only an introductory stage to general disarmament. Article 8 of the Covenant called for the reduction of national armaments to the lowest point consistent with national safety and the enforcement by common action of international obligations. Article 8 did not single out Germany.

Chancellor Brüning was conciliatory. The disarmament of Germany should be followed by general disarmament; legally and morally this was Germany's right. The German people," he said, "look to the present Conference to solve the problem of general disarmament on the basis of equal rights and equal security for all peoples."[16]

He spoke, therefore, of equality in terms of general disarmament rather than German rearmament.[17]

The other nations presented their positions. At the close of the general debate on February 24, 1932, the issues raised were assigned to a series of special commissions. These included in addition to the General Commission, the Land, Naval, Air, and National Defense Expenditure Commissions. A Political Commission was established at French insistence to consider the issues of security. The French terms of reference for this Committee were designed to exclude any question of German equality. At Poland's request, a special committee on Moral Disarmament was established.

The task of the commissions was difficult because what appeared to the technical commissions to be issues of principle to be decided by the General Commission often appeared to the General Commission to be technical issues. This was frustrating to those who believed that all that was needed was to lay down clear-cut, basic principles of peace. They tended to believe that the problems were caused by the technical experts, likely to be men who wore stripes on their sleeves or stars and crowns on their shoulders.[18]

What were offensive weapons and what were defensive weapons? Seapower enabled Great Britain to lead an Empire upon which it was said the sun never set. It was clear to Lord Cecil that battleships were purely defensive; submarines, on the other hand, were offensive. Powers which had no battleships tended to consider them aggressive. The German view was simple: all weapons forbidden to Germany were offensive.[19]

The deliberations of the Air Commission illustrated the difficulties. By June, it had arrived at these conclusions, neither startling nor useful: that aircraft could be used for offensive purposes, without prejudice to the question of their defensive use; that whether aircraft were offensive weapons depended on certain construction characteristics; that the most threatening to civilian populations were bombers. The Commission concluded that the danger represented by an aircraft was proportional to its useful load and its range. The Air Commission, after lengthy deliberation, was able to conclude that aerial bombing constituted a grave menace to civilians and that the dangers arose from poison gases, bacteria, and incendiary and explosive devices.[20]

The Committee on Effectives could make no progress until it could define the term effectives. What was "premilitary training" and to what extent were paramilitary or police organizations effectives? In the end, the Committee confessed defeat and so reported to the General Commission.[21]

Beyond the technical difficulties lay the omnipresent French claim that, instead of trying to make war more humane, the Conference would achieve more by organizing the peace on a stable basis, which to France meant providing security against the German threat.

These were lengthy and complex deliberations, interrupted from time to time as the statesmen were called upon to address issues outside the Conference and as the Conference indulged in lengthy recesses. Progress was difficult to perceive, but the crises and problems of the world outside the Conference hall in Geneva would neither recess nor adjourn until the Conference had brought forth its results.

The World Outside—2

Heavily reinforced, the Japanese stepped up their offensive against the Chinese at Shanghai. The Chinese rebuffed a demand that their troops be promptly withdrawn from the Shanghai region and resisted stoutly. This was real war. By early March, the Chinese were in retreat. Negotiations finally produced an armistice agreement on April 27, 1932. Signature was delayed by a bomb incident on April 29 during a review of Japanese troops in honor of the Emperor's birthday. This cost the Japanese minister, Mr. Shigemitsu, his leg. So it was that thirteen years later, he limped painfully aboard the USS Missouri to sign the Japanese act of surrender. By the end of May, the

Japanese troops were withdrawn save for a small garrison.[22]

The Japanese pressure in Manchuria took on a more permanent cast. Under Japanese impulse, a declaration of independence was published on February 18, 1932 by which shortly thereafter the Manchurian provinces became the state of Manchukuo. It was declared to be a republic. Henry Pu Yi, the last Mongol Emperor of China, was named first acting President and then Regent. The new state, he said, would be founded on the bases of "morality, benevolence, and love."[23]

Thus did Japan tender the issue to the Lytton Commission which had set out upon its labors on February 3, 1932.

As lurid as the flames of Chapie were the torchlights of Nazi rallies and processions. Adolf Hitler presented himself as candidate for President in opposition to Hindenburg. In the election of March 13, 1932 the Nazi vote increased to 11.5 million from the 6.5 million of 1930.[24] Hindenburg failed to gain the requisite majority by 0.4 percent of the vote. It needed a second election on April 10, 1932 for Hindenburg to gain his 53 percent majority.

This time Hitler campaigned over all Germany by plane—a dramatic innovation. The Nazis increased their poll to 13.4 million, taking votes from the Conservatives on the one side and the Communists on the other.[25]

Winston Churchill was alert to the German challenge. The talk of equality for Germany, which commended itself to large segments of the public, the clergy, and the press, was to him a clear and present danger. He told the House of Commons in May, 1932 that to grant equality of arms to Germany was to invite war. This was Churchill's first warning:

> I am sure that the thesis that they (the Germans) should be placed in an equal military position with France is one which, if it ever emerged in fact, would bring us to within practical distance of almost measureless calamity.[26]

Prophecy began its steady march to reality. Chancellor Brüning, lacking a stable parliamentary majority, had been compelled to govern under Hindenburg's emergency presidential powers. The President and the army represented the bases of power in a state where Parliament could not assemble a working majority. General Schleicher, who commanded the allegiance of the army and the ear of the President, led the assault on Brüning and offered Hitler substantial political advantages in return for Hitler's benevolent neutrality. These included a removal of Brüning's ban on the SA and early Parliamentary elections from which the Nazis might hope to benefit.[27]

On May 30, 1932, Hindenburg asked for and received Brüning's resignation.[28] He was succeeded as Chancellor by Franz von Papen, as confirmed an aristocrat and conservative as Brüning had been a democrat. Of ten members, his cabinet of barons included seven noblemen whose views paralleled Papen's. Democracy was in full retreat in Germany.[29]

The lifting of Brüning's ban on the SA was followed by riot, violence, and murder across Germany as the Nazis battled the Communists in the streets. Seizing upon these as a pretext, Papen, using dubious presidential decree powers, deposed the Social Democratic government of Prussia, Germany's dominant state on July 20, 1932. This was another critical step in the collapse of Weimar democracy.[30] The pace quickened in the Reichstag elections of July 31, 1932 when the Nazis with 13.7 million votes gained 230 seats in the Reichstag, becoming the largest party in Germany, far outweighing the 8 million Social Democratic ballots.[31]

The Conference Continues

It soon became clear that Papen's view of German equality differed from Brüning's. Rather than leveling down by the other parties to match Germany, the new Chancellor preferred an equality in which treaty restrictions were removed and Germany leveled up to her rivals.

The Conference was nearing a standstill. Herbert Hoover submitted a plan which he hoped would cut through the brush and at the same time promote economic recovery by saving vast sums wasted on armaments.[32] He proposed reducing all arms by one-third. Once again, the British suspected an American assault on British seapower. But Britain tabled its own proposal in deference to the Hoover plan. France thought the proposals "so attractively simple that they might appear to be too simple in view of the complexity of certain problems"; and again called attention to the French proposal for security.[33]

While the Hoover plan was under discussion, the Lausanne Conference on Reparations was also underway, complicating the work of the Disarmament Conference. Chancellor Brüning had stated firmly in January that Germany was no longer able to pay reparations; his successor was equally firm. The Lausanne Conference agreed that reparations should be terminated and that Germany should issue three billion marks ($2 billion) of 5 percent bonds, the proceeds to be placed in an escrow subject to an allocation agreement among the creditors. Germany's obligation was thus reduced from $25 billion to $2 billion which few ever expected to be paid.[34] Adolf Hitler promptly declared that he would not pay three marks, much less three billion.[35] The British were pleased; the French thought they had made a great sacrifice; the Germans were indignant that the slate had not been wiped clean. Their indignation was wasted. No payment was ever made.

The Hoover plan failed in its turn to gain approval.[36] The Conference now attempted to put on the table a resolution stating that some agreement had been reached. This resolution provided that air attacks against civilian targets should be forbidden and the numbers and characteristics of aircraft limited in ways later to be determined; that heavy artillery should be confined to calibers later to be determined; that the maximum tonnage of tanks should be limited as later determined; that chemical and bacteriological war should be prohibited under conditions to be recommended; and finally that a permanent Disarmament Commission should be established.

The resolution was long on principles and exceedingly short on specifics which were simply deferred to a more agreeable day and climate.

Forty-one delegations voted for the resolution; eight abstained; Germany and the Soviet Union voted nay.[37] Germany now announced that she would no longer participate in the work of the Conference until there was a clear and definite recognition of equality of rights between nations. Germany not only firmly maintained this stance, but General Schleicher from time to time announced that Germany, threatened by the enemy would in any case do what was necessary to defend herself.[38]

Germany now left the Conference. Her action was endorsed by a large segment of British opinion. The churchmen whose warnings and blessings had attended the opening of the Disarmament Conference concurred with Germany. The Archbishops of Canterbury and York, the head of the Methodist Church, and the General of the Salvation Army headed a delegation of spiritual leaders which called on the Prime Minister and the Foreign Minister on September 20, 1932. They were deeply disappointed at the lack of progress at the Conference:

> The problems involved are of a moral, not a juridical character. . . . The promises given at Versailles by virtue of which the compulsory disarma-

ment of Germany ought to constitute the first step to general disarmament have not been fulfilled . . . .The British government should formulate a definite disarmament policy, based on legal equality of all League of Nations members.[39]

The World Outside—3

The Lytton Commission report came before the League of Nations in September. It rejected Japanese pretexts for the invasion of Manchuria, labeled the state of Manchukuo a fiction; but at the same time criticized Chinese attitudes and provocations. It recommended that Manchuria become an autonomous state following negotiations between Japan and China under League auspices.[40] Again the principle was pronounced; the difficult questions were left to be determined.

The British Cabinet had by now agreed in principle to equality of status which would bring Germany back to the Conference. But Stanley Baldwin understood the consequences of such a course of action. On November 9, 1932, he declared that "the time has now come to an end when Great Britain can proceed with unilateral disarmament."[41]

And on the following day he made a memorable statement to the House of Commons: the bomber will always get through. To which he added: "The only defense is offense, which means that you have to kill more women and children more quickly than the enemy if you wish to save yourselves."[42] The Government, he said, would be guilty of criminal neglect if it did not make adequate preparations.

Even so, Churchill found in Baldwin's statement a sense of fatalism, of helplessness. "Tell the truth" he urged, "tell the truth to the British people. They are a tough people and a robust people."[43] The issue of British rearmament was now joined.

In Germany, in November, 1932, the fifth election in a year produced a modest setback for Hitler. The Nazis lost 2 million votes of the 13.7 million in July; their Reichstag seats were reduced from 230 to 196.[44] Hitler remained, nevertheless, master of Germany's largest party. Fifteen years before he had been a corporal on the Western Front, ten years before he had been the leader of a petty group of political outcasts. Now Papen and his barons sought Adolf Hitler's support in the Reichstag for their regime. Hitler, by setting impossible terms, effectively declined. Papen tendered his resignation to Hindenburg on November 17, 1932.[45]

Now it was the turn of the venerable Field Marshal become President to call on the erstwhile corporal to ask if he would lead a coalition government. This was precisely what Hitler did not want, perhaps remembering his days as a youthful spectator in the Austrian Parliament. Hitler wanted full power, effective power. He wanted the sweeping emergency powers Hindenburg had given Papen. He declined, confident the day would soon come when such powers would be placed in his hands.[46]

Schleicher now declared that the army no longer had confidence in Papen and that Papen's policy, opposed by both the Nazis and the Communists, would result in civil war. "I am an old man," Hindenburg said, "and I cannot face a civil war of any sort in my country." He withdrew his support of Papen. Schleicher became Chancellor on December 3, 1932.[47]

The Conference Resolves

At Geneva, the search continued for a formula which would resolve the basic issue raised by Germany—equality. The American delegate, Norman Davis, suggested that the Conference should give the world a Christmas present: an agreement incorporating whatever could be agreed upon, leaving the rest to the Permanent Commission.[48]

In the end what was found was a formula, not a solution:

> The Governments of the United Kingdom, France and Italy have declared that one of the principles that should guide the Conference on disarmament should be to grant to Germany, and to the other Powers disarmed by treaty, equality of rights in a system which would provide security for all nations.[49]

What precisely this meant was left to the Conference to determine, to be included in the proposed Disarmament Convention. Germany was asked to return to the Conference on this basis and accepted on December 11, 1932.

Arms Control, 1932—An Interim Assessment

The formula of December 11, 1932 comforted those who wished to be comforted and gave hope to the hopeful. On a more stringent analysis, the Disarmament Conference at this stage was not an unqualified success.

Its goal had been disarmament. Germany had successfully defied the Conference and had been wooed back by a declaration which effectively gave to Germany the right to rearm. Germany was to be given equality; how security would be assured remained to be seen. The burden of armaments was not reduced.

Vital provisions of the Versailles Treaty had been opened to modification—those limiting German arms. If these provisions of Versailles could be revised, might not Germany hope for liberation from every onerous chapter and clause?

Reparations had expired, too. For these signal accomplishments, the Weimar Republic gained no credit. Brüning was gone; Papen and Schleicher had presided over these events.

These were hammerblows to the peace settlement for which France had fought and to the security which she believed had been bought and paid for in the blood and devastation of 1914–1918. The Treaty of Guaranty had gone first. The occupation troops had been removed from the Rhineland in 1930, not 1935, at British insistence. The reparations which were to have restored the ruin of war were now at an end. What now would German military equality mean to France?

What remained alone and untouched of France's security barriers lay on the West bank of the Rhine, the strategic border which Foch had sought. The demilitarized Rhineland, created by the Peace Treaty and voluntarily confirmed by Germany at Locarno, now assumed an even greater importance as the keystone of French security.

The world was becoming more dangerous. Japan stood in unassailable possession of the Manchurian provinces and neither the indignation of the world nor the reports and resolutions of the League of Nations had been to any effect. The Lytton Commission report was adopted by the League Assembly on February 24, 1933; on March 27, 1933 Japan left the League of Nations, an ominous precedent.

Germany had been the consistent winner. But there was little evidence that the concessions granted to her had led to any real satisfaction. Instead they were looked on as signs of weakness and precedents for the next German demands.

The principle of equality remained to be translated into reality. In the wings, confidently calculating his support and Schleicher's weakness, stood the supreme realist—Adolf Hitler.

8

The German Challenge

"My programme was to abolish the Treaty of Versailles. It is nonsense for the rest of the world to pretend today that I did not reveal this programme until 1933, or 1935, or 1937. Instead of listening to the foolish chatter of emigres, these gentlemen would have been wiser to read what I have written and rewritten thousands of times. No human being has declared or recorded what he wanted more often than I. Again and again I wrote these words—the Abolition of the Treaty of Versailles."
—Adolf Hitler[1]

Hitler in Power

Papen now sought to turn the tables on Schleicher. He met Hitler on January 4, 1933 and suggested a joint chancellorship. Though Hitler said he must be head of government, the two men, united in their dislike for Schleicher and their desire for power, found common ground.[2]

They continued their discussions, significantly importing into them Oskar von Hindenburg, the President's son. Meanwhile, Schleicher found that he could, no more than Papen, construct a workable majority without the largest party in the Reichstag. He asked Hindenburg, as Papen had, for the power to dissolve the Reichstag and govern by emergency decree. Hindenburg told Schleicher what he had told Papen: that it was essential to obtain National Socialist support, but Hitler rebuffed Schleicher.[3]

It was under these circumstances, on January 31, 1933 that Hindenburg appointed Hitler Chancellor, with Papen as Vice Chancellor, and Hindenburg's nominee, General von Blomberg, Minister of Defense.[4]

The remarkable transformation of Adolf Hitler has often been noted. The drifter and dreamer, the failed artist of Vienna days, the wartime corporal, the street corner and beer cellar orator, the petty politician who had attracted his full share of derision and contempt, had now become the Chancellor of the German Reich. More remarkable were the characteristics that had brought Hitler to this point: the sheer will-power, the dedication, the toughness, and the self-confidence fueled on the one hand by his fanatical hatreds and on the other hand by his incandescent visions of German glory and conquest. To these were added his intuitive perception of the inner thoughts and emotions of the German people, his uncanny ability to communicate directly with them, and an equally intuitive grasp of the concerns, the hesitations, and the weaknesses of the statesmen with whom he would be called upon to deal.

Hitler had built Germany's largest party and made it indispensable to the governance of the state. He had achieved office by strictly legal and constitutional means. He had no intention of governing that way.

Hitler Prepares for War

Immediately on becoming Chancellor, Hitler sought a meeting with the army leaders. This took place on February 3, 1932 at the Bendlerstrasse apartment of General von Hammerstein-Equord. Hitler's message to the generals was as precisely tailored to their interests as had been his speech to the industrialists.[5]

The first aim was to regain political power. Democracy, his hearers must have been gratified to learn, was of as little use in government as it was in the army—or in industry. The whole political situation in Germany had to be reversed, and Marxism exterminated root and branch. Pacifism would not be tolerated. The cancer of democracy would be removed. There would be the tightest authoritarian state leadership and those who would not be converted would be broken.

If the generals were apprehensive of the SA formations, millions strong and noisily on the march throughout Germany, Hitler set their minds at ease. The task of the Nazi party was educational. The party was not created to bear arms. Thus, Hitler assured the generals that he did not seek, through the SA, to supersede the army. Instead he would battle against Versailles for equality of rights. He was committed to the build-up of the armed forces and especially the reintroduction of conscription. What message could have been more welcome to the leaders of the 100,000–man army?

The conscripts must be imbued with the fighting spirit without which equality of rights would be useless. They must not be poisoned by pacifism, Marxism, or Bolshevism.

In the realm of economics, the solution was not in an increase in exports in a world plagued by overproduction, but in a settlement policy, since German living space was too small for the needs of the German people. When political and military power had been regained, they would be used to conquer and ruthlessly Germanize new living space in the East.

For all this, the armed forces were, Hitler assured the generals, the most important institution in the state. The most dangerous period would be during the build-up of the armed forces. For this reason, the build-up had to be carried out with the utmost secrecy until it was an accomplished fact. On that day Germany would have regained its freedom of decision. In the interim, Hitler warned, if France had real statesmen, she would not stand idly by but would attack, probably through her East European allies.

What Hitler was plainly telling his generals was that he intended to carry out the policy he had so clearly enunciated in *Mein Kampf*.

On February 7, 1933, Hitler reiterated these goals to his cabinet:

Every publicly supported project for creating employment," he said, "must be judged by one criterion alone: is it or is it not requisite for the restoration of the German nation's fighting capacity?[6]

He pronounced his bedrock position:

Everything for the Wehrmacht. Germany's world position will be a factor of its Wehrmacht position, and of that alone.[7]

It was now necessary to put in place the foundations of the new armed forces. Facilities had to be built. The civil aviation budget deliberately camouflaged the building of the new air force. The military budget of April 1933 called for two-front armed forces to be ready in five years.[8]

Hitler Consolidates Power

Hitler now turned to the task he had set for himself in his speech to the generals. The Nazis and Nationalists lacked a parliamentary majority. The Nazis held only three of eleven cabinet posts, and Papen, the Vice Chancellor, was Minister-President of Prussia and confident that real power lay in his hands.

For a parliamentary majority, the support of the Center Party was needed.[9] In his negotiations with its leader, Monsignor Kaas, Hitler made sure that no agreement would be reached, thereby forcing another election. The Nazis now had advantages they had lacked in previous elections. "The struggle is a light one now," Goebbels wrote,

> since we are able to employ all the means of the State. Radio and Press are at our disposal. We shall achieve a masterpiece of propaganda. Even money is not lacking at this time.[10]

The industrialists again rallied in response to Hitler's plea, pledging three million marks to the coalition which in essence meant to the Nazis.[11]

The Nazis had sought from the first moment of Hitler's chancellorship to find a pretext for crushing the Communists. This they found, whatever the true facts may have been, in the Reichstag fire of February 27, 1933. The arrest of the Communist leaders for subsequent trial was promptly followed on the day after the fire by an emergency decree, promulgated by Hitler and signed by President Hindenburg "for the protection of the People and the State."[12]

By this law, the guarantees of individual liberty under the Weimar Constitution, including the freedom of the press, the right of assembly, of privacy and communications, and protection against warrant less searches and confiscation of property were suspended. The Reich Government was authorized to take over full power in any state. The death penalty was reinstituted for high treason, arson and sabotage, and even for grave breaches of the peace. These were powerful weapons in the hands of an authoritarian leader and party, as Goering made clear:

> Fellow Germans, my measures will not be crippled by any judicial thinking. My measures will not be crippled by any bureaucracy. Here I don't worry about Justice, my mission is only to destroy and exterminate, nothing more.[13]

As Minister of the Interior of Prussia, Goering was in a position to carry out such a pledge, to dismiss his opponents, and place the administration of Prussia which was, after all, two-thirds of Germany, solidly in Nazi hands.

The election campaign was electric; Nazi parades, demonstrations, brutality and violence backed up by Hitler's announced determination to crush Marxism and the parties of the left. The sheer mass and naked power, the force and intimidation employed made as profound an impression on the German electors as the Nazi campaign themes of German pride and German power.

Despite all this, when the election results were counted on March 5, 1933, the Nazis had not gained a majority. They polled 17.3 million votes, 5 million higher than their highest prior total, or 43.9 percent of the total vote. The Center and Social Democratic parties maintained relatively steady totals; the Communists lost a million votes in counting 4.8 million ballots. This was Germany's last multiparty election. Hitler needed the 3.2 million Nationalists votes and their fifty-two deputies added to his own delegation of 288 Nazis to command a majority in the new Reichstag.[14]

When the new Reichstag assembled, Hitler had his weapon in hand. It was the Law for the Protection of the People and the State. He could now arrest any of the eighty-one Communist deputies who appeared to claim his seat. He entered into negotiations with the Center Party for the passage of the fundamental law of the Nazi regime—the Enabling Act, or, as it was more colorfully and formally titled, the Law for Ending the Distress of the People and the Reich.[15]

The Enabling Act empowered the Government to pass laws without reference to the Reichstag and specifically provided that such laws might deviate from the Constitution. It also granted to the Government authority to enter into treaties affecting international affairs without any of the approvals required for domestic legislation. The term of the proposed grant was four years expiring April 1, 1937.

At the Reichstag session held in the Kroll Opera House on March 23, 1933, all of the symbols of Nazi power were on full display; the black-shirted SS troops and the brown-shirted SA were a massive presence. The Social Democrats, some of whose members had already been arrested, bravely announced their opposition to the Enabling Act. The Center Party understood the danger. In addition to Hitler's promises, they had obtained a letter from Hindenburg who wrote: "The

Chancellor has given me his assurance that, even without being forc-ibly obliged by the Constitution, he will not use the power conferred upon him by the Enabling Act without having first consulted me."[16]

The President was then eighty-seven and unlikely to survive the four-year term of the Enabling Act. It is a tribute to the comfort to be found in paper promises by those who wished to find them there that, on this basis, Monsignor Kaas announced the Center Party's support of the Enabling Act.[17]

This was Hitler's triumph. The Enabling Act had conferred on him powers which Brüning, Papen, and Schleicher had never possessed and what is more made him independent of the President. Hitler was now in control and he used that power to destroy any vestiges of opposition.

Under the process called *Gleichschaltung*, or coordination with the Nazi state, office holders in the German states were displaced and replaced with Nazis, first in Bavaria, then in Baden, Wurtemberg, and Saxony. On March 31, the diets of all of the other states were dis-solved to be replaced without election by members representing the voting rolls of the Reichstag election, with all Communist votes nulli-fied.[18] Shortly thereafter, even this vestige of independence disap-peared as Hitler appointed governors for each state with the power to make law, dismiss diets and remove the state governments. Naturally the new governors were all Nazis.[19]

On May Day, 1933, the government held a huge worker's rally in Berlin. The next day, the SS and the SA invaded all trade union offices, beating and arresting trade union officials, many of whom formed the first contingent in the concentration camps. The unions were then declared part of the German Labor Front. Goebbels exulted that with the trade union movement in Nazi hands, no party or group would be able to hold out for long.[20]

The formal end of political opposition came with the Law Against the Formation of New Parties of July 14, 1933. The provisions were simple:

Article I
The sole political party existing in Germany is the
National Socialist German Workers Party.

Article II
Whoever shall undertake to maintain the organization of another party,
or to

found a new party, shall be punished with a sentence of hard labor of up to three years, or of prison between six months and three years, unless other regulations provide for heavier punishment.[21]

By a law of July 20, 1933, the jurisdiction of the civil courts over the army was abolished to the army's immense satisfaction.[22]

Gleichschaltung meant more than the subordination to the will of government by the organs of politics, of the military, and of trade unionism. All organizations and associations of whatever complexion, profession, trade, purpose or outlook were co-opted to the ends of the Nazi state. Mathematics had a long and proud tradition in Germany as one of the ornaments of German and world scholarship. The German Mathematical Association heard this address, on September 20, 1933, from its President:

> We wish thus to conform to the spirit of the total state, and to cooperate loyally and honestly. Unconditionally and joyfully, we place ourselves— as is a matter of course for every German—at the service of the National Socialist movement and behind its leader, our Chancellor Adolf Hitler. And we hope that we have something to offer. What mathematics and natural science mean in today's state, too, for patriotic education, will be indicated in the address by Senior Counselor Ernst Tiedge.
>
> But we also know that even in a merely advisory capacity, we are in a position to be heard only if in external matters, too, we adapt ourselves to the demands of the movement.
>
> Hence, we decided to submit these three points for your approval:
>
> 1. The leadership principle. You are to elect a leader, who is to bear the sole responsibility.
>
> 2. The leader then is to appoint his assistants, and especially the members of a leader's council. In so doing, he shall be obliged to observe the requirements of Aryan ancestry in their strictest form, i.e., as they apply to leading government officials.
>
> 3. The Association's board is to be dissolved. It is the prerogative of the leader to organize that institution in a new form.[23]

The pattern had been set by Mussolini: the acquisition of emergency powers, the artificial creation of a parliamentary majority followed by the laws which would destroy the concept of law and leave all powers in the hands of the head of state. The difference was the speed with which Hitler had acted. It had taken Mussolini three years finally to subordinate all public and private organs to the state. Hitler had accomplished the same in his first six months in power.

If there remained a potential source of danger, it was in the heart of the National Socialist Movement. It had been founded on the concepts of Feder and the notion of interest slavery. The party had been proud to incorporate "Socialist" in its name; and its first program made strong appeals to the proletarian masses with its call for the abolition of unequal incomes, profit sharing, nationalization of trusts and department stores, and land reform. Many of its adherents and not a few of its leaders were deeply committed to a program of this left-wing character. They worried, as Hitler's powers grew, that he had lost interest in their goals.

The other discordant element was found in the paramilitary forces of the SA and the SS, headed by Ernst Roehm. They had been in the vanguard of the struggle for power; they had furnished the indispensable manpower, the physical force, the intimidation, the glamor and appeal of armed might on which Hitler had built his party. Hitler acknowledged this in his 1934 New Year's greetings to Roehm, addressed to "My dear Chief of Staff":

> The fight of the National Socialist Movement and the National Socialist Revolution were rendered possible for us by the consistent suppression of the Red Terror by the SA. . . . It is primarily due to your services, if after a few years this political instrument would develop that force which enabled me to face the final struggle for power and to succeed in laying low the Marxist opponent.[24]

For this, his gratitude was inscribed "in true friendship and grateful regard" by Adolf Hitler.[25]

Roehm found the state of affairs distinctly unsatisfactory. His SA and SS forces of between two and three million men vastly outnumbered the army. Roehm's logic dictated that the army and the SA be combined and it seemed even more logical to him that he should lead the combined organization.

Hitler had made his choice and had announced it to the generals. He would not, he had promised, call upon the army to act in the political field. For the tasks he had in mind, for the conquest of space in Russia, for the gigantic responsibility of world power, the street fighters and brawlers, the part-time troopers of the SA and SS were inadequate. The professional skills, the organization, the traditions, and the discipline of the German army were the vehicles by which Hitler's program would be fulfilled.

It was for these reasons that, when Anthony Eden, clearly concerned over Germany's growing military might, visited him in February 1934, Hitler offered to reduce the SA by two thirds and insure that the remainder had neither arms nor military training.[26]

Both Schleicher and Papen were dismayed and disgruntled by the speed and finesse with which Hitler had seized effective power. Hitler later claimed that Roehm had intrigued with Schleicher to unite the army and the SA under Roehm. Papen publicly proclaimed that the time had come for the revolution to define its aims and to represent all of the people and not simply the revolutionary elite.[27]

Beyond the struggle between those elements of National Socialism whose vision emphasized socialism and those whose vision emphasized nationalism, beyond the tension between the military forces of the regular army and the paramilitary forces of the Nazi party, there lay the personal rivalries among Roehm, Goering and Himmler. The latter two were pleased to take charge of arrangements for eliminating a feared rival. The army remained as firmly loyal to Hitler as it had been in the days when he was called to power.

It was under these circumstances that Hitler struck, personally telegraphing Roehm for a rendezvous at Weissee. It was there that Roehm was picked up and brought to Munich. He refused to commit suicide: "If I am to be killed" he declared, "let Adolf Hitler do it himself." Hitler did not do it himself; but Roehm was shot as dead as if he had.

Goring and Himmler supervised the executions in Berlin. Their victims included Schleicher and his wife and Gregor Strasser, Hitler's chief party rival. Papen's colleagues were executed and his house wrecked, but he himself was spared.

While Hitler entertained at tea, the executions went on in Berlin, in Breslau, and in Munich. The total number of victims of the celebrated Night of the Long Knives has been estimated from 100 to 400.[28]

Two days later, General von Blomberg telegraphed Hitler to convey the congratulations of the Cabinet. As for the army, in a special order of the day, it expressed its loyalty to Hitler and its readiness to establish new relations with the SA.[29]

When Hitler appeared before the Reichstag on July 13, 1934, he emphasized the nature of Roehm's plot against the state and his own reluctance to act. He also emphasized his loyalty to the army, which alone should be the bearer of arms in the state, while the Nazi party would be the bearers of its political will.

This was the army's bargain—that it should have a monopoly of military power. To the army's Dr. Faustus, Hitler proved an unyielding Devil.

Hitler defended the bloody and arbitrary manner of his exercise of power:

> If anyone reproaches me and asks why I did not resort to the regular courts of justice for conviction of the offenders, then all that I can say to him is this: in this hour I was responsible for the fate of the German people, and thereby I became the Supreme Justiciar of the German people.

Hitler made his point perfectly clear:

> And everyone must know for all future time that if he raises his hand to strike the State, then certain death is his lot.[30]

Now occurred the climactic event in Hitler's ascent to supreme power. On August 2, 1934, Hindenburg died. All had been prepared. The Law Concerning the Head of the German State had been passed on August 1, 1934. It provided that the offices of President and Chancellor should be combined and that the powers exercised by the President should be transferred to the Führer and Chancellor, Adolf Hitler. The law was to take effect on the date of Hindenburg's death.

This was the law that was promptly proclaimed on August 2. In addition, Hitler was named Head of State and Commander-in-Chief of the Armed Forces of the Reich.

The effective implementation of the law for the Army took place the same day. The officers and men of the German Army swore this oath:

> I swear by God this holy oath: I will render unconditional obedience to the Führer of the German Reich and People, Adolf Hitler, the Supreme Commander of the Armed Forces, and will be ready, as a brave soldier, to stake my life at any time for this oath.[31]

The oath was not to the state, but to Adolf Hitler personally. On August 19, 1934 the German people in a plebiscite, in which 95.7 percent took part, by 89.9 percent of the votes cast, affirmed Hitler's assumption of Hindenburg's offices.[32]

Hitler and the Disarmament Conference

When Hitler outlined his plans to rearm to the German generals on February 3, 1933, the Disarmament Conference had completed its first year. With its ponderous deliberations, its obvious procedural and more glaring substantive problems, and with its many adjournments, the Conference would, Hitler saw, be an ideal cover for German rearmament. It might be possible to prolong the discussions while Germany laid the technical and economic bases for rearmament, and to play upon hopes for peace in order to prepare Germany for war.

If the Conference offered Germany a cloak under which to further its rearmament, it also offered opposite and unattractive dangers. It was possible that the Conference would decide on a general disarmament down to Germany's level; or on the other hand, offer Germany a genuine equality at a controlled level. Hitler clearly wanted neither disarmament nor equality. From the first day of his chancellorship, his goal was to achieve decisive superiority which alone would enable him to carry out his grandiose program.

Here was the first test of Hitler's political ingenuity and propaganda skills: to make the Conference serve his own ends of rearmament while staying clear of any unwelcome obligation or limitation. If he could successfully portray himself as a man of peace, the task would be much easier. From the start, Hitler perceived that, given the divergence between his acts and his words, there would always be those, and they were numerous and influential, who preferred to accept his words at their face value.

The French plan then before the Conference rested on the French thesis that in order to have equality and a system of security, the system of security should be created first. This the French plan provided for elaborately with three layers of obligations, the first involving all signatories to the Kellogg-Briand Pact (which included the United States), the second involving all members of the League of Nations (which did not), and the third involving the continental European powers. At each level, there would be automatic, interlocking obligations to enforce in turn, the Paris Pact and the Covenant of the League of Nations; in Europe there would be a special mutual assistance organization involving political and military arrangements.[33]

Notwithstanding that Britain was not included in the third level of continental European powers, the French plan raised the usual British objection to increased commitments. At Geneva, on February 3, 1933, Anthony Eden said,

I can give no hint of encouragement that it would be possible for us to. . . . undertake new obligations to which, I believe, the public opinion of my country is unalterably opposed.[34]

But Eden thought that something must be done else the Germans would proceed to rearm. He persuaded the Prime Minister to present a detailed plan to the Conference, fixing the manpower and armaments of the continental European armies. The MacDonald Plan provided short-service European armies of 200,000 men for France, Germany, Italy, and Poland, and 500,000 for the USSR. Maximum artillery calibers were provided, though no limitation of numbers. Aerial bombing was prohibited and the number of aircraft limited to 500 each for Britain, France, Italy, Japan, the USSR, and the United States, but none for Germany.[35]

MacDonald presented the Plan in person in Geneva on March 16, 1933. In Britain, criticism of the Plan took two distinctly different forms. Gilbert Murray wrote to Lord Cecil:

I think Ramsay's speech hollow, ranting and inadequate and the Foreign Office scheme rotten as usual. Not a single sacrifice by England; all the reductions to be made by others.

Cecil replied that he entirely agreed.[36]

Winston Churchill entirely disagreed. "Thank God for the French army," he told Parliament on March 23, 1933, as he described the resurgence in Germany of the war spirit, the persecutions, the abandonment of civilized standards by a gifted and formidable nation. He pointed out, the next month, that Germany no longer was parliamentary democracy, but a grim dictatorship. To grant Germany equality would, he said, bring Europe within measurable distance of a general European war.[37]

The MacDonald Plan was the subject of numerous amendments. Germany continued to demand equality, notwithstanding that the reduction of the French army to a 200,000 equality with Germany enormously enhanced the German position. At the German Cabinet meeting of May 12, 1933, Hitler concluded that Germany would leave the Conference.

After President Roosevelt's firm backing of the MacDonald Plan in a speech of May 16, 1933,[38] Hitler changed his mind. When he spoke on May 17, it was as a man of peace.[39]

After cataloguing the evils of the peace settlement, which, he said,

Germany had nevertheless faithfully observed, he seized the higher ground of Germany's moral right to equality in arms. Germany would do more than accept the MacDonald Plan as a basis for negotiation, and would participate in a five-year transition period for German rearmament. Germany would abandon not only offensive weapons but would be prepared to disarm completely if only the other nations would do the same. Germany would reject no disarmament plan as too drastic which applied in the same manner to other states.

This was premised on grounds of humanity, justice and understanding. Hitler waxed lyrical:

> [W]e in this new Germany are filled with deep understanding for the same feelings and opinions and for the rightful claims to life of other nations. The present generation of this new Germany, which, so far, has known in its life the poverty, misery, and distress of its own people, has suffered too deeply from the madness of our time to contemplate treating others in the same way.
>
> Our boundless love for and loyalty to our own national traditions makes us respect the national claims of others and makes us desire from the bottom of our hearts to live with them in peace and friendship.[40]

Germany, said Hitler, would be willing to enter any solemn nonaggression pact "because she does not think of attacking but only of acquiring security." Moreover, Germany desired to heal the wounds caused both by the war and the Treaty of Versailles.

> The German people wishes to come to a peaceful agreement with other nations on all difficult questions. They know that in any military action in Europe, even if completely successful, the sacrifices would be out of all proportion to any possible gains.[41]

In the end, there was a warning note. Any attempt to do violence to Germany by a majority of the Convention would be tantamount to excluding from the Conference a Germany possessed of sufficient character, though with heavy heart, to draw the only possible conclusions.[42]

Further discussions led to amendments and, on June 29, the inevitable adjournment until October 16, 1933. Meanwhile, the President, Arthur Henderson, was commissioned to embark on a pilgrimage for peace to the principal European capitals in search of agreement on which a new draft convention could be based.

The more the French thought about a German army equal to their own, the less they liked it. They had followed the progress of German rearmament and had submitted to a joint meeting of cabinet ministers on September 25, 1933 a well-developed dossier on the subject. Again, the French had a plan. Under it, the disarmament convention would span two four year terms. In the first, supervisory controls would be established and tested. Having proved effective, the substantive provisions for disarmament/rearmament would then follow.[43]

Sir John Simon reported to the Conference on October 14, 1933 on the conflict between the five year term of the MacDonald Plan and the two-phase French plan. When he announced that his government would support the French plan,[44] Germany was ready.

Hitler now employed a combination tactic as effective in the field of international politics as the tank-Stuka team would one day prove in battle. The first element, surprise, was at his dictatorial command, utterly disconcerting diplomats shackled by parliaments. The second was to couple the act, however violent, with loud and fervent protestations of peace and good will.

Germany announced that she would leave both the Disarmament Conference[45] and the League of Nations.[46] This was a violent repudiation of Germany's obligations under the Covenant of the League of Nations. Germany would no longer be accountable under the Covenant, thereby escaping the consequences that would one day be visited on Signor Mussolini. Germany had turned her face from the principal vehicle of international order, the League of Nations, and rendered meaningless the Disarmament Conference of which she was the chief subject.

In so doing, Hitler adopted the most elevated moral tone. He scathingly attacked the Conference's refusal to accord Germany equal rights in accordance with the Declaration of December 11, 1932. He lauded the German people's "unalterable will for peace,"[47] adding, with a fine rhetorical flourish his conviction that "the final pacification of the world which is so necessary for all, can be attained only if the ideas of conqueror and conquered give place to the noble conception of equal rights to life enjoyed by all."[48]

To demonstrate the force of public opinion behind him, Hitler announced that the Reichstag would be dissolved and elections held, including a plebiscite on Germany's withdrawal from the Disarmament Conference and the League of Nations.[49] Hitler's principal election theme was the desire for peace: by radio on October 14, pleading for an end to hostility between France and Germany: "After the return of the Saar territory to the Reich, it is only a madman who could conceive of the possibility of a war between the two States"[50]; in an interview with G. Ward Price on October 18, 1933: "No one in Germany thinks of going to war with Poland over the Corridor"[51]; in Stuttgart on October 28: "We do not wish to subjugate any foreign peoples."[52]

The other themes of the plebiscite campaign were familiar: valiant and undefeated Germany betrayed by Woodrow Wilson and the Fourteen Points[53]; the impossibility of reconciling inequality and German honor[54]; the fight against Communism in Germany[55]; the economic achievement which had reduced unemployment from 6.2 million to 3.8 million; the final appeal to the German people to restore on November 12, 1933 the honor which had been lost on November 11, 1918.[56]

It was true democracy, Hitler said, for a government with a four-year mandate to submit to the electorate after only seven months; but effective policy could only rest on public opinion: "The people itself must give its own witness before the world. The statesman can only be the spokesman."[57]

The results of the plebiscite showed what mastery Hitler had gained over the German people in less than a year. Not only did 95.1 percent of the votes cast affirm Germany's withdrawal from the Disarmament Conference and the League, but the Nazi vote of 92.2 percent in the Reichstag election wiped out the indignity of the failure of the Nazis to obtain a majority on March 13.[58]

It had been Hitler's genius to link a foreign policy issue—Germany versus the world—with a parliamentary election, securing the overwhelming approval that had escaped him in March.

It may have been dedication, it may have been optimism, or it may have been a failure to connect to reality that moved the French, the British, the Italians and the Americans to carry on the work of the Conference. They agreed on November 21, 1933 that the Conference should be adjourned until January and that meanwhile "parallel and supplementary" efforts should be made to reach an agreement using diplomatic channels.[59]

All this was to Hitler's benefit, enabling him to prolong discussions which could only have the effect of delaying an effective response to the German rearmament program. Thus, on December 18, 1933, Hitler offered France a ten-year nonaggression pact conditioned upon the immediate return of the Saar to Germany and a German buildup to an army of 300,000.[60] The French had hopes in the Saar and declined, at the same time signifying their willingness to accept modifications of the British plan which made it, in effect, the French plan.[61]

Hitler's next surprise took place on January 26, 1934. No more bitter hostility had existed in Europe since the founding of the Polish state than that between Poland and Germany. Germany accepted neither the Polish Corridor nor her eastern boundary and viewed Poland with ire and contempt. But Hitler now announced a nonaggression pact of ten years, moving Poland into the German orbit. More than that, it totally disconcerted France's eastern policy of which Poland, as France's chief ally, had been the linchpin. Having secured his eastern border, Hitler could now contemplate new adventures.[62]

When Hitler reviewed his first year in office on January 30, 1934, he could point with pride to having defused Polish-German enmity. He rejected as "absurd" any assertion that Germany would undertake or was planning an attack on Austria. He reiterated his keen desire for a reconciliation with France. After the settlement of the Saar question, there would be no issue between the two nations. Germany would, he said, then accept "not only the letter, but the spirit of the Locarno Pact."[63] Nothing could be better calculated to allay French and British concerns; each time the provisions of the peace treaties were modified or reversed in Germany's favor, the more important became the Locarno undertakings of nonaggression, the guaranty of the Franco-German border, and of the demilitarization of the Rhineland.

The British government remained determined to bring Germany back to the Conference. On January 29, 1934, it published a plan whereby, in addition to an army at a strength to be negotiated between 200,000 and 300,000, Germany would be allowed tanks and artillery hitherto forbidden, and, if after two years a convention had not been signed abolishing military aircraft, an air force. German parity in ten years was the ultimate goal.[64]

Eden now visited Hitler in Berlin. Hitler again affirmed that Germany would honor treaties freely signed, and, very specifically, Locarno. Eden was not unimpressed. Hitler was friendly, listened well, and was master of his facts. They exchanged war experiences. Old soldiers, Eden suggested, should be the very last to wish for another war. Hitler was hearty in his agreement.[65]

Hitler offered assurances that the SA and the SS would be demilitarized. He proposed that France retain, rather than reduce its heavy weapons for the first five years of the convention. But Hitler wanted aircraft—30 percent of the total of her neighbors, but not more than fifty percent of France's—and an army of 300,000. His disclaimed any aggressive intent. These weapons would be used only in self-defense.[66]

Mussolini readily assented to Hitler's proposal.[67] But for the French, the problem was more difficult. They did not accept German assurances as readily as did Eden. They did not think the sanctions contained in the British memorandum offered adequate security. They would deliberate further, but were not ready to agree.

On his journey back to London, Eden mused on the differences between the leaders of Germany and Italy, informed, decisive, ready to act, and the preoccupation with politics, the lack of knowledge, the unreadiness to make decisions, the difficulty of translating them into action, of the leaders of the democracies, such as France.[68]

France finally replied to the English memorandum on March 19, 1934. It could not accept a German army of 300,000. What was needed were adequate provisions for supervision of the disarmament/rearmament process, and, more important, there must be guarantees of execution, the all important guarantees that the essence of an agreement would not be confined to paper.

When the vital interests of States are at stake, general affirmations, however great may be the honesty of those who express them, cannot suffice.[69]

While the British and French debated the meaning of guarantees of execution, Germany published its military budget on March 28, 1934.[70] To France this made public what she had already known—that Germany was fast rearming. Britain still pressed Germany on its memorandum until on April 16, 1934, Hitler shrewdly announced that he would accept the British memorandum as a basis for negotiation.[71] Clearly, he had nothing to lose by prolonging the discussion.

This was too much for France. Louis Barthou, the Foreign Minister, Pierre-Etienne Flandin, and Pierre Laval, each in his turn to become Foreign Minister and Prime Minister, urged that the negotiations proceed. They were overruled by Prime Minister Doumergue, supported by Andre Tardieu and Edouard Herriot. France stated its position:

The French government refuses to legalize German rearmament, which has made all negotiations useless. France will henceforth ensure her security by her own means.[72]

The Disarmament Conference had a life of its own. In the absence of any agreement at the policy making level, it maintained the appearance of reality by assigning work to four committees on Security, Guarantees of Execution, Air, and the Manufacture of Armaments. Perhaps in the end some limitation on the international trade in arms could redeem the Conference.

The gallant and lonely efforts of Arthur Henderson did not succeed. Perhaps typical is a portrait drawn at an earlier stage of the conference:

[T]here have been few more pathetic figures than that of Mr. Henderson sitting alone in one of the lounges in the delegates' foyer and gazing enviously at the milling groups of representatives who surged up and down the floor and cast not a glance at the lonely, rubicund, kindly figure in the corner. On the outskirts of these scrimmages hung, like a half-back, Mr. Henderson's faithful Achates, M. Aghnides, Director of the Disarmament Secretariat, who spared no effort to 'collar' delegates as they broke away from their groups and to transform the picture of Mr. Henderson from 'Solitaire" into 'Conversation Piece.' But even when M. Aghnides' efforts were crowned with success, his prey would vanish from his clutches into another group before they had crossed the brief distance to Mr. Henderson's sofa.[73]

The subcommittees produced many texts, but no agreement. By the second half of 1935, they had ceased to meet. The Conference never formally concluded; but the death of Arthur Henderson on October 20, 1935 signaled not only its end, but the end of the hopes with which it had opened. The difficulty, Henderson had said, was that none of the political problems had been worked out in advance among the Great Powers, without which the Conference was bound to fail. This was a confession that principles and ideals, detached from the facts, are an insufficient basis on which to resolve conflicts of power. The issues, it appeared, were not exclusively of a moral character.

Lord Cecil drew another conclusion. He was sympathetic to the French need for security. If, at the outset of the Conference, he said, the British government had courageously declared that, under a system of disarmament based on security it would join in guarantees to disarmed powers against disloyal attacks by convention-breakers, an agreement could have been reached.[74] This was precisely the kind of guarantee from which British governments habitually shrank on the grounds that public opinion would not support it. This was a vital issue that Lord Cecil would address in the Peace Ballot.

Hitler Confronts Mussolini

When Hitler reviewed his first year in office in his speech of January 30, 1934, he paid special attention to Austria. He regretted that German-Austrian relations were not more satisfactory; but he characterized the assertion that Germany intended to coerce Austria as absurd. That Germany would ever undertake or even plan an attack on Austria he emphatically denied.[75]

In an interview the next month with an English journalist, Hitler repeated this theme.[76] If some people believe Germany had anything to do with the troubles in Austria, that was entirely false. At the same time he hoped that resort to arms between Germany and Poland had been abandoned, not for ten years, but forever, adding: "What! We take territory from Russia? Ridiculous!"[77]

Such pronouncements went far beyond what Winston Churchill liked to refer to as terminological inexactitude. That Austria must unite with Germany was Genesis 1:1 of *Mein Kampf.*

Hitler knew he needed to build a mighty armed force to achieve his ultimate goals. He saw the takeover of Austria as a simple, more immediate task. He could bring to bear immense economic pressure against the feeble Austrian economy. He had at his disposal an Austrian Nazi party which was not a separate national entity but merely a branch of the German party, owing its allegiance directly to Hitler.[78] The well-honed skills of party organization, of street fighting, of intimidation, and of propaganda, which had been crowned with success in Germany, were all ready to hand.

Hitler could also hope for electoral success. Ever since the collapse of Austria-Hungary, there had been a strong desire on the part of Austrians, probably at any time a majority of them, for a union with Germany, not simply because it was forbidden by the terms of the peace treaties and subsequent financial arrangements, but because it seemed to them both natural and beneficial.

Across the Austrian border lay Italy. Hitler had not only expressed his admiration for Mussolini in *Mein Kampf,* but he also had designated Italy as Germany's natural ally. Immediately upon becoming Chancellor, Hitler had sent a cordial message to Mussolini, conveying "admiration and homage," suggesting the benefit of closer relations between Germany and Italy and seeking a personal meeting.[79]

Mussolini reciprocated with his own congratulations. He liked the idea that Fascism had succeeded in Germany; he saw himself as its inspiration and Germany as a kind of a junior partner. This was a feather in his cap as a political philosopher and opened interesting possibilities in the world of power politics, especially in Danubian and Southeastern Europe.

The speed with which Hitler crushed his opponents and achieved supreme power and the startling ferocity and inhumanity of the Nazi regime soon evoked second thoughts in both the Austrian people and Mussolini.

The Catholic and Social Democratic parties which commanded the allegiance of a great majority of Austrians saw that they would have a far different role and fate in Hitler's Germany than in Brüning's. Nazi rule was a direct threat to many segments of the population. Hitler did not necessarily inspire respect in Vienna where he had not distinguished himself. Rather than a local boy who had made good, Hitler appeared in many Austrian eyes as a parvenu and an embarrassment. The ancient and glorious Austria of the Holy Roman Emperors had been humiliated and overshadowed by the upstart Prussians and their Hohenzollern kings, but they were, after all, kings. That an habitue of Viennese soup lines and flop-houses, a sometime corporal should assume not only the mantle of the Hapsburgs, but powers they had not wielded for centuries was not a welcome prospect for many Austrians. An astute historian has pointed to the paradox that Hitler should, in his first year in power, have reconciled the Poles and alienated the Austrians.

After a dozen years in power, Mussolini had become a knowledgeable observer of the international scene. He did not lack intelligence or a Latin clarity of mind. As Hitler gained in power and Germany recovered her economic and military might, it became apparent to Mussolini that in a partnership with Nazi Germany, the junior partner might well be Italy. Italy might thereby lose the goodwill of England, which Mussolini had assiduously cultivated, and of France, still the arbiter of the European scene.

The principal reasons lay on the Brenner Pass, on the Italian-Austrian border. Italy's chief gains during the war had been the Austrian provinces of the Adriatic Coast and the South Tyrol, including 250,000 German speakers who did not aspire to become Italians. Austria was a comfortable neighbor for Italy, posing no threat. Germany on Italy's border was a distinctly uncomfortable prospect for Mussolini.

Unmoved by optimism and unaffected by idealism, Mussolini saw what British and French statesmen could not see—or what public opinion would not permit them to admit—that the Disarmament Conference was in early 1933 a failure. There would be rearmament, first in Germany, then the world. The League of Nations had been as unsuccessful in revising the territorial provisions of the peace treaties as it had been in achieving disarmament. After Versailles, Italy had always regarded herself as a have-not, as an unsatisfied and hence revisionist power.

Out of the combination of these elements, Mussolini proposed a solution that seemed to him eminently practical. He presented his proposed Four Power Pact to Britain and France in March, 1933.

It provided that four powers—Britain, France, Germany, and Italy—would combine: to cooperate to maintain peace, to carry out treaty revision within the framework of the League of Nations, to permit to Germany effective equality of rights by stages, in the event of failure of the Disarmament Conference, and generally to act together in all economic, political, and colonial affairs.

To Mussolini, it seemed clear that four powers could more easily agree than fifty. In this he anticipated Henderson's conclusion that the League or the Disarmament Conference could succeed only by the prior agreement of the Great Powers. Italy would be promoted to full partnership in the management of Europe; German rearmament would be effectively controlled; and Italy might well profit, directly or indirectly, by the process of treaty revision and colonial arrangements. Best of all, to Mussolini would accrue the prestige of leadership and Rome would be the seat of the new directorate of Europe.

The fact that there was a certain logic to the plan did not avoid difficulties. To balance the clauses on treaty revision, the British insisted on clauses affirming the sanctity of treaties and of the Covenant under which alone treaty revisions could be made.

France's clients, Poland and the Little Entente, the winners at the peace settlement, had ominous presentments that any treaty revision would necessarily be at their expense. If there were to be treaty revisions, they wanted to be directly party to agreements freely consented to, without pressure or blackmail, and they insisted, in the event of revision, on adequate compensation.

In the end, a meaningful four-power agreement was as difficult to achieve as an effective result from the Disarmament Conference. When the Pact was signed in Rome on June 7, 1933, the first and fourth provisions had all but disappeared; the provisions for the revision of treaties were reduced to favorable references to Articles 10, 16, and 19 of the Covenant; and the provisions concerning German rearmament emerged as a right to reexamine the questions with a view to ensuring their solution through the appropriate channels.[80]

All this was no great help and the Pact was never ratified. Mussolini had tried to exert a meaningful control over the development of Germany in Europe by a collaborative effort. Now as he watched the growth of German influence in Austria and the escalation of the German threat to Austrian independence, he embarked on a purely Italian policy to protect Italy's interests in Austria and in Central Europe.

The Austrian Chancellor, Engelbert Dollfuss, had proclaimed Austria an authoritative corporative state. Here was another tribute to Mussolini's corporate state and an attempted bulwark against Nazi pressure. Neurath told the German cabinet on April 7, 1933 that Mussolini's opposition would currently frustrate a campaign for Austro-German union. The Nazis pressed for parliamentary elections in the hope of winning a majority. At the same time, the hostile activities of the Nazis on both sides of the border convinced the Austrian government that the German government was directly implicated in its attempted overthrow.

Germany now stepped up economic pressure; on June 1, 1933 it imposed a tax of 1,000 marks on Germans leaving Germany to enter Austria, a blow to the lucrative tourist trade.[81]

Dollfuss again turned to his mentor, Mussolini. They met on August 18 and 19; Mussolini promised to support Austrian independence. He advised Dollfuss to suppress the Social Democratic party to deprive the Nazis of their anticommunist argument and to enable him more effectively to deal with Germany.[83] Such was the turmoil in Austria that on November 10, 1933, martial law was declared to forestall the demonstrations which might attend the German election of November 12 and the anniversary on the same day of the Austrian republic.[84]

Austria assembled the massive evidence of Nazi activities against the Austrian state and made a verbal protest on January 17, 1934 to the German government.[85] Germany denied that there had been interference, intervention, or violation of treaty obligations. The Austrian dossier was forwarded to Britain, France, and Italy who were amply persuaded of Austria's peril.[86]

Meanwhile, on February 13, 1934, Dollfuss followed Mussolini's advice. A brutal assault, complete with artillery, was levied on Social Democratic strongholds in Vienna. There was fighting in provincial cities; but after two days, the Socialists surrendered on a promise of amnesty. Austria had solved one problem but had created another.[87]

It was Italy to whom the Austrian issue was most significant and it was Italy that pressed Britain and France into action. On February 17, 1934, the three nations issued a joint declaration that they had a common view of the necessity of maintaining Austria's independence and integrity in accordance with the peace treaties.[88]

Italy followed up the Three Power Declaration with practical steps. On March 17, 1934, it entered into the Rome Protocols with Austria and Hungary, providing for a consultative pact, an economic development pact, and a new Austrian-Italian trade agreement.[89] This was more than commerce; it was, in effect, a warning to Germany. On the following day Mussolini was explicit. He proclaimed to Rome and the world that Austria could rely on Italy for the defense of its independence.[90]

It was as the defender of Austrian independence that Mussolini finally met Hitler in Venice on June 14 and 15, 1934. Mussolini was at his grandest, uniformed and bemedalled, the master of ceremonies of military parades and ceremonial concerts. He was confident he had upstaged Hitler, who in his raincoat and soft hat has been described as looking like a traveling salesman. But the parade was chaotic, the concert wrecked by an organized claque which shouted "Duce, Duce" throughout the performance, and the Hitler-Mussolini conversations were a disaster.[91]

Out of vanity, Mussolini insisted on dispensing with an interpreter. The meeting produced numerous reports, virtually none agreeing with the others. Hitler asked Mussolini to withdraw his protection of Austria and thought Mussolini had agreed so long as there was no Anschluss. Mussolini, on the other hand, thought he had made it clear that Italy still backed Dollfuss. It was variously reported that Hitler had talked of attacking France and said the British had no political leader to compare with him.

Italian sources reported that Hitler had been immensely gratified to find himself treated as an equal by so great a man as Mussolini. Mussolini said that Hitler was like a gramophone, with just seven tunes; when they were done, he played them over again. He thought Hitler a buffoon, slightly mad, lacking the strength and the presence Mussolini had expected.[92]

Mussolini had misjudged his man, as Hitler proved with savage ferocity on the night of June 29–30, when he personally ordered the liquidation of his rivals in the Blood Purge.

When blood next flowed, and it was soon after, it was in Vienna, and at Hitler's bidding. On July 25, 1934, a Nazi gang seized the Austrian Broadcasting Company and announced the overthrow of Dollfuss and his cabinet. Learning of the plot, Dollfuss suspended a cabinet meeting and remained in the Chancery. There the Nazis found him and shot him down. But the other ministers had escaped the plotters' web, organized an effective response, and captured the plotters.[93]

All this horrified Europe but none more than Mussolini. Mussolini had looked on Dollfuss as a personal friend as well as a protege. On the day of her husband's murder, Frau Dollfuss and her children were on vacation, as guests of the Mussolini family.

Mussolini acted immediately. He ordered four army divisions, 100,000 men to the Austrian border to guard against complications. He telegraphed the Austrian government the assurance that Italy would strenuously defend Austrian independence and broadcast to the world his declaration that all those who had been responsible for the murder of Dollfuss, and he was careful to add, directly or indirectly, had incurred "the moral condemnation of the civilized world."[94]

Mussolini's private comments were more colorful. He was furious. Hitler was "a horrible sexual degenerate, a dangerous fool." He did not hesitate to lay responsibility directly at Hitler's door. "Hitler is the murderer of Dollfuss. Hitler is the guilty man, he is responsible for this."[95]

Hitler, the putsch failed, now adopted an attitude of correctness and concern. The German border was closed to the Nazi fugitives and Hitler joined Hindenburg in condolences. With expressions of condemnation and regret over the assassination of Dollfuss, he appointed

Papen ambassador to Vienna.[96] Thus, having escaped assassination himself a few weeks before, Papen took up the task of liquidating the consequences of the assassination of the less-fortunate Dollfuss.

Kurt Schuschnigg was appointed Chancellor and a measure of calm returned to Austria.[97] On September 27, 1934, Britain, France and Italy renewed their declaration of February 17. It would, they said, after fresh examination, remain in full effect and continue to inspire their common policy.[98]

Mussolini drew his conclusions and they were stark. It was all to be expected, this "revolution of the old German tribes of the primeval forest against the Latin civilization of Rome." No civilized country would tolerate Hitler's behavior.

"Perhaps the Great Powers will recognize the German danger," he said. The time for action had come. Mussolini spoke with prophetic clarity:

> Hitler will create an army. Hitler will arm the Germans and make war— possibly even in two or three years. I cannot stand up to him alone. We must do something, we must do something quickly.[99]

9

France and the German Challenge

"Refuse to disarm, take our stand on the Trea-
ties, bring Russia into the League, re-knit East-
ern alliances, and by improving relations be-
tween Italy and Yugoslavia open up a French-
Italian front that would pin Germany down."
—A statement of French policy[1]

France in Crisis

Political instability was the normal condition of the Third French
Republic, but never was it more pronounced—nor more dangerous—
than in the years which followed the 1932 elections. Between May,
1932 and February, 1934, there were six ministries; the longest lasted
nine months, the shortest only a week.

This reflected the deep cleavage of French society between left and
right. The division of Europe between the Fascist and Communist
ideologies was faithfully reflected in France, and every interest and
party was represented in the spectrum between.

In these fragile circumstances, a scandal broke involving Serge
Stavisky, a swindler with a lengthy criminal history, and the bonds of
the municipal pawnshop of Bayonne. Fuel was added to the fire by
revelations of corruption in high places. Prime Minister Chautemps,
resigned to be replaced by Daladier. His was the ministry of one week.

In the Chamber of Deputies on February 6, 1934, Daladier was
greeted with riotous catcalls, whistles, and cheers as the ushers intervened to prevent physical confrontations. He obtained a vote of confidence. The next speaker was Tardieu. The Right burst into the

Marseillaise, the Left responded with the Internationale, the speaker could not be heard, and the session was suspended.

The same drama was played on a grimmer scale in the Place de la Concorde across the Seine from the Chamber of Deputies. The immense, hostile, divided crowd did not confine themselves to singing the Marseillaise or the Internationale. The battle of words was followed with paving stones; a bus was burned; shots were fired. The deputies were under seige in the Palais Bourbon; the respected Herriot, recently Prime Minister, attempting to go home, was barely saved by the police from being thrown into the Seine.

It was an assault on the Government. But there was no organization, no leader, no program. The mob was a swirl of conflicting interests and parties who, antagonistic, one against the other, were only united in their antagonism to the Government. But there were results—nine dead, 412 wounded; and the resignation on the following day of the Daladier government. Gaston Doumergue, a former President of the Republic, was called back from his retirement to form a national government including elements of both left and right. Among the most brilliant and energetic of his colleagues was seventy-two-year-old Louis Barthou, the Foreign Minister.[2]

Barthou's Grand Strategy

From the start, the brutality, the persecutions, the violence of the Nazi regime, and the ferocity with which it crushed its opponents caused a sensation throughout the world. Not only the rule of law, but the normal usages of civilized society were shattered and the gods that the new regime worshiped were not the gods of Western Christendom. Indignation at the Nazi regime and sympathy for its victims were widespread and nowhere more so than in Britain.

If there was equal sympathy, there was perhaps a calmer response in France to the new Germany. If the British were shocked and surprised, the French were not. After all, so far as they were concerned, the Germans were simply behaving like Germans. The Weimar Republic had been an aberration; the Nazi regime represented the uninterrupted continuity of German ambitions and mirrored the German soul. This was the portrait of Germany which Clemenceau had painted for his fellow countrymen years before:

I have sometimes penetrated into the sacred cave of the Germanic cult, which is, as everyone knows, the *Bierhaus*. A great aisle of massive humanity where there accumulate, amid the fumes of tobacco and beer, the popular rumblings of a nationalism upheld by the sonorous brasses blaring to the heavens the supreme voice of Germany, "Deutschland Uber Alles!" Men, women and children, all petrified in reverence before the divine stoneware pot, brows furrowed with irrepressible power, eyes lost in a dream of infinity, mouths twisted by the intensity of willpower, drink in long draughts the celestial hope of vague expectations. These only remain to be realized presently when the Chief marked out by Destiny shall have given the word.[3]

The French were gratified to think that they had been right. Germany was a menace as the French had always said; her ambitions were exactly as Hitler had proclaimed. The provisions of the peace treaties limiting and restraining Germany had been wise, the warnings of French statesmen, unheeded though they may have been, had proved true, and the need for a system of security against a resurgent Germany was demonstrably clear. All this seemed to vindicate French policy and make it a standard to which the sensible ought quickly to repair. It was a continuing disappointment to France that it didn't work out that way.

The English didn't see it that way and they did not wholly approve of Louis Barthou. There was no more able, dedicated, nor effective exponent of the French view of Germany. To the French historian of the Second World War, Maurice Baumont, he was a man of superb intelligence, courage, firmness, and confidence, a luminous figure whose policy of erecting a common European front against Nazi Germany could have saved Europe. This did not sit well with those in England who preferred to arrive at an accommodation with Germany. In 1934 Anthony Eden was one of these:

I cannot shake off the conviction—shared I believe by the great majority of my fellow countrymen—that it is the Barthous of this world who have made Hitler inevitable.[4]

To Lord Cecil, Barthou had "a genius for being wrong" because he did not regard the League of Nations as the ultimate arbiter of international issues.[5]

Baumont said of Barthou: "A pure patriotic flame gave youth as well as vigor to this seventy-year old minister."[6] Arnold Toynbee saw it differently. To him Barthou was "a man who had acquired the mental rigidity of age without having lost the animal spirits of youth."[7]

This reference to M. Barthou's mistress reflected the enduring cross-channel cultural and social gap that bedeviled relations between England and France. Among these, a differing perception in morals, as well as in the formation of policy, was a serious barrier to understanding and effective collaboration.

Vansittart pungently etched the basis of some British prejudices against the French:

> Victorian England was vaguely convinced that nineteenth century France had too good a time; that France laughed too much and cooked too well for this vale of tears. . . . More serious still, Victorian England suspected that the French put more into, and got more out of sex than the English. Victorian England had not the vaguest idea how this was done, but was fairly sure the advantage was not fair and quite sure that it was not nice.[8]

The French Government had, against Barthou's recommendation, terminated disarmament discussions with Germany on April 17, 1934. France would insure her security by her own means. It fell to Barthou to find those means.[9]

The task was familiar to Barthou, who had worked at it before. When the Treaties of Guaranty had failed, when France's proposals for a strong and armed League of Nations were rebuffed, he had helped to erect the alliances with Poland and the Little Entente by which France sought to balance the German threat.

This time, Barthou embarked on a more ambitious program. Poland aspired to be a Great Power, but she was not, nor were Czechoslovakia, Rumania, and Yugoslavia. Barthou wanted nothing less than to add to them the Soviet Union and Italy in an overwhelming combination that Germany must respect. The first step would be an Eastern Pact of Mutual Assistance, an Eastern Treaty of Locarno. Just as Locarno had guaranteed the critical French-Belgian-German border, so finally would a new pact stabilize Germany's eastern borders by a similar system of guarantees. A second step would be the entry of the Soviet Union into the League of Nations.

Since the revolution, the Soviets had played a lone hand in international relations, scorning the League of Nations as a hostile association of the capitalist victors of 1918. As Lenin's dream of world revolution gave way to Stalin's nationalism, the Soviet Union began to renew its ties with the world outside its borders. The advent of Hitler accelerated this process. The Soviets not only read *Mein Kampf*, they believed it.

They had signed a nonaggression treaty with France in 1932. For those whose logic queried a pact between capitalist France and communist Russia, Herriot said in the parliamentary debate:

> What has happened is a happy thing for France. Do I need to remind the House of the broad lines of our national policy—the traditional policy as I will make bold to say, of the Kings of France? Remember how Francis I allied himself with Turkey not only in the face of but actually against the whole of Christendom, because this was what the interests of France required?[10]

Stalin had a similar orientation. He told the Seventeenth Congress of the Communist Party on January 26, 1934 that Russia's alliance policy would not be subjected to ideological tests. He said that if the interests of the USSR demanded a rapprochement with any countries interested in peace, it would make the necessary rapprochement without hesitation.[11]

Barthou visited Warsaw on April 22–24, 1934. Hitler had anticipated his mission with the bilateral German-Polish Pact, and the Poles were aggrieved that the Four Power Pact should have relegated them to a secondary role. If the meeting did not advance the proposed pact, nevertheless the official communique announced that the Franco-Polish alliance remain "absolutely immutable."[12]

In Prague, Barthou found a more cordial reception. The Czechs had no illusions about the German threat and felt the need for security as keenly as did France.[13]

In May, Barthou met with the Soviet Foreign Minister, Maxim Litvinov. They discussed not only an Eastern European Pact, but the question of the admission of the Soviet Union to the League of Nations.[14]

The French prepared their plan as assiduously as they had prepared so many plans over so many years. At the same time they promoted Soviet admission to the League of Nations. Barthou journeyed to Bucharest and to Belgrade to gather Rumanian and Yugoslav support. This done, he appeared in London on July 8 and 9 for critical discussions with Sir John Simon, the British Foreign Secretary.

This is the plan that emerged from their discussions: There would be a mutual assistance pact among the USSR, Germany, Poland, Czechoslovakia, and the three Baltic states, Estonia, Latvia, and Lithuania, by which each would support any of the others who was a victim of aggression, and withhold any support from the aggressor. France and the Soviet Union would enter into a separate mutual assistance pact. Germany would be invited to join this pact which would in turn be tied to Locarno so that France could aid Germany if attacked by Russia and Russia would aid France if attacked by Germany. To all this was added a General Act stating that these treaties, specific in intent, were fully compatible with the Covenant of the League of Nations.

Sir John approved. The proposed plan had a double charm for him: there was absolutely no British commitment and Germany was now invited to become a party. He did not wish to antagonize Germany, but instead to find common ground. Britain now actively championed the pact. More than that, Sir John Simon announced that the entry of the Soviet Union into the League of Nations was an essential component of the Eastern Security Pact.[15]

Italy responded favorably to the proposed pact. Germany, having departed from the League of Nations, had no desire to become enmeshed in multilateral pacts. Surely it gave added pleasure to announce, on September 10, 1934, that Germany could hardly be a party to new security arrangements when her right to equality in arms went unrecognized. Poland followed the German lead.[16]

Barthou was not without his successes. He pleaded with the League of Nations:

> Do not turn Russia back outside into adventures, into the advocacy of a doctrine which you dislike. Accept her since she comes on the conditions you yourselves have set.[17]

On September 18, 1934, The Soviet Union become not only a member of the League of Nations, but also a permanent member of the Council of the League as befitted its great power status.[18]

Despite the German and Polish rebuffs, Barthou had made real progress. He had secured British backing for his Eastern European project, and the close collaboration of Czechoslovakia and the Soviet Union. He did not despair of Poland. What he really needed was the adherence of Italy and Yugoslavia.

The inherent rivalry between these two countries was based on their conflicting claims to Trieste and the Adriatic coast. Yugoslavia was one of the great beneficiaries of the peace settlement; Italy was disgruntled and supported the revisionist aspirations of Austria and Hungary. France's consistent support of Yugoslavia was a continuing cause of estrangement between France and Italy.

If Barthou could compose into a harmonious alignment the rivalries and antagonisms which had separated Italy from France on the one hand and from Yugoslavia on the other, and at the same time secure an Eastern European Pact, the German threat would be largely contained. It was with this in mind that Barthou arranged a visit to France by King Alexander of Yugoslavia. Barthou would next visit Rome where he might hope to put in place the final piece of his grand design.[19]

Arnold Toynbee may have remarked on Barthou's animal spirits; but he was indeed seventy-two and in the past months had crisscrossed Europe in pursuit of his design. He was tired and secured permission from the President of the Republic not to make the long trip by train from Paris to Marseilles for the ceremonial welcome of King Alexander. Pietri, the Minister of Marine was delegated to head the reception. But Pietri, for reasons of protocol, insisted on Barthou's presence. Wearily and reluctantly, he made the journey.

On the scene Barthou entered the spirit of the occasion. He disparaged the closed car provided for the King's procession. The King is a friend of France; let's not hide him, he said. An open car was found.

The welcome honored protocol. There were flags, bands, and aircraft overhead when the King disembarked on the quay, national anthems and the obligatory wreath deposited at the monument to the French soldiers who had been the King's comrades in arms during the war. The King did not like the open car. In the rivalry between the Karageorge and Obrenovich dynasties for the Serbian throne, assassination was a practical method of succession. This was how Alexander's father had obtained the throne thirty-one years before. Assassination was always on the mind of a Serbian monarch.

He had received reports from his consul on the quay that an attempt was imminent. There was no special escort of motorcyclists. The Director of Protocol thought they would distract from the spectacle.

The King was in full naval dress, plumed and cocked hat, epaulets, belt and sword, garnished with the Grand Cordon of the Legion of Honor, the Medaille Militaire, and the Croix de Guerre. M. Barthou was the picture of antique dignity; his neat spade beard and pince-nez appropriately set off the Prince Albert coat and top hat.

The dignitaries were seated side by side when the assassin, shouting "Vive le Roi" jumped on the running board and emptied his pistol. Alexander died without having regained consciousness. In the confusion, Barthou, bleeding profusely, was calm. He hailed a taxi; but the crowds made traffic difficult. Finally arrived at the hospital, he died from loss of blood on the operating table. A simple tourniquet could have saved his life.[20]

The evidence soon disclosed that the assassin was an agent of Ante Pavelich, the Croat fanatic and veteran enemy of the Yugoslav state. In the imperfect union of the Serbs, Croats, and Slovenes that made up Yugoslavia, an assassination attempt was no more unexpected than that the perpetrator should be a Croat. What made the situation in equal degrees more complicated and more distressing was that the trail of the assassin led to a training camp in Hungary via Italy and the aid, comfort, and financial support of Benito Mussolini's secret service.

The task upon which Barthou had embarked was now infinitely more complicated. After deliberating on three candidates, President Doumergue chose a former Prime Minister, Pierre Laval, to become Barthou's successor as Foreign Minister.

Pierre Laval

The Auvergne lies nearly at the center of France. Geologically it is its oldest part, a land of volcanic origin, of mountains, timber-clad hills, strange volcanic outcrops, deep valleys and rivers, a hard, gray land over which broods an air of mystery. It has always been poor; its people are tenacious and tough as they had to be to survive, thrifty as poverty taught them to be, but at the same time sharp witted. Because the land would not support them all, many were compelled to leave. In Paris they formed their own community and returned home whenever they could.

The village of Chateldon is not to be found in the Guide Michelin. It lies in a valley surrounded by hills. There are fifteenth and sixteenth century houses and a chateau which overlooks the town.

Pierre Laval was born here on June 28, 1883. His father turned his hand to a variety of callings. He was an innkeeper, the proprietor of a cafe, a butcher and the owner of some vineyards. To these he added the civic function of postmaster. He was successful, and it seemed natural to him that his son should succeed him.[21]

He therefore took Pierre out of school, where he had been an apt scholar, at the age of twelve, putting him in charge of the mail cart which ran between Chateldon and Puy-Guillaume. Pierre saw things differently; he was ambitious, bright, and eager to continue his education. This he did while driving to and fro with the mail. The priest, the magistrate, and his former teachers encouraged him, but none more than Dr. Claussat, a local dignitary and political figure.[22]

Persuasiveness was one of Laval's most notable characteristics. He persuaded his father to send him to Paris at fifteen to enroll in the Lycee St. Louis. After a year, he continued his education in Bayonne and Moulins.[23] He then became a *pion*, or monitor, in a series of lycees while studying zoology. At St. Etienne, he joined the Socialist Party.[24] He found in debating societies a congenial atmosphere where he could expound his left-wing views. All this was natural in a spirited and ambitious young man who looked at society from his modest estate and relied on his own resources.

Laval shifted his course of study, concluding that the law offered a more direct path to prosperity and power than zoology. As a monitor, Laval was subjected to the usual hazing, disorder and disrespect as the students tested his limits. His response exemplified Laval's talent for mutual accommodation. He would wink at infractions of the rules; his pupils might smoke or leave the school grounds if they would give him the peace to concentrate on his legal studies. The arrangement seems to have given satisfaction.[25]

Self-confidence was another basic quality in Laval. When the issue was still debated of the unionization of teachers, Laval formed a union of seven members. He obtained an audience with Gaston Doumergue, then Minister of Public Instruction, whom he managed to persuade that he represented not seven, but 775 or 800 monitors in Paris. If nothing came of it, Laval had measured himself against a cabinet minister and was not dissatisfied with the result.[26]

With the help of his students, Laval qualified as a lawyer in Paris in 1909. He had a profession; now he thought to take a wife.[27]

Pierre Laval was not a handsome man. He had the broad head and squat physique of an Auvergnat peasant. His swarthy complexion had gained him the nickname of the Jamaican and many a schoolyard fight.[28] He was often disheveled and paid little attention to the neatness or style of his dress.

But he was persuasive and engaging; he had charm. He married well; his bride was the daughter of Dr. Claussat, his Chateldon sponsor.[29] The marriage brought him great happiness. That Pierre Laval was passionately devoted to his wife, his only child, and to the soil of his native Auvergne his bitterest enemies never denied.

A young lawyer who is poor and friendless, a stranger in the metropolis, will not likely embark on a corporate practice, or the representation of the well-to-do, their affairs, their properties and their estates. Criminal cases and trade union matters, which were neither dignified nor lucrative enough for the more established and better connected members of the bar, gave Laval a modest start.

His first offices were humble enough, in the workers quarter of Faubourg St. Martin. A colleague recalled:

> The old house, dating from the time of Louis Phillippe, was flanked by a tripe shop, and a cobbler's booth; each step of the narrow twisting stairs evoked memories of Balzac and Zola. The neighbors were a midwife, a three-franc dentist, and a disbarred notary, half scribe and half pawnbroker.[30]

From the notary, Laval borrowed from time to time the white tie that was to become his trademark.

A childhood in his father's inn made Laval comfortable with his workingmen clients and their Socialist views. He was one of them:

> I am a comrade among comrades, a worker among workers. I am not one of those lawyers who are mindful of their bourgeoise origins even when attempting to deny it. I am not one of those high-brow attorneys who engage in academic controversy and pose as intellectuals. I am proud to be what I am. A lawyer in the service of manual laborers who are my comrades, a worker like them. I am their brother, comrades, I am a manual lawyer.[31]

A celebrated criminal case, in which he secured an acquittal from a charge of sabotage for a dedicated trade unionist with anarchist leanings, brought him notice.[32] He built a practice and gravitated into politics where he was as assiduous in participating and cultivating useful friendships and alliances as he had been in union circles. With union backing, he became, in 1914, the Socialist Deputy for the working-class suburb of Aubervilliers, and at thirty-one, the youngest member of Parliament.[33]

As a deputy, he was exempt from military service in 1914. He observed, he was assiduous as always behind the scenes, and he learned the ways of Parliament. He was flexible enough to seek to throw Socialist support to Clemenceau. If he did not succeed, he forged friendships and connections. Yet he could be independent; he voted against the Versailles Treaty.

As a Socialist he was defeated in the *horizon bleu* election of 1919.[34] He returned to the law and the representation of labor unions. In 1922, as an Independent Socialist, affiliated with neither the Socialist or Communist Parties, he was elected mayor of Aubervilliers, which he had represented in Parliament.[35] This triumph gave him a solid political base and, while sitting in Parliament, he retained the mayoralty year in and year out until 1945. He was diligent in serving his constituents, always approachable without appointment, easily establishing rapport with the humblest among them.[36]

He returned to the Chamber of Deputies in 1924 as an Independent. He climbed the political ladder as Minister of Public Works and Undersecretary of State. He gravitated from left to right. In 1927 he was elected to the Senate on the National Republican Union slate. But he managed to retain the loyalty of his many one-time Socialist supporters.[37]

He built a successful law practice and moved from the Faubourg St. Martin to more elegant and fashionable quarters. He was not a scholar of the law. A colleague rendered this judgment:

He trusted his instinct and intelligence. He was not out to discover ideal solutions, to attain scientific truth, which, even for the most learned, is illusory. He was concerned with wriggling out of difficulties, settling things, getting along. To replace reasoning by sleight-of-hand, method by tricks— "in brief, my dear Torres, whether you like it or not, to use art instead of science, that's my system. It has its merits. At any rate, it works."[38]

His legal fees gave him the means to invest, and he invested shrewdly. Among his holdings were two newspapers in his native Auvergne and in Lyon. If they supported his political line, he also made sure that romantic serials and increased sports coverage made them commercially successful. He bought a radio station in Lyon. He was prudent, thrifty, a good manager, turning marginal properties into profit-makers. The ultimate symbol of his success was his purchase, in a run-down condition, and at a good price, naturally, of the chateau overlooking Chateldon.[39]

There were charges that his affluence was corrupt and ill-gotten, but this was not the case.[40] Nevertheless, the accusations, which persisted, did his political career no harm. This again illustrates the vast difference in attitudes and values on the two sides of the English Channel. In France, it has been said, the people expect the politicians to be dishonest, but would be appalled if they were stupid. In England, on the other hand, people expect their politicians to be stupid, but would be appalled if they were dishonest.[41]

In 1930, Laval became Minister of Labour in Tardieu's second government. His great achievement was to secure the passage of a social insurance bill.[42] There had been debate and discussion for ten years; when such a bill last came to a vote, it was defeated.

Laval studied the matter. His method was simple, direct and concrete. He did not lose himself in the accumulated statistics, drafts, and proposals. "Suppose I'm a worker who pays four francs a month and the boss pays the same. What do I get when I'm sixty?" Laval asked the experts. He discussed the matter with the workers and with the employers to work out an agreed plan of contributions. The state was to pay its share. With agreement in hand, he ran the law through Parliament with a minimum of debate.[43]

There was a method in this. Of course, the law was imperfect, even crude. There would be time for "honorable amendments." But the first thing was to create an irreversible fact, acknowledgment of the fundamental rights of the workers. The method was to secure the maximum agreement possible and to create a process in which the unsettled issues could continue under discussion. This was the method Laval would apply to international affairs.

As Minister of Labor, he quickly settled a major textile strike in the North. Again, the method was face-to-face talks with labor and employers. He extracted from the employers the concessions which made settlement possible:

> I did it in three days. You can't talk to workers with Marxist slogans, you have to talk to them as workers. If you don't know the language of the working man, you're not a socialist. And the socialist party has become Byzantine—endless congresses, black and white resolutions, debates until it ceased being a worker's party.[44]

In the shifting kaleidoscope of French politics, Laval's ability to conciliate and reach out to opposing factions was invaluable. Where others failed, on the invitation of Gaston Doumergue, President of the Republic, Laval formed a cabinet and on January 31, 1931 became Prime Minister.[45] He was forty-seven, and his rise to power was as remarkable as had been those of Mussolini and, shortly, Hitler from the total obscurity of twenty years before.

In his term of office he dealt with the Germans on the question of German reparations and with the Americans on the related issues of the Allied debt, all complicated in the extreme by the economic crises which had engulfed, first the United States, then Austria, then Germany, then Great Britain. He liked to recall that he had acted promptly and quite on his own authority in the middle of the night, to authorize a loan to Great Britain to support the pound, which evoked the immense gratitude of the British Ambassador. On the eve of the 1932 elections, on an issue of electoral reform, Laval lost a vote of confidence and resigned on February 19.

He had made an impression. Henry Stimson, the American Secretary of State noted his straightforwardness. "Laval stands in a class by himself for frankness, and directness and simplicity," he said, "and he is different from all other Frenchmen with whom I have negotiated in these respects."[46] To Sir John Simon he was a man of "directness and stability of mind."[47] His bitter enemy, Henri Torres, granted him these qualities: solid and sharp intelligence, tenacity, reflective calm, positivism, and a sense of the commonplace and concrete, all joined by a subtle instinct.

His colleague in government, André François-Poncet, who became during crucial years the French Ambassador to Berlin, was well placed to pass this judgment:

> He believed stoutly in himself and in his genius. . . . He dreamed of appearing in old Briand's place as peacemaker. At once more realistic than Briand, he would not rely solely on the League of Nations. He was none too fond of this assembly. He professed that the only prompt and fruitful method lay in direct conversation, in personal contacts, man to man. According to Laval, a free exchange of ideas, in tête-a-tête, stripped of elaborate terminologies and of such childish timidity as inspires professional diplomats, must surely lead to the solution of the most complex problems. Laval shared the mob's prejudice against diplomats. He was smart, though less smart than he often supposed, and his smartness was vulgar.[48]

Laval, Foreign Minister

Pierre Laval fully shared prevailing opinions on the devastating effect of another European war. Only two weeks before becoming Foreign Minister, he told a German visitor:

> War means the end of us all. Mankind is morally incapable of enduring another war, the horror of which will surpass everything that has occurred hitherto. War would mean the end of Christian civilization.[49]

The spectrum of policies to avoid war ran from pacifism to rearmament. The middle course was conciliation and this was the course most congenial to Laval's temperament and outlook. The occasion to employ it was immediately at hand. The murder of King Alexander had raised once more in its most grievous form the tension between Yugoslavia and Hungary. The assassin had come from a Yugoslav refugee camp in Hungary; he and his colleagues there enjoyed the hospitality of the Hungarian government which stubbornly pressed its territorial claims against Yugoslavia. Worse still, there was every chance that Italy, Hungary's defender, would be implicated. If in the League of Nations Yugoslavia should press charges against Hungary, implicating Italy, Barthou's program for a French—Italian rapprochement would be at an end.

Laval was fully alert to the danger. He told Anthony Eden he had come to Geneva to calm the Yugoslavs and he impressed on Eden the seriousness of the situation. Here was a case in which Laval excelled. Together with Eden he patiently worked with each of the principals involved, Jevtich, the Yugoslav Foreign Minister, Kanya, the Hungarian, Benes, the Czech, representing the opinion of the Little Entente, and Aloisi, the Italian. Constantly amending and compromising, in the end they managed to produce a resolution with substance enough to assuage Yugoslav feelings, and responsibility modest and indirect enough to be acceptable to Hungary. Direct charges were omitted and Italy was not involved. The path was now clear for Laval to proceed to forge new ties and resolve old conflicts between Italy and France.[50] There was, in the meantime, another item on the Barthou agenda to which Laval attended. This was the tightening of bonds between France and the Soviet Union of which the proposed Eastern European Locarno was a major element. On December 5, 1934 a French-Soviet protocol was signed at Geneva by Laval and Maxim Litvinov. It simply pro-

vided that neither France nor the Soviet Union would enter into negotiations with any other power that would prejudice the proposed Eastern Pact without prior consultation with the other.[51]

As 1935 began, Laval was now in a position to carry on negotiations by which he hoped to make Italy and the Soviet Union integral
parts of a system of security not only for France, but for Europe.
German strength was rapidly increasing. 1935 would see whether or
not Germany could be contained.

10

Britain and the German Challenge

> *"The German problem, like so many others, has been complicated by the very comprehensible reluctance of human nature to face inconvenient facts."*
>
> —Sir Eric Phipps, January, 1934[1]

Britain Faces Hitler

The British people were appalled by the violence and savagery of the Nazi regime. The brutal suppression of the opposition, and the cruelty wreaked on the weak and helpless by the strong and armed violated British principles and stirred British consciences. What made it more painful yet was the memory of British generosity to a defeated foe and British willingness to help her regain her rightful station.

These feelings were widely shared throughout the Government and the population. That they did not give rise to any unified response was due to the deep divisions, political, economic, and social, that separated the British people.

The Government itself was a source of unprecedented bitterness. Stanley Baldwin and Ramsay MacDonald had alternated as Prime Minister since Baldwin first took office in 1923. Labour had returned to office in 1929. Again, the devastating world depression dominated the political scene. MacDonald presented an austerity budget unacceptable to his Labour colleagues. In a dramatic moment, he reached out to the Conservatives and formed a National, or coalition government. Stanley Baldwin, as Lord President of the Council, became in essence his partner. In the 1931 election the coalition secured a stunning victory, notwithstanding that only a handful of MacDonald's Labour colleagues supported him. The bitterness of Labour's defeat at the hands of its longtime leader and champion injected a poison into British politics that would distort, among many other issues, the British response to Germany's challenge.

What Britain Knew

Hitler's basic determination was to rearm as quickly as possible. German rearmament would, of course, breach the Versailles Treaty and upset the peace settlement under which Europe had operated for fifteen years. Hitler wanted Britain as an ally. But if Hitler were to carry out the program of *Mein Kampf*, the program he had preached up and down Germany for a decade and more, the implied threat to the interests and safety of Britain and the British Empire were as grave as were the express threats to France, to Austria, to Czechoslovakia, and to Russia.

From the start, all this was well known to the British Government and that knowledge was readily available to the British people. In the annals of diplomacy, there are few examples of clear, informative, and prescient reporting to equal the dispatches which the British Ambassador to Berlin, Sir Horace Rumbold, sent to his Foreign Secretary after Hitler became Chancellor.

Sir Horace had been born to his profession in St. Petersburg where his father, Sir Horace Rumbold, was then Ambassador. The father had also been Ambassador to the Hapsburg Court in Vienna which Adolf Hitler so despised. In his leisurely, multivolume memoirs of a Victorian diplomatic career, the father portrays a Europe startlingly different in its standards and usages from the Third Reich his son was to confront.

It was at the end of his father's era, in 1891, that Sir Horace Rumbold entered the diplomatic service. He had served in Cairo, in Teheran, in Vienna, in Tokyo, had headed British legations in Switzerland and Poland and had served as Ambassador to Spain. He knew Germany; he had been in the British Embassy in 1914; he arrived as Ambassador in 1928. When Hitler became Chancellor in January, 1933, Sir Horace's retirement was close at hand.[2] This did not affect his interest, his keenness of vision, or the quantity or quality of his reporting.

In Hitler's first month he reported: "The forces of reaction ruling the country with an irresponsible and frivolous disregard for all decent feeling which is without precedent in history." The Nazi election campaign, then in progress "would be regarded in most civilized countries as deliberate incitement to violence." He took Hitler's measure: "Hitler may be no statesman, but he is an uncommonly clever and audacious demagogue and fully alive to every popular interest."[3]

On March 7, 1933, he reported on the results of "the most remarkable election ever held in this country." He pointed out that if the Communists were suppressed, the Nazis would have a clear majority.[4] This is, of course, exactly what happened.

He followed Hitler's swift consolidation of power. On March 15, 1933, he had "the honor to report that the counter-revolution which began when the President appointed Herr Hitler to the chancellorship on the 30th January has now come to an end with the capture of the entire administration of this country." Hitler renounced pacifism and rejected internationalism. "A policy of ruthlessness," Sir Horace observed, "will always appear in Germany to be a strong policy and therefore a wise one."[5]

Sir Horace first reported on concentration camps on March 21, 1933.[6] On April 26, 1933, he sent to London a remarkable summary and analysis of Nazi Germany. Hitler was now, Rumbold reported, in a position of unchallenged supremacy. He had only to express a wish to have it fulfilled by his followers. Germany was rearming, "which can only end in one way." The new Reich would attempt to gather in all Germans and recover the lost territories and this would be done by force of arms. For all this a great army was needed, not a brownshirt militia. He outlined the Nazi philosophical basis of rearmament: man as a fighting animal, the survival of the fittest, and hence total rejection of pacifism, internationalism, and intellectualism. In their place would reign a nationalism based on "the driving force of fanatical and hysterical passion."

For those who had neither his perspicacity nor his command of German, Rumbold outlined the basic foreign policy principles of *Mein Kampf*: Increased territory in Europe which meant that Germany must look to the East; the desirability of Britain and Italy as Germany's allies; Hitler's aversion to a two-front war on the one hand and commercial and naval rivalry with Britain on the other.

Sir Horace foretold the result of all this—the restoration of militarism, the institution of the War State in which there would be little resistance to conscription and the expansion of the manufacturing of war materiel. He quoted a Government spokesman who said, if this did not mean war at a moment's notice, it did indeed mean war in the long run.

He measured Hitler's shrewdness and exposed his method: "Herr Hitler has, of course, sufficient natural cunning to realize the necessity of camouflage." His task was complicated. Germany had to rearm, and "as Herr Hitler explains in his memoirs, they have to lull their adversaries into such a state of coma that they will allow themselves to be engaged one by one."

Sir Horace noted with unerring accuracy the goals of Germany policy:

> The aim of this policy is to bring Germany to a point of preparation, a jumping-off point from which she can reach solid ground before her adversaries can intefere and to do all this without violating Article 173 to 179 of the Treaty.

This is precisely what Hitler set out to do—and did.

What were the chances that Hitler would deviate from this policy? To Sir Horace, literally none. Sir Horace knew his man and his *Mein Kampf*. Hitler was above all a man of "fanatical conviction and uncompromising resolution":

> I fear it would be misleading to base any hopes on a return to sanity or a serious modification of the views of the Chancellor and his entourage. Hitler's own record shows that he is a man of extraordinary obstinacy.

Sir Horace closed with an appreciation of the source of Hitler's power: he had restored pride and self-respect to the average German. "The German people today no longer feel humiliated and oppressed."[7]

In June, Sir Horace reported on the buildup of the German air force which was the immediate threat to Britain. The buildup, he observed, was hardly a new development. What was new was how little effort Germany was making to conceal it.[8]

Sir Horace Rumbold filed his last dispatch on June 30, 1933. He analyzed the Nazi chiefs, Hitler, Goering, and Goebbels as "notoriously pathological cases." He concluded:

> I have the impression that the persons directing the policy of the Hitler government are not normal. Many of us, indeed, have the feeling that we are living in a country where fanatics, hooligans and eccentrics have got

the upper hand and there is certainly an element of hysteria in the policy and actions of the Hitler regime. . . . Asked by a member of my staff what they thought about their new duties, three members of the Prussian police force on duty at His Majesty's Consulate said that they had long since ceased to think. They had returned to the war mentality of 1916 when they obeyed any order without troubling about the sense or meaning of it.[9]

While Sir Horace was reporting from Berlin, the Disarmament Conference was in session. The chief military advisor to the British delegation was Brigadier Temperly. With equal precision he outlined the totality of the Hitler revolution, and the military buildup which started, for want of immediate arms, with labor service and defense sport, "the merest camouflage for intensive military training." He reported on the development of the German air force, including its training activities and in the Soviet Union and the increased tempo in the armaments industry.

His reports were read by the Cabinet on May 16, 1933. If things were allowed to drift, Temperly said, in five years, war would be inevitable:

There is a mad dog abroad once more and we must resolutely combine either to ensure its destruction or at least its confinement until the disease has run its course.[10]

At the Foreign Office, Sir Robert Vansittart, the Permanent Undersecretary, read and approved these reports. The keen intelligence of Sir Horace Rumbold was masked by a stolid exterior; the plump pink cheeks and white mustache were reminiscent of David Low's Colonel Blimp. Of Vansittart's brilliance, there was never doubt; and it was not always to his advantage. He had grown up in the security of Victorian county society and had led his class at Eton. His mastery of languages was unusual even in the diplomatic service. When he conversed with Hitler, he had no need of an interpreter. He wrote plays, not only for the English stage, but one in French which ran for four months in Paris. He was equally fluent in Spanish, in Turkish, and in Arabic. He published poetry and could never resist an epigram. He was a commanding figure in London society and at the same time vice president of the Civil Service Boxing Club.[11]

Vansittart measured Hitler's challenge. His prediction was early and apt: "Austria, Czechoslovakia, Poland, then West or East or both."[12]

In May, 1933, he told the government:

The present regime in Germany will, on present form, loose off another war just as soon as it feels strong enough. Their only fear is that they may be attacked before they are ready.[13]

In August, 1933, he combined reflection and warning in a memorandum to the government on the imminent crisis. Hitler would persist in the destruction of Austrian independence. Were France not to cultivate Italy, Italy would turn to Hitler. But Austria was only the beginning. Having destroyed Poland, Germany would then realize Hitler's dream—war on one front. To prevent all this Vansittart counseled Anglo-French-Italian cooperation, "the only real bulwark of peace."[14]

Knowledgeable statesmen throughout Europe agreed. Benes told Lord Cecil much the same thing in May, 1933 at Geneva. Hitler would, Benes said, absorb Austria and Czechoslovakia, reduce Poland to subservience and create an independent Ukraine.[15] He had read *Mein Kampf* and believed it.

Professor Thomas Jones, sometime Deputy Secretary of the British cabinet, was Stanley Baldwin's intimate friend, advisor and speech writer. Like so many who frequented the higher levels of power in Britain, he had correspondents abroad who kept him well informed. In May, 1933, he knew that conditions in Germany were worse than the press reported and by August he was well aware of Nazi militarism, the concentration camps, and German's eastward territorial ambitions.[16]

In May and June of 1933, B.H. Liddell Hart detailed the progress of German rearmament in articles in the *Daily Telegraph*. When Professor Toynbee came to write, in 1934, the *Survey of International Affairs* for 1933, he included among his speculations a graphic picture of a triumphant Germany, astride Europe from the Saar to the White Sea in the North and to the Black Sea in the South.[17]

Sir Horace Rumbold had been succeeded in Berlin by Vansittart's brother-in-law, Sir Eric Phipps. In early January, 1934, Phipps cabled to Simon that Germany had no interest in disarmament but a firm intent to rearm. Two courses were possible—sanctions, or a convention which would legitimize and control German rearmament. Which to take became a key issue of British policy.[18]

A week later Phipps reemphasized the German program: fusion with Austria, rectification of the Eastern frontiers, an outlet for German energy in the South and East, and the recovery of the German colonies. All this was complicated by the fact that ". . . . Nazi Germany believes neither in the League nor in negotiation." It was doubly complicated "by the very comprehensible reluctance of human nature to face inconvenient facts."

The sum and essence of the German program was rearmament. Phipps pointed out that Hitler's prestige had been vastly enhanced by the curious passivity of the ex-allies, Britain, France, and Italy. Hitler had seized power: nothing had happened. Against dire prophecy, Hitler had left the League of Nations; nothing happened. Worse yet, instead of blockade, sanctions and occupation of the Ruhr, with each step Germany was the more assiduously courted.[19]

The Foreign Secretary endorsed on this dispatch the notation: "This is a most illuminating document—and terrifying."[20] He showed it to the Prime Minister.

In February, 1934, there were detailed memoranda and reports on the progress of German rearmament, especially in the air. On February 24, 1934, Phipps gave Simon his estimate of German military aircraft and observed that "convention or no convention, they mean to use them."[21]

Thus fortified, on March 9, 1934, the Foreign Secretary told the cabinet that "Germany was tearing up the Treaty of Versailles."[22] The progress of German rearmament was carefully noted. The issue was not one of knowledge but of what to do. On March 21, 1934, the Foreign Office again reported to the Cabinet in specific detail on Germany's surging might. Her army was now three times that permitted by Versailles. The memorandum fastened on a critically important point of policy. No longer was the issue French security; no longer was it an issue of an international convention on armaments. The issue was far more direct; it was nothing less than "the future organization of British security against the impending menace of Germany's uncontrolled rearmament."[23]

On April 7, 1934, Vansittart laid out for the Cabinet his views on the German threat. He reviewed the warnings of Rumbold and Phipps. His information on German rearmament, the arms industry, and the drive for economic self-sufficiency was the latest. He reviewed Hitler's program, reiterating that Hitler meant to carry it out in full. One ought therefore to view Hitler's protestations of peace with appropriate skepticism.

All this came down to a very concrete issue:

The French are right as regards the demilitarized zone. It is only a question of time, at most until Germany is strong enough to prevent reoccupation before some overt breach of treaty obligation occurs there—a matter directly concerning this country.

Vansittart's eyes were firmly focused on the most strategic area of Europe. With Germany rearming, the demilitarized zone of the Rhineland was France's most critical defense, the last, and the most vital vestige of all that France had fought for at Versailles. Nor was it only France to whom the demilitarized zone was a matter of life and death, as Vansittart so clearly perceived.[24]

That Vansittart's warnings had not resulted in the action he thought vital was a source of continuing agony to him. He knew he had acquired the reputation of being stubbornly anti-German and what was worse, pro-French. He thought fit to close his memorandum with these observations:

> It goes without saying that no trustworthy public servant can be either pro- or anti- any foreign country. It is his business to think of the interests and policy of his country and of the government that directs it. It is his responsibility to record and present facts, however unpalatable, nor is it his fault or desire that the facts should point in one direction.[25]

As 1934 progressed, Germany provided the world with gruesome evidence of its methods and its goals. The Blood Purge and the assassination of Dollfuss followed each other within a month. Of the former, Winston Churchill observed,

> This massacre, however explicable by the hideous forces at work, showed that the new Master of Germany would stop at nothing, and that conditions in Germany bore no resemblance to those of a civilized state. A dictatorship based upon terror and reeking with blood had confronted the world. Anti-Semitism was ferocious and brazen, and the concentration camp system was already in full operation for all obnoxious or politically dissident classes. I was deeply affected by this episode and the whole process of German rearmament, of which there was now overwhelming evidence, seemed to me invested with a ruthless, lurid tinge. It glittered and it glared.[26]

The Committee on Imperial Defense reported in November that the German army now numbered 300,000 men; that 300 munition factories were in full production and that within a year the German air force would be as large as the RAF.

All this was duly considered by the British cabinet on the following day, November 21, 1934. The issue was put again by the Foreign Secretary: should Britain ignore German rearmament or seek to arrive at an agreement while Germany was still weak. The alternative of action, of the kind that Temperly had recommended, was not seriously considered. Indeed a decision had been taken a month earlier and communicated by the Foreign Office in a message to Ambassador Phipps in Berlin.[27]

The message reported that there was no prospect of a Disarmament Convention which would legalize Germany's illegal arms. The directive recognized the difficulties of tacitly ignoring flagrant treaty breaches over long periods. But there was no desire, by arraigning Germany, to press her into denouncing what was left of Versailles. Britain's representatives were, therefore, tacitly to acknowledge the German air force:

> But naturally in the exercise of this new freedom the members of the Embassy will have to use the utmost discretion so as to avoid making the Embassy particeps criminis. It will also be highly desirable that the subject of this letter should not be mentioned outside the Embassy.[28]

There is no record that this decision was communicated to France.

On Armistice Day, 1934, Sir Robert Boothby, M.P., addressed an audience of 2,000 at a memorial service at his home, Corstorphine, near Edinburgh. He was blunt. Germany was rearming. In eighteen months she would be able to strike blows at the heart of the British Empire.

There was still time, he said, for resolute action. Failing that, Britain would be exposed to an attack which might pulverize its heart in a few hours. All that makes life worth living would be swept away and Britain would have broken faith with those who lay dead in Flanders.

There was shocked silence, broken only by the cry "No, No," from Lady Haig. No one, Boothby said, wanted to speak to him; five clergymen refused to shake his hand. He walked solemnly home and reflected: "We are going to betray them all."[29]

Mixed Views

Clearly, the government had received vast amounts of accurate information about Adolf Hitler, the Nazi regime, its programs, its goals, and the threat to Britain it represented. Such information had been widely published and the nature and character of the Nazi state were well known to the British public.

This did not mean that there was a uniform response. In a vigorous democracy with an active press, fiercely contending political parties, and a vehement tradition of freedom of opinion, there was a full spectrum of reaction to Hitler's Germany. Outright supporters of Hitler were rare, but there were many who, for reasons that satisfied them, took a very different view from Sir Robert Vansittart, Sir Horace Rumbold, Brigadier Temperly, or Winston Churchill.

Lord Allen of Hurtwood was a dedicated pacifist who thought disarmament was the key to peace. On May 18, 1933, only a day after the Cabinet had considered Sir Horace Rumbold's dispatch from Berlin, his letter appeared in the Manchester Guardian:

> [O]ur duty is to call for the disarmament of the old allies and not to join in the hue and cry against Germany's rearmament. . . . Germany is but little interested either in re-arming or disarming; her one concern is to secure equality. Herr Hitler has declared his willingness for his country to abandon her own armaments if other countries would do likewise.[30]

Sir John Wheeler-Bennett was an eminent historian who visited Berlin in 1933. He concluded that Hitler was "a man of sense . . . who did not want war." The *Economist* told a wide audience in December, 1934, that Hitler's Germany posed no threat.[31]

More important, Geoffrey Dawson, editor of the *London Times*, far from seeing Germany as a threat, looked to her as a prospective ally for peace. The editorial columns of the *Times*, and its letters furnished a forum of first importance and enormous influence in the formation of opinion in Britain in the thirties.

The news pages contained, day by day, broad coverage of the emergence of Nazi Germany as they did of the world at large. But the coverage was not always totally objective and disinterested since the news from Germany was not always what the correspondents had sent. Dawson wrote,

> I do my utmost, night after night, to keep out of the paper anything that might hurt their (Germany's) sensibilities. . . . I shall be more grateful than I can say for any explanation and guidance, for I have always been convinced that the peace of the world depends more than anything else upon our getting into reasonable relations with Germany.[32]

The Blood Purge of July 1, 1934 was graphically reported in the news pages of the *Times*. On the editorial page, it took on a strange significance:

The story can best be read in the graphic messages which we published this morning from Berlin and Munich; the explanation shows that Herr Hitler, whatever one may think of his methods, is genuinely trying to transform revolutionary fervor into moderate and constructive effort and to impose a high standard of public service on National Socialist officials. He charges his new Chief-of-Staff, HERR LOTZE, with the task of reha- bilitating the Nazi movement. Its discipline is to be rendered more strict. Its members are to be examples to all of good behavior. . . . The move- ment, in fact, has been purged, and is to be worthy to represent the elite of the nation. Having reached power by violence, HERR HITLER is now fighting extremism with violence and trying to establish moderation by force.[33]

Here was a characterization of Hitler and his regime which was welcome in many quarters. To reasonable men, to men of good will, it was pleasant to conclude that Hitler was a reasonable man, a man of good will, with whom one could discuss the issues and arrive at rea- sonable agreements. There were good men who saw Hitler in their own image; it seemed to them only natural. To conclude otherwise would have required them to analyze the facts, worse still, to read *Mein Kampf* and the German press, and worst of all, to contemplate uncongenial courses of action, such as rearmament, and rapproche- ment with the likes of Italy and the Soviet Union. To those, and there were many, who persisted in advocating disarmament in the face of a rearmed Germany, the picture of a reasonable and peaceful Hitler was more than a desire; it was a necessity.

Hitler saw all this clearly. He entertained a steady stream of distin- guished British visitors and cannily reinforced in them the prejudices and the policies which they had brought to Berlin or Berchtesgaden. He sent them away with a gratifying conviction that they had been right all along.

The contrast to German virtue was French vice, and this was a theme that survived and even flourished in the Hitler era. Malcolm Muggeridge lent his admirable talents to the bastion of Liberal jour- nalism, the other great ornament of the British press, the *Manchester Guardian*:

In the view we propounded of Europe in the *Guardian's* columns in those just pre-Hitler years, the villain was France, armed to the teeth, and we insisted, ruthlessly pursuing selfish national ends; the hero, a much wronged Germany, disarmed, bankrupted, victimized by the greedy, vengeful vic- tors of the 1914–1918 War. No view could have better pleased the then emerging Dr. Goebbels, or been more conducive to the disaster of September, 1939.[34]

This was precisely the view Lord Allen took as he wrote to Ellen Wilkinson on April 30, 1934 after more than a year of the Nazi regime:

> I incline to think it would be a mistake to seem to be on the side of France, about the secret rearming of Germany under the Versailles Treaty. To do that means, however carefully we put it, that we appear to reendorse that wicked treaty and justify the evil policies of France toward world conciliation during the last ten years.[35]

What is apparent from this is that the rearming of Germany was not, in April, 1934, particularly secret. It is also apparent that Lord Allen like many others in Britain, viewed foreign policy in moral terms. His judgment on the Versailles Treaty was that it was wicked and on the policies of France that they were evil. These are stated in absolutes unrelated to the question whether the Treaty defended and advanced British interests or the policies of France were in her best interests. Hitler looked at such things differently. For him, foreign policy was a means to an end guided by self-interest and the only question as to a policy was whether in the present or in the future it would benefit Germany.

Added to the moral criterion, there appears in Lord Allen's critique an element of score keeping. If France had pursued evil policies for ten years, this was somehow to be cast into a balance which would excuse or absolve Germany until the score had been evened. Such an approach was inimical to policy making based upon the hard facts as they existed at the time a decision was demanded.

If there was irritation and dismay in Britain over French policy, there was a far deeper level of discomfort with the policy of Britain herself. Here moral analysis produced a sense of guilt that pervaded large and influential segments of the leadership and the public.

George Lansbury was no longer leader of the Labour Party when he visited Hitler in 1936 and expounded his principles of peace and love. Hitler listened well and found the chink in Lansbury's moral armor. His repressive acts, his persecution of the Jews and Communists, Hitler said, were in Germany's best interest:

> It is however true [Lansbury wrote],that Herr Hitler and his friends believed they are serving the best interests of the Germany people by ruling

in this way. Again and again as I listened to him, I imagined myself listening to speeches I have heard in the British House of Commons defending concentration camps in South Africa and the actions of the Black and Tans in Ireland.[36]

This was a view that found adherents in the Foreign Office as well as in the ranks of the pacifists. Lord Lothian, who was to become British Ambassador to the United States, excused Nazi persecutions as "largely the reflex of the external persecution to which the Germans have been subject since the war."[37] This outlook was at the roots of the editorial philosophy of the *Times*. It was the expressed conviction of Barrington-Ward, the assistant to Dawson, that the mistake of Versailles had to be paid for. "The conclusion drawn," British contemporary historian A.L. Rowse observed, "was that nothing Hitler did, however immoral, was to be resisted."[38]

To some, British responsibility was graver still. Britain had, in this view, created Hitler. This is what Tom Jones thought, in February, 1933:

The responsibility for Germany's plight today lies upon those who made the Treaty of Versailles—England, France and President Wilson. If they had pursued the policy Wellington had pursued after Waterloo, the moderates would have, in my judgment, permanently controlled.[39]

The belief that England was herself to blame not only chilled the prospect of a realistic view of Nazi Germany and Britain's response to it, but gave rise to comforting illusions. Nevile Henderson was to be Ambassador to Berlin at the outbreak of war in 1939.

Moreover, I believed that there was no real prospect of stability, either in Germany or in Europe generally until the grievances arising out of the Treaty of Versailles had been rectified so far as the Germans were concerned. This done, I trusted that Hitler, and the reasons for his existence and the methods of his regime, would disappear.[40]

Had Sir Nevile Henderson read and pondered *Mein Kampf* and his predecessor's dispatches?

There were those who believed that Hitler was a man of peace and there were those whose visions stopped at French wickedness and British guilt. Beyond them were the pacifists who, however much they might fear and despise Hitler, saw war as incomparably the greatest evil. Lansbury thought that the ideas, Fascism and Communism, could never be crushed by force of arms but only by allowing "the ideas that are right" to prevail in those countries. How he would secure freedom for the dissemination of such ideas he did not explain. The League could not check aggression by arms and the influence of the League, he believed, would wax if only the elements of force were removed wholly from the Covenant.[41] His ultimate confession of faith was this:

I will add that the first nation that disarms and refuses to participate in any international conflict will find that it has thereby gained complete security.[42]

It would, moreover, send a message to the world based on morality and common sense. It was in this faith that the Reverend Dick Sheppard, the Canon of Westminister, founded the Peace Pledge movement in 1934, asking the men of Great Britain by written pledge to renounce participation in any war. He promptly secured 100,000 adherents. That same pledge on the part of women was sought by the Women's International League for Peace and Freedom. The No More War Movement flourished in Britain; its international counterpart was the War Resisters International.

Dick Sheppard was a determined optimist. He later wrote a letter to Hitler asking his permission to travel to Germany to preach pacifism.[43]

In the field of popular pacifist literature, the 1934 successor to *Cry Havoc* was *Peace with Honour* by Christopher Robin's creator, A. A. Milne. He proceeded from the basic thesis that war would, it was absolutely certain, extinguish civilization. It followed, therefore, that preparations for defense were as dangerous to peace as preparations for war. Milne was not blind to the threat of Nazi Germany and Fascist Italy; he recognized their disdain for peace and their dramatic appeal to popular sentiments.

What then was the way out of this dilemma? It was the assumption that Germany was: "as amenable to reason as Italy (or any other nation) and that. . . she is at least as anxious as any other nation for the security of peace."[44]

This greatly facilitated the solution Milne proposed. At an international conference each nation would renounce war subject to the condition its discontents were remedied. The method of remedying all discontents was not supplied. All this would be followed by an oath to renounce both aggressive and defensive war and to submit all disputes to arbitration. The delegates to the conference would be responsible, not merely to their countries but to civilization. This suggested, of course, that the latter duty was the higher.

Milne proposed that security had now passed beyond the security of armaments to "the security of a country's honour; a moral force that has never yet been allowed expression." Disarmament could now look after itself.

Technical provisions were offered. A new dictator would, Milne suggested, renew the oath his predecessor had sworn. Certainly the King of England would never renounce *his* oath. But what of Germany?

> I can do no more than say that I feel quite certain that she wouldn't, and that she couldn't; that it would be as surely a moral impossibility for her to break the pledge as it would be for France or England.[45]

And if the worst were to befall Britain, conquest by a pledge-breaking Germany, there would be ample compensation to Britain in having kept her pledge of honour. She would have merely suffered "a defeat which she has deliberately risked for the sake of the world."[46]

These ideas were taken seriously. There was however an attitude less deliberate and far simpler than a favorable opinion of Hitler, a concern for morality, or devotion to the cause of peace. Larger numbers of people lived their daily lives unconcerned with foreign affairs than those who gave to them their deliberate and involved attention. In times of economic hardship, people had livings to earn, careers to make, families to form and to cherish; these were urgent, immediate, and infinitely more absorbing than the complicated, mostly unintelligible affairs of Central Europe.

And the British people had much in which they could take satisfaction. Their Empire was the largest the world had seen. London was the world's greatest capital. They lived in a free and open society which offered avenues for the pursuit of every interest and the gratification of most fancies. If they thought about foreign affairs, they might first be affected by a sense of disillusion and by the idea that their lives would be simpler and happier without them. The ideas that power politics were by their nature evil, that the balance of power insured war, and that arms were inherently to be suspected as agents of Mars, made it comfortable to do nothing in particular. To all this, membership in the League of Nations gave the satisfaction that someone out there was safeguarding the peace and that Britain was doing her share.

Britain had always muddled through and there was no reason to suspect she wouldn't continue. The thing was to keep calm, don't rock the boat, keep your hair on,[47] and maintain that characteristic combination of phlegm and mild and superior disinterest with which Britain viewed a world of which she did not really approve.

All this was human enough. "Right or left," Vansittart said, "everybody was for a quiet life."[48] Those who disturbed the peace were not always welcome. "Here," said A.A. Milne,

> is Mr. Winston Churchill. Indeed, no one so fearless as he, nor so ready to die heroically for England. But he would like to die heroically first. If war comes, he would like to head a forlorn hope somewhere. . . one that would leave him free to lead another forlorn hope afterwards, somewhere else. He would die gloriously for anybody or anything. . . . But might he? . . . Dead men are never Prime Ministers.[49]

No, there were limits, and the idea that the human race was not only capable of but engaged in material and moral progress had survived, though hardly intact, the World War. It is fair to say that the ultimate horrors of Nazi Germany were beyond the imagination of the world in 1933 and 1934.

Phillips Gibbs was Britain's dean of war and foreign correspondents. He had seen more than his share of slaughter, and he knew Germany and the continent. Whatever Hitler might say, whatever he might see or hear in Germany, he was comforted to think:

> It is rather too much to massacre 15 million people in cold blood or even a few million, or even five hundred thousand. There would be an outcry of public opinion. People would make 'a fuss about it.' A nation might be considered uncivilized if it adopted such measures.[50]

This was a climate of opinion which the government was bound to take into account. It comprehended diffuse views from every segment of the political spectrum and every interest, sometimes overlapping, for very different reasons, sometimes conflicting, always vocal, always present.

There was, however, one center of organized public opinion on foreign policy and that was to be found in the Labour party which constituted the Opposition to the National Government. Its foreign policy was rooted in its socialist and trade union antecedents. It could be philosophical and deliberate, but at election times it could also be shrill:

The Unionist Party wants war. Your husbands and sons will be cannon-fodder. More poison gas will mean dearer food. Register your distrust of the warmongers by voting Labour.[51]

When the Labour Party held its annual conference at Hastings in 1933, it endorsed disarmament and collective security. If it came to war, Labour washed its hands of such imbecility. The National Executive of the Labour Party would confer with the trade unions to determine the steps to be taken, including a general strike, to organize the workers against war.[52]

By December, 1933, Labour was well aware of the character of the Nazi regime. It responded with a manifesto and a peace campaign, all under the sponsorship of the Labour Party, the Trades Union Congress, and the Cooperative Union. The goal was the Socialist dream: a world where nations worked together for the common good, abolishing war and poverty, and establishing the golden rule of fellowship and cooperation.

Liberty, personal and intellectual, parliamentary institutions and the League of Nations were all threatened. There were ogres abroad in the world and Labour named them:

The masses in countries stricken by fear are being asked to bow down once more to War and Mammon, the old gods of the frenzied nationalism and greedy imperialism of the past.

War profiteers are once more at their devilish work spreading panic among the nations in order that their ghoulish profits may be increased. War preparations are being made on a scale even greater than before 1914, and with weapons far more terrible than were then known. Science at the service of madness threatens to destroy humanity itself.[53]

The manifesto proposed that, under British leadership, the moral forces of the world would be irresistible. What was needed to fight dictatorship and war, even beyond constructive peace measures, was "the frank acceptance of the higher loyalty to the world community of mankind."[54]

A solution grounded in morality was consistent with a higher loyalty to mankind in the sense that no influence of national interest should be allowed to corrupt it. It remained to be determined who would lay down the principles of international morality and who would enforce them.

By the time of the 1934 conference, the leaders of Labour had come to realize that there was little hope of a general strike in Germany, Italy, or Japan. They did not abandon the idea of a general strike in Britain. But, as is natural under such circumstances, when one cannot influence other nations, one seeks to achieve his goal by influencing policy at home.

If Labour could not obtain action abroad it would achieve its aims by hobbling the British Government. It now proposed, as its contribution to the peace of nations, the Peace Act of Parliament. This would make it illegal for the British Government to use force as an instrument of national power. It would, at the same time, empower the government to use economic or financial measures which, it was confidently hoped, would prevent war.[55]

All this was contained in an overall statement called *For Socialism and Peace*. Labour would do all those things that had been talked of, debated, hoped for, and never attained since Armistice Day: the settlement of all international disputes by peaceful means; drastic disarmament and the replacement of armies and navies by an international police force; abolition of the private manufacture and sale of arms; the internationalization of civil aviation; an international air force; an international agreement on tariffs, trade regulation, and conditions of labor. The result of all this would be the abandonment of the old and infamous balance of power and the substitution of a World Cooperative Commonwealth. All this, the Labour leadership announced, was in the long-term mainstream of Socialist foreign policy.[56]

It was all very spacious and inclusive, and the policy gained large but not total support of Labour. One faction, led by Lord Ponsonby called for complete unilateral disarmament, irrespective of any action taken by any foreign country. Sir Stafford Cripps led Labour's militant wing, denouncing participation in the League of Nations, since it was essentially a capitalist organization to which no honest class warrior could pledge his allegiance. All capitalism did was to pile up armaments, thereby "helping the bloody, ferocious rule of British imperialism."[57]

Against these subcurrents, the mainstream resolution might appear positively conservative; but it offered little encouragement to a government faced with a practical task of formulating a foreign policy to meet the German challenge.

There were dedicated members of the Labour Party who saw things differently. They realized that, with the advent of the Nazis, principles and policies that might have been appropriate to the Germany of Brüning were no longer appropriate to the Germany of Hitler. There were those who saw the threat and even began to perceive the need to rearm.

But too many of them fell victim to the intense bitterness that the breakup of the Labour Party and the triumph of the National Government led by Ramsay MacDonald, had caused. It was all sham and trickery, dishonest and fraudulent, the same charges they were to bring against the Baldwin government after its 1935 election victory.

One of them was A.L. Rowse, a young Oxford professor of working-class antecedents, but now a fellow of All Souls College, moving in the company of the elite of the National Government and its supporters, including the Foreign Secretary, Dawson of the *Times*, and Stanley Baldwin himself. He knew Germany; he saw and felt the danger; he knew that the policy of Labour was not the answer. He struggled, but he was loyal to his party:

> After the trickery of the Red Letter scare in 1924, after the trickery of 1931, repeated in 1935, no decent Labour man would accept anything from these men, even when they were right—as, too little and too late over armaments.[58]

Danger clearly lay ahead, knowledge of the danger was widespread, and yet Labour concluded in 1933 and 1934 that disarmament, not arms, was the correct policy. This posed a problem for which a responsible government must find a solution. The problem was clearly put by a leading advocate of peace:

> The worst of all disservices to disarmament would be to become defeatist. . . . To press on, undeterred, with disarmament, in the face of the German situation is dangerous and difficult and to try to fall back on the one-sided regime of Versailles—that would be not only dangerous but assuredly disastrous.[59]

The Government Responds

On October 14, 1933, Germany had withdrawn from the Disarmament Conference and given notice of its withdrawal from the League of Nations. There could have been no more dramatic evidence of Germany's repudiation of the postwar system of security and international relations. Henceforth, Germany would look to her own interests, pursue her own way.

A Parliamentary election campaign was then underway in the East Fulham constituency, to replace the recently deceased Sir Kenyon Vaughan-Morgan. In the 1931 National Government landslide, Sir Kenyon, a Conservative, had polled 23,438 votes and overwhelmed his Labour opponent with the majority a 14,521.

The Conservative and National candidate, W.J. Waldron, was well known as Alderman and a Town Councillor since 1906. The Labour challenger, J.C. Wilmot, was a newcomer to the constituency.[60] Superficially, astute observers commented, it would be difficult for Mr. Waldron to lose a seat never before held by Labour and won two years before by a vote of 23,438 to 8,917. Yet the *Times* correspondent conceded it was not impossible; the Labour candidate could poll 15,000 votes "so popular had Mr. Wilmot and his peace propaganda proved."[61]

The issues of the Wilmot campaign were peace and housing. The peace movement recognized the significance of the election and rallied to him. Labour's brochure featured a picture of Mr. Wilmot with Arthur Henderson, Labour's Foreign Secretary and President of the Disarmament Conference. The caption was homely and appealing: "Uncle Arthur tells John Wilmot that peace men must 'stand together.'"[62]

Uncle Arthur was not the only national leader to enter the campaign. George Lansbury, leader of the Labour Party, came to Fulham Town Hall to address Wilmot's election rally. The warmongers were on the warpath, he told his audience, when the real duty of the Government was to abolish war. In supporting Mr. Wilmot, the East Fulham electors would be striking a blow on behalf of true peace.[63]

To the campaign Lansbury also contributed another ringing message:

> I would close every recruiting station, disband the Army and disarm the Air Force, I would abolish the whole dreadful equipment of war and say to the world 'do your worst.'[64]

The East Fulham Liberal Association urged its members to vote for Mr. Wilmot on the peace issue. Mr. Wilmot welcomed this support. "I stand for peace" was the headline of his election poster. He did not state his program for securing peace but instead he attacked what he alleged was his opponent's advocacy of rearmament.[65]

Stanley Baldwin had come to the aid of Mr. Waldron. His message to East Fulham emphasized the degree of British disarmament, and Britain's contributions to the Disarmament Conference. The Government, he added, would not be discouraged by Germany's actions from pursuing peace.[66]

When the votes were counted, Mr. Wilmot, the stranger, had surpassed every expectation with a vote of 17,790 to Mr. Waldron's 12,950, a turnaround of more than 19,000 votes. Clearly domestic issues were important, but equally clearly the Labour candidate had chosen peace as the critical issue and one that secured his party's wholehearted endorsement. Mr. Wilmot promptly became a national celebrity, and journeyed to Kilmarnock and Skipton, where November Parliamentary elections were scheduled, to rally support for Labour on the peace issue.[67]

East Fulham involved one seat in Parliament, where the Labour Party was a small minority indeed. But East Fulham had sent a message which the Government could only ignore at its peril. This was not Hitler's German democracy where the elected leader made all the decisions. This was the rough and tumble of British politics where policy, to be effective, had to command public support.

The Government now had a complex task. It had to deal in a practical way with the German challenge while the Disarmament Conference was still underway and commanded widespread support, and all this in a manner that the public would accept.

Stanley Baldwin had said in November, 1932, that the bomber would always get through. He had also said that it would be criminal neglect to fail to make preparations.[68] On March 2, 1933, he had told the Cabinet's Disarmament Committee that the safety of Great Britain was their first consideration.[69] On October 6, 1933, he told the Conservative Party conference in Birmingham that disarmament had to mean real limitations; Britain could not afford to be weaker than its rivals and would have to arm up to that level. But the Cabinet concluded on October 23, 1933 that, despite German withdrawal from the Disarmament Conference, it was still useful and desirable to continue to pursue some agreement for arms limitation.[70]

This conclusion was reinforced by the dramatic results of the East Fulham election. On November 2, 1933 at Kilmarnock, the Government candidate prevailed, but the swing against the Government was greater than at East Fulham. The 7,036 majority of 1931 was reduced to a slender 2,653.[71] Again, at Skipton, on November 7, 1933, the Government's 1931 majority of 14,960 was reduced to 3,979, an adverse swing of 25.2 percent.[72] At Ruisholme, on November 21, 1933, a 1931 Conservative majority of 18,448 was reduced to 2,899.[73] On the same date, the election at Rutland recorded an 18.6 percent swing against the Government, its 1931 majority of 11,640 votes being reduced to only 1,787.[74] At Harborough, on November 28, 1933, the Conservative's candidate saw his margin of victory reduced from 19,578 in 1931 to 6,860.[75] As the year turned, the story was much the same at Cambridge where, on February 8, 1934 the Conservative majority was reduced from 14,795 to 2,720[76] and at Lowestoft, on February 15, 1934, from 11,992 to 1,920.[77] Only at Portsmouth, home of the Royal Navy, did the candidacy of Admiral Sir Roger Keyes, one of the Navy's greatest living heroes, result in holding the swing against the Government to 8.8 percent.[78]

Judgments on the meaning of elections are as complex as the issues involved. The size of the Government majorities in 1931 had clearly been unusual. Domestic issues were important. Nevertheless, the appeal to peace by opposition candidates had won an interested response; that there was a strong tide of opinion running against the Government seemed plain. Baldwin's biographers made a claim which is worthy of consideration, if not definitive: "A General election. . . would have turned the National Government's huge majority into a Labour one of at least one hundred seats."[79]

The Government, the Cabinet, and the executive departments kept themselves continuously informed about international developments. But ultimately it was in Parliament that the facts—or contentions as to what the facts were—were aired and the issues joined. In Parliament lay the power to determine the questions of disarmament and security, war and peace. This was a continuing process in 1933 and 1934.

Winston Churchill, of course, was eloquent in describing the progress of German rearmament. He had no information, he told the House of Commons, on November 7, 1933 save what he read in the papers but that was more than sufficient. Did the leader of the Opposition think, he asked, that Hitler would ask him for his consent before rearming? He might, Churchill said, go ahead without the formality of obtaining a card vote from the Trades Union Congress.[80]

This provoked laughter, but the debate made clear the German rearmament was a generally acknowledged fact. The question was not whether Germany was rearming but what to do.

British security was again debated on November 29, 1933 on the motion of Rear Admiral Sir Murray Sueter, "That this House views with grave disquiet the inadequacy of the provisions made for the air defense of these islands, the Empire overseas; and our Imperial communications."[81]

Mr. Wilmot, the new member for East Fulham, promptly opposed the motion which he thought might mean the end of the Disarmament Conference. The *Times* correspondent had reported that day the observation of several members of Parliament that the electors were against rearmament. They ought not, he said, to allow the opinion of the electors to affect their duty to assure the safety of the country.[82]

Stanley Baldwin was sensitive to all sides of the issue. Germany had withdrawn from the Disarmament Conference the month before, and the message of East Fulham seemed to be that she ought to be brought back. He would accept the statement relating to inadequacy of defense if it were not put to a vote. He did not wish, by an affirmative vote, to send the message to Germany that Britain had given up on disarmament and was proceeding to rearm. An amendment in this sense carried.[83]

That Germany was rearming had been acknowledged. To this was added widespread agreement that British defenses were inadequate; and on this basis the debate continued.

The urgency of the issue was underlined, on November 12, 1933, by Hitler's overwhelming success in the plebiscite on German withdrawal from the Disarmament Conference and from the League of Nations. During the debate on foreign affairs of December 22, 1933, Clement Attlee asked the Foreign Secretary about the progress of disarmament discussions and again clearly stated Labour's position. They recognized that the situation of the Disarmament Conference was critical; but they were unalterably opposed to any rearmament.[84] Here was the paradox, which members noted in debate after debate: if collective security was indeed the answer, how could collective security be enforced by nations without arms?

Attlee returned to his theme in the debate of February 7, 1934. The real problem of the disarmament conference was not a failure to agree on tonnages and calibers; it was instead that there was never an acceptance of the principle of the disuse of force.[85] Whether Hitler would agree to such a principle, and, having agreed, whether he would abide by it were questions necessarily inherent in this formulation.

When the debate continued the following day, the positions taken were familiar. Mr. Clarry moved,

That this House, while appreciating the several efforts of His Majesty's Government to secure world-wide disarmament, considers that the growing disparity in armaments of the United Kingdom in relation to other powers has brought about a situation which seriously imperils the security and independence of the British commonwealth and endangers peace; in consequence this House, though anxious to cooperate in a universal policy of peace and disarmament, either through the League of Nations or by direct international agreements, urges His Majesty's Government to pursue a course which will adequately safeguard our industrial, political, and national existence.[86]

Would the country, Mr. Clarry asked, accept the views of men who knew or would it be led astray by a small but potent group of callow university youths and those who would exploit the peril of the nation?

Members again asked if such a motion might not prejudice the cause of disarmament. The issue of cost, always present, was examined. And as always, there were members who rejected military preparations and wanted "to go back to the hopes of international agreement. . . . The idea of security lying in armed forces was exploded."[87]

Mr. Churchill did not agree. The situation caused by the emergence of Nazi Germany was entirely new. The Disarmament Conference had simply failed. Britain needed an air force as strong as that of any power which could attack her. He would vote against the motion so "temporizing, vaporizing and paralyzing." The Government had an immense majority. They needed only to state what should be done, and the country would support them.

Stanley Baldwin paid tribute to his collaboration with Churchill in the past. At present, Churchill spoke, he said, from a position of greater freedom and less responsibility. He would persist in the effort to find agreement on disarmament. He laid down a warning for those who supposed that, failing agreement, sanctions were the answer. "A blockade was an act of war and any country, unless it was absolutely impotent, would fight against it":

If we fail. . . there is no need for me here to say a word to this House of the dangers of that situation, but I would say this—if we do fail, the Government will feel that the duty of the Government is to look after the interest of this country first and quickly.

Sir Herbert Samuel showed that Churchill had no monopoly of picturesque speech. Rearmament only meant an arms race without end and he would paraphrase Mr. Churchill's remarks: "Long live anarchy, and let us all go rattling down to ruin forever."[88]

Outside Parliament, Nazi pressure was unrelenting in Austria, Hitler's first goal. Under Italian prompting, Britain joined with France and Italy on February 17, 1934 in the declaration stating their common interest in the preservation of the independence and integrity of Austria.[89] In the same month, Anthony Eden made his first acquaintance with Adolf Hitler and Benito Mussolini.

In November, 1933, the Cabinet had established a Defense Requirements Subcommittee in response to reports and developments in Germany. On February 28, 1934, the Subcommittee made its first report, recommending a five-year expansion program which would add forty squadrons to the RAF. This was based on the assumption that Germany could not soon challenge Britain in the air. The total defense budget recommended over the five year period was at £70 million. Vansittart formally disagreed. Germany "will not be inferior to us in the air for any appreciable time," he wrote to Hankey, the committee's chairman. The issue now was not the fact of a German air force, but the rate of its development and hence the immediacy of the threat to Britain.[90]

The program was debated in the House of Commons on March 8, 1934. Attlee stuck to his guns. Air defense was a contradiction in terms; what it really meant was the threat of counterattack powerful enough to deter. To think Britain could achieve air parity was "absolutely useless and insane." The great mistake had been not to internationalize aviation and create an international air force: "we on our side are out for total disarmament because we are realists."[91]

This was calculated to arouse a stirring response from Winston Churchill. Germany was arming fast, he said, and no one would stop her. No one was proposing a preventive war. But Germany could develop a powerful air force in a short time. He dreaded the day when Germany should be able to threaten the heart of the British Empire. "We should be in a position which would be odious to every man who loved freedom of action and independence, and in a position of utmost peril for our crowded, peaceful population."[92]

And that day was not far distant, perhaps eighteen months.

Stanley Baldwin was no orator, but masterful in the intimate and familiar tone of the House. He valued the moderation of Mr. Churchill's speech. He agreed that the situation had changed in the past year. He appreciated the potential peril and knew Britain had to take care that it did not become actual. Again, the bomber would always get through, though the possibility of retaliation could lessen the danger.

Baldwin would pursue an air convention. He was not prepared to admit defeat:

> But I do say that, if all efforts fail, and if this equality be not possible to be attained in such matters as I have indicated, then any Government of this country and the National Government more than any, and this Government, will see to it that in air strength and air power this country shall no longer be in a position of any inferiority to any country within a striking distance of our shores.[93]

But no progress was made on an air convention and on March 19, 1934, Germany published its defense budget showing increases of over a third and a 250 percent increase for the air force. Baldwin was forced to conclude that there were few realistic hopes of an air agreement.

What the public thought was indicated in the Parliamentary elections. In Basingstoke on April 21, 1934, the Conservative majority of 17,417 in 1931 was reduced to 6,885.[94] At Hammersmith, the Labour candidate campaigned on peace and disarmament through the League of Nations as well as public ownership and control of industry and finance. The problem of disarmament had grown more acute, he said, because of Britain's failure to give a courageous lead to the world. In the vote on April 24, the swing against the government was repeated[95] and, again, on May 14, 1934 in West Ham.[96]

In the debate in the House of Commons on May 18, 1934, the parties played out their accustomed roles. The radical Labour view was put by Sir Stafford Cripps. He asked if His Majesty's Government was prepared to sacrifice the country's independence of action and decision to attain security.[97]

The Liberal view, stated by Sir Francis Acland, refused to believe that the Disarmament Conference could die. It should go on in the spirit of the leaders of the churches, subordinating all party and national interests to the peace of the world.[98]

For the Government, Captain Cazalet firmly recommended a strong policy of friendship and alliance among Britain, France, Italy, and the Little Entente to restrain Germany. But the Government ought not to undertake obligations without the force needed to fulfill them. The

Foreign Secretary was not sanguine about economic sanctions. And as to the hopes of Sir Frances Acland he replied:

> Peace and disarmament were the subject of every good man's discourse on Sunday and week days. There was not a sentence of the admirably phrased speech of Sir Francis Acland which would not be perfectly appropriate at any peace meeting, whether in a sacred or secular edifice at any time in the last 20 years.[99]

Stanley Baldwin again emphasized that sanctions meant war. Nothing, he said, would be a worse guaranty or a crueler deception than for a country to say it would guarantee peace by arms and not be ready to do so. And finally, no democratic country could possibly wage war unless the people were behind it. All these were considered thoughts that the oncoming years would validate time and again.

He asked the House and the people to trust the Government as they prepared a program for their defense. Perhaps, on a softer note, he said, there was less danger than was imagined and in any case, preparations were afoot in more than ample time.[100]

The Hankey report recommending a five-year expenditure of £72 million for defense was reviewed often by the Cabinet. Neville Chamberlain, Chancellor of the Exchequer, thought this sum too high and with customary tenacity argued for a reduction to £50 million. Baldwin would not agree. He told the Disarmament Committee of the Cabinet on June 11, 1934 that the public had to know the truth, that from an air point of view Britain's border had moved from Dover to the Rhine.[101]

The Cabinet agreed with Baldwin. At its meeting on July 18, 1934, the cuts proposed by Chamberlain were restored and the full Baldwin program approved. On July 19, Baldwin announced the new program to the House of Commons. It provided for forty-one new squadrons, thirty-three to be allotted to home defense, making a total of seventy-five squadrons, the rest for the Fleet Air Arm and abroad.[102]

The debate on the new program took place on July 30, 1934. Only the day before, the Austrian Chancellor, Dollfuss, had been buried in Vienna. The Austrian President, in his eulogy, said that Dollfuss had "spared Austria from losing her soul, her inmost essence, in so-called Nazi 'conformity.'"[103] Frau Dollfuss then returned to her children who were Mussolini's guests. In Italy, fierce indignation gave rise to a flood of anti-German criticism and abuse. The Nazis were depicted as "barbarians addicted to all the most shocking vices and breaches of normal Christain and civilized morality." At the same time, Italian military forces were massed on the Austrian border. It was the nadir of German-Italian relations.

The debate was on a motion of censure against the Government's air rearmament proposal. Over the course of two years, little that was new was said in these debates. Baldwin again noted that the vote of censure was based on a faith in collective action. But how was this to be carried out without means of enforcement? He acknowledged that the program was modest enough. But it would not, he thought, jeopardize the cause of or prospects for disarmament.

There were those who called him inconsistent, reminding him of his 1932 pronouncement that there was no defense, the bomber would always get through. He had, he said, read his speeches—some of them were rather good—but there was no inconsistency. Because defense was not absolute did not lead to the conclusion that there should be no defense. An air deterrent could lessen the chance of attack. You could not guarantee that no enemy submarine would ever sink a British ship; but this was no reason to abandon the Navy.

Baldwin's speaking manner was underated but his ending left no room for doubt:

> The greatest crime to our own people is to be afraid to tell the truth. . . . We are far too apt in this country to believe that all the peoples of the world are animated by the ideals which animate us. That is not true at this moment. There are in the world signs of a form of force being used which shows the spirit which if it became powerful enough might mean the end of all that we in this country value and which we believe makes our life worth living.
>   Let us never forget this—since the day of the air the old frontiers are gone. When you think of the defense of England, you no longer think of the chalk cliffs of Dover, you think of the Rhine.[104]

Attlee made his accustomed response. What possible relevance could armaments have in a world where the renunciation of arms as an instrument of policy had been solemnly sworn to? The question was simple enough: "Were they for national defense or were they for collective security?" Mr. Mander thought the fault lay with Britain for never sincerely seeking a Disarmament Convention while Mr. Adams would vote for the motion because war was evil. To this, Mr. Banks rejoined that it was unjust to blame the Government for having failed to teach Germany Christian morality. Winston Churchill put the danger picturesquely:

We were a rich and easy prey. No country was so vulnerable, no country would better repay pillage. This rich metropolis, the greatest target in the world, was a kind of valuable great cow, tied up to attract a beast of prey.[105]

His concern was not that too much was being done, only too little. Britain was the sixth air power. Any move to rearmament would be attacked by pacifists "with all that interested and unscrupulous vituperation which they saw in the squalid election at Fulham some time ago."

Germany, Churchill said, had created a powerful air force and was rapidly increasing it. In 1935 it would be equal and at the current rate of increase, in 1936 it would be stronger than Britain's. That was the danger.[106]

Sir John Simon closed the debate with the observation that the estimates had been framed on the principle that at no moment should Britain fail to have an air force adequate to the circumstances. The triumph of the government was never in doubt. The vote of censure was defeated by 344 votes.[107]

That vote did not necessarily match the sentiment of the country. The electorate was unconvinced. At North Lambeth, on October 23, 1934, Labour gained a Parliamentary seat that had been won in 1931 by a Liberal candidate. The National Government candidate won only 2,927 votes of 19,499 cast.[108]

Information on Germany continued to pour in. On November 20, 1934, the Committee of Imperial Defense reported on German rearmament and stated that within a year the German air force would be as strong as the RAF. On November 26, the Cabinet determined that the time had come to speed up air defense.[109]

On November 28, 1934, the polling took place in Putney where the Labour candidate, Dr. Edith Summerskill told her rally:

My party is pledged to work for peace. That is the most important issue in the election. It eclipses all other questions. If we are not peaceminded now, another war is inevitable. Another war! It may cost 10,000,000 lives— perhaps more. Your cross on the ballot paper will be a direct message to the Government that you wish for peace. This message will reach Westminster, where the voice of Putney will be heard.[110]

When, on the same day air defense was debated in the House of Commons, the motion was not Labour's protesting rearmament but

Churchill's on the inadequacy of the government program. He graphically described the threat to London. 30,000 to 40,000 killed in a week or ten days, and an unmanageable mass of three or four million driven out into the countryside, docks and facilities destroyed and in the end, absolute subjugation. The decision lay with a handful of men—the men of June 30.

Churchill returned to his thesis. Germany had an air force, deny it though she might. In 1935 it would be as strong as Britain's, and in 1936 stronger. More needed to be done: "Let the House do its duty, let the Government give the lead, and the nation will not fail in the hour of need."[111]

The difference with Baldwin was again not on principle but on facts. Baldwin cited his facts. Was it the case that Germany was nearing air equality? If she continued her air program without acceleration and Britain carried out its announced rate of expansion, Britain would have a 50 percent margin of superiority in the next two years.

With Baldwin's conclusion, Churchill could agree

> that His Majesty's Government are determined under no condition to accept any position of inferiority with regard to what air force may be raised by Germany in the future.[112]

Labour introduced an amendment deploring the increase of arms. It was supported by the usual arguments: collective security and a return to the provisions of Versailles. Churchill withdrew his motion; the Labour amendment was overwhelmingly defeated by 241 votes.[113]

The Government did not fare quite so well in the Putney election. Its candidate won but with a 2,663 majority, a far cry from the 21,146 triumph of 1931.[114] The National Government still had to look to its left at the electorate and to its right at Mr. Churchill.

After the debate, the Foreign Secretary, Sir John Simon reflected on the issues it had raised, issues which would have to be faced promptly. The primary issue was this: whether to legalize German arms and, if not, what position to take when Germany formally renounced Versailles. And if the former, what ought Britain to say to France?

Sir John concluded that the best course would be to recognize German rearmament while terms were still available, thus making Germany an honest woman. The conditions would be Germany's return to the League and the Disarmament Conference, though not on the basis of Versailles.

The French would of course complain that blackmailers and wrong-doers ought not to be rewarded; but Britain had to look at things in a practical way. The alternatives might be disastrous.

Of course there would be a division of Europe into opposing camps, but again, what was the alternative? British public opinion knew of German rearmament and would not for long acquiesce. Let us, Sir John concluded, get rid of the lumber while it will still fetch a price. The retribution, if a definite policy were not adopted, would be severe.[115]

Hitler was now completing his second year in power. Hitler's aims had been widely proclaimed and were well known. His progress in pursuing those goals was equally well-known to those who did not wish to avert their eyes. He had suffered a temporary setback in Austria. But his grip on Germany was complete and the most odious features of the Nazi regime were in place. The progress of German rearmament had been swift.

The yearning for peace remained strong in Britain and a swelling tide of votes against the Government in parliamentary elections made its position uneasy.

Assailed alike by those who thought the Government had done too little and those who thought it had done too much in matters of rearmament and defense, the Government had nevertheless some real accomplishments to its credit. The debates in Parliament had educated both the Government and the public. The threat had been clearly recognized and described, though there was no agreement as to its immediacy and size.

The Government had staked out important positions. Britain's frontier was the Rhine. There was no mincing of words in defining the enemy. The policy was clear: no inferiority in the air to any nation in striking distance. The issues that remained were less policy than implementation.

Vansittart appreciated what the Government had accomplished and what Baldwin's contribution had been when he wrote,

> The Government's fat majority had come of fear and fickleness. In so unstable an electorate fat melts quickly, 'and then [he quoted Baldwin] you will have the Socialists who will give you no rearmament at all, instead of me who will give you not enough.[116]
>
> Baldwin was in truth a paragon compared to the Opposition. . . . He had to contend with a time of recoil so powerful that simple men like Dick

Sheppard could be canonized for helping to endanger lives by the million. It can truly be said that most of Baldwin's contemporaries would have done worse. . . . Yet with all allowance made for everyone, the deathwatch beetle was ticking in the structure of democracy.[117]

11

Voting For Peace

"Therefore let me beg my readers to do their utmost for the success of the Peace Ballot. There is no single thing which they can do of greater value for Peace. . . . Every vote is wanted and may contribute to prevent war and save the lives of countless thousands of our fellow citizens."
—Lord Cecil[1]

Cecil at Seventy

As 1934 opened, Lord Cecil was in his seventieth year. It seemed that everything he had worked and fought for was going down to defeat. Since his key role in drafting the Covenant of the League of Nations, through his years as a delegate to the League Assembly, as a member of the Preparatory Commission for the Disarmament Conference, as President of the League of Nations Union in Great Britain, and as President of the International Federation of League of Nations Unions, he had devoted his life to the cause of peace through collective security.

The League of Nations had failed in Manchuria, where Japan now stood in undisputed practical possession. After Japan, Germany had left the League of Nations in which only Britain, France and Italy of the Great Powers were represented. The Disarmament Conference had failed. Germany had walked out; and since the problem of disarmament was essentially a German-French issue, the prospects of agreement outside the Conference were remote.

Worse still, Europe was clearly falling into the hands of the dictators, whether of the right or the left, men who ridiculed democracy and pacifism, extolled nationalism, militarism and brute force, and were busily and openly engaged in building up their armed forces. They proclaimed their ambitions, crushed opposition, and dismissed out of hand the openness, the freedom, and the human values which Lord Cecil had dreamed of promoting through the League of Nations.

Lord Cecil was not discouraged. He had formidable resources in hand and he had unlimited courage, vigor, and imagination, all of which he would deploy in the fight for peace and world order.

His resources included the League of Nations Union of which he was the embodiment. From a peak of 600,000 in the 1920s, depression and international crises had reduced membership to some 400,000 in the 1930s. The LNU reached even broader audiences through its church and corporate memberships. In 1934 for instance, 2,650 church congregations were members. Some 3,000 local branches gave on-the-ground representation and a presence that could be effectively mobilized, as the Peace Ballot was to show.[2]

The LNU responded to the international crises of the 1930s with a wide and imaginative array of programs in support of the League of Nations. Branch meetings were basic. A monthly magazine, *Headway*, discussed international issues competently from the League point of view.

A steady stream of publications backed the League cause—*The Covenant Explained, Traffic in Arms, The Problem of the Air, Social and Economic Planning, Christian Churches and the League of Nations, Coal, British Foreign Policy, The Price of Peace*—these testify to the breadth of the LNU's interests.

There were conferences—a Conference on Training for World Citizenship, an International Conference of University Students; there were Junior Summer Schools; and there were Leaders' Training Camps. Conferences for teachers were another way to reach large indirect audiences.

At youth camps in the New Forest, swimming and hiking enlivened lectures and discussions, ending with singing around the campfire, where international representatives shared their songs.[3]

Economical tours to Geneva showed public and secondary school groups the League in operation. Other groups toured the United States and the Soviet Union; these and a combined Anglo-German tour were ways to reinforce like spirits and combine the League message with the pleasures of foreign travel.

The resources of modern merchandising were imaginatively employed. There were LNU diaries and calendars, Christmas cards, assorted postcards from foreign lands, and, inevitably, the LNU tie.[4]

The leadership was always aware that foreign policy was not in and of itself particularly titillating to a mass audience. To make its programs agreeable, entertaining, and socially rewarding was a prime way to stimulate not only membership, but active participation.

The Wanstead branch reported in 1933 that it had held an invitation dance, a dramatic performance, and a sports meeting. Its membership, unwearied by these events, could participate in a history society, a study circle, and pen entries for an essay competition.[5]

Youth could meet and mingle at the Paddington LNU Youth Group, which danced, debated, and visited a newspaper office. The Hampstead Youth Group enlivened the prosaic matter of canvassing for new members by organizing the hunt in couples.[6]

At garden fêtes across the land, the League message was spread. At the garden party and open-air fête sponsored by the Dewsbury branch, inclement weather necessitated a drastic change in the arrangements at the last minute, but the attendance was highly satisfactory.[7] At Harrowgate the feature was "a heavily contested water polo match in the open air bath." The satisfied organizers reported to *Headway* that the contest drew many who would not otherwise have attended an LNU event.[8] At Ealing's garden fête, Dame Margaret Lloyd George's speech on peacemaking as part of the education of the young was balanced by "excellent entertainments and side-shows."[9]

Lord Cecil, as readily as anyone, knew the value of a peer as a drawing card. The autumn, 1933, meeting of the East of Scotland Branch, held in the bracing precincts of the Waverly Hydro, was hosted by the Earl and Countess of Home.[10] At Poole,

> Mrs. Samways easily walked away with a first prize for her clever and attractive fancy dress at the annual Charity Carnival. . . . Mrs. Samways was robed in silver with silver wings, each huge feather bearing the name of a member of the League.[11]

Mrs. Samways' talent for creating a dazzling visual impact was shared by other branches. At Wembley, the Youth Group participated in the Whitsun Carnival Hospital Procession with a tableau representing Big Ben, captioned: "Every time Big Ben ticks, the country spends £213 on preparations for war."[12]

Amateur theatricals were pressed into the service of the LNU. The Kenton Youth Group gave three plays which contributed £8 to Peace Week. The LNU made available three original plays in June, 1934: *If the League Should Die, At the Bar of Public Opinion*, and a new pageant, all three items from the talented pen of Mrs. Dowbiggin, the energetic secretary of the Lancaster Branch.[13] Typical of other plays was *The Eleventh Hour* in which a munitions manufacturer learns that his son has been killed by his own invention,[14] and *Gas Masgue*, in which a highly militaristic old lady decides that extensive drilling of her family and servants is the best way to achieve victory in the next war.[15]

More publications flowed from the LNU presses: *Patriotism, Critics of the League Answered, The League and War, Now is the Time to Prevent Another War.*[16]

For those branches where the available talents indicated that a tableau would be more practical than a play, there was no lack of imagination or good will. The Aldeburgh Branch's prize-winning tableau featured colorful national costumes, each surmounted by a League slogan.[17] The Whitstable and Tarkenton Branch's tableau, *The Old Way—War; the New Way—Law*, was more dramatic:

The old way was conveyed by man with a model machine gun (cleverly contrived in wood) and other weapons crouching behind sandbags, his head being bandaged as for a wound. The New Way, of course, was presented by a judge, counsel and two litigating parties in court. . . . It should always be remembered that such entries appeal also to vast numbers of spectators who are not already converted and in whose mind the seed is thus planted.[18]

The women of Scotland were more direct. The North of Scotland District Council of the LNU organized twenty-five women's organizations and 3,000 women in a march through the streets of Aberdeen.[19] The tone of this event varied distinctly from the Drayton Park rally opened by Lady Winfrey, but boasting Jan Christian Smuts as speaker, where "dancing and competitions added to a delightful gathering."[20]

All of these activities were inspired by the same goal. The great membership drive held in 1934 made that goal explicit:

If there is a vast increase in the membership of the LNU, ruthless dictators abroad and cautious Parliamentarians at home will know for certain that the British people (in the words of the King's speech of November 20 last) is determined to uphold the work of international cooperation by collective action through the machinery of the League of Nations.[21]

The Kingston Branch enthusiastically echoed this proposition. It announced that it had enrolled one-third of the local population as LNU members adding, with pardonable pride: "If only the entire country could challenge that position, the Fight for Peace would be practically won."[22]

If Lord Cecil was too experienced to share Kingston's heady optimism, yet he ardently believed that the LNU could make the difference. The time had come to act.

On the steps of the Ilford Town Hall in February 1934, Lord Cecil had seen his opportunity and seized it. With the LNU as his basic vehicle, he would take the principle of the Ilford poll and apply it nationwide. He would show dictators abroad and cautious parliamentarians at home where the British people stood—and that they stood for the League of Nations and collective security he never for a moment doubted.

By March 1, Lord Cecil had secured the approval of the Executive Committee of the LNU for a national poll so long as the cooperation and financial backing of others could be had. In a week Lord Cecil rallied other organizations to support the proposed poll and by April 19, the organizing committee was established. In another week Lord Cecil had organized a conference of delegates. He knew where to look: the churches, peace societies, women's organizations, and cooperative guilds. The political parties were included, but it was significant of Lord Cecil's belief in the public that the political parties had to compete with large numbers of vocal and determined citizens. At the meeting of March 27, 1934, questions were drafted, a plan of campaign adopted, and an executive committee appointed. It was only natural that its chairman should be Lord Cecil.

The Executive Committee met on April 11, 1934, to prepare detailed plans. There were cautious members who thought that a lukewarm response to the poll might adversely affect the prestige of the LNU. Lord Cecil would have none of it. The *Official History* relates that "vision and courage won." There can be little doubt whose vision, whose courage. The Ballot would proceed on a national scale.[23]

The official name chosen for the poll was the National Declaration on the League of Nations and Armaments. It was a formal title; it was long on the tongue; and it was complex, comprehending two different subjects. Moreover, it was neutral, unlikely to command attention or compel response.

In an inspired moment, the National Declaration on the League of Nations and Armaments became the Peace Ballot. This was more than a name; it was a battle cry. It announced and explained itself in the absolute minimum of two words. It was direct and visceral, it spoke to every man of the uppermost concern of the time. It was at once a challenge and an opportunity to take a stand. You can declare for peace, the title said, and your voice, which alone would mean little, could mean everything when joined with legions of others.

So was born, expeditiously and publicly, the Peace Ballot, which was to become, in 1934 and 1935, a meteoric phenomenon of public participation in international affairs. The public response and the immediate impact upon British policies were all its founders hoped and asked for. Whether in the long run the Peace Ballot furthered the goals of its sponsors is a far more complex question. Generous impulses do not always produce happy outcomes; virtue is not always rewarded; and in the end, the dazzling success of the Peace Ballot produced results quite the opposite of what its proponents had intended—and this through the operation of factors they could not have known or taken into account when they launched their poll.

The Questions

These are the questions put by the Peace Ballot:

1. Should Great Britain remain a member of the League of Nations;
2. Are you in favor of the all-round reduction of armaments by international agreement?
3. Are you in favor of the all-round abolition of national military and naval aircraft by international agreement?
4. Should the manufacture and sale of armaments for private profit be prohibited by international agreement?
5. Do you consider that, if a nation insists on attacking another, the other nations should combine to compel it to stop by
   a) economic and non-military measures?
   b) if necessary, military measures?[24]

The publicly proclaimed goals of the Peace Ballot were what Lord Cecil's goals had always been. It would lead the nations away from the failed nationalism which had only ended in war, and promote internationalism in its place. The League of Nations was founded on the principle that the interests of each nation were best served by the well-being of all and Lord Cecil said "nationalism must not be allowed to infringe this principle."[25]

The Ballot would demonstrate that the British people looked on the League of Nations as the cardinal point in British foreign policy. It was especially important to demonstrate their loyalty to the collective system after the deadlock of the Disarmament Conference. All this would combat that strain of isolationism which always found powerful support in Britain.[26]

The Peace Ballot would educate. It would generate discussion and show the British people what was involved in being a member of the League of Nations. Convinced of the unrivaled influence of Great Britain in the councils of the nations, Lord Cecil was sure that the success of the Peace Ballot would not only inspire the peace movement at home but would also powerfully influence peace movements abroad.[27]

Lord Cecil had always believed that the ultimate sanction behind the Covenant and the League of Nations was the force of public opinion. This is why he had fought the French quest for an effective executive and a League military force. In a true democracy, the opinion of John Smith and Mary Smith, and the sum of their opinions were what mattered. They are the rock, the *Official History* said, upon which the fabric of government is based and upon their response all else depends.[28]

The election at East Fulham had proved this point. An aroused electorate had reversed a large Government majority and had sent a determined foe of the Government into Parliament. Subsequent events made it clear that the Government had heard the message and that the message was not without influence on policy.

The Government respected public opinion. To raise the great voice of public opinion, then, gave rise to the delicious anticipation of a major impact on policy.

Another aim was to involve people, to give them an outlet for political energies in a way that was not open under the system of indirect representation. Participants are activists; to create a role in which the public could function was to heighten the intensity of public feeling and enhance public effectiveness.

Behind all this lay Lord Cecil's deeply felt and strongly held religious convictions. To him the Europe of the dictators, the Europe of racialism was a continent "drifting back into the tribalism from which it had been rescued by Christian civilization."[29]

In the literature of the LNU, God and the League had always been firmly linked. In April, 1933, *Headway* had reported to its readers a resolution adopted by fifty church leaders who "convinced that God at this time is calling all nations of the world to live as one family," announced also:

That the machinery of international cooperation provided by the League of Nations, while not yet perfect, affords the best available means of applying the doctrine of the Gospel of Christ to stop war, to provide justice and to organize peace.[30]

The League of Nations assuredly was not perfect. But, looking back at the origins of the Peace Ballot, Lord Cecil saw the League "however imperfect it might be," as "in the direct line of Christian progress."[31]

Having due regard for the religious basis of the League, it was a logical step to conclude that "a policy of international isolation was both futile and immoral."[32] This was a powerful inducement. To those who were so minded, a vote for the Peace Ballot could be a vote to vindicate Christian morality.

More powerful yet was the ultimately compelling message which the National Declaration Committee sent to the British public. That message was emblazoned on the poster which announced the Peace Ballot, a plowman and his team superimposed over a sword. More compelling yet was the headline with its stark and simple challenge: "Peace or War?"[33]

Here was the theme and it was powerful: not peace, but Peace. When a test ballot was completed at Luton, *Headway* enthusiastically reported: Luton has cast a decisive vote for Peace.[34] Indeed, *Headway* editorialized, to obtain "an overwhelming vote for Peace is the Ballot's whole purpose.[35]

The League of Nations Union was at the heart of the Peace Ballot. In turn, Lord Cecil hoped that the Peace Ballot would result in a large increase in its membership. Beating the drums for the LNU was a congenial task for him. Increased membership enhanced its prestige and shored up its platform. The Peace Ballot could produce a double victory for Lord Cecil.

Beneath all this lay Lord Cecil's inmost conviction. He was a Cecil, descended from one of the greatest families in the land. He was the son of a Prime Minister; in his generation four brothers sat in the House of Lords. He had himself been a member of the House of Commons and a Cabinet Minister.

Yet Lord Cecil deeply distrusted Prime Ministers and indeed all ministers of state, as well as peers, civil servants, naval and military officers, and all other inhabitants and ornaments of the Establishment. What he believed in was the will of the people of which public opinion was the legitimate and potent expression.

There could be no greater contrast to Lord Cecil than Sir Maurice Hankey, longtime secretary to the Cabinet, classic civil servant, whose biographer chose as his title *Hankey, Man of Secrets*. To Lord Cecil's condemnation of secret diplomacy, Hankey wrote to him that he was restrained by his position from writing to the press but could address Lord Cecil as an old friend. He pointed to cases where agreements arrived at in private had been effective and doubted the same solutions could have been reached in public.

Lord Cecil ably argued the facts of the cases, but admitted that in the end, what counted was the principle:

> You, as you have often told me, are not in favor of the abolition of war. You perhaps wish to limit it, but as a valuable method of evolution you approve it. . . . Consciously or unconsciously, you dislike any method which will bring the whole force of public opinion into play against the professional advisors of the various governments on military and naval affairs. We, on the other hand, who desire a complete transformation of international relations, are confident we shall never get it by a perpetuation of the methods of the Congress of Vienna.[36]

Hankey rebutted Lord Cecil's factual arguments, but thought that on matters of method and procedure they ought to have been able to agree. But Lord Cecil did not yield:

> The point of view which you seem to me altogether to ignore is that nowadays, with modern means of communication and education it is not really sufficient for distinguished ministers and distinguished civil servants to come to an agreement unless they have behind them the support of their people; and conversely, in many cases, particularly those which affect peace, the peoples are more and more taking strong views on the questions involved in international conferences, and the fact that these views exist is an important feature in producing or preventing agreement.

Your technique was no doubt the best in the days when foreign affairs were left either to the King or a few of his most trusted advisors; but that day is past for good or ill, and I am profoundly convinced that we have got to conform to these new political conceptions or bring great disasters upon the world.[37]

Behind the stately language lay Lord Cecil's vision of the ultimate impact of the Peace Ballot. It would, by the thundering voice of the people, take the power of decision out of the hands of kings and sovereigns of every kind, of their distinguished ministers and civil servants, and of their naval and military advisors. The affairs of state would no longer be conducted behind curtains; the corridors of power would be thoroughly ventilated and illuminated. The ultimate decisions would be made in the fullest glare and blare of public discourse, and in the end, the people would decide.

This would be nothing less than a revolution in the conduct of government. Lord Cecil had long believed that the British people were deeply committed to the League of Nations and collective security. He believed with equal sincerity that the will of the people had been frustrated by governments, by ministers, civil servants, and advisors who were pursuing their traditional roles and interests. This was, he thought, a principal reason for the failures of the League, whereas, under strong British impulse, it would surely have succeeded. The Peace Ballot could change all that and make the people, in the great matters of state, the policymakers and the ministers, the civil servants, and their advisors the executants of that policy. This was Lord Cecil's vision; he soon created an effective organization dedicated to making that vision a reality.

How the Peace Ballot was Organized

What enabled the Peace Ballot to get underway quickly and efficiently was the structure, the facilities, and the talents of the League of Nations Union, all of which were, of course, firmly in Lord Cecil's hands.

The LNU lent the National Declaration Committee one of its department heads, complete with secretary and office, and these became the heart of the operation. All of England outside London, the west of Scotland and the north of Ireland were organized from this head office. The north and east of Scotland were organized by the district councils of the LNU. London and Wales were organized on a decentralized basis.

The whole area was divided, first into two and then three sectors, each reporting to a responsible officer to whom fell the task of setting up a local committee in each parliamentary constituency.

This task was facilitated by using as the nucleus of each committee the local branch of the LNU or, in rare cases, one of the other cooperating societies.

The local committee would convene a constituency conference, open to all who were interested and willing to cooperate. Here again, the organizers of the Peace Ballot clearly understood the wisdom of using established organizations rather than attempting to create a new entity from scratch. The cooperating societies included political parties, churches, peace societies, women's organizations, cooperative guilds, and trade unions. Each had its leadership, its facilities, its membership lists, and what was more important, members of proven dedication and devotion to their own causes, who were apt to be well-disposed to the Peace Ballot.

Displaying a vivid instinct for publicity, the local committee would seek to induce some well-known local figure, a Mayor, or the Chairman of the District Council, to preside over the Conference. Twenty-five London mayors acted in this capacity. Two objectives would be achieved. The Chairman would lend the prominence and dignity of his office to the Conference and hence to the Peace Ballot; and at the same time emphasis would be given to the nonparty nature of the proceedings.

This had been a fundamental decision. Like the LNU, the Peace Ballot would be nonpolitical. As it happened, the Labour and Liberal parties promptly endorsed the Peace Ballot and functioned as cooperating societies. The Conservative Party declined to take an official position, leaving the decision to its local constituencies. The matter was not free of controversy. There were those who viewed the Peace Ballot as antigovernment. But many prominent Conservatives, including members of Parliament, endorsed the Ballot; and its timing was deliberately disassociated from any general political election.

The Conference then became a steering committee responsible for the local campaign. It would elect an executive committee and officers and take on the mundane functions of raising money and recruiting canvassers. It would also undertake to establish relations with the press.[38]

Four traveling secretaries coordinated the efforts of the headquarters' offices and the local committees. In the end, there were more than 1,000 local committees covering, if not all, the great bulk of the Parliamentary constituencies in the country.[39]

At headquarters, there was a literature department to prepare not only ballot forms, but the accompanying explanatory materials and circulars. The press department played a critical role. It created and disseminated news of the Peace Ballot, interviews, events, and results. An official press release was issued every day; the results were tabulated and announced weekly. This offered the escalating drama of a continuing event and the press department made the most of it.[40]

In February, 1935, as the results began to mount, *The Ballot Worker* appeared weekly, with detailed facts, figures, and diagrams illustrating the Ballot's progress. Nor was this all; in London and Wales the local committees issued their own publications.[41]

The statistical department was responsible for checking, tabulating, entering, and analyzing the vote as it came in. A special department, headed by two appeals secretaries, coordinated the fund raising which would support the National Committee.[42]

This was an enormous, intelligently conceived, and efficiently organized effort. Yet, in the last analysis, everything depended on the foot soldiers in the field, the canvassers, and the volunteers who distributed and collected the ballots and performed all the tasks between the conception of the Peace Ballot and the final count.

Operating on a limited scale in search of a limited result would have greatly lessened the need for volunteers and the risk of failure. The decision to go national was more than justified by the overwhelming volunteer response. The numbers were vast: 35,000 volunteers in London alone; in the great cities of Glasgow and Birmingham, 7,000 and 6,500 respectively; 3,000 in Edinburgh, 3,600 in Manchester, 3,500 in Bristol. The proportions held good in the smaller cities and towns.

In the end, the astounding total of more than a half million people volunteered their time and effort to the Peace Ballot.[43] This was not an election where the electors came to the polls. Instead, the poll had to come to the electors via whatever method was available, which most often meant the feet of the volunteers. Each home was a polling station, each elector had to be approached individually. Nothing daunted, working in groups, each with a trained leader, using lists of houses from local directories, the canvassers called on millions and millions of homes, from the crowded tenements of London and Glasgow, to scattered rural dwellings in remote dales. It fell to them to explain the Peace Ballot, to answer questions, to collect ballots which had been left for consideration and discussion, and to return them for counting and analysis. The sponsors understood that enthusiasm could become the zealous pursuit of a result. They were sensitive as well to the issue of pressure tactics as they were to political partisanship. The canvassers' training included a working understanding of the very real difference "between legitimate explanation and unjustifiable persuasion." It was also vital to the integrity of the enterprise that the volunteers should learn to respect the absolute secrecy of the ballot.[44]

The lot of the canvasser was seldom easy and often thankless. The average volunteer called on thirty to forty homes; many called on far more. One volunteer in Nottingham collected over 3,000 ballots. Often the same home required several visits, to distribute the ballot, to explain it, to replace lost ballots, to answer further questions, and, if the volunteers were persistent, to collect the completed ballot.[45] The record, it was reported by the *Official History*, was set by the persevering canvasser who had failed to collect a ballot on nineteen visits:

> "I haven't signed it yet," the housewife said.
> "Come now", responded the canvasser. "All your neighbors have signed this paper, and are watching out of their windows to see if you are going to."

At this, the housewife yielded and delivered her ballot.[46]

In rural areas, hours on foot were sometimes needed to yield a few ballots There was recorded the gallant march across a distant dale to canvass a field laborer seen from afar who turned out to be a scarecrow.[47]

Lord Cecil had always believed that there was in the country deep-seated support for the League of Nations and for the cause of peace. With great satisfaction he could later write: "This army of workers is far stronger evidence of the depth of feeling for peace in this country than even the number of voters."[48]

All this had to be paid for. This was a private, not a public undertaking. There were no party funds, no public facilities to ease the task of the election workers. The National Committee supplied literature, publications, and ballots to the local committees. The rest was a local responsibility. Whether it was office rentals, equipment, supplies, postage, travel, the rental of halls for meetings, and whatever compensation was paid to local officers, the local volunteers had to finance as well as operate the poll. That they managed to do it all was added proof of their dedication.

The national headquarters received what contributions the cooperating societies could make, far less than its operations needed. The balance of some £12,000 or $60,000 in 1934–35 dollars was raised by the two appeals secretaries, aided by Lord Cecil. The National Committee was proud of the range of its contributors, large and small, from public figures, industry, labour unions, commerce, schools, and countless individuals, not only in Britain, but from throughout the Empire and from foreign lands. There were touching tales of modest contributions such as a shilling from an old age pensioner; an eight year old who, accompanied by his younger sister, came to the Liverpool committee rooms with 4d "as his contribution to the sinews of peace."[49] The Committee could take pride, too, in the economy of its operation. The change in time and economic values since 1934–35 could not be better illustrated than by the estimate that in those years a General Election in Britain would cost, at the party headquarters level, some £500,000, or $2,500,000 in 1934–35 dollars. The Peace Ballot's national headquarters conducted a national election, in almost every constituency in the land, on the £12,000, plus cooperating society contributions, that it raised and spent.[50]

The Peace Ballot Goes Public

In an age when the polling of public opinion is a basic ingredient of policymaking and political leadership, it is easy to forget that comparatively recently it did not exist. The Peace Ballot was in every sense a pioneer effort. It was only in 1936 that the Gallup Organization inaugurated public opinion surveys in Britain.

Moreover, the Peace Ballot did not aim for a limited but scientifically respectable sampling of public opinion. Its founders' vision was more spacious. They would conduct a national election, not on candidates, but on complex issues of foreign policy.

From the start, they showed keen appreciation of publicity. They understood that celebrities and stars had a vastly greater public following than issues of foreign policy and they pressed the celebrities and stars into their service. These endorsements called attention to the Peace Ballot in the most favorable way.[51]

Youth and classic English beauty were represented by Diana Wynyard, who had appeared in Noel Coward's *Calvalcade* and most recently played Charlotte Brontë in *Wild December*. Sir Cedric Hardwicke, knighted only the year before, upheld the great tradition of English acting and Miles Malleson its comic genius. St. John Ervine was the prototypical actor- manager of the great era of the English stage.

Among the writers who lent their names and pens to the Peace Ballot were A.A. Milne, the author of the best-selling *Peace with Honour*, Margaret Kennedy, whose *Constant Nymph* had retained its popularity, E.M. Delafield, chronicler of county life, and Rose Macaulay. Dame Laura Knight represented the painters.

Those who turned first to the sports pages would recognize the greatest stars of their day, Jack Hobbs, the cricketer and W.W. Wakefield, captain of the All-England rugby team.

No name was more eminent or indeed more relevant than that of Arthur Henderson, former Foreign Secretary and President of the Disarmament Conference. That the Peace Ballot was nonpartisan was made clear by the backing of the Attorney General, Sir Thomas Inskip, J.A. Thomas, Secretary for the Dominions, Lord Rochester, the Paymaster General, the Earl of Lytton who had chaired the League of Nations Committee of Inquiry in Manchuria, Lord Davies, the founder of the Union of Democratic Control, Sir Herbert Samuel, the veteran Liberal wheelhorse, and members of Parliament from all of the political parties.

To these were added the Lord Mayor of London, and among the preeminent academicians of their time, Professor J.B.S. Haldane, Dr. A.D. Lindsay, the Master of Balliol, Professor Winifred Culles, and the historian H.A.L. Fisher. Sir Arthur Salter and Sir Norman Angell were men who had devoted their careers to promoting the cause of peace.

The Peace Ballot was conducted in the odor of sanctity with the enthusiastic backing of religious leaders of every denomination. The Archbishop of York issued an appeal to the public to vote, signed by thirty bishops. The Archbishop of Canterbury was equally supportive and in the end more than fifty bishops lent their names. Inevitably, Dick Sheppard was in the van. The ecumenical appeal of the Peace Ballot was amply demonstrated by the support of the Moderator of the General Assembly of the Church of Scotland, the President of the National Association of Evangelical Free Churches, the General Secretary of the Baptist Union, the Moderator of the English Presbyterian Church, and the Chief Rabbi.

A manifesto was signed by sixty-one leading physicians and surgeons supporting the Ballot.

Surely there was someone here to impress and gain the sympathy of almost any prospective balloter. To translate this glittering array into an American constellation of the same era (without intimating they would have supported the Peace Ballot) will give some idea of the impact.

Representative American endorsers might have been as stars of the stage and screen, John and Ethel Barrymore, Norma Shearer, Clark Gable, and Joe E. Brown. From literature, Edna Ferber, Pearl Buck, and Margaret Mitchell with Georgia O'Keefe representing painting.

From public life, the former Secretary of State, Henry L. Stimson; Postmaster General James A. Farley; Attorney General Homer Cummings; the Mayor of New York, Fiorello LaGuardia; and for good measure Herbert Hoover and Senators George W. Norris and Robert LaFollette.

To these, add, from the world of sport, Babe Ruth and Bronko Nagurski, Bill Tilden and Bobby Jones; from the academy, Nicholas Murray Butler, Abbott Lawrence Lowell, and Ray Lyman Wilbur; from the clergy an impressive delegation including the Rev. Harry Emerson Fosdick, the Rev. Norman Vincent Peale, the Rev. John Haynes Holmes, Cardinal Hayes and Rabbi Stephen S. Wise.

The founders of the Peace Ballot knew that their principal medium of communication would be the press, then at its zenith in British life. Four national newspapers, the *News Chronicle*, the *Daily Herald*, the *Manchester Guardian* and the *Star* gave the Ballot almost daily mention. If the *Times*, the *Daily Telegraph* and the *Morning Post* did not afford such continuous coverage, they nevertheless reported the parliamentary debates, the Archbishop of York's appeal for votes and Lord Cecil's appeal for funds.

The provincial press covered the Peace Ballot thoroughly; readers of the *Northern Echo*, the *Birmingham Gazette*, the *Nottingham Journal*, and the *Yorkshire Observer* could be well informed of its progress.

At the height of the balloting, a weekly stream of 1,750 press clippings attested to the breadth of coverage.

The great weekly journals of opinion furnished an ample debating platform. *Time and Tide* published a special supplement by Sir Norman

Angell, and the *New Statesman* and *Spectator* regularly featured ballot news and opinion as did the religious press. The publications of the cooperating societies added importantly to the news coverage.[52]

In March 1935, Lord Cecil debated the issues of the Peace Ballot with Leopold Amery over the BBC and the debate was subsequently published in the *Listener*.

A final service of the press occurred in the last week of the Peace Ballot when the *News Chronicle,* the *Star*, and several provincial newspapers published newspaper ballots enabling many who had yet been reached to vote.[53]

All this amply illustrated the skill and professionalism of the Ballot's press section in creating and distributing the story of the Peace Ballot.

The Questions

The National Declaration Committee showed equal sensitivity to public opinion in framing the questions.

The first asked whether Great Britain should remain in the League of Nations. The public was here offered collective security as the alternative to the balance of power and the inevitable result of the balance of power—war.

An affirmative vote on the second question—are you in favor of an all-round reduction of armaments by international agreement?—would support the Disarmament Conference and the hope that arms, themselves believed to be a prime cause of war, could be controlled or, better still, eliminated.

The third question—are you in favor of the all-round abolition of national military and naval aircraft by international agreement?—touched a special fear of the British public—the specter of mass destruction and loss of life by aerial bombing. For the first time Britain was, as France had always been, exposed to the direct impact of enemy arms.

If arms caused war, and if, as many thought, the profit motive stimulated and sustained the trade in arms, then an affirmative answer to the fourth question—should the manufacturer and sale of arms for private profit be prohibited by international agreement?—would also further the cause of peace and security.

The fifth question offered interesting possibilities. It asked, first, in the event a nation insists on attacking another, whether the other nations should combine to stop it by economic and nonmilitary measures, popularly understood to be economic sanctions. If indeed the causes of war were economic, then by making it economically unprofitable and in the end impossible, you could, it seemed to many, forestall or quickly end it. The experience of the blockade in the First World War and the growing notion of economic interdependence lent substance to this concept. There was an added charm that one could vote at one and the same time for disarmament and collective security.

The second segment of the fifth question raised the ultimate issue of military sanctions. This emphasized the point that the Peace Ballot did not raise the issue of unilateral disarmament, nor was it intended to.

The Peace Ballot accorded well with a series of public perceptions about international affairs, economics and arms that were increasingly widespread and had captured considerable public attention. On the surface, it was all quite plain. Even beyond the simplest level of "You shall decide War or Peace," the Ballot presented propositions which presumably thoughtful, interested citizens could authoritatively answer to the immense benefit of the public and the government.

But, it proved to be not that simple. Complexities lurked in every question, which in the end would render interpretation of the results difficult.

Overall, it will be noted that each inquiry was presented as an issue of principle and not as a factual situation. Inherent in this was the notion that it is the principles that count and not the facts.

Whether the issue was the League of Nations, disarmament, aerial bombing, or economic or military sanctions, the Peace Ballot never asked the British public to what extent any of the questions, or the principles for which they stood, affected the well-being, security, or national interest of their country.

Undoubtedly, this stance was deliberate. As Lord Cecil noted, the whole concept of the League of Nations was that the interests of each nation were best served by the well-being of all; hence consideration of the national interests could only subvert this concept. So long as one believed this, one could dismiss the idea of national interest.[54]

The concrete proof of this lies in the deliberate change from the Ilford Poll. It had asked whether the respondents supported the Locarno Treaty which bound Britain to go the aid of Germany or France if either was attacked by the other. The public voted resoundingly in the negative, by 18,498 to 5,898.[55] Presumably, many of the Ilford electors remembered 1914 and how deeply their lives had been affected when Britain came to the aid of Belgium and France. This seemed to show that specific cases could evoke quite different responses; to the other questions of membership in the League of Nations, continuation of the Disarmament Conference, and the prohibition of the private manufacture of arms, Ilford had voted overwhelmingly in the affirmative.

Lord Cecil was frank to admit that he had been surprised by this result of the Ilford Poll.[56] The *Official History* is honest on this point:

> Although the general idea of the Ballot had been inspired by the Ilford plebiscite, the Questions, it will be seen, were more comprehensive and drafted on a wider basis. The one regarding collective security, for example—the last—made no mention of the Locarno Treaty but raised instead the whole matter of combined action against the aggressor nation in its wider and more inclusive aspects—with the result that a large negative majority was turned into a large affirmative majority.[57]

The phrasing of the questions in terms of principle rather than factual situations was in keeping with a moral view of foreign policy where good ethics and sound principles could resolve the power struggle. It offered a basis of foreign policy congenial to all those who shrank from a more realistic view while, at the same time, offering the satisfaction of both virtue and efficacy.

Whether Britain should be a member of the League of Nations seemed a simple enough question; and indeed Lord Cecil said a principal object of the Peace Ballot was to educate the British public as to what this membership meant.

But there were questions that the League had never been able to resolve. What indeed was the meaning of Article 10 of the Covenant in which the members of the League undertook to respect and preserve as against external aggression the territorial integrity and existing political independence of all members?

What was the meaning of Article 16 under which a member resorting to war would immediately be made subject to the severance of all trade and financial relations, the prohibition of all intercourse whether financial, commercial or personal with that state and, in the last event, military action? Simple membership did not answer these questions.

The League had been shown to be ineffective in Manchuria, and the question of its authority would soon be tested in even more dramatic circumstances. The League, by its own constitution, had to act unanimously. It had no executive or enforcement power. What if the nations were unable to agree upon a policy, or having agreed, were unwilling to unite to enforce that policy? A very practical question, in 1934 and 1935, would have been how to remedy these by then obvious defects of the League and make it an effective contributor to, if not a guarantor of, collective security. This was not a question the Peace Ballot asked.

Surely, an all-round reduction of armaments by international agreement was desirable and, in principle, could hardly be opposed. Here again, the question was severely practical. Suppose there were nations—one did not have to think long to identify Germany, Japan, Italy—that would not agree to a limitation of arms? In such case, was the answer to rearm? This was the crucial issue of British politics in 1934–36; yet the Peace Ballot did not ask this question. The related question was equally plain: if there were to be effective collective security, were not arms needed to guarantee it? If so, what level of arms, and in whose hands?

The same was true of the limitation of air forces by international agreement. This was immensely desirable and was a principal goal of British governments and the British public in the mid-1930s. But here again, suppose there were nations who simply would not agree, who insisted that they alone were to be the judges of their own military and aerial needs. What, then, was the appropriate response?

A ban on the private manufacture of arms was popular, and, as the Peace Ballot was to show, would even command large majorities in towns like Sheffield and Portsmouth where local economies were tied to the defense industry. A Royal Commission had recently met, amid great publicity, to consider this issue. And yet, unless on grounds of absolute pacifism one opted for unilateral disarmament, there would be arms and a need for arms. If collective security required arms to enforce it, by whom would such arms be produced? And if some nations declined to share the all-round agreement to limit arms or aircraft, and if a measure of rearmament were deemed prudent, then by whom would the needed arms be supplied? Here again, the Peace Ballot stood silent.

Nor was the question of economic sanctions free of complexity. Again, the League of Nations had to depend upon the voluntary compliance of its members, and how could economic sanctions be successful if they were not universally applied? But universally applied they could not be. The greatest economic power in the world, the United States, was not a member of the League and hardly likely, in those isolationist years, to bind itself to League action.

Moreover, the economic impact of sanctions could vary widely, depending upon the countries involved. For close neighbors and trading partners, economic sanctions could be as devastating to the virtuous as to the aggressor while more remote, perhaps less-developed nations would hardly be affected. Here was a fundamental issue of fairness and sharing burdens.

The problem of economic sanctions ran deeper. By separating the issue of economic sanctions from military sanctions, the Peace Ballot left the clear implication that economic sanctions could prevent war and that hence one could vote yes to 5a and no to 5b.

Stanley Baldwin had said clearly that sanctions meant war; there were many who agreed and would raise this point forcefully in the debate over the Peace Ballot. The Ballot, nevertheless, was phrased as if there could be meaningful economic sanctions without war.

Suppose, however, that economic sanctions were ineffective and did not stop the aggressor. That was a legitimate question to ask those, and there were millions, who voted for 5a and against 5b. The Ballot confused rather than offered a resolution to this difficulty.

It did offer a resolution on a vote for military sanctions. Nonetheless, the Ballot, in a seeming contradiction, permitted a vote for both disarmament and for military sanctions.

The practical issue here was who would bell the cat. Who, indeed, would supply the equipment, the fleets, the aircraft and above all the men to enforce the sanction? Even more than in the economic sanction, issues of geography and proximity would bulk large and the issue of equity was bound to arise in every case. But no one could compel a contribution to the military sanction, and, if not, how was it to come into being?

As always, there lurked in the background the final question: What to do if the military sanctions adopted and put into action by the League failed to deter the aggressor?

These were formidable difficulties. But at the start of the Peace Ballot, they did not seem so and it took time to develop a keener analysis. Surely both Lord Cecil and the LNU had a clear idea of the results they hoped to attain and the goals they hoped to achieve; and the good faith of the Peace Ballot was never seriously doubted. If these questions can be raised and were not addressed by the Ballot, a good faith answer can be found in the state of mind of the proponents.

There was inherent in the Peace Ballot the idea that an international system *did* in fact exist and with it a working degree of cooperation among the nations of the world, all in contrast to the bad old pre-1914 days of the balance of power. This was the sincere belief of Lord Cecil and the supporters of the League of Nations. To believe otherwise might have been to confess that their labors since the Peace Conference had been in vain.

Inherent also was the idea that collective security existed or could be made to exist independent of the great powers. To believe otherwise would again to retrogress to the balance of power.

There was, as always, the religious view. Canon Thompson Elliot had told the readers of *Headway* in 1933 that the fault lay not in the League of Nations but in themselves:

> If there is anything wrong with the League of Nations it is with the nations rather than with the League. The defects have been moral defects in statesmen and peoples much more than technical defects in the organization of the League. . . . The issue before the nations today is not one of politics, still less one of machinery, but a moral issue. The principles of Gospel of Christ have to be applied.[58]

These pious views were not shared by Adolf Hitler, nor by the Japanese, and they had made this clear by abandoning the League of Nations. Such was the strength of belief in the League of Nations and faith in collective security that these events did not discourage the Peace Balloters.

The initial challenge was "Peace or War?" To many it must have seemed their vote could indeed make the difference. After the issue was raised, the leadership of the Peace Ballot conceded that that simple question asked, or promised, too much, and it was dropped from the literature. It was never intended, they said "to make the superfluous query as to whether people preferred peace to war."[59]

And yet the impression lingered. At the least, the choice was often seen as one between international cooperation and peace as against nationalism and rearmament.

The huge gap between simply being a member of the League and

applying force to insure collective security was not always understood, much less appreciated. So long as this issue was not plainly
raised and clearly faced, there were legions of those, including sincere
pacifists, who could enthusiastically lend their support to the Peace
Ballot, secure in their own consciences that the ultimate issue would
never arise. The belief that somehow collective security could be
achieved without the risk of war was a powerful aid to the Peace
Ballot.

The Peace Ballot was novel in many respects; it was most original
in that it addressed the issues directly to the people. In the British
system, elections were simple. They involved neither the initiative nor
the referendum of which American progressives were so proud, nor a
vote for the executive as distinguished from the legislators. In British
single-member Parliamentary constituencies, where the winner was
the first past the post and took all, the electors were accustomed to
voting for their member of Parliament and their member only. A vote
for a candidate implies some knowledge of his stance on the issues.
The issues are not always so clearly defined and range across the
international, the national, the domestic and the local. A vote pre-
sumes a judgment on the character and intellect of the candidates and
the influence they might be likely to bring to bear. To vote, therefore,
on specific questions of international policy was a novel and challenging experience for that British electorate which the Peace Ballot called
into being.

Counting the Vote

To maintain the integrity and authority of the Peace Ballot, a fair
and accurate count was essential. The ballots had to be uniformly
analyzed, interpreted, and counted. Instructions were clear and stern.

Local ballots were sent to the head office of the constituency committee for counting under four headings: Yes, No, Doubtful, and No
Answer. In any case where the answer was not clear, the ballot was
classified as Doubtful.[60]

The organizers understood that the volunteer canvassers would elicit
and receive across the nation a wide variety of responses in an endless
array of formats, notwithstanding the clear presentation of the Ballot.
Indeed, many electors responded at length and added their own papers
commenting on the issues. It was thus decreed that the Yes and No

ballots would be retained locally for six months in the event that a question should be raised or there should be need for verification.

All Doubtful ballots were sent for interpretation and classification to the head office in London. This gained the immense advantage of their treatment on as uniform a basis as possible. A special committee, headed by Lord Lytton, made the final classification of the Doubtful answers thereby affording a triple test of fairness.[61]

The official form sent to each constituency asked the local committee to state the parliamentary electorate for the constituency. On the advice of the National Committee's actuaries, 9 percent was added to the electorate to recognize that the Peace Ballot was tendered to those between the ages of eighteen and twenty-one; thereafter 10 percent was deducted to cover plural votes in Parliamentary elections, the old, the infirm, the military, and others unlikely to vote. This presumably gave an accurate indication of the eligible voters against which the percentage actually polled could be calculated. From the start, it was the aim of the sponsors to obtain, more than any given result, a "good poll"—that is to say, a high, or at least representative selection of the Parliamentary electors of the constituency.[62]

Strict confidence was enjoined. The forms were signed by the scrutinizing committee or the heads of the local committee and sent to headquarters there to form a permanent and accurate record of the Peace Ballot.[63]

It is indicative of the organization and the care with which the ballots were counted that, however controversial and contentious the Peace Ballot became, no question was ever raised as to the integrity of the canvass.

Opponents of the Peace Ballot

No such enterprise could possibly receive unanimous approval; and the Peace Ballot had its determined opponents from the start. The very fact that it was endorsed immediately by the opposition parties, by Liberals and Labour, gave rise to the opinion that it was an antigovernment lobby.

Anthony Eden called it tendentious; but he supported it, as did many Conservatives on a calculation of political expediency.[64] In 1934, Eden had not yet become Minister for League of Nations Affairs.

Vansittart was more blunt. It was he said "a free excursion into the inane." Not half, he thought, really understood what they were doing; but they enjoyed the pleasant feeling of thinking "we have done something by signing something." Lord Cecil had administered to the public "a beaker of what it fancied." Such things were hard for the more cynical electorates of the continent to understand and "The continent concluded that the British hardly needed to be fooled, so long as they would fool themselves."[65]

Harold Nicholson thought that "Care was taken also that the questions should be phrased in such a manner as to elicit the wished for response."[66] This may have not been completely fair, though far from groundless as the alteration of the Locarno question showed. What was important is that this impression was abroad in the land.

But surely Duff Cooper was less than fair when he wrote in his memoirs:

> The forces of the Left in Great Britain were still preaching disarmament and circulating the idiotic Peace Ballot with the alleged object of discovering whether people preferred war or peace, an inquiry which hardly justified the time and stationery devoted to it.

This was precisely what, as the *Official History* states, the organizers disclaimed as superfluous. More to the point was Duff Cooper's assessment of the state of mind of many of the balloters:

> To them naturally the news that the most powerful people on the continent were arming was unwelcome. It was a fact they preferred to ignore.[67]

Sir Austen Chamberlain took a more practical view. The National Committee had at the outset distributed with the Peace Ballot a green folder entitled "Notes on the Five Questions" supplied by the Union of Democratic Control which had the tendency of supporting the Peace Ballot. Sir Austen considered this a blatant attempt to influence the poll.[68] He therefore created his own blue leaflet which discussed "some aspects of the various problems which have not been included" in the green leaflet. This was the "rainbow controversy" and the LNU finally resolved it by refusing to distribute any but the official ballot. At the same time, it created a yellow sheet designed only to tell the prospective voter "why he should fill in the Ballot form."[69] This series of events did not increase Sir Austen's respect for the Ballot, notwithstanding which he continued as a board member of the LNU. The

LNU in turn consoled itself that the rainbow controversy had had the constructive effect of educating the public on the true issues.[70]

Lord Beaverbrook was a fierce opponent. He dubbed it the Blood Ballot. The epithet did not take and the Peace Ballot justified the hopes of its sponsors almost as soon as the first ballots came in.

The Peace Ballot Underway

The original hopes had been modest and Lord Cecil had spoken of 500,000 votes. But the army of workers swelled in devoted service to what the *Official History* dubbed "The Cause." They were treated to a colorful variety of experiences. A worker who called on a colonel "of the fiery type" became the audience for a tirade on the glory of imperialism. Nevertheless, as he left the house, the Colonel said to him: "It may interest you to know that I have answered all of the questions 'Yes.'"[71]

The distinction between upstairs and downstairs was still clear in 1934 London. A Kensington canvasser was told by the mistress of the house that neither she nor the staff were interested in the Ballot. At the downstairs door she was handed the completed ballot forms of the entire staff.[72]

The churches provided both a pulpit and a mass audience for the Peace Ballot. In churches across the land, the Sunday before local balloting was dubbed "Peace Sunday" with special sermons to bring out the faithful to church and poll. Rev. Mr. Marks, Plymouth's well-known Fisherman's Bishop, donned a blue fisherman's jersey over his canonicals to preach out the vote.[73]

In Birmingham, an independent-minded balloter rebuffed the canvassers' two polite offers of information about the Ballot. "Gertcha," she firmly objected, "we ain't all fools in Birmingham, if you think we are."[74]

We can imagine the experiences that led veterans like "Sergeant at Eighteen" to appeal to all to sign the Ballot and the emotions of the father who pointed to his little son and told the canvasser "It's him I'm thinking of."[75]

The first of the Peace Ballot's great days came on November 22, 1934. The tiny village of Scaldwell in Northhamptonshire, like a small New Hampshire town casting its ballots in the opening minutes of an

American election day, reported large affirmative majorities for every question.[76]

More returns came in, from Scotland, from small towns in England, from part of Oxford. In the one week of voting in November, 60,000 votes were received. What was of greater interest, the first four questions had recorded affirmative votes of over 90 percent and 5b, which was to remain the most controversial, received an average vote of 81.1 percent.

This was exciting. But the organizers asked themselves: "Was this a preliminary burst of unsustainable enthusiasm, a rocket whose blaze of splendor would leave only a trail of sparks?"[77]

The answer was not long in coming. Meanwhile, far away, at an obscure water hole amid the wastelands on the Horn of Africa, shots were fired and men died in a conflict among armed nomads and colonial troops that would in the year to come escalate and magnify the votes of the Peace Balloters into a prominence of which they could have scarce dreamed.

12

An Abyssinian Incident

"The people of Abyssinia . . . have seldom met with foreigners who did not desire to possess themselves of Abyssinian territory and to destroy their independence. With God's help, and thanks to the courage of our soldiers, we have always, come what might, stood proud and free upon our native mountains."
—Haile Selassie[1]

The Boundaries of Empire

Few places in the world could have been more remote or more uncongenial than the Ogaden Desert in southeastern Abyssinia which lay between British Somaliland on the north and Italian Somaliland on the east. The region had been annexed by the Abyssinian Emperor Menelik in the last decade of the nineteenth century. When he sent a military force of 7,000 men into its arid wastes, only seven lived to return. Wandering tribesmen constituted the sole population, dependent upon scattered wells for their subsistence. Brigandage and banditry were commonplace. Sporadic attempts by the Abyssinian government to collect taxes in kind, camels and cattle, were the extent of Abyssinian government in the territory.[2]

While the first returns of the Peace Ballot were anxiously awaited, a joint British-Abyssinian commission, which had been at work marking the boundary between Abyssinia and British Somaliland, was proceeding south into the Ogaden. The British section of the commission was headed by Lt. Col. E.H.M. Clifford, assisted by two other British officers, a corporal, and a civilian from the Colonial Office. An armed escort, always considered wise in such rough, remote country, was furnished by a platoon of the Somaliland Camel Corps.[3]

Lt. Col. Clifford was going about the business of empire. Just so, at the same time, detachments as indigenous and colorful as the Somaliland Camel Corps would have been patrolling the Northwest Frontier of the Indian Empire while divisional and district officers carried on its administration and "men still heard cases under a tree." Patrol officers would have been penetrating the stone-age jungles of New Guinea; and from the Cape to Cairo, from the Straits Settlements and the South Seas to the Caribbean and remote islands of the Atlantic, the administration of territories, of justice, of economies, and of the lives and fortunes of the native populations would have been carried out in the name of the King-Emperor, and, as most British people thought, for the benefit and advancement of those same native populations.

Lt. Col. Clifford's specific task was to survey the grazing grounds of the Ogaden and to determine which nation, Great Britain or Abyssinia, had jurisdiction over the nomadic tribes. An additional purpose was to collect information which might be useful in the event of an exchange of territories. The Emperor, Haile Selassie, concerned over the threat of encroachment from Italian Somaliland, contemplated ceding a triangle of the Ogaden to British Somaliland, establishing a buffer between Abyssinia and the Italians, in exchange for a corridor across British Somaliland to the Red Sea. Abyssinia would then no longer be landlocked.[4]

The Emperor had grounds for his concerns. The border between Abyssinia and Italian Somaliland remained undemarcated despite the provisions of a 1908 Treaty that it should be marked out on the ground as soon as possible. In 1929 the Italians pressed inland to Wal Wal, which with its 359 wells was the Ogaden's chief source of water and to Wardair. In 1930 they fortified Wal Wal and established a subsidiary post at Wardair.[5]

Haile Selassie made fitful and wholly abortive attempts to regain control of the territory in 1931 and 1933. No official protest was made. The Italians were firmly in command and made it clear that any Abyssinian or British approach to the wells at Wal Wal required their permission.[6]

By 1934, the government of Abyssinia thought the time had come to react. Renegades find their natural habitat in borderlands. Omar Samantar was a Somali who, having killed an Italian captain in 1925, found it healthy to leave Italian Somaliland and take Abyssinian pay. He had the modest price of 25,000 lire on his head when the Abyssinians offered him a further mercenary opportunity. The negotiations were protracted, and were broken off when Samantar held out for a higher price. In the end agreement was reached. Samantar would recruit and lead a force armed by Abyssinia to recapture Wal Wal and Wardair.[7]

There was method here. In the event of failure, Abyssinia could disclaim the mercenaries; in the event of success, it could promptly follow up with action bearing its own authority. This Abyssinia prepared to do.[8]

Italian intelligence was excellent. The Italian consul at the provincial capital of Harar, was as effective as his colleagues throughout Abyssinia. The existence of Omar Samantar's force and its goals were accurately reported to Rome. Especially galling was the fact that the force should be headed by a fugitive from Italian justice.[9]

In early November, Samantar's band was joined by regular Abyssinian troops commanded by Governor Shiferra of the Ogaden who bore the title Fitaurari, Commander of the Advanced Guard. The combined force of 600 men met the British-Abyssinian border commission on November 20, 1934 at Ado, twelve miles from Wal Wal. It now functioned as the commission's military escort.[10]

They marched to Wal Wal. The shrewd Emperor was not unaware of the advantage of using a British commission to assert his authority over Wal Wal. The British knew that the Italians occupied Wal Wal; at the same time, it was the opinion of the Foreign Office that Wal Wal was clearly in Abyssinian territory.[11]

Lt. Col. Clifford knew that the Italians would not permit him to water at the Wal Wal wells without their express authority as Captain Cimmaruta had earlier advised him. The outlook of the British Empire of the time is reflected in Lt. Col. Clifford's later comment: "It goes without saying that the British Government did not even reply to such a communication."[12]

On November 22, 1934 Fitaurari Shiferra and Omar Samantar arrived at Wal Wal. The possibility of an armed clash was clear. Captain Cimmaruta's outnumbered garrison consisted of 160 Somali soldiers, known as dubats. On the next day, the joint boundary commission arrived at the scene. The Union Jack was raised over the British camp; but at Abyssinian suggestion, it was planted, not on the ground, but in a can as a token recognition of Abyssinian sovereignty.[13]

Lt. Col. Clifford now formally protested that he could not move freely about Abyssinian territory to which Captain Cimmaruta replied that as a soldier, he was not competent to discuss political concerns.[14]

Indignant though he was, Lt. Col. Clifford readily saw the risk of becoming embroiled in an Italian-Abyssinian dispute that could rapidly degenerate into a bloody confrontation. He was wise and well enough informed to understand that policy lay behind both Italian and Abyssinian intransigence and that neither was likely to give way.

On November 25, both the British and Abyssinian sections of the commission decamped and returned to Ado, accompanied by a portion of their escort. This left Fitaurari Shiferra and some 400 men at Wal Wal, facing the Italians along a brushwood line at a distance that was in places not more than six feet. Abyssinian reinforcements swelled the force to 1,400 men.[15]

The Governor of Italian Somaliland, Maurizio Rava instructed Captain Cimmaruta: "[S]o long as the armed Ethiopians do not use arms against our military post, refrain from any hostile act whatsoever."[16]

After ten days in which the Italian garrison and the Abyssinians faced each other at close quarters, the inevitable happened. Perhaps, it has been speculated, a soldier fired idly at a passing bird. At any rate, a shot was fired, by whom it was never determined. Inevitably, the battle was joined on December 5, 1934.[17]

The Italians held their ground. After a fierce combat, the Abyssinians withdrew to Ado. They had suffered 107 dead and 45 wounded. The Italians lost 30 dead and 100 wounded.[18]

"Quarrels at watering places have been commonplace occurrences of desert life since the days of Abraham"[19]; such skirmishes on the fringes of empire were usually of no great consequence except to the participants. The dead and wounded at Wal Wal were all humble Africans with whom Europeans of that time would not normally have concerned themselves. For the British, such clashes with the Afghan and Waziri tribesmen of the Northwest Frontier were routine. In this very area, the Mad Mullah of British Somaliland had eluded his British pursuers from 1899 to 1920 when, never captured, he expired in his bed of influenza. The Italian pacification of Libya had been long, arduous, and cruel.

But Wal Wal was not to be forgotten. For two proud and domineering men, there was too much at stake. To Emperor Haile Selassie, it was the independence and integrity of his kingdom. To Benito

Mussolini, it was Italy's place in the world and more than that, the ultimate triumph of the Fascist state.

An African State

Among the countries of Africa, Abyssinia was unique in many respects. It was genuinely and fiercely independent and had always been. In the first half of this century that could not be said of any other African state; the questionable independence of Liberia had resulted from an American initiative with colonial overtones.

Moreover, Abyssinia was a Christian country and had been since the fourth century A.D. The Abuna, the head of its Coptic Church had, since the Council of Nicea, been appointed by the Egyptian patriarch in Alexandria.

Abyssinia was forbiddingly remote. The mountainous heart of the country, roadless and inaccessible itself, was surrounded by formidable barriers: the Danakil deserts to the north and east, the Ogaden deserts of the southeast, on the west the Blue Nile flowing from Lake Tana to join the White Nile amid the wastelands of the Sudan at Khartoum.

The history of Abyssinia stretches back to Biblical times. Its Emperor claimed descent from King Solomon and styled himself the Conquering Lion of Judah. The Queen of Sheba was thought to have figured in its history. The true Abyssinians, the Amharas, were Semites in their origins and for centuries their history was part of that of the Biblical lands on the far side of the Red Sea. The triumph of Islam, which in time occupied the Red Sea shores, cut Abyssinia off from the west for a thousand years. When the opening of the Suez Canal in 1869 made the Red Sea a vital artery of commerce, and when the European powers in the succeeding decades carved their colonial empires out of Africa, Abyssinia found itself, whether it wished it or not, an object of the attention and interest of the European powers.

There was much about Abyssinia that was picturesquely medieval. An English observer remarked of Haile Selassie in his coronation robes and headdress that he looked like a processional statue from Seville.[20] His military chiefs were caparisoned in leopard cloaks and helmets of lion's manes; the chain mail and antique weapons of the warriors colorfully recalled times long past to European eyes.

Uniquely, too, while the Europeans were carving up the map of

Africa, Abyssinia had joined them as a conquering power, but only after having tasted the force of European arms and ambitions.

The Emperor Theodore II was crowned in the historic capital of Aksum in the north in 1855. Never a stable character, he engaged, as Abyssinian emperors had done out of necessity from time immemorial, in a series of wars with his rivals, and victories alternated with cruel repressions. This was all very well so far as local customs were concerned, but Theodore had the temerity to engage in conduct which was unacceptable to Lord Palmerston's Britain. Palmerston had appointed a British consul to Gondar. It was an era when there were few places so wild and so remote from the prospects of commerce that they did not support a British consul.

Theodore was implicated in the murder of the consul. He imprisoned the consul's successor and numerous other Europeans. Retribution followed. Sir Robert Napier was dispatched with an elephant-supported expedition which in heroic Victorian fashion, penetrated the trackless mountains that lay between the Port of Massawa and Magdala, and secured the release of the prisoners, while Theodore, now completely mad, committed suicide.

Perhaps the most remarkable aspect of this remarkable expedition is that it promptly turned about and marched off the stage of Abyssinian history, a rare example of a European conqueror in nineteenth-century Africa who did not come to stay.[21]

Abyssinia remained independent, but no longer unnoticed. The Egyptians pressed down from the north but withdrew; their enemies, the Dervishes attacked and were rebuffed. The Italians appeared on the Red Sea coast in 1882. They were at first encouraged by Menelik, a rebel against the Emperor John IV and, after John's death in battle with the Dervishes, his successor. The Italians established their colony of Eritrea and signed the Treaty of Ucciali in 1889 which, by the Italian text, gave Italy claims to a protectorate over Abyssinia. The Italians next moved into the Somali coast and established the colony of Italian Somaliland on Abyssinia's southern border.[22]

This was too much for Menelik, now Emperor. Italian friendship could no longer confer personal advantage on him, and his outlook became national. When he denounced the Treaty of Ucciali, the Italians determined on war.

The Abyssinian chiefs, the rases, who were accustomed to warring among themselves, now stood firm behind Menelik. The Italian garrisons at Amba Alagi and Makalle fell to the Abyssinians. Italy persisted with new armies.

At Adowa, the ancient capital of Tigre, General Oreste Baratieri, Governor of Eritrea and his army of 16,000 faced the Emperor Menelik who led a host of 100,000. These were considered normal odds for a nineteenth-century European army on colonial campaign. The roster of Menelik's chieftains was a kaleidoscope of the history of Abyssinia: Ras Makonnen of Harar, the Emperor's cousin; Ras Mangushu of Tigre; the Imperial Fitaurari Gabreishu; Ras Mikail of the Wollo Galla; Wagshun Gwangul and Hailu of Lasta; the Janitrari Astari of Wag; Ras Mangushu Alikum of Ifrata; Ras Wule of Beghender; the Liguemaguas Abate; and the Negus Tekle Haimamot of Gojjam. Such were the names and ranks and provenances of the leaders of Africa's most ancient kingdom.

It was St. Georges Day, March 1, 1896, the feast day of the patron saint of the Empire. The Abuna celebrated the mass and forgave his congregants. By mid-afternoon the battle was decided. The Italians had been decisively defeated with a loss of 262 Italian officers and 4,000 Italian soldiers. In full retreat, the Italians were relentlessly harassed by the Galla tribesmen of Ras Mikail in their traditional red cloaks. They were fulfilling their time-honored role of turning defeat into butchery. 1,900 Italians were taken prisoner with 1,000 Eritrean Askaris.[23]

No European nation had ever suffered a greater defeat in Africa. Young Benito Mussolini read of it with the same grief and anger that seized so many of his countrymen. It was now Menelik's time to play the conqueror, which he did with resounding success. He expanded his territories to the south and to the west and established a new capital at Addis Ababa. Thus, the Abyssinia of 1934 had at its core the old Christian and Amharic provinces of the northern highlands, girded about with the newer provinces where either the Moslems or the negroes predominated. Thus arose the paradox that Professor Toynbee noted when war came between Itay and Abyssinia. Abyssinia was hailed as the defender of black men everywhere, when, in fact, the Amharas were of Semitic origin and had conquered large populations of Hamites to secure their empire.

Abyssinia and the Great Powers

Italy recognized Abyssinia as a sovereign and independent state and by the Treaty of Addis Ababa abrogated the Treaty of Ucciali. That was not the end of foreign interest in the country. Great Britain and France had agreed after Fashoda to the division of Africa into spheres of interest and each was Abyssinia's neighbor.

The Nile had always been the life of Egypt and the Sudan and the Blue Nile and its tributary, the Atbara, both had their sources in Abyssinia's Lake Tana. This guaranteed a lively British interest. Under a concession from Menelik, the French built the railroad from Djibuti in French Somaliland to Addis Ababa and looked long and hard for a return on their investment. Italy continued to see Abyssinia as the logical arena for the expansion of her modest colonial empire.

In 1906 these three powers, in the spirit of the colonial era, entered into a treaty defining their interests in Abyssinia: for Britain, the Nile sources, for France the railroad. This left large areas in the north, south and east of the country as an Italian sphere of influence. It was specifically recognized that Italy might require expansion to preserve its east African colonies and Italy was by treaty granted the right to a "territorial connection" between the two. All three nations agreed that they would abstain from intervention in the internal affairs of the country and that they would not act independently in Abyssinia. Should military action be needed, it would be jointly undertaken.[24]

It was also in the spirit of the times that no one thought it necessary to consult Abyssinia in matters deeply affecting its integrity and sovereignty. For Italy, notwithstanding the defeat at Adowa, the 1906 Treaty was a recognition by Britain and France that she had not only interests, but also expectations in Abyssinia.

When the firm rule of Menelik ended with his death in 1913, the country plunged into the usual disorder under Menelik's incompetent grandson, Lij Yasu. Menelik's daughter, Queen Zauditu, came to the throne in 1916. She was childless, an acceptable figurehead. The moving spirit of her reign was the regent and heir to the throne, Ras Tafari.[25]

He had been born on July 23, 1892, the son of Ras Makonnen, Menelik's cousin and trusted advisor. He had been governor of Harar province. As regent, his goals were those he would pursue throughout his career: to create a strong central government of which he would be the undisputed arbiter, and to bring Abyssinia, insofar as he could, into the world of the twentieth century.

This was a difficult task. Loyalties were local and the rases traditionally powerful and independent minded. The clergy numbered almost a fifth of the population. Slavery was firmly established and nothing incurred Abyssinia more odium abroad. Slavery was a special interest of the League of Nations. Kathleen Simon carried on the vigorous antislavery tradition of nineteenth-century Britain and included a graphic description of Abyssinian servitude in her 1929 study *Slavery*. It detracted nothing from the issues she raised when her husband, Sir John Simon, became Foreign Secretary of Great Britain.

The regent was keenly sensitive to the pressure of foreign encroachments and in 1923 wisely sought the protection of membership in the League of Nations, under French sponsorship. With characteristic changeability, Mussolini first opposed and then endorsed Abyssinia's application. More determined opposition came from Great Britain. A League of Nations investigation of slavery had reported particularly appalling conditions in Abyssinia, not only with respect to the institution of slavery itself, but also as to slave raiding and slave trading. In addition, Britain expressed serious doubts as to the ability of the central government to rule effectively and its capacity to carry out the commitments inherent in membership in the League.[26]

When Abyssinia was, after prolonged debate, admitted to the League, special conditions attached. Its government was required to sign a declaration denouncing slavery and the slave trade and pledging effective efforts towards their abolition. This was not all. It was recognized that the League had a continuing right, in this matter, to intervene in the affairs of Abyssinia as the facts warranted. Finally, Abyssinia was required to sign other declarations aimed at suppressing the arms trade, always a concern to Europeans in Africa.[27]

Ras Tafari was now more than ever keenly aware that the fate of Abyssinia lay in European hands. Since the rulers of Europe were unlikely to appear in Addis Ababa, Ras Tafari embarked upon a ceremonial tour in 1924. He was accompanied by two of his principal chiefs, Ras Seyoum and Ras Hailu, perhaps on the grounds that he was safer with them in his entourage than at home. Emblematic of the title to the Abyssinian throne, he also took with him six lions.

He paid his respects to the Coptic patriarch in Cairo, confirmed his Christian faith in a visit to Jerusalem, and made the acquaintance in

Rome of Benito Mussolini. The party called at Athens, Geneva, Brussels, Stockholm, and Amsterdam. In Paris, Ras Tafari divested himself of four of the lions, two of them to the Jardin Zoologique and two to President Poincaré whose response is not recorded.

Royalty to royalty, he presented the remaining two lions to King George V, receiving, in return, the imperial crown of the Emperor Theodore which had been captured in 1868 by Sir Robert Napier.[28]

The favorable notice that the tour generated not only in Europe but in Abyssinia, was for Ras Tafari a valuable lesson in the arts and rewards of publicity.

Abyssinian membership in the League of Nations did nothing to dampen foreign interest in the country. Italy had long sought additional privileges and indicated its approval of a British dam on Lake Tana in the light of Italian interest in building a railroad to connect Eritrea and Italian Somaliland.

By a 1925 exchange of letters, the two countries agreed that, if Britain could indeed obtain a concession for the dam, it would recognize exclusive Italian influence in Western Abyssinia and in the territory to be crossed by the railroad.[29]

This time, in addition to failing to consult with Abyssinia, the parties also neglected to bring into the discussions their other partner in the 1906 Treaty, France.[30]

When copies of the agreement were sent to France and Abyssinia, Ras Tafari's response was prompt and entirely in character, both in substance and tone. He immediately protested the threatened infringement of Abyssinian sovereignty to the League of Nations. He found it hard to believe, he said, that the members of the League would enter into special agreements to impose their will on another member. He noted Abyssinia's commitment to both progress and independence:

> The people of Abyssinia are anxious to do right and we have every intention of guiding them along the path of improvement and progress; but throughout their history they have seldom met with foreigners who did not desire to possess themselves of Abyssinian territory and to destroy their independence. With God's help, and thanks to the courage of our soldiers, we have always, come what might, stood proud and free upon our native mountains.[31]

Both Britain and Italy promptly disclaimed any aggressive intent. But Italy single-mindedly pursued further opportunities in Abyssinia. The only question was whether greater influence could be gained by subversion and the support of the rases or by helping to build a strong central government where Italian influence might predominate. It was in pursuit of the latter policy that Italy and Abyssinia signed in 1928 a twenty year Treaty of Friendship, pledging each country to increased trade with the other and providing for a new road from Abyssinia to the Red Sea at Assab in Eritrea. The road was never built, perhaps because Ras Tafari suspected it would furnish an easy invasion route.[32]

As an expression of amity associated with the Treaty, Ras Tafari was dignified with membership in the Order of Annunziata, Italy's most exalted honor. He could reflect, in later years, that by his investiture, he had become cousin to the King of Italy and to Benito Mussolini himself.[33]

On October 27, 1928, Ras Tafari advanced a step further to his goal. He was crowned Negus, a rank second only to that of Emperor. The response was prompt. Just as in the first year of the reign of Queen Zauditu, a powerful local noble, Ras Mikail of Wollo, had risen in revolt and had been crushed, so now Ras Gugsa Wule led the Raya Galla uprising. He represented the ancient traditions against the reforming tendencies of the Negus. The scene of Abyssinians arrayed in battle against each other was a familiar one. Ras Tafari and the rases loyal to him won the day. Ras Gugsa's death in battle ended the revolt.[34]

When the Empress Zauditu died two days after the battle, the Negus was ready. On April 3, 1930, he proclaimed himself Emperor, taking the title His Imperial Majesty Haile Selassie I, Negus Negesti, or King of Kings.

The young regent who had toured the Near East and Europe had arrived. His splendid coronation was the occasion for the world to come to his capital. Britain accorded him the honor of a Royal emissary, the Duke of Gloucester, who presented the Emperor with a pair of scepters. Britain's encircling imperial interests were represented by Sir John Maffey, Governor-General of the Anglo-Egyptian Sudan, Sir H. Baxter Kiddermaster, Governor of British Somaliland, and Sir Stewart Symes, Governor of Aden. Much appreciated, also, was the Marine band under Major Simpson.

Italian royalty was present in the person of the Prince of Udine, cousin to the King. The Italian gifts were practical, an airplane and, from Mussolini, a light tank. Franchet d'Esperey, Marshal of France, also presented an airplane. Baron von Waldthaussen contributed 800 bottles of hock and a signed photograph of President von Hindenburg.[35] Egypt's delegation numbered twenty. Not only were Sweden and Belgium represented, but also Turkey and far-off Japan.

When the lengthy ceremonies were done, Haile Selassie returned to his task of centralization and modernization.

He proclaimed a constitution in 1931; but the Parliament had no real power and the provincial nobles found that during their stay in the capital, the Emperor had dispatched his own administrators to their territories. He engaged Belgian instructors to train as army. He imported foreign advisors. Maître Auberson was a Swiss constitutional lawyer. He turned to an Englishman, de Halpert, to assist in the abolition of slavery. Most important was the American, Everett Colson, who became his shrewd, practical and highly effective expert on foreign affairs.[36]

Haile Selassie did his best amid unique conditions to advance his country. When a commission under Sir John Maffey weighed Britain's interests in Abyssinia, it reported:

> [T]here had been a sincere though unhappily only partially successful attempt to improve frontier administration, to eradicate slavery, brigandage, and other abuses. Cruelty, crudity, and confusion can still be found. . . but it does not appear reasonable or just to write off the Ethiopian Empire as irremediably barbarous and uncivilized without any hope of eventual reform.[37]

In the early 1930s, both Britain and Italy expanded their presence in Abyssinia. In addition to the British legation, British consuls operated at Maji on the Kenya-Sudan border, at Dongola in Gojjam near the headwaters of the Nile, at Moyale in the south, Gore and Gambele in the west and Harar in the east.

Italian consulates were established in the provincial capital cities of Adowa, Gondar, Dessie, and Debra Markos, at Moyale, and Harar where Italy could keep herself well informed on developments in the country, nurture contacts and allegiances with the provincial nobles, and generally keep a sharp eye open to such opportunities as might come along. If there was no specific Italian plan for Abyssinia, there were always advocates of expansion who saw in Abyssinia the core of empire.[38]

Abyssinia was concerned and requested confirmation of the 1928 Treaty. A joint statement was issued in Rome on September 29, 1934:

Italy does not have any intention that is not friendly toward the Ethiopian government with whom we are bound by the Treaty of Friendship of 1928.[39]

The Duce Changes His Mind

This was less than the whole truth. Mussolini's calculations in 1934 ranged from the Brenner Pass to the Abyssinian highlands. Mussolini had no illusions. The Disarmament Conference had failed. His plan for the Four Power Pact to regulate rearmament and treaty revision, far from impractical, had failed, too. To his immense indignation, Hitler had procured the murder of Mussolini's Austrian protégé, Dollfuss, in an attempt to take over Italy's buffer state.

Mussolini saw the future clearly and spoke with equal clarity: Hitler would create an army; he would arm the Germans and make war—in two or three years. Something had to be done, and quickly.

His hostility to Germany was at a peak. It was Mussolini who had sent his troops to the Brenner Pass and Mussolini who pressed Britain and France to renew, on September 27, 1934, their February pledge of support for the independence and integrity of Austria.

At the same time, Haile Selassie was strengthening his position and building a modern military force. If these did not in fact threaten the Italian colonies, they might well interpose growing obstacles to Italian ambitions.

Chief among the advocates of an aggressive policy in Abyssinia was the Minister of Colonies, General Emilio de Bono. This picturesque, white bearded septuagenarian's lust for military glory had not been sated by his undistinguished performance in the World War. He had asked, and in 1933 Mussolini had casually granted him the honor of leading the Italian army in an Abyssinian campaign. This did not mean that a settled plan existed.

But in the summer of 1934, Mussolini began to see that if he were indeed to move into Abyssinia, time was of the essence. He must do it before the threat of a fully rearmed Germany at the Brenner could become a reality. If he moved at the earliest feasible date, he could create his African empire and then restore the military balance in Europe while there was still time.

Mussolini asked his Chief of Staff, General Pietro Badoglio, to report on the prospects of an Abyssinian campaign. Badoglio was pessimistic but planning went ahead, followed by actual preparations.[40]

These were well enough known by September to inspire Abyssinia to request assurances under the 1928 Treaty.[41]

As the plans matured, logical and formidable objections were raised: problems of water and supply, the distance, the long sea routes in waters controlled by the Royal Navy, and the necessity to use the British-controlled Suez Canal. Mussolini was firm. The order to march would be given, he said, only when by political action neither the democracies, aided by the Little Entente, nor Germany would interfere.[42]

The affair at Wal Wal fitted neatly into these plans. As was natural, both Abyssinia and Italy charged the other with responsibility for the incident. Italy demanded not only reparations but an apology. This again was normal conduct for a European power dealing with African state. And indeed, in November, when an Italian consular officer had been killed in an imbroglio in Gondar, the government of Abysinnia, though in no way involved, had tendered both an apology and reparation. Abyssinia in turn on December 9, 1934 sought arbitration or conciliation under the 1928 Treaty of Friendship. Italy disdained to reply, and pressed its demand for an apology, including an Abyssinian act of homage to the Italian flag at Wal Wal, turning over Omar Samantar to Italy, and payment of 200,000 Maria Theresa dollars. On December 14, Italy formally refused to arbitrate the matter under the Treaty.[43]

Britain and France were fellow colonial powers; they were Italy's co-signers to the 1906 Treaty. The potential for trouble was obvious. Both nations, through their ministers in Addis Ababa, did their best to pursuade Haile Selassie to yield to Italian demands.[44]

Haile Selassie was a proud and obdurate ruler. More than that, he really could not impose his will on the rases who were incensed, and, remembering Adowa, far from cowed. His foresight in securing Abyssinia's membership in the League of Nations now appeared providential. Here was an impartial body, remote from the scene of the quarrel, in which an equal vote was accorded small powers as well as large.

Promptly after receiving Italy's rejection of arbitration under the 1928 Treaty, Abyssinia formally brought the quarrel to the League of Nations Council under Article 11 of the Covenant. This provided a "friendly right" to each League member to call the attention of either the Council or the Assembly to any situation which might threaten to disturb international peace and understanding.[45]

What had been a skirmish at a watering hole in the remote Ogaden desert now became an international issue. It raised serious questions of the meaning of the Covenant and the functioning of the League of Nations. The ultimate issue was whether the League could or would effectively restrain a great power from taking action it had firmly determined upon. Had Abyssinia not been a member of the League, the result of the quarrel would be predetermined by size and strength alone. Whether collective security could supplant the test of the might of individual nations was the issue inherent in Abyssinia's request.

Mussolini reacted with the speed and decisiveness that were to characterize his conduct over the whole affair. He drew up his action plan on December 20, and ten days later sent secret copies to his aides. He minced no words.

First and foremost, Italy would solve the Abyssinian problem, not by diplomacy, but by force of arms. Abyssinia was gaining strength and could be a threat to Italy's colonies. It was modernizing and centralizing. Time worked against Italy. The solution would be "the destruction of the Abyssinian armed forces and the total conquest of Ethiopia."

Mussolini stated clearly that he needed a free hand from the European powers. He could not carry out his plan if Britain and France opposed him. Germany needed two to three years to rearm; the only threat from Germany would be in Austria. An understanding with France would greatly enhance European stability while Italy fought an African war.

The operation must be adequately manned with at least 100,000 troops. Mussolini would not be caught short. This was important because speed and decisiveness would resolve political problems:

> The speedier our military action the less will be the danger of diplomatic complications. . . . No one in Europe would raise any difficulties provided the conduct of operations resulted rapidly in an accomplished fact. It would suffice to declare to England and France that their interests would be recognized.[46]

Main strength was not enough. The policy of subversion of the Abyssinian chiefs should begin at once. The date of the campaign was set for the end of the rainy season in October 1935. Until then, it was the task of diplomacy to provide any delay or advantage that would enable the military plans to mature.

The conflict was declared inevitable. Fascist morale was high. Abyssinia was the last part of Africa not owned by Europeans. The Gordian knot of Italo-Abyssinian relations would be cut, and the problem which had existed since 1885 would be settled once and for all.

Mussolini's Goals

Many of Italy's goals antedated Mussolini and Fascism. Italy was poor and overpopulated. A colonial empire might furnish room for expansion without which Italy's demographic capital was lost by emigration. Italy was a have-not nation, disgruntled by the sharing out at the Peace Conference. She had wanted the right to economic participation in the world's resources included in the Covenant; the possessors would not agree.

To avenge Adowa was a desire that was not peculiar to Mussolini but deeply felt and widely shared. Winston Churchill might conclude that Italy's Abyssinian ambitions were unsuited to the ethics of the twentieth century and that for white men to subjugate men of color by superior strength and weapons was obsolete and reprehensible. He had not yet developed these moral insights when as a lieutenant in the 21st Lancers he had led the charge at Omdurman to avenge the death of Gordon at Khartoum and, incidentally, to place the Sudan under the British flag.

Mussolini had mastered domestic politics and gained credit for enhancing Italy's strength and stability. For Italy, which had always occupied a position on the fringes of power, to emerge as incontestably one of the great powers would be a fitting continuation of the Risorgimiento. And it was permitted to dream dreams grander yet, of a new imperial Rome retracing the boundaries of the Empire of the Caesars. For Mussolini to envision himself as the descendant of the Caesars would have been neither out of character nor unnatural as he looked over the trajectory of his fifty years.

He had never ceased to look upon the colonial empires of Britain and France with envy, mixed with a keen appreciation of their tactics and accomplishments. How Britain effectively ruled a nominally independent Egypt and how France had achieved the same in Morocco were useful object lessons to him.

Churchill's latter-day mastery of ethics mystified Mussolini who lacked any pretentions in this area. It made him angry to think that, having by whatever means were necessary acquired great territories and imperial riches, Britain and France should suddenly declare the season closed and the pursuit of empire a wicked and immoral occupation. To his clear Latin mind, this was sheer hypocrisy and the notion that foreign policy was, or ought to be, based on moral and spiritual principles totally escaped him.

More to the point, Fascism had not proved the high road to prosperity and economic development. The Fascist state created rhetoric but not solutions and the world depression deeply affected Italy. To solve Italy's economic problems with the gold and grain, the minerals and manpower of Abyssinia was a seductive enough vision. It was enhanced by the serendipitous consequence that the glory of the triumph would thoroughly distract the Italian people from the shortcomings of their regime.

All this accorded well with Fascist philosophy. Mussolini had written in 1932:

> War alone keeps up human energies to their maximum tension and sets the seal of nobility on those peoples who have the courage to face it. . . Fascism carries this antipacifist attitude into the life of the individual. 'I don't give a damn'—the proud motto of the fighting squads. . . sums up a doctrine which is not merely political; it is evidence of a fighting spirit which accepts all risks. It signifies a new mode of Italian life.[47]

And he had told the quinquennial Fascist congress in March, 1934 that Italy's historic objects were in Africa and Asia; that she was of all the Western powers closest to them and had nothing to gain in the North and in the West. It was not a question of territorial conquest, but of natural expansion whereby Italy would bring culture to Africa. In the rhetoric of the time, this was Italy's historic function, not only its right but its duty. Those nations which had arrived and were satisfied had no right to block this expansion.[48]

Mussolini had recognized that he could not carry out his Abyssinian project against the will of Britain and France and stated explicitly that he would assure them that their interests would be protected. Because he calculated Italian foreign policy in terms of Italian interests as he saw them, it was natural for him to conclude that Britain and France would do the same.

He would make it crystal clear that in no way would their interests be prejudiced or threatened and offer them the necessary assurances.

Why, then, should they object, especially when the friendship of Italy was valuable to them? They must see the threat of Hitler; Mussolini had done everything he could to call it to their attention. The critical area was Europe itself. To Mussolini, on any rational calculation, it was inconceivable that a colonial campaign in Africa should alter or affect the fate of Europe. What would determine the fate of Europe would be Hitler and Germany. And the sensible policy for Britain and France would be to give Italy a free hand in Africa in order to preserve the status quo in Europe.[49]

Mussolini confidently prepared to take out the necessary policies of insurance with France and Britain.

Later, on the eve of war, Mussolini said: "I have reflected well; I have calculated all; I have weighed everything."[50] He had made many calculations that proved correct and in the end, the victory was his. But there was one element he had not taken into his calculations.

This was Edward Algernon Robert Cecil, Viscount Cecil of Chelwood and the national campaign he was now launching to demonstrate British support of the League of Nations. Mussolini did not, indeed in December could not, have taken into his accounting the Peace Ballot.

70,000 votes had come in in November. This was encouraging but left unanswered the question whether this was an initial burst of enthusiasm.[51] In December, Mussolini's month of decision, the proportions of the tidal wave of votes began to become apparent. 400,000 ballots were received. In five weeks, the Peace Ballot had almost reached the early goal of its sponsors. The quality of the vote was significant. Returns of over 50 percent of the electors were common; in Bury the vote attained 66 percent. The ballots continued to show high percentages of affirmative votes on every question though the ayes on question 5b tended to be distinctly lower than the others.[52]

And yet, the main effort did not begin until after Christmas. The returns had mostly been from the smaller towns. The great cities remained to be heard from.

The New Year came. The sponsors of the Peace Ballot could have increasing confidence that the voice of the British people would be heard in 1935.

13

A Double Challenge

"The realization of Germany once again fully armed and a menace to the world's peace has come home to most people at last and has produced a profound sadness. Millions have been voting in the Peace Ballot and it is difficult for the rank and file to think ill of any country's intentions. This country has never been more peaceful and they are accepting the small increases in the programme of the services because SB assures them there is no help for it in the present mood of Europe."

—Tom Jones[1]

Two Challenges

Mussolini had determined to create a new Roman Empire in East Africa. Hitler had determined to reverse the verdict of 1918 and to create a Great Germany that would dominate Europe for a thousand years. To each, either the threat of arms or the force of arms was the logical method to attain his goals. Each now pursued this course with a will.

The problem for Britain and France was to assess these challenges. Were they equal? To what extent was Germany a direct threat to them? To answer this, it was necessary to measure her population, her industrial and economic prowess, her military potential, and her geographic position. In the heart of Europe, Germany confronted France in the West where she could also bring overwhelming force to bear on the Netherlands and Belgium. These were, with France, guardians of the Channel coast that had long been England's prime security interest, and now, with the advent of aircraft, even more important. Germany faced Austria and Italy to the South and all of Central and Eastern Europe to the East.

To what extent was Italy a direct threat to Britain and France? Here again, it was important to measure population, economy, and geography. Ringed at her northern borders by the Alps, Italy was essentially a Mediterranean power. Could Italy threaten Britain or France directly? And even supposing that Italy dominated Abyssinia, did this involve a meaningful conflict with British or French interests?

For Britain and France, the other side of the Italian coin was to inquire to what extent Italy was a valuable prospective ally. Mussolini had raised the alarm; he had responded to Hitler's threat to Austria; he said that something must be done. Was Italy important, or even useful, in doing it?

Both Hitler and Mussolini had to make the opposite calculations. How would Britain and France respond to their moves? Mussolini thought it was a matter of timing. Time worked against Italy; the Abyssinian deed could be done if it were done quickly enough to become an accomplished fact. Hitler had already acted; there had been no reaction, making him more confident. The gamble for both Mussolini and Hitler was that if they moved swiftly and decisively, they would win.

Whatever the computations of Britain and France may have been, one thing was certain. For them the worst of all possible worlds was a combination of Germany and Italy joining their resources and their arms, at the same time denying to France and Britain the possibility of effective collaboration with France's friends and allies in Central and Eastern Europe.

All these were matters of rational calculation. The issue was to what extent British and French policy would be based on the rational calculation of national interest and to what extent it would be based on other, less easily determined factors. Chief among these factors was that combination of values, standards, morals, information, ignorance, passion and prejudice, reason and sentiment which make up public opinion.

In France, Pierre Laval, as Foreign Minister and then as Prime Minister, adhered to the steadfast goal of French policy since Versailles—security. To France, the threat was Germany, as it had always been, a Germany whose economic resources, population, and military potential far outstripped those of victorious France. Neither Laval nor his predecessors for a moment lost sight of the German threat; and he was as preoccupied as they to construct an adequate defense. Clemenceau had said that the Treaty of Guaranty was the ultimate sanction of Versailles, but that was long gone. What remained, as France's first line of defense, was the demilitarized zone of the Rhineland which at the same time protected France and gave potency to its Central European alliances.

Again and again, as French statesmen faced the crises caused by the Italian adventure in Africa and Germany's steady military renaissance, it was the German border, the Rhineland, and the guarantees of the Treaty of Locarno which would be the foundation of their policy.

To counter the German threat, France spared neither expense nor exertion. She built the great Maginot fortifications on her border with Germany, conscripted her youth, and maintained a military establishment that alarmed her friends more than her prospective foes. She sought allies and commitments to balance German preponderance. This was the policy of the note of April 17, 1934 refusing to legalize German rearmament: "France will henceforth ensure her security by her own means."[2]

Britain followed another path. Her army remained small and weak; the defenses of Singapore, vital to the protection of British interests in the Far East, were delayed; and only in the air was there a modest and hotly contested response to the German threat. Britain was careful not to enter into any continental commitments over and above Locarno, and what the Locarno commitment meant was a lively topic of debate. Britain was not in a position to ensure her security by her own means.

The means she preferred, then, was an understanding with Germany. This would happily spare rearmament, the threat of war, continental embroilments, and their attendant expense and inconvenience. There was this difficulty: an understanding with Germany could not be achieved unilaterally. It required the cooperation, understanding and loyal adherence of Nazi Germany.

Mussolini Makes His Move—France

Mussolini had measured Hitler and had arrived at his conclusions: Germany was preparing for a war which it would launch as soon as it was ready. There was a window of two years while Germany rearmed and trained. In that period, Italy could achieve a decisive victory in Abyssinia and then return to the watch on the Brenner—so long as Great Britain and France raised no obstacle.

To Mussolini, the solution was prudent and uncomplicated. He would make clear to Britain and France that their interests would be recognized and respected. That they had, with Italy, a joint interest in restraining Hitler was to him self-evident. It did not occur to him, as it had to Professor Toynbee, that the sin of aggression had become mortal instead of merely venial; nor did he consider himself bound by the moral judgments laid down by the Archbishops of Canterbury and York or by Lord Cecil. He would and did dismiss all that as classic British hypocrisy designed to justify ill-gotten gains, at the same time denying to others what Britain had acquired.

To arrive at an understanding with France was not without problems. Relations had been strained since Versailles. Italy regarded herself as a have-not, unjustly deprived of her share of the spoils of victory. Her friends were Austria and Hungary, the defeated Central Powers with whom Italy shared revisionist aspirations. Their rivals were the winners of 1918, Poland and the Little Entente, who were France's allies. In the case of Yugoslavia there were longstanding, bitter disputes about title to the Adriatic shores and hinterlands. In Africa, Italy had not shared in the parceling out of German colonies, notwithstanding secret promises of equitable compensation. Britain had recognized Italian claims and ceded lands of modest size and dubious value bordering Italian Somaliland in 1925; but France had stood aloof.

The French protectorate in Tunisia had always caused problems and aroused emotions. There was a large Italian colony that retained Italian citizenship, identity, and the unfulfilled hope that Tunisia would become Italian. Finally, there were not inconsiderable numbers of Italians who could remember the day when Nice and Savoy had been Italian.

These were difficulties; but they would not stand in the way of determined men whose agendas now converged. As Barthou's successor, it was Laval's task to carry out Barthou's grand design—the classic French task of erecting safe barriers against German aggression. Laval had deftly managed the perils arising out of the assassination of King Alexander. He had mollified Yugoslavia, validating Little Entente adherence to French policy, and at the same time avoided implicating Italy in the crime.

The critical link in the defense against Germany was Italy itself, angered and alerted by the threat to her Austrian client and buffer. French diplomats had begun conversations in Rome while Laval was attending to the Yugoslavian crisis. The affray at Wal Wal had spurred Mussolini's Abyssinian plans. He now wanted to extend to France assurance that her interests would be protected, both in Europe and in Abyssinia. At the same time he wanted to associate France with Italy in taking a clear stand on preserving the independence and integrity of Austria, and ruling out unilateral treaty revision and rearmament by Germany. To both Mussolini and Laval, here were clear and convincing cases of mutual self-interest.

The French and Italian negotiators had arrived at several understandings. It was easy to agree that France and Italy would act jointly if Germany denounced the disarmament promises of Versailles and that in any case Italy would support French superiority in arms. Both would publicly support Austrian independence; the only real issue was whether France's Little Entente allies should join in the guaranty. Tunisian matters proved amenable to discussion; in the end it was the remaining African issues that required urgent attention before an accord could be reached.[3] Perhaps further negotiations would have produced a full agreement. In any case, Pierre Laval told the French cabinet on January 2, 1935 that he would go to Rome. It must have seemed to him an ideal opportunity to apply his powers of intimate personal negotiation and persuasion to achieve his ultimate goals.

On January 3, 1935, Haile Selasse followed his December 15, 1934 message to the League of Nations with a telegram reporting Italian military measures and asking action by the League Council.[4]

Laval arrived in Rome on January 5. An exchange of decorations preceded the ceremonial speeches. Mussolini wore the Legion of Honor and praised the foreign policies and principles of his own regime. Laval, now decorated with the green sash and ribbon of the Order of Sts. Maurice and Lazare, prepared to negotiate with Mussolini. He emphasized the importance of French-Italian cooperation to the peace of the world. "Duce," he said, "you have written the fairest page in modern Italian history; you will bring assistance indispensable to maintaining peace."[5]

Mussolini's reply recognized Franco-Italian, European, and world problems. In Europe, he said, France and Italy had to be prepared for any eventuality. A crucial year was commencing; it would take intelligence and perseverance to give the world what it waited for.[6]

Beneath the ceremonial regalia of the state occasion these were two country lads, born in the same year, ardent Socialists once, who had risen by their talents and their efforts to become heads of state. They instinctively recognized that they could do business with each other.

They lunched with King Victor Emmanuel and began discussions that day. Mussolini was not impressed with the territory France proposed to cede to Italy—54,000 square miles on the border of Libya and French Equatorial Africa. "I am not a collector of deserts," Mussolini said, ". . . I sent Marshal Balbo to take photographs of the areas. . . . I have them here for you. They are lunar landscapes."

All the same, Laval told him, there were two towns. He was putting his case in the most favorable light. They were in fact two oases. "Two towns!" Mussolini exclaimed. They weren't Rome, Laval smilingly confessed, nor even Aubervilliers.[7]

The negotiations continued on the 6th and some doubted they would succeed. The issue was Abyssinia. After dinner at the French Embassy on the 6th, the Duce and Laval retired together. This was the natural setting for Pierre Laval, the man who believed in direct conversations, man to man, who had dealt face-to-face with labor on the one hand and management on the other, distrusting the complexities and formulas of professional diplomats and bureaucrats, superbly confident of his own abilities, always seeking an agreement in principle. The agreement might not be perfect—he disdained ideal solutions—but it would be subject to "honorable amendments" in an ongoing process whereby the parties would continue to find the interests served and the benefits gained that the process afforded.

The late-night meeting of Mussolini and Laval constitutes a celebrated gap in historical knowledge. We have no record of what they said. What is known is that Pierre Laval emerged from the meeting smiling and said to a French journalist: "C'est fini." For his part, the Duce instructed his negotiators to proceed to a conclusion on terms that the French found highly acceptable.[8]

On the following day, the two nations signed a series of agreements that were published on January 8, 1935. Modest colonial concessions were made by France to Italy. They included, in addition to the expanses of Libyan desert, 13.5 miles of coastline on the Red Sea strait of Bab el Mandeb and an offshore island. Italy was granted the right to buy about 7 percent of the shares of the Addis Ababa-Djibuti railway. For this, Italy gave up important rights in Tunisia where, in matters of citizenship and schools, the Italian nationals would over time become exclusively French.

Laval had said, in his official declaration, that the African agreements were equitable and that the two nations had examined all the problems which concerned the maintenance of European order. In Europe, they called for mutual central European undertakings among Italy, Germany, Austria, Hungary, Czechoslovakia, and Yugoslavia— that is to say, Austria's neighbors—not to try to change by force the territorial integrity or political or social regime of any of those states.

France and Italy for themselves affirmed the necessity of maintaining the independence and integrity of Austria. If it were threatened (and by whom other than Germany?), they would consult among themselves and Austria as to appropriate measures.

As to German rearmament, the real threat to the European balance, the two governments referred to the declaration of equal rights of December 11, 1932 and declared that no country could modify its obligations on armaments by its own unilateral act; if so, Italy and France would confer.[9]

A secret protocol on disarmament named Germany as a potential aggressor and pledged Franco-Italian cooperation in any future disarmament negotiation to preserve mutually advantageous positions vis-à-vis Germany. An exchange of letters on Abyssinia stated that France did not look to Abyssinia for the satisfaction of any interests other than those relating to the zone of the Djibuti railway, rights enjoyed by French nationals under previous treaties, and the renewal of existing concessions.[10]

Both Mussolini and Laval expressed satisfaction in their accomplishment. In the World Map Hall of the Palazzo Venezia Mussolini paid tribute to Laval:

> Before concluding I want to render homage to M. Laval's clear intelligence, open-mindedness, practical sense and good methods of negotiation. It is a pleasure to talk to him. I venture to believe that there is a personal sympathy between us as, because our tormented youths had something in common, because our experiences have been similar, because a similar evolution has led us from a somewhat Utopian universalism to profound and indestructible realities.

Laval responded in kind:

> I do not want to leave Rome without telling the Italian Press all my admiration for Mussolini. A sympathy has been born between us. I shall know how to use it in promoting Franco-Italian friendship.[11]

Laval proceeded to an audience with the Pope, who decorated him with a Grand Cross of Pius IX, and to whom Laval gave the assurance: "France will remain the eldest daughter of the Church."[12]

Laval had achieved his immediate goals in Rome. He had liquidated the causes of Franco-Italian rivalry and dissension. He had secured important declarations concerning European security—the maintenance of Austrian independence and the unacceptability of unilateral German rearmament. The military consequences were notable. With Franco-Italian friendship, the need to garrison the Italian border no longer existed; instead substantial troop components—ten divisions of infantry and two brigades of calvary—could be posted to the German frontier. Free communication with Africa and the safe passage of troops from her African empire in a tranquil Mediterranean were important considerations for France.

There had been talk between Mussolini and Laval of military cooperation and conversations. In fact, in the spring and summer of 1935, air and military conventions were signed.[13]

The military advantages, Laval claimed, went further. The military conventions, he later said, would provide

> a corridor which would permit us to rejoin the 100 divisions of the Little Entente armies. Italy was the corridor through Middle Eastern Europe towards Moscow, that is to say, toward the Soviet army. I put into effect the policy of encirclement.[14]

Nor had Laval paid an excessive price. The very real claims of Italy in Tunisia had been compromised with some barren acreage and minority shares in the Djibuti railway. With evident satisfaction, Laval told an American journalist that he had come home with Mussolini's shirt and studs.[15]

But Mussolini was satisfied, too. He had said, in announcing the agreements, that they were a compromise of opposing views. What truly concerned him was the threat to Austria, and hence to Italy; and it was here he saw the greatest value in the Rome Pacts. A later press statement reflected his view:

Many newspapers have described the French accords signed in Rome on January 7 as one of the most important events since Locarno. It is precisely from this overall European standpoint that Italy regards the accords.[16]

But in addition, Mussolini surely wanted, perhaps not so much an assurance, but a signal that he could now proceed with his Abyssinian campaign and that France would not raise obstacles. He did not want to undertake the adventure in the face of British and French opposition. Their combined power was significant; and they had geography on their side. He preferred to conciliate, to negotiate, and to make concessions to France which, in addition to the published agreements concerning European security, must redound to his benefit in Africa.

Whether Pierre Laval gave any direct assurances to Mussolini that France would stand aside while Italy conquered Abyssinia has been a matter of surmise and fierce debate. In the bitterness of 1943, when England was at war with Italy, Vansittart wrote:

He [Laval]. . . paid a visit to Rome at the beginning of 1935 and I have no doubt that he sold Abyssinia on the sly. He was accompanied by my 'opposite number' and close friend, Alexis Leger, Berthelot's successor as Head of the French Foreign Office. Nothing reprehensible took place at the meetings attended by Alexis, a man of notorious integrity; but Laval arranged meetings from which his subordinate was excluded. No agreement was consigned to writing; but 'a wink is as good as a nod' and Laval always had a brace of eyelids which droop with facility toward Berlin or Rome at the expense of France.[17]

Leger later said he had no idea of the extent of concessions made privately by Laval to Mussolini; only that he was sure they existed.[18]

Pierre Laval always maintained the contrary. He told the French Senate on March 26, 1935:

As for Ethiopia, it has been asked whether I may not have forgotten the role of friend and protector which France has always played toward her. I reply that I have forgotten nothing and on this point I have not conceded anything with which I may be reproached. Nothing in the Rome Agreements tampers with the sovereignty, independence and territorial integrity of Ethiopia, as these are guaranteed by the Anglo-French-Italian Agreement of 13th December 1906, and also—it should not be forgotten—by the Covenant of the League of Nations.[19]

Flandin, who was Prime Minister at the time, flatly denied the existence of any secret agreement. "This is absolutely wrong," he declared.[20] Laval was consistent in his claim; and in the end even secured an acknowledgment of his position from Mussolini.[21] Nevertheless, the absorbing question lived on and influenced the thoughts and actions of the statesmen as the Abyssinian crisis developed.

The parties had both left the negotiating table satisfied and confident that they had advanced their causes. Yet each had a different understanding of what had occurred. Perhaps there was a secret agreement concerning Abyssinia; perhaps there was none. Another possibility would occur to seasoned negotiators who know or sense that to press a given point to its absolute and final conclusion will destroy the agreement they hope to reach. In such a case, wise negotiators, who are at the same time optimists concerning their positions and their negotiating adversaries, will preserve the essence of the agreements and delicately leave the difficult point in just such posture as each wishes to see and understand it, confident that the process of the agreement and the spirit in which it is entered will modify, mollify, and finally resolve the issue. Each is then free to carry on in his understanding and to parley and negotiate another day.

A foundation had been laid for Laval's further work. Recognizing that Britain was above all France's ultimate, however reluctant ally, he had to secure British endorsement of the Rome Pact. He then had to carry out the final and fundamental piece of Barthou's plan—a treaty of friendship and alliance with the Soviet Union. With all these in place, he earnestly believed the peace of Europe could be secured.

Mussolini, too, had a full agenda after the signing of the Rome Pacts. He was as conscious as Laval of the role of Britain. The Royal Navy had long dominated the Mediterranean; Britain's African possessions—the Sudan, Kenya and British Somaliland—ringed Abyssinia; and above all, Britain controlled the Suez Canal through which each and every Italian vessel, soldier, sailor, vehicle, airplane and weapon, not to mention the supplies and ammunition to make them effective, must transit en route to a campaign on Abyssinia.

Abyssinia was pressing her case before the League of Nations. Mussolini had made his deal with France and was satisfied with it. Now was the time to reach the accommodation with Britain which Mussolini deemed prudent before he could confidently move forward with his plan.

Mussolini Makes His Move—Great Britain

On January 15, 1935, the Abyssinian government notified the League of Nations that Italy had refused conciliation under the 1928 Treaty and asked the League, under Article 9 of the Covenant to examine the situation.[22]

Britain was not disinterested in this corner of the world. Indeed, since the spring of 1934, the British Ambassador in Addis Ababa, Sir Sydney Barton, had been conducting discussions with Haile Selassie looking to an exchange of territories in which a portion of the Ogaden Desert would be added to British Somaliland in exchange for an Abyssinian outlet to the sea at the port of Zeila.[23] These talks were the reason for Lt. Col. Clifford's presence at Wal Wal. Britain had not informed its partners to the 1906 Treaty, France and Italy. But the Italians seemed well-informed and there were suspicions of British designs on the oases at Wal Wal and Wardair. Had the Italians learned of the British negotiations with Haile Selassie, Sir Eric Drummond, the British ambassador in Rome, asked Vansittart? He thought it highly likely.[24]

If the Italians were concerned over British designs, the British were concerned where the Abyssinian appeal to the League of Nations could lead. Indeed, Drummond had met with Mussolini the day before and pressed for a settlement. Mussolini was ready to waive punishment of the guilty, but he insisted on the Italian demands for an apology, an indemnity, and a salute to the Italian flag. Yielding to these, Drummond thought, might endanger Haile Selassie's position which, he pointed out, was an element of stability in Abyssinia. Mussolini was unimpressed. What was stability in Abyssinia, he inquired? Was it the number of slaves, he asked, quoting statistics on slavery in Abyssinia from Lady Simon's book.[25]

The next day, Simon wired Drummond that the matter must not go to the League. He urged Drummond to press Mussolini for a settlement.[26] Meanwhile, Grandi, Italian Ambassador to Britain, was concerned, "for he could not regard these Abyssinian questions as having the importance of the really great European issues in which we are so vitally interested."[27]

These concerns were for the time being resolved. Anthony Eden and Pierre Laval worked with Joseph Avenol, Secretary-General of the League of Nations, and with Baron Aloisi, Italy's representative, to get the Abyssinian appeal dropped from the League docket. The solution, pressed by Eden and Laval, came on January 19, 1935 in the form of a joint letter from Italy and Abyssinia, each undertaking conciliation under the 1928 Treaty.[28]

Abyssinia had been foresighted enough only to postpone its request for a discussion under Article 11 of the Covenant. The matter would remain on the League agenda. Abyssinia had persisted in its complaint and superficially had achieved a forum in which it could pursue it. On a more practical level, the delay was costly to Abyssinia. Mussolini went forward with his preparations. On January 16, 1935, General de Bono landed at Massawa, to take command of the prospective campaign. On the same day Mussolini added to all of his other posts and titles the Ministry of Colonies. The military preparations and the arbitration with Abyssinia could go forward hand and hand. Indeed there was for Italy the enticing possibility that, shielded from the impartial gaze of the League, the negotiations could be paced precisely so as to aid the military preparations.

Italy was not alone in her incident on the Abyssinia border. Late in January, a Danakil raiding party of 3,000 men crossed into French Somaliland. The youthful French district officer, a twenty-four-year-old civilian on his first assignment, had tried to intervene. He was killed along with his thirty-man escort and some accompanying tribesmen. France, too, was demanding the restoration of stolen property, the punishment of the guilty, and indemnities paid to relatives of the victims.[29]

It was under these circumstances that Leonardo Vitetti, Counselor of the Italian Embassy in London, called on Geoffrey Thompson of the Foreign Office on January 29, 1935. The meeting had been arranged by Grandi, Vitetti said, specifically to keep Britain informed of the recent agreements between France and Italy. Thompson supposed it may have been occasioned by leaks concerning Sir Sidney Barton's talks with Haile Selassie. If secrecy had shrouded the British-Abyssinian talks, Italy, to the contrary, wanted to remove any suspicion of operating behind the backs of her Tripartite Treaty partner. Vitetti emphasized the friendly nature of the Franco-Italian agreements, pointing to the French undertaking not to seek new economic interests or concessions in Abyssinia. He said that Italy's intentions in Abyssinia were pacific; he then invited a discussion of British interests in that country "so as to explore the possibility of the development of such interests in a mutual and harmonious manner."[30]

The British did not accept this invitation. They took refuge in the classic method of avoiding a decision. They appointed a committee to study the issue. After all, they reasoned, the Vitetti talks could hardly be disassociated from the Italian-Abyssinia dispute and it would be wise in any future talks "to guide Italian requests away from points which His Majesty Government will be unable to concede." It would also be wise to consider actual British interests in Abyssinia and how Italian absorption of Abyssinia would affect them.[31]

The Chairman of the Committee, Sir John Maffey, represented the richness of the human resources the British Empire had at its disposal. The son of a traveling salesman, he had passed through Oxford to the Indian Civil Service in 1899 where he found his metier. He served on the Northwest Frontier and eventually became its Chief Commissioner, a great expert on the country and its people, who became "a sort of honorary Pathan" and always pressed for the independence and autonomy of the native tribes. He had equal success from 1926 to 1933 as Governor-General of the Sudan. He was a dedicated naturalist and traveller who took advantage of his post to travel widely in Eritrea, Abyssinia, and to the sources of the Nile. In 1933 he was appointed Permanent Undersecretary of State for Colonies. Few people could have been as well prepared to analyze and determine British interests in Abyssinia.[32]

While Vitetti talked to Thompson, Grandi and Vansittart met on the same day, and the day following.[33] They had much upon which to agree. Grandi shared Vansittart's fear of Germany. To make the German threat real, Vansittart believed, Germany needed an ally, just as Hitler had said in *Mein Kampf*. It was precisely as an ally that Grandi most feared Germany. He had no illusions where the balance of power between them would lie. Whatever may have been Vansittart's personal evaluation of Pierre Laval, he wholly agreed with Grandi on the usefulness of a Franco-Italian-British combination against the German threat, a goal both would pursue tenaciously in 1935.

The Foreign Secretary, Sir John Simon, had no illusions either. He told Thompson: "The Italians intend to have Abyssinia."[34] Whatever the Maffey Committee might eventually say about Britain's direct interests in East Africa, it was clear that an Italian aggression in Abyssinia would raise myriad problems for Britain, at home and abroad.

At home there could be no mistaking the fervent activity on behalf of the League of Nations led by the League of Nations Union and exemplified by the nationwide canvass in progress—the Peace Ballot. Its "Peace or War" posters and its ballots bearing that headline had spread across the land. The Foreign Secretary, who had criticized the Peace Ballot in the House of Commons, promptly felt the pressure of Lord Cecil's forces. On December 27, 1934, in a letter to a LNU branch, he now denied that he opposed the Peace Ballot. His sole purpose, he said, had been to make certain comments on Question 4 dealing with the private manufacture of arms.[35]

The first flood of Peace Ballots was pouring in; the effort was at its peak. Certainly any effort to flout the authority and procedures of the League of Nations would not go down well with a vocal and apparently growing segment of the British public.

The issues abroad involved calculations of risks, dangers, and opportunities that turned on the impact of an African adventure upon the great issues of European power relations. What that would mean for Great Britain and France vis-à-vis Italy, in the first instance, vis-à-vis Germany in the second, the latter depending upon relations between Germany and Italy—all these were subjects which the Foreign Secretary could well ponder—and did, without any immediate response to Italy.

Mussolini did not press the issue. As usual, he was exceedingly well informed. He knew about the Peace Ballot and queried Anthony Eden on the significance of Parliamentary elections. His information was sometimes less than accurate. He had read studies of England that emphasized the number of spinsters, the excess of deaths over births, and the prevalence of homosexuality, from which he concluded that the British had lost the vigor that had gained an Empire. He knew, too, about the Oxford Union's celebrated resolution not to fight for King and Country and he contrasted the pacifism of England unfavorably to his own militaristic passion.[36]

Perhaps he felt he had made his position clear. With France there had been issues and grievances and these, and other issues, had been resolved in a series of formal documents. With England, it may be that he felt entitled to take the silence that followed his approach as a form of consent to conduct that the Foreign Secretary clearly understood.

This was the position he later took: "I was ready to table my case—I wanted to do that. Your Minister of Foreign Affairs acted evasively. In the face of silence," Mussolini added, "there was only one road which remained open to me and I took it."[37]

Britain and Germany

Great Britain had deflected the Italian approach. The critical issue on the agenda of the British Cabinet in January, 1935 was not Italy but Germany. The Cabinet were well informed and keenly aware of the threat posed by rapid German rearmament and equally well aware of the limitations on their response imposed by the state of public opinion.

The issue was emphasized by the impending visit of Pierre Etienne Flandin, the French Prime Minister and his Foreign Minister, Laval, later in the month to review the Rome accords. When the Cabinet met on January 9, 1935, they were informed that Laval wished to clear positions on an Eastern pact and any agreement they might propose to Germany to limit arms before entering into discussion with Germany. Laval maintained the traditional French stance; such discussions should take on the wider aspects of a "regime of security."

The Cabinet reviewed the joint Franco-Italian declaration that no country could unilaterally modify its obligations as to armaments. They wondered what to do if the French asked what action Britain would take should Germany not agree to proposed limits on arms. Germany was unlikely to agree to earlier proposals since it was well known that Germany already possessed a bomber fleet.

The Cabinet considered the perennial question of Britain's Locarno obligations and especially interpretations whereby Britain would be the judge of its own obligations. As the Secretary for Dominion Affairs plainly stated, public opinion was not ready for anything more than a declaration that Britain would intervene only if its vital interests required it.

The Cabinet deferred further consideration of other issues but firmly concluded that, convinced as they were of the illegality of Germany rearmament, it was better that it should be acknowledged and controlled rather than uncontrolled.[38]

On January 13, 1935, the Saar plebiscite returned an enormous majority in favor of reunion with Germany. This was a great German triumph in the face of an extended French effort to secure an opposite result. It was also a triumph for Anthony Eden, who had joined Pierre Laval in mollifying the antagonisms and difficulties inherent in the plebiscite and in securing the participation of an international force including British troops to keep the peace.

The British Cabinet met again on January 14, 1935. Once again, the principal topic was British obligations under Locarno. Was Britain automatically obliged to come to the aid of its Locarno partners in the event of an attack? The question that had been theoretical in 1925 was now severely practical. If, the Prime Minister said, "we now entered into an agreement which public opinion held to have weakened the existing safeguards, strong public objections might be raised." To which the Secretary for Dominion Affairs added that "there was a strong public opinion opposed to being drawn in to assist France."

What to do then, if the French Ministers upon their arrival in London, insisted on some firm statement of British obligations under Locarno? To this Sir John Simon replied that,

> if the negotiators were faced with French proposals to 'put teeth into Locarno' they would have to make it clear that it was necessary to carry British opinion with the Government and that from this point of view it was necessary to speak of a 'vital British interest' without mentioning Locarno. . . . He thought also that care ought to be taken about the demilitarized zone, as the time was certain to come when the Germans would not be willing to put up with it.

The issue was thus faced directly. Should Britain reaffirm that it considered the demilitarization of the Rhineland as a vital British interest and treat it as such in accordance with the Locarno treaty?

Few British Cabinets have ever made so fateful a decision. Upon it turned, as the decade would tell, the fate of Europe and the lives of tens of millions of its inhabitants. Ultimately it involved the fate of the British and French Empires and the world of today.

It was pointed out in the Cabinet record

> that as the demilitarization of the Rhineland was included in the Locarno Treaty and that in certain circumstances we might be compelled to fight for it, we could not repudiate the point if raised by the French Ministers. The view of the Cabinet, however, was that demilitarization of the Rhineland was not a vital British interest and that if the French raised the question of the demilitarization of the Rhineland, the British negotiators should state that we were bound by the Locarno Treaty and had no intention to repudiate it.

Suppose the French negotiators asked for regular consultations among the General Staffs of Great Britain, France and Belgium? The answer was "that the British Ministers had to consider public opinion in this country and from that point of view could not enter into any such engagement."

These, then, were the conclusions of the meeting:

> That no attempt should be made for a redefinition of our obligations under Locarno. If the French Ministers should make proposals to put teeth into Locarno' the British negotiators should make it clear that it was necessary to carry British public opinion, and from this point of view it was necessary to avoid any actual reference to the Treaty.

And

> That the negotiators should avoid a statement that Great Britain considers the demilitarization of the Rhineland as a vital interest. If the French Ministers should raise the question of the Rhineland the British negotiators should be authorized to state that we were bound by the Locarno Treaty and had no intention of repudiating it.[39]

More than the Maginot Line, more than the arms limitations of the Versailles Treaty (which Germany had already shattered), the security of France rested upon the demilitarized zone of the Rhineland. It was France's first and most vital line of defense. It denied to Germany a jumping-off point for an attack on France and offered to France a pledge of vital German territory by which France could respond to German breaches of treaty obligations and through which, equally importantly, France could come effectively to the aid of its Central and Eastern European allies.

Not only had the British Cabinet now declared that the demilitarized zone of the Rhineland was no longer a vital British interest; not only, in anticipation of a meeting with the French Prime Minister and Foreign Minister did the British government fail to communicate to France that critical fact; but instead, a careful formula was adopted to evade a direct and truthful reply if the very question were put by the French Ministers.

All this was notwithstanding the firm and repeated pronouncements by Stanley Baldwin that Britain's frontier was no longer the English Channel but the Rhine and that the security of Britain lay not on the white cliffs of Dover, but in the Rhineland. Did not these declarations still ring in French ears and form a basis for French policy?

Instead, the British Cabinet adopted as its negotiating position that German rearmament was an accomplished fact, that Germany would continue to insist on equality, and that it was necessary to arrive at an arms control agreement with Germany. If the French Ministers were to ask—what about security?—they should be asked for their own proposals to satisfy this condition. And in fact, the Cabinet noted, Britain had in progress a rearmament program, especially in the air, which was a real contribution to European security.[40]

If the British Cabinet was deeply affected by the state of British public opinion, few people appreciated that fact more keenly than Adolf Hitler. He made it his business to cultivate influential British contacts and through them to influence the British public. He was extraordinarily successful.

In January, 1935, he met two very different leaders of British public opinion. Lord Allen of Hurtwood, the veteran pacifist and National Labour peer was received by Hitler on January 25, 1935. Allen told Hitler of a "strong change of opinion in England favorable to Germany," of the concern about German encirclement raised by the Rome agreements, and of the need for an understanding between Britain and Germany.

Hitler told Allen that Germany needed forty to fifty years of peace. She was ready to conclude an arms agreement with Britain. He specifically suggested limiting the Germany Navy to 35 percent of Britain's. All this would be the first step toward a general arms limitation agreement. These tidings Lord Allen was glad to bear home to England.[41]

Lord Lothian was, unlike Lord Allen, a hereditary aristocrat of impeccable connections and wide influence, which reached far beyond the Liberal Party. He was, Germany's ambassador to London remarked, "the most important non-official Englishman who hitherto has requested an audience with the Reich Chancellor."[42]

Lord Lothian was also pleased with his reception. He reported directly to Sir John Simon that Germany was not thinking of war—at least for ten years. He opined that Germany would never attempt to interfere in the affairs of Austria by force; nor did Hitler want to include any non-Germans in Germany—which would seem to exclude, among others, the Czechs. What was truly opportune was the chance for a general settlement:

The central fact is that Germany does not want war and is prepared to renounce it absolutely as a method of settling her disputes with her neighbors provided she is given real equality.[43]

Not only did Lothian so report to the Foreign Minister, but he exposed the same report and the same opinions in widely read and highly effective correspondence in the columns of the *Times*, which in turn endorsed these views on its editorial pages.

Britain and France

In preparation for the meeting of the British and French Ministers on February 2, 1935, the French had secured the prior approval of the Rome agreements by their Little Entente and Balkan Allies. In the end, a Franco-British declaration was issued on February 3 in which both parties found grounds for satisfaction.

For its part, the British Government cordially welcomed the declaration of Franco-Italian friendship and mutual interest and congratulated the two nations on the Rome agreements. More than that, the British government would consider itself as one of the powers who would consult if the independence and integrity of Austria were menaced.

The British Government also associated itself with the declaration "that neither Germany nor any other Power whose armaments have been defined by the Peace Treaties is entitled by unilateral action to modify these obligations."

To a very real degree, then, France and Italy had obtained British approval of the Rome agreements. The declaration immediately following reflected to British views:

But they [Britain and France] are further agreed that nothing would contribute more to the restoration of confidence and the prospects of peace among nations than a General Settlement, freely negotiated between Germany and the other Powers.

Such a General Settlement would include an Eastern European Pact and arrangements for Austria and Central Europe as foreshadowed in the Rome agreements. The arms limitation provisions of Versailles would be replaced by a negotiated agreement with Germany providing for equal rights in a regime of security and Germany would rejoin the League of Nations.

Moreover, especially impressed by the danger of air attack, the British and French Ministers urged consideration of a reciprocal regional agreement in Western Europe whereby each nation would aid the victim of an aerial attack. They invited Germany, Italy and Belgium to consider such a pact.[44]

Stanley Baldwin had little interest in the fine points of diplomacy, but on this occasion he outdid himself. He arranged a special lunch for Pierre Laval and Eden at Downing Street:

> I gave him good English food and plenty of it. I didn't attempt to compete with French cooking. We had salmon trout, mixed grill, very mixed, Kentucky ham which tasted like crystalized nectar, plum pudding and brandy sauce. But for that luncheon we should never have got the important Declaration of February 3.[45]

Such a repast should have made a good impression on a hotel keeper's son. In his broadcast reporting the results of the London meeting, Laval took pains "to underline in what spirit of friendship and strict unity" the French and British colleagues had faced all problems.[46] He could not know of the British cabinet's decision concerning the Rhineland.

The British Government had advanced its pursuit of a General Settlement with Germany, controlled rearmament, and an air pact that addressed the most immediate threat to the country. Approval of the declaration was not unanimous. Lord Cecil disliked it because to him it was a blow to the authority of the League of Nations.[47] This was consistent; he was in the midst of a huge nationwide campaign the professed aim of which was to demonstrate British support for the League. Labour attacked the Declaration for the same reason; it was a special arrangement outside the League of Nations.[48]

The German reply, on February 14, 1935, to the invitation contained in the London Declaration emphasized Germany's desire for peace and willingness to discuss the arms race, especially the threat of an air attack. To that end, Germany invited Britain to participate in direct talks which might lead to solutions to European problems satisfactory to all states.[49]

Voting for Peace-2

Meanwhile an army was marching the streets and roads of Britain. These were the canvassers for the Peace Ballot: "In one town, it was suggested that an allowance should be made for shoe leather worn out in the Cause."[50] They were spurred on by Lord Cecil's exhortation that "to obtain. . . an overwhelming vote for Peace is the Ballot's whole purpose."[51]

The enormous success of the Peace Ballot became apparent in January. The first large city, Bristol, reported on January 6, 1935. The Bristol organizers thought nothing would be gained by prolonging the campaign. They made certain that for three weeks the town should be gay with banners, advertisements, and posters so that "not a man, women or child in Bristol will have an excuse to be ignorant that a National Declaration is being held on behalf of the League of Nations." The Bristol vote of 132,773, 51.5 percent of the eligible voters, more than justified the local plan.[52]

Hull's vote of 83,914, a 44 percent poll, was registered at the end of January. January recorded 750,000 ballots. February was the first million ballot month.[53]

Here was a chance to work for Peace, a challenge eagerly accepted. Reporting spurred competition. Before the Ballot was over, one worker collected 3,000 signatures, another distributed more than 10,000 ballots.[54]

In crowded urban neighborhoods workers collected all the families in a tenement to explain and distribute forms while in the country it sometimes was a day's work to distribute a half dozen ballots.[55] In the remote Shetland and Orkney Isles, on Skye and Lewis, there was no official organization; the Ballot relied on the initiative and effort of local citizens.[56]

There were bound to be differences of opinion. In Sussex, a ballot worker recounted with evident delight the story of the family in which the husband answered yes to the six questions while his wife answered no to them all.[57] Questions arose. In the north of England, at Thirsk-and-Malton, a keen respondent asked how military sanctions could be applied (question 5b) if the country were first denuded of its arms (question 2).[58]

There was discomfort. People thought the government was prying into their affairs. "No, I'm not signing nothing no more. Government's not going to get to know no more about me," was not untypical.[59]

By common consent, the working-class districts were returning the highest polls. Less successful results were reported from middle-class areas; and the least productive were areas of wealth. These were results for politicians to ponder.[60]

There was objection to the green leaflet, the explanatory materials first distributed with the ballot. Independent souls felt they were being regimented, that the answers were being supplied to them—rather like the "Ja," some suggested, in a Hitler plebiscite.[61]

There were comments aplenty that accompanied the ballots:

> Is it worse for a nation to be governed from a foreign capital than for half the world to be wiped out by poison gas?
> We should advocate that no person under the age of 40 must bear arms. Men of such mature age and judgment would insure that there be no future wars.

One comment indicated an honest effort to respond:

> I do not consider it possible to answer a plain Yes or No to any particular question.[62]

The evident success of the Peace Ballot attracted imitators and competitors. On February 18, 1935, the *Morning Post* announced a series of thirty questions on foreign policy which appeared over ten issues of the paper. A total of 45,182 votes was received—hardly to be compared, of course to the massive results of the Peace Ballot.

The *Morning Post* questions were put differently. To the question, should Britain rely mainly on the League of Nations to prevent war, the response was 30.7 percent yes and 60 percent no. To the question, should Britain increase her defenses, the response was 82.4 percent yes, and 10.6 percent no.[63]

These were questions the Peace Ballot had never asked. It would have been consistent to vote in the affirmative on Peace Ballot question 2—are you in favor of an all-round reduction of armaments by international agreement—a hypothetical question, and for an increase in British armaments, an intensely practical issue. The Peace Ballot presented to the British public in the first quarter of 1935 the former question but not the latter.

It was not only in Bristol that the claim could be made that no man, woman, or child could be excused from knowing the Peace Ballot was in progress. Press coverage was intense with headquarters receiving

1,750 clippings a week.[64] The Peace Ballot was a national happening and a national phenomenon, gaining momentum right up to the date of the final announcement of results, and it was an event which neither the British Government nor the British Parliament could ignore.

The White Paper

The British ambassador in Berlin had warned that Germany would reoccupy the demilitarized zone of the Rhineland as soon as she felt strong enough.[65] The British Government hopefully pursued a General Settlement with Germany and eagerly awaited the planned visit of Sir John Simon and Anthony Eden to Berlin.

The adequacy of British arms had been a subject of continuing discussion and Parliamentary debate in 1933 and 1934 as the German threat become clearer. The Government had formed a special committee charged with determining defense requirements. It had, in July, 1934, secured Parliamentary assent to a forty-one-squadron expansion of the Royal Air Force and in November announced the acceleration of that program. All this aroused bitter dissent, from the right who thought the provisions tardy and inadequate and from the left who believed there should be no increase at all.

In March, the Government once more submitted the full issue to debate by issuing its Statement of Defense Policy, known as the British White Paper of March 1, 1935.[66] It opened with an obligatory statement of British dedication to peace. This was followed by an equally plain statement that Britain required adequate defenses for its own security and to enable it to play its part in maintaining peace. Britain had substantially disarmed. It had taken risks for peace. But there were serious deficiencies in British defenses; and these deficiencies had not contributed to general disarmament and had left Britain approaching a point when it would not have the necessary means of defending itself against an aggressor.[67]

The Disarmament Conference had failed. Germany was rearming. The value of the Locarno Treaty as a deterrent would be seriously weakened if there were no means to enforce it.

Rearmament, the White Paper said, especially German rearmament, could put peace in peril. The spirit of the Nazi regime and its regimentation of German youth added greatly to feelings of European insecurity. The British Government would be failing in its responsibilities if, while continuing to seek peace and disarmament, it did not put its defenses on an adequate basis. Failure to maintain an adequate navy could doom Britain. More cruisers were needed to protect British trade. Britain would welcome naval limitations, but ineffective defense would mean not only waste, but defeat.[68]

The Government proposed a further expenditure of £10 million. It pointed to the Royal Air Force as the country's principal defense and the great danger if Germany acquired air bases along the English Channel. Civil defense measures were necessary. An increase in arms was urgently required to preserve peace, to maintain security and to deter aggression.[69]

The French, too, were looking to their defenses. Twenty years after the World War, France had entered upon its empty years when the annual contingent of conscripts would be at record low numbers. This was part of the price of victory. On March 5, 1935, the French Government proposed the extension of the term of military service from eighteen months to two years, not to increase, but simply to maintain the number of her effectives. No new arms accompanied the measure.[70]

These actions so aggrieved Adolf Hitler as to make him ill. At least, so he reported to Great Britain: a sore throat and general indisposition had left him unable to meet with the British Ministers on their scheduled visit.

To Lord Cecil, the White Paper was a grievous disappointment, all the more so as it coincided with the growing success of the Peace Ballot. On March 8, 1935 he reported to a luncheon meeting of the National Council for Equal Citizenship that three million votes had already been cast and that these represented only a seventh of the constituencies to be polled. High affirmative votes were being recorded on all questions, led by 97 percent in favor of the League of Nations. Indeed, a proposal had been made for a world ballot to be organized through the churches which would show what the people of the world really wanted.

What could the White Paper mean, he asked, but that the League of Nations had failed, that it could not be relied on as a defense against aggression, and, most terrible of all, that it heralded the abandonment of the collective system and a return to military preparedness as the nation's only safeguard?[71]

There were many who shared Lord Cecil's concerns. Mrs. Ayrton Gould was the Labour candidate in a Parliamentary election at Norwood, to be held on March 14. To her the White Paper was "The most tragic document since the War, a diabolical one, for the policy it announces heads straight for a new war."[72]

Stanley Baldwin's rebuttal was contained in a letter to the Conservative candidate, Duncan Sandys:

> I am informed that your Socialist opponents are once more accusing the National Government of a warmongering policy. The very reverse is the truth. No Government has striven more earnestly to promote peace and disarmament. We trust that the conversations with other nations on which we are now entering may pave the way to a real advance toward the consolidation of international peace and security in which the proposal for an Air Convention will, we hope, play an important part.
>
> In the meantime the Government of the day is the trustee for the safety of the nation, and there is nothing more certain than that our influence for peace would be eno+-rmously weakened if, in the present condition of the world, we attempted to pursue a policy of one-sided disarmament.[73]

Britain had published the White Paper. Hitler had his own announcement to make. On March 9, Reichsmarshal Goering, notified the air attachés accredited to Berlin of the existence and organization of the German air force. What almost all had known, heard, seen and wondered how to treat was now confirmed, official. Hitler now publicly proclaimed to have in hand the weapon Britain feared most, the weapon which would in the event devastate France even more than the British Isles.

This was a shattering blow—an absolute, outright and deliberate breach of the terms of the Treaty of Versailles which explicitly denied military aviation to Germany. It was a deliberate challenge to Britain and France, to determine not how much vitality Versailles still had, but what will the victors had to maintain it.

It was under these circumstances that two days later the British Parliament debated the White Paper. Before it was Clement Attlee's motion that the Government defense policy contradicted the spirit of the League of Nations, jeopardized the prospects of a Disarmament Convention, and far from ensuring national security, would lead to war.[74]

The White Paper, Attlee said, amounted to a repudiation of the League of Nations. Yet the country was overwhelmingly for peace: "Among the people of this country," he pointed out, "the expressions of opinion were tremendously strong."[75]

The German announcement had not profoundly affected Attlee, who maintained that "the world had grown so small that there was no longer room for national armed forces." Security was not to be gotten by national defense, but only by moving forward to a new world—"a world of law, a world of the abolition of national armaments, with a world force and a world economic system." To all this one member promptly replied: "Tell that to Hitler."[76]

No, said Attlee, the policy of the White Paper was disastrous. Let Mr. Baldwin go to the young men of the country and ask them what they thought. The young people would reject his policy not only in England but throughout the world.

Attlee had been eloquent. He had not, however, explained how a world of law, a disarmed world, a world air force and a world economic system were to be brought into being—or what policy would protect Britain until that happy and eventful day.

Stanley Baldwin was forthright in his reply:

> If this house expected me today to stand in a white sheet because of the White Paper it will make a great mistake. I think that this document will be one of historic interest. It is one in which a Democratic government tells what it believes to be the truth to democracy, and I hope to show in my speech that one of the greatest perils that have met democracy in the past and meet them today, is when their leaders have not the courage to tell them the truth.[77]

He reviewed the progress of British disarmament, the fifth rank of its air force, and renewed the pledge that Britain must be equal to any air power in striking distance. Of course, he said, you could not insure immunity from air attack. What you could do was to make it unprofitable to the point of deterrence.

Democracy, Baldwin said, was a difficult form of government. "It cannot function unless the whole people are sane and think and come to considered conclusions and are not swayed by propaganda and sentiment." Did the five questions of the Peace Ballot lead to considered conclusions? Was the question "Peace or War?" an appeal to sentiment?

If Britain were not ready to endorse this modest program, Mr. Baldwin put the consequence squarely: "I believe the risks of our democracy perishing are great." A country, he concluded, unwilling to defend itself will never have force, moral or material, in this world.[78]

The numbers of the Liberal Party had shrunk but its leader, Sir

Herbert Samuel, preserved intact its idealism. He referred to the powerful peace movement in the country which was vehemently opposed to any increase in arms. The League of Nations Union, the churches, the women's organizations all felt that peace was the supreme issue in the world and that disarmament was essential as the way to pursue it. If Britain must rearm to fulfill its Locarno obligations, then Germany could make the same case. The result would be an arms race. Not armament, but disarmament was the only road to security.

Sir Herbert Samuel's final plea was a familiar one. The £10 million would be far better spent on social programs. Aneurin Bevin did not aspire to Sir Herbert Samuel's gentility. Mr. Baldwin and his class, he thundered, would one day lose their heads in a violent revolution. Only when the country turned aside from policies of economic exploitation would there be hope for peace.[79]

Sir Austen Chamberlain's amendment to the Attlee motion spoke of faith in the League, arms limitation, and disapproval of unilateral breaches of treaty obligation but wholly approved of the government's defense programs whereby Britain could discharge its international obligations.

He made the significant point that the Covenant and the League structure had been designed to prevent wars which arose out of incidents and accidents. Against a predetermined plan of aggression, only the deterrent force of real collective security could avail. When that day came, he asked, would Denmark supplement the deficiencies of the Royal Navy, or Switzerland furnish airplanes, or Belgium the troops Britain could not find?

If that day came, Sir Austen said, it was the business of the House that men of courage should tell the truth to the country—that sacrifices were necessary for Britain's defense, and that the promises of Locarno and membership in the League of Nations were worthless without forces adequate to the present danger.[80]

Sir Austen was strongly supported by Leopold Amery. It was not enough, he said, to publish the White Paper and debate it in Parliament. It ought to be sent to every home in the country that also had received the well-intentioned but highly misleading Peace Ballot. The Government had to make it plain to the public what the real position in the world was and what the duty of Englishmen was in dealing with it.[81]

Amid the speeches came there was a clamor in the Strangers Gallery. Two women flung leaflets to the floor of the House, shouting "Women want peace," and "Not a penny for war," and "Scrap the White Paper." They were quickly ushered out by plainclothesmen.[82]

Sir Stafford Cripps railed that the Government was deserting the League of Nations. The policy of Labour was to stop aggression by recalling ambassadors; if that failed, by economic pressure; if that failed, in collaboration with other nations equally bound, by force of arms.[83]

This was met with jeers and laughter from the Government side of the House and provided an irresistible target for Sir John Simon in his closing speech.

He found it difficult, Simon said, to understand the Labour view that Britain should intervene with armed force in any quarrel while at the same time Labour voted against all proposals to provide the necessary arms—with the added attraction, that any war in which Labour did not believe should be met by a general strike.

Simon paid dutiful tribute to the League of Nations, and to the sentiment for peace. But he clearly presented the Government's case, lauded the proposed air pact and the London Declaration and looked forward to the visit he and Mr. Eden would make to Berlin.[84]

The House overwhelmingly rejected the Attlee motion and by a similar margin adopted Chamberlain's amendment.

There was one capital in Europe where the White Paper and the action of the British Parliament were firmly approved. The correspondent of the *Times* reported from Rome on March 13, 1935 that:

> The criticism has frequently been heard here that the policy of Great Britain toward disarmament was too obstinately idealistic in the face of certain steadily accumulating facts and that it needed to be corrected by the realism of a Mussolini.[85]

Lord Cecil did not agree. This was not the time, he told the House of Lords on March 14, 1935 to increase the air force. To accept air warfare as a normal part of the future seemed to him the most shocking thing in the world. Was Britain to reject the collective system? Any threat to peace was a danger to all Europe. He was alarmed, he said, that someone might declare that the question of the Rhine affected Great Britain. He did not believe the Rhine affected Britain anymore than a great many other questions.[86]

The Parliamentary debate was echoed in Norwood the following day when the Parliamentary candidates made a joint appearance at the Roupell Park Methodist Church, presided over by the veteran pacifist Dr. Maude Royden. The sole subject of the meeting, she said, was peace and the views of the candidates on peace.

Mrs. Gould advocated collective security, the abolition of naval and military aircraft, and the prohibition of the private manufacture of arms. Far from forthrightly supporting rearmament, Mr. Sandys presented the Government's policy as a peace policy and suggested that accusations of warmongering would not help the Government's quest for peace.[87]

Mr. Sandys was returned, but the 23,634 Conservative majority of 1931 was reduced to 3,348. True, 1931 had been an abnormal year and an Independent candidate had taken votes away from Mr. Sandys. The results of the March 14 election, nevertheless, gave the Government cause for reflection.[88]

There were echoes of the Parliamentary debate in the French Chamber on March 15. Prime Minister Flandin explained the necessity of extending to two years the term of active service. Germany had rearmed. Everyone knew that. In 1936 Germany would have 600,000 men in service; France, even with extended service, could count only on 208,000.

Leon Blum led the left's attack on the law. It was all a matter of militarism trying to impose its policy on the government. The Maginot Line had been sold to the public as saving manpower. The army of 1936, solidly established behind impenetrable fields of fire, was more than enough.

What France did not need, Blum said, was an army like Germany's— a professional, long-term army of shock and speed, always ready for offensives and attacks. To what strategic conception did that relate? Certainly not the defense of the national territory.

Paul Reynaud had recently met Lt. Col. Charles de Gaulle. Convinced of the merit of de Gaulle's ideas, he became his spokesman. The program Reynaud urged on the deputies on March 15 was for an armored corps, capable of striking hard and fast, in joint operations with French aviation. That was the kind of war, he predicted, Germany would wage tomorrow. How would France respond?

Reynaud pointed to two contradictions in French policy. How, first, could France honor her obligations to Poland and Czechoslovakia without the means of coming to their aid? More important, how could

France defend the Belgian frontier, where there was no Maginot line, thanks to indecision and lack of funds? The military policy of France could neither aid her allies nor protect herself.

The term of service was extended, but Reynaud's plea for a very different kind of army failed for want of support from either the Government or the military establishment.[89]

Another Challenge

Exactly a week after announcing the new German air force, Adolf Hitler made an even more dramatic announcement. Germany would have an army of 600,000 men, organized into twelve army corps and thirty-six divisions, supported by universal military service. He had chosen his timing carefully. It was Saturday, March 16, Hero's Day when tribute would be paid to the German dead of 1914–1918. The English were away for the weekend.

The announcement was greeted with wild enthusiasm which the attendant ceremonies were carefully designed to arouse. At the Prussian Opera House, Hitler occupied the central box. He was flanked on the one side by Field Marshal von Mackensen in the uniform of the Death's Head Hussars, representing the old Imperial Army and on the other by General von Blomberg, the Defense Minister, representing the new order.

The curtains parted to reveal a rainbow woven of color and sentiment—the massed standards of eighty-one regiments of the Imperial Army in tiers, ascending from the front to the back of the stage, born by motionless soldiers of the new Reichswehr. Behind them for a backdrop was a huge Iron Cross in black and silver.

The band played the Funeral March from Beethoven's Eroica Symphony. General von Blomberg's address paid tribute not only to the dead, but to the new Germany and its "heaven-sent architect."

After the national anthem, Hitler proceeded to Unter den Linden to take the salute of the passing troops. The smart appearance of the air force drew special comment.[90]

Hitler did not lose sight of his audience outside Germany. He had learned that many people were far more impressed by what he said than by what he did. He had torn up the principal military limitations of Versailles and had lifted the veil for the world to see his grandiose rearmament program. Now he proclaimed his fervent devotion to peace.

Germany, he said, had proposed bilateral nonaggression pacts with its neighbors. It had signed such a treaty with Poland. It had assured France that it had no territorial demands now that Saar was settled. He had read Stanley Baldwin's speech and now echoed it. Germany must have arms to command respect as a co-guarantor of peace.

Hitler renewed his assurance that Germany would never "proceed beyond the safeguarding of German honor and the freedom of the Reich, and especially does not intend in rearming. . . to create any instrument for warlike attack, but on the contrary, exclusively for defense and thereby for the maintenance of peace."[91]

This was not the program Hitler had argued so fervently and passionately in *Mein Kampf*. Had he abandoned his primary goal—bread and soil which the German sword would obtain for the German plow; had he given up hopes of recovering, by force of arms, the lost territories; had he lost the conviction that German posterity would applaud the blood sacrifice by which Germany's rightful place in the world would be won?

These were issues of first-class importance for statesmen and citizens alike to ponder. For some the choice was easy. The *Daily Herald*, organ of the Labour party, was captivated by Herr Hitler's assurances. The future was "bright with hope," the poison of Versailles was at last draining from Germany's blood.[92]

Hitler had indeed torn the Treaty of Versailles to pieces and flung those pieces in the faces of France and Britain. Nothing of importance remained save the borders of 1919 and the demilitarized zone of the Rhineland.

Hitler had his reasons. He had needed two years to build the requisite economic and industrial base for his war machine. He had needed the coal mines and factories of the Saar before publicly denouncing the Treaty. He had proceeded with some discretion when Germany was weakest and least able to cope with any action to enforce the Treaty. There had been natural limits on how fast he could proceed from the start. Importantly, in his diplomacy, in leaving the League and the Disarmament Conference, in his Austrian adventure, he had tested the will of his adversaries and taken their measure. He had carefully monitored the trends of public opinion and taken care that his own position had solid public support.

Now the time had come to turn the tables. He would proclaim to the world German might and German determination. If it were useful to exaggerate, then so be it. Fear would become an instrument of Germany foreign policy along with the hope which the Chancellor's pacific assurances would engender.

British opponents of rearmament were not moved by the spectacle of thirty-six divisions of German soldiers and a German air force. Clement Attlee told a Yorkshire audience that the world was heading for another war. The White Paper was a gross deception. There was no defense in armed forces. The people wanted peace and their governments talked war to distract them from economic conditions. What was needed was to abolish national armaments altogether.[93]

Sir Stafford Cripps persisted in his theme that only a radical restructuring of the world economy could lay the foundation for peace.[94]

There were those, however, who now began to see things in a new light. Herbert Morrison spoke plainly. The armaments race was a fact. British Socialists had better have no illusions that Hitler and the Nazi regime were friends of peace. And Hitler was, he warned, irresponsible and reckless of consequences.[95]

On the continent, reactions were sharp and anguished. Suvich, the Italian Undersecretary of Foreign Affairs, called on the British Ambassador in a state of high excitement and argued for a military bloc against Germany composed of as many European countries as possible. Germany was obviously presenting Sir John Simon and Anthony Eden with a fait accompli on the eve of their visit.[96]

Laval took a grave view and urged immediate consultation among Britain, France, and Italy before any step was taken in response to Germany's actions.[97] To France, Hitler was running true to form. The paean of joy with which Germany greeted its new armed forces was alarming; Germans would probably respond in the same way to the appeal to war. Describing the French position, the British Ambassador wired to Sir John Simon on March 17, 1935:

> It is only [by] remaining united in the face of this challenge [and] speaking to Germany in tones free from weakness—the only language she understands—that it will be possible to arrest the madness which is obtaining an ever increasing hold on the German people. There is a general demand for immediate consultation under the Rome and London declarations between Great Britain, France and Italy with whom in some questions the Soviets are associated.[98]

As to the proposed trip of the British ministers to Berlin, the British

Ambassador wired Simon the next day that Laval would regard such a trip as an encouragement to Germany to further acts of defiance.[99]

The French Ambassador to London was equally precise:

> The decision of the German Government, the state of mind which it publicly reveals, constitutes a new fact. In these circumstances the French Government would be glad to know whether the projected visit of Sir John Simon to Berlin still offers in the eyes of the British Government the same justification or the same usefulness.[100]

These were vain protestations. On March 18, 1935, the British Government sent its note to Berlin. There was no prior consultation with France or Italy. The note contained the protest that Hitler expected. In a tone of pained indignation, the note reiterated British desire to arrive at a General Settlement with Germany and plaintively noted that Herr Hitler's action had made this more difficult.[101]

The forcefulness of the British note was considerably weakened when, in the end, it inquired whether Germany would still receive Simon's and Eden's visit. Germany graciously acceded. If the sole price Hitler had to pay for the demolition of Versailles was a visit from the British Foreign Secretary and his youthful colleague, he could look forward to the meeting with pleasant anticipation and a growing sense of mastery.

Britain now attempted to explain to France that its unilateral response had been compelled by the exigency of a scheduled debate in the House of Commons. Laval was shocked and disappointed; the British action had placed him in a very awkward situation. He would, he told the British Ambassador, be attacked for being too lenient to Germany. Yet he was calm and practical. He was not one to boggle over details of procedure. Here was an entirely new situation. He was gravely alarmed at the prospect of the exhilarating effect upon Hitler in his present exalted state of mind of the decision to maintain the visit to Berlin notwithstanding what had occurred and without further consultation with France and Italy. This could only lead to further acts of defiance.[102]

The French press rendered a unanimous verdict. *Le Populaire*, the Socialist organ, thought the proposed visit constituted a legalization of German rearmament. *Ere Nouvelle*, asked how many snubs it took to make an impression on the British mind. *L'Oeuvre*, a Radical paper, spoke of a complete German diplomatic victory. *Le Figaro* was more understanding, but equally concerned. It did not think the British Government Hitler's dupes, but the move had been costly.

The Italians were equally indignant and alarmed. British action was, plainly and simply, a breach of the common front among France, Italy, and the United Kingdom which Mussolini had said was the only chance of keeping Germany in order. Germany, he added, would rejoice.[103]

On a more practical basis, Italy called the class of 1919 to the colors. It would have, the Duce said, an army of 600,000 by April—a figure that curiously mirrored Germany's. The new recruits would bring up to full strength two divisions destined for East Africa, but Mussolini spoke in more general terms.

> In political weather that is cloudy and unsettled like the sky of today, Italy offers the world a spectacle of calm because Italy is strong both in spirit and in arms.

Italy would face the future with an "incomparable will"—this was a Mussolini staple. Italy was ready for any task: "The millions of bayonets borne by the people of the Blackshirts accompany our desire for sincere European collaboration."[104] Adolf Hitler might have noticed the word European.

Nowhere was indignation greater than in Moscow. *Pravda* charged Britain with foolishly abetting German rearmament. It was the British Government which had enabled Germany to denounce Versailles. The Lothian and Allen visits had paved the way. Instead of a strong protest, Britain had sent a humble request.[105] Britain, Moscow complained, was the weakest link in the chain of defense against Nazi Germany.[106]

None of these opinions moved the British Government to alter its plan. The lure of a General Settlement with Germany was too strong. At this stage the power of hope remained stronger than that of experience.

In Parliament, the issues were sharpened. The Government presented its air budget on March 19, 1935. Winston Churchill pounced on the omission of any estimate of Germany's air strength. The Prime Minister had assured the House, he reminded them, that his government would never suffer inferiority in the air to any country within striking distance. He had admitted German air rearmament but claimed British superiority now—and what was more important had claimed that Britain would have a 50 percent margin of superiority over Germany in November, 1935.

What was the position now, Churchill demanded. The difference was not of principle—they agreed on that—but on the plain facts. His own showed Germany equal to Britain and building faster, en route to superiority. Would the Government deny that?

The Government spokesman said he was unprepared to give precise figures, that the coming visit would clarify matters. In any event, he claimed present British superiority and gave the assurance that no stone would be left unturned to maintain an adequate defense. Churchill was not persuaded.[107]

The opposite point of view was eloquently expressed in the House on March 21, 1935 when George Lansbury spoke for Labour of the coming visit. The arms race, he said, must ultimately lead to war and the destruction of civilization. The Labour Party had an imperative duty to save civilization. In any question of disarmament, Britain had the most to give and Mr. Lansbury wished to give that, in full measure, pressed down and running over. Britain must take the lead and say to the world: "We are willing to lay on the altar of disarmament this business of aerial warfare; we are willing to give up for good and for all with other nations."

Once again he made Labour's solemn declaration of faith, that peace was to be had not by rearmament but by disarmament.[108]

Clearly, Lansbury hoped that Adolf Hitler would respond in a similar vein when he met Simon. A year later, still full of hope, he embarked on his own mission to carry the very same message to the German Chancellor.

As Mussolini contemplated the proposed visit, he had another practical impulse. The visit of the British Ministers to Berlin, like Hitler's defiance of Versailles, was, or would shortly be fait accompli. What was really needed was an in-depth consultation among Britain, Italy, and France whereby all the issues could be faced and a united front created. That meeting should take place in Rome or in a town in northern Italy.

Such an arrangement, Sir Eric Drummond wired to the Foreign Secretary, would allow Mussolini to participate in person. This was the genesis of the Stresa Conference.[109] On March 22, 1935, before he and Anthony Eden had left England, Simon asked Drummond to inform Mussolini that Britain cordially accepted his suggestion and that Anthony Eden, in Paris, en route to Berlin, would so inform Pierre Laval. Simon trusted that the Duce would attend personally; he would look forward to seeing him again.[110]

Vansittart had insisted on Eden's visit to Paris. There must be a gesture before Berlin. Eden's position was uncomfortable. It was with foreboding that he prepared to meet not only Laval, but also Fulvio Suvich, the Italian Undersecretary of State.

Eden met with Laval alone. Laval was practical and unemotional. There were few of the reproaches that Eden had expected and which were in fact deserved. Of course, Laval said, his task would have been far easier had Britain consulted him before sending its note to Germany. But Laval, characteristically, was not disposed to look back, nor to recriminate, but instead to tackle the job at hand with the optimism and self-confidence native to him.

They were joined by Suvich. Eden was impressed by the close unity of the Italian and French Ministers. Suvich was more alarmed than the French. Mussolini, he said, insisted that limits must be placed on concessions to Germany. If Germany were permitted to violate one treaty after another, she would soon try to absorb Austria and that would mean war. It was essential, in Mussolini's view, that Britain, France, and Italy "take steps to immediately stop the rot." That was why the Stresa meeting would be so important.[111]

Laval had a special concern. The three Governments had to be prepared to meet a German move into the Rhineland. If the idea should get abroad that Britain and Italy would be indifferent to such a violation, it would inevitably take place. The Germans would find a pretext—perhaps Laval's visit to Moscow. Laval hoped the British Ministers could take a strong stand on this subject in Berlin.

Anthony Eden did not in turn inform Laval and Suvich of the decision taken by the British Cabinet on January 14 that the Rhineland was not a vital British interest and that any inquiry was to be met by no more than a formal statement of Britain's continued adherence to Locarno.

Eden did give Laval three assurances: that the Berlin meeting was purely exploratory, that the conversations would be within the scope of the February 3 Declaration, and that he would fully report the discussions and their results to the French and Italian Governments.[112]

When Simon and Eden met Hitler on March 25, 1935, Eden observed how Hitler had grown in assurance over the past year. He was more authoritative, less anxious to please. He spoke clearly and well without notes, and reveled in the maps, charts, and diagrams that he used to make his points.[113]

Simon opened with a statement of Britain's desire for peace, its preference for a General Settlement rather than the division of Europe into two hostile camps. He felt bound to report that British opinion was disturbed, not only by Germany's recent acts, but by Germany's withdrawal from the League and the Disarmament Conference, and the whole process of unilateral rearmament.

He specially called to Hitler's attention this vital element in British policy making:

> Great Britain was a country where the general opinion of the people was of great importance and where the spirit and character of the people made it important for the future of Europe that their opinions should be taken into account.[114]

The Peace Ballot would fully demonstrate this truth in the coming months. Hitler rejoined that his government was similarly grounded in the opinion of the German people who overwhelmingly approved all that he had done. After all, 94 percent had approved withdrawal from the League.

Hitler mixed firmness with assurances. Germany had never threatened Austria. Germany would respect the territorial clauses of Versailles, however terrible they might be. Germany had no further claim on France.

Beyond that, Simon and Eden encountered only rejection. Germany would not enter an Eastern European Pact. Why should she? Germany would never attack Russia. Anthony Eden was young enough to inquire as to Herr Rosenberg's plan. This was a polite reference to the conquest of Russia as set forth in *Mein Kampf*. At this point the Chancellor and Baron von Neurath smiled.[115] But the point was not pursued.

Instead Hitler said Germany had neither need nor desire of Russian protection under an Eastern European pact and never, should another country attack the Soviets, could he envision National Socialists fighting for Bolshevism.[116]

As to Austria, Hitler was the soul of innocence. No one in Germany, he protested, had any thought of annexation, of depriving Austria of self-determination, or imposing a union with Germany. It was true that Germany would be glad enough to see Austria disappear from the chessboard of European politics. But Germany would leave Austria severely alone; others must do the same.

Germany, Hitler said, really had no interest in a Central European pact. She might accept the idea on principle, but doubted its practicality. After all, what was noninterference, and who could define it? No, Germany was indifferent to Austria, and the Austrian issue would exact neither German concessions nor German sacrifices.

Simon had no better luck with the League of Nations. He emphasized how attached the British people were to the League. He could hardly have been unaware that, after recording a million votes in February, the Peace Ballot was well on its way to polling two million votes in March.

Hitler was stonily indifferent. Germany could never return to the League under conditions of inferiority. He now raised the issue of colonies as an example. He pointed to the map, comparing Germany to the British Empire. How could Japan, which had left the League, continue to hold League mandates while Germany was deemed unfit?[117]

Hitler was raising the ante. This was a sensitive point. Simon stiffened. The Dominions, he replied, were not quite the same as colonies; the interests of other nations were involved; and the mandated territories were not at Britain's sole disposal.[118]

Firmness made a better impression on Hitler than weakness. Eden thought he noted an underlying friendliness beneath the sometimes heated discussions and respect for the British Empire, its sway and its power. At an elaborate dinner that night, Eden sat between Frau Hess and Frau Goebbels and told them of his experiences in the great German offensive of 1918. Hitler, to Frau Hess's right, joined in enthusiastically. Maps were drawn on the menu, place names recalled. They must have been, Hitler and Eden concluded, opposite each other at La Fere on the River Oise.

François-Poncet, the French ambassador was a party to the conversation. After dinner he asked Eden if it were true that he had faced Hitler across No-Man's-Land. When Eden said that it was probable, François-Poncet replied: "And you left him there. You ought to be shot."[119]

The next morning Simon invited Germany to participate in a general naval limitations discussion. Hitler coyly responded that this came as great surprise, which was in itself surprising since he had proposed an exact figure to Lord Allen in January. Hitler disclaimed any interest in naval rivalry with Britain and, after some debate as to the size of the French fleet, the discussion centered around a German navy 35 percent as large as Britain's.[120]

On land, Hitler was insistent. There were more diagrams, more statistics, and Hitler was firm that Germany needed all of the forces she had announced. All the more so, he added, because Germany had undertaken at Locarno to respect the demilitarized zone of the Rhineland.

The discussions now reached the critical issue of air armaments and what Britain most desired, an air pact. Simon asked Hitler his concept of air parity. Air parity with France, Hitler replied, and if Britain were to increase to the French level, that would be satisfactory. Simon had advised Anthony Eden that a good cross examiner always saves the most important question for the last. The official record shows to what degree Sir John was acting as cross examiner rather than as a diplomat:

> Sir John Simon said there was one more question he must ask. When he had asked Herr Hitler what air force he claimed, the Chancellor had said air parity with Britain and France. Now it would be very material to the discussion if Herr Hitler was able to state the strength of the German air force as it was. He felt obliged to put the question.[121]

There was, Eden recorded, no note of triumph in Hitler's voice, but his reply heralded the doom of a generation of Europeans:

> HERR HITLER replied that Germany had reached parity with Great Britain.[122]

The session ended.

At the outset of the final session, Sir John made a special request: that neither party say anything about the proposed naval meeting. Germany agreed.[123]

The last topic was the air pact. Hitler had scored his point. German air power had become a critical factor, perhaps the critical factor in European affairs. He could now afford to be conciliatory. Germany, he said, would look with favor on an air pact; he was particularly appalled at the thought of indiscriminate bombing of densely populated areas and especially the bombing of women and children. By all means let there be a pact in principle. But Hitler did not see the need to combine it with a limitation on air strength. It was, he said, like the cinematic practice of block booking whereby film companies combined good and bad movies to assure the widest distribution.[124]

This was the end. Sir John expressed his disappointment that they had not been able to progress further toward a general agreement. Hitler replied that he would sign nothing he could not accept; but that, if he gave an undertaking, he would never break it.[125]

The communiqué issued at the close of the conference revealed its futility:

> It was established that the aim of the policy of both governments is to secure and strengthen the peace of Europe by promoting international cooperation. Both the British and German Ministers are satisfied as to the usefulness of the direct conversations which have been taking place.
>
> Sir John Simon will leave Berlin by aeroplane tomorrow on his return to London while Mr. Eden will proceed as arranged to Moscow, Warsaw, and Prague.[126]

The climate was warmer in Moscow where Eden found the Soviets deeply fearful of Germany and supportive of an Eastern European Pact. Eden reported on the Berlin talks. Had Hitler asked the abolition of the demilitarized zone of the Rhineland as the price of a return to Geneva? No, Eden replied, reporting instead that Hitler had specifically said he would abide by Locarno.[127]

Could Britain do anything more to add to security in Eastern Europe? Could Britain guarantee the Baltic states? Eden replied truthfully that there was no possibility. The Soviets saw British forbearance of Germany as an encouragement to Germany to turn against them. This Eden denied.

Stalin impressed upon Eden that hesitant policies in a time of great tension could be dangerous. Eden pleaded that the British Government had to take into account "an active and impressionable public opinion which closely followed events."[128]

Upon the principal theme of the meeting—the German threat and the need for collective security—there was never disagreement. Toasts were drunk to His Britannic Majesty and the orchestra played "God Save the King," all for the first time since the Revolution. Eden was thrilled to see the state's fabulous art collections. Evenings of formal dinners, theater, and ballet added cordiality to the atmosphere.

The official communiqué noted that the organization of peace in Eastern Europe and the proposed Eastern Pact did not in any way aim at the isolation or encirclement of any state, but equal security for all; and that the adherence of Poland and Germany would be welcome. After a full exchange of views, the communiqué said that there was at present no conflict of interest between Britain and the Soviet Union who would collaborate in the cause of peace, loyal to their obligations as members of the League of Nations.[129]

In Poland, the Foreign Minister, Col. Beck, was confident of his relations both with Germany and the Soviet Union, and little interested in the proposed pact.[130] Eduard Benes in Czechoslovakia was more forthcoming. Czechoslovakia's fate lay with the West; he was favorable to both the proposed Central and Eastern European pacts.[131]

Pierre Laval would soon follow Eden's journey to the East. He had entered into the Rome accords with Italy and these had been ratified by the French Parliament on March 26, 1935. He had secured Britain's adherence to the Rome Pact and its approval of an Eastern European pact. It remained for him to sign the Treaty of Friendship and Mutual Assistance with the Soviet Union which would complete the alignment of the European powers on the basis of mutual support against a German threat daily becoming more dangerous. In Parliament, on March 26, Laval announced his planned trip to Moscow. Meanwhile, Britain, France and Italy would meet at Stresa, in northern Italy, in April to implement their already well-developed plan of mutual support. Pierre Laval did not strive for eloquence, only directness. "Let us be strong and let us be united," he told his Parliament, "that we may live in peace."[132]

Mussolini looked forward to this meeting with special interest. In the framework of European security and the German menace he had his own personal piece of business to forward. That business was Abyssinia.

Meanwhile, at Geneva

On March 17, 1935, Abyssinia once more appealed to the League of Nations.[133] She had agreed to conciliation and arbitration under her 1928 Treaty with Italy and what is more to accept any award resulting therefrom. But Italy had shunned negotiations, declined the good offices of a third party, and rejected arbitration. Instead, Italy had sent troops and war material to East Africa.

Abyssinia now claimed its due as a member of the League. Under Article 10, all members were bound to maintain against external aggression the independence and integrity of a fellow member. Under Article 15, Abyssinia laid the dispute before the League and asked for prompt action.

Hitler's actions of March 16 had preempted the League's attention. France had requested a special session of the Council to consider German violations of Versailles. Italy had a stake in this, too. On March 22, 1935, Italy wired the Secretary General of the League denying the truth of Abyssinia's appeal, protesting good faith and promising to proceed with the mediation. Should direct talks fail to produce any result, Italy would join Abyssinia in the formation of a commission of arbitration.[134]

Mussolini had his reasons. Weather conditions would not permit a campaign in Abyssinia to start until October. He had no intention of underestimating the task. At least 300,000 men would be needed. He wrote to De Bono:

> You asked for three divisions by the end of October, I intend to send you ten, I repeat ten; five from the regular army, five of volunteer formations of Blackshirts, who will be carefully selected and trained. These divisions of Blackshirts will be the guaranty that the undertaking will obtain popular support. . . . In view of the possible international controversies (League of Nations, etc.) it is wise to speed up our tempo. For lack of a few thousand men we lost Adowa. I will never commit that error. I am willing to err in excess, but not in deficiency.[135]

Abyssinia understood the threat and the uses of delay. On March 29, 1935, it once more pressed its appeal to the League, and proposed a thirty day limit on arbitration.

The League's processes were complicated. The Secretary General said the matter would be considered at the next Council meeting in mid-April, which had been called in conjunction with the conference to be held at Stresa on April 11–14. There, France, Britain, and Italy would discuss a common front against the German menace.[136]

Time had its uses. Adolf Hitler sensed the attraction of a naval agreement to the British government and the appeal of an air pact to the British public. His war machine had developed rapidly, but several more years were needed for it to attain its designed complement and strength. Hitler might claim air parity with Britain but the Luftwaffe was still a fledgling force and the Panzer divisions were in process of formation. Negotiations would be useful to provide time to develop the ultimate force and Hitler would negotiate from the position of strength he had thus far obtained—or claimed.

He had much to gain; how much by negotiation, how much by the other means remained to be seen. He had taken the measure of Britain and its ministers. The quest for a General Settlement was to him an admission of weakness. He could wait.

Mussolini, too, needed time to prepare his forces. The procedures of the League of Nations were well suited to this need. Meanwhile, at Stresa, perhaps two birds could be killed with a single stone—the restraint of Germany organized and the decks cleared for his conquest of the new Roman Empire. To his practical mind, considering how much he was willing to give and how modest were his requests, it must have seemed a fair and logical transaction.

14

Stresa

*"Diplomacy has to determine which difficulties
will resolve themselves and which will spread
their rot when shoved under a rug."*
—Anthony Eden[1]

Looking to Stresa 1—Mussolini

The problem Mussolini faced at Stresa was Britain. More specifically, he suspected that Britain was dealing behind Italy's back, both
in Abyssinia and in Europe.

The alert Italian consul in Harar had noted the passage of Lt. Colonel Clifford on his way to see the Emperor in Addis Ababa, as he
understood it, to sign a convention concerning the Ogaden. In fact,
Clifford's purpose was to sign the report of the Boundary Commission. The Italians thought they should have been consulted before any
steps were taken. Without further information, suspicions were height-
ened.[2]

The Duce worried that Simon and Eden had been unduly conciliatory in Berlin. Certainly there had been no firm denunciation of
Germany's action, and he suspected a continuing British urge to arrive
at some kind of bilateral agreement with Germany. Mussolini, Sir Eric
Drummond reported to Simon, favored a policy of firmness. This
included discussion at Stresa of the specific steps to be taken in the
event of another treaty violation by Germany, whether in the Rhineland,
Austria, or Memel.[3]

The Duce's outlook was dutifully reported in the Italian press. On
April 2, *Popolo d'Italia* spoke of the need for common action in the

face of certain eventualities. At Stresa, it said, the necessary responsibilities must be assumed, despite election results in England and France that were competitions in pacifism. The Duce, like the Supreme Court, followed the election returns. Stresa ought to be "a steadfast rock in the agitated sea of European politics." Britain and France should renounce the utopia of disarmament as Italy had done since 1922. Concrete results must be obtained at Stresa before any bells were rung.[4]

On April 8, *Giornale d'Italia* published a report from London that in Britain there was a growing tendency to disassociate her policy from France and Italy which it would be blindness not to see.[5]

The Italian press, on the same day, admitted Britain's strength. But it was not enough to be strong: "It is necessary also to be resolute and to avail oneself of one's strength. Irresolution is tantamount to weakness."

Mussolini had another item for the Stresa agenda. The defeated Central Powers, Austria, Hungary, and Bulgaria still remained under the arms limitations of the postwar treaties. To give them some consideration in the face of German rearmament seemed to him only prudent.

Abyssinia was, of course, much on his mind. He was concerned about reported German and Czech shipments of arms to Abyssinia and the possibility that Germany would try to establish influence there and elsewhere in Africa. There was potential, he thought, for mischief which boded ill not only for Italy, but for Britain and France.[6]

Abyssinia was not on the formal agenda at Stresa. There never was any doubt that the prime purpose of the conference was to face the problems raised by Germany's unilateral denunciation of the peace treaties and by her menacing, fast-growing war machine. But the thought occurred, and to many, that Stresa might be a useful forum for the discussion of Abyssinia and perhaps for some friendly agreement among the Tripartite Treaty powers.

Thus, on March 27, 1935, Signor Vitetti, who had approached the British Government in January hoping to establish an Abyssinian dialogue, told Geoffrey Thompson that the Italian authorities thought Stresa might offer important opportunities for informal discussion of the Abyssinian problem. Thompson replied that the same thought had occurred to him and to his colleagues.[7]

The First Secretary of the Italian Embassy in London, Signor Fracassi, again approached Thompson on April 5, 1935, suggesting that the ancient problems of grazing rights in the Ogaden ought to be resolved; he hoped, too, that he might see Lt. Colonel Clifford's report. Vitetti had clearly got Rome's ear; Rome suggested that the proposed discussions could, as Italy had earlier suggested, cover "the mutually harmonious development of economic rights in Ethiopia."

Thompson sidestepped the main issue; it was, he said, a question for Ministers to discuss, though informal discussions could be helpful. As to mutual interests, he informed Fracassi of Sir John Maffey's committee which would lay the basis for any such talks.

Thus it happened, that at the particular request of the Italian Ambassador, approved by Vansittart, Thompson was instructed to go to Stresa. "I trust some good may come out of it," Vansittart endorsed.[8]

The Italian authorities would hardly have proceeded in this matter without Mussolini's consent. He was perfectly willing to discuss Abyssinia at Stresa. Indeed it seemed to him natural enough. The immense importance of the issues facing Europe, and the steadying and unifying role which Italy could play all seemed to him reasons why the Abyssinian issue should be amenable both to reasonable discussion and solution.

He was confident of his military preparations. An Abyssinian campaign would be consistent with much of Mussolini's ideology and oratory throughout the Fascist era. Mussolini made a clear distinction: a European war would be an irretrievable disaster and he was willing to put Italy in the forefront of the effort to prevent one. But a colonial campaign, a campaign such as France had recently concluded in Morocco, and such as Britain waged regularly on the fringes of her great Empire, was to Mussolini different not only in size, but also in kind.

Inflated as he was with his own oratory evoking the grandeur of Rome and the civilizing mission of Fascist Italy, he could readily view a colonial war, far from being a disaster, as bringing the blessings of law, order, discipline and restraint, not to mention Italian culture, to a backward, benighted, corrupt, slaveholding land.

But perhaps the campaign would not be necessary. On April 10, 1935, the day before the Stresa conference convened, Italy informed the Secretary General of the League of Nations that it did not consider the procedure under the 1928 Italo-Abyssinian Treaty exhausted and that it was prepared to enter into direct talks and name negotiators.[9] Mussolini was now prepared for Stresa.

Looking to Stresa 2—France

France shared Italian views on the European situation and Italy's desire for the Stresa conference to confront concrete cases and produce workable results.

Laval laid out France's concerns and prepared France's position. Germany's action, he said, revealed the progress of German rearmament, and hence the German danger. It obliged the Western powers to confront the issue of unilateral treaty denunciations. Italy and France could not, he said, accept as a basis of negotiation that Germany should set its own military limits.

Moreover, the issue of the Rhineland was critical. Germany had so far promised to respect Locarno. But what were German assurances worth? One day there would be another fait accompli. It was important to be prepared, and to react immediately. The Locarno powers must know in advance what they would do. For France, it was to put the procedures of the Locarno Treaty immediately into effect.[10]

Thus it was that France went to Stresa with a full dossier of facts and figures showing German military and paramilitary activity in the Rhineland and the immediacy of the threat.[11]

Like Italy, France was concerned about the British attitude. François-Poncet, French Ambassador to Berlin, painted for Pierre Laval a withering picture of Sir John Simon in Berlin. Before arriving, Hitler had subjected him to three insults: his purported illness, the announcement of the air force, and the army law of March 16, completely disposing of the principal subjects which Simon had come to discuss. But Simon, he reported, made a mild protest and came to Berlin full of smiles, looking at the triple insult through rose-colored glasses. Throughout the meeting he had, far from complaining, been full of politeness and gentility. He congratulated himself on having made the acquaintance of Führer and quitted Berlin full of eulogies and thanks to his host.[12]

The British ambassador in Paris took pains to brief Simon on French attitudes prior to the Stresa meeting. France no longer believed that Germany had rearmed solely to impose its will by the threat of arms. Instead, Germany would carry out the policy of *Mein Kampf*, deliberately and remorselessly preparing a war of revenge on France for which France was ill-prepared. The French Government had concluded that the time for seeking a General Settlement had passed. Such a search would only encourage Germany to tear up more treaties. No firm action had been taken, convincing Hitler that he was right and the German people that Hitler was right. The time for wavering had passed; the time for action had come.[13]

French soundings in Rome were more encouraging. Charles de Chambrun, the French ambassador, reported to Laval Mussolini's interview with the editor of *Temps*. The Duce had told the editor that he did not exclude another German coup, whether in Austria, Memel, Czechoslovakia or the demilitarized zone of the Rhine. To avoid it, unity among the Western powers was indispensable. The real point, Mussolini declared, of the Stresa conference was to arrive at concrete solutions for each of the concrete cases to which he had referred. He added that Italy had 8 million men under arms; France therefore ought not to worry if some small fraction were employed to reinforce the security of Italian East Africa.[14]

Laval telegraphed Chambrun the same day that no occasion should be given to Germany to claim a lapse of Locarno, and that the powers at Stresa must be prepared to act immediately and jointly in a breach of the demilitarized zone.[15]

Chambrun in turn reported to Laval his later discussion with Mussolini, occasioned by Laval's wire. All depended, Mussolini said, on the attitude of Britain, which appeared to him highly equivocal. It was hardly to be expected that the English would bring any solutions to Stresa.[16]

If there were to be concrete solutions, there would have to be concrete preparations. The French military staff carried on detailed discussions in March with the Italian General Staff, elaborating mutually reinforcing troop movements in four specific cases of German action.

France would go to Stresa with logical, clear, carefully considered programs—programs for a European security pact, proposals for an air pact, and a memorandum on the use of economic and financial sanctions to brake German rearmament. It was this last element that intrigued France.[17] France had always sought some automatic and effective response to a breach of the Covenant. The economic sanction was the legitimate scion of French initiatives since 1919, and the proposal would enliven the proceedings at Stresa.

Looking to Stresa 3—The British Cabinet

The connection between Abyssinia and Europe was evident. Vansittart had in a memorandum of February 25, 1935, put the problem with crystal clarity. Italian expansion in Abyssinia was inevitable.

> *We* have got comfortably and richly over that period. I have sometimes thought it was a pity we didn't let Italy have a German Colony in 1919. We were really imprudently greedy. The impending episode is the sequel of our hogging policy then.

What to do? In the first instance, try to dissuade Italy from going all the way for the triple reasons that she would need her hands free to face graver issues in Europe; that a deadly blow would be dealt to the League of Nations; and that there would be an enormously adverse impact on British public opinion when Italian confidence and collaboration were most needed.

It all had to be done in the quietest, most friendly way:

> And for the gravest and highest of reasons, reasons which concern the maintenance of peace in Europe and therefore the lives and safety of our people, we cannot afford to quarrel with Italy and drive her back into German embraces.

This would be, Vansittart warned, not only folly but "a grave and foolish departure from the policy of realism, on which our existence depends."

However unpleasant, then, Britain must look to her interests and decide what "precise representations" to make—a euphemism for a deal—when the real forward movement began. On such a policy Vansittart pronounced a regretful judgment:

> The action foreshadowed in this letter is out of keeping with the modern world as we would wish it, but not, alas, as it is.[18]

There could be no greater contrast between the realism and clarity of Vansittart and the thoroughly muddled state of mind of the British Cabinet in session April 8, 1935 to consider its Stresa policy.

If France and Italy asked for an end to British discussions with Germany which they thought both unprofitable and inflammatory, the Cabinet would not agree. Furthermore, "If France and Italy asked us to join them in a statement that we would not stand a breach of the peace anywhere, that meant in effect that we would be prepared to take forcible action anywhere." Before this suggestion the Cabinet retreated to its habitual stance—no new commitments.

Nor did the Cabinet see Stresa as determining policy. It was, in their eyes, a necessary stage in clarifying the position and educating public opinion at home and abroad: "To adopt Signor Mussolini's view would be to throw German public opinion more behind Hitler than ever, and to drag us into escapades which we had no intention to follow."

No, instead it would be advisable to keep Germany fully informed of the Stresa proceedings, "so as not to undo the good of the Berlin visit." Moreover, British considerations ought to be put in the friendliest way to Germany, "so that the German people may be impressed morally and spiritually."

Nothing daunted, the Cabinet would, at the same time as it was morally and spiritually uplifting the German people, try to "convince M. Flandin and Signor Mussolini that we had no intention of leaving them in the lurch." With the cheery confidence of a practiced swindler, the Cabinet observed: "The idea of this was to get their confidence without isolating Germany at Stresa."

There was one shrewd observation: the British people had concluded from the last war that war was foolish. The Germans had concluded that the mistake was to fight everyone at once.

The Cabinet drew lines of policy that were consciously vague. Emphasize, it admonished, the solidarity of members of the League of Nations and support of the Covenant. (The Peace Ballot had registered two million votes in March. The week in which this Cabinet meeting took place was the first million vote week.)

There should be no commitments in Eastern Europe—only moral support for arrangements of other powers. Any such arrangements should be entered under the auspices of the League.

Finally, Britain could undertake no special responsibilities in Austria; anything that was to be done there should be also done under League auspices.

There was a special warning:

> The cabinet were reminded that the Naval part of the German conversations had not yet been reported to the other Powers.

So Britain would go to Stresa with two cards face down—naval talks with Germany and British policy on the Rhineland. The decision of January 14 that the Rhineland was not a vital British interest stood. The Foreign Secretary made this clear:

> 3. I should prefer not to make a specific declaration about the 'demilitarized zone' though this would be included in the general reference. It would be better to speak of the obligations of the Treaty as a whole instead of picking out one set of obligations to the exclusion of others.
> 4. We should avoid making any public declaration or giving any private assurance which defines exactly what we would do in a particular hypothetical case. . . . '(Even) If the French persist'. . . it is surely most undesirable to be drawn into the discussion of these distinctions.

What the Cabinet had in mind was words, not acts, as the final paragraph makes clear:

> 5. We should remember throughout, and remind the French, that the main purpose of any pronouncement about the sanctity of Locarno at Stresa is to give the Germans notice that, though they may have disregarded Treaty obligations about armaments, they had better be warned about disregarding Locarno.

As for an air pact, the Cabinet thought there should be no attempt at mutual support arrangements among Britain, Italy and France; this might be inconsistent with Locarno, and Germany should be brought in.

A plea, then, for discussions with Germany and an obligatory obeisance to the League of Nations and collective security (always provided Britain accepted no new commitments) concluded this remarkable meeting.[19]

Stresa

On the day following the Cabinet meeting, Simon assured the House of Commons that Britain would undertake no commitments at Stresa or at the League Council meeting which was to follow. This caused equal disappointment in Rome and Paris, where the need for firmness and a common front were emphasized. *Popolo d'Italia* thought that it would be "incredible and inadmissible" if no concrete discussions of any kind should take place at Stresa. It was reported from Stresa that the choice of experts suggested that the Abyssinian questions would come up for review.[20]

The Duce was to preside at the conference and he outdid himself with the arrangements. The Borromeo Palace occupied Isola Bella, an idyll of art, architecture, and nature set down in the blue waters of Lake Maggiore. It was spring. Azaleas, camellias, hyacinths, oranges and magnolias, which filled the gardens and lined the streets of Stresa, furnished soft scents and softer contrasts to the majestic snow-capped Alps surrounding the lake. Added color was supplied by the reds, the whites, the greens, and the blues of the flags of Great Britain, France, and Italy, everywhere to be seen. The arrangements had been plain and simple for Hitler's visit to Venice the year before and the contrast was evident.

Prince Borromeo had lent his palace for the conference which would take place in the Music Hall. Featured among the rich furnishings and statuary were the paintings of Tempesta, who was given asylum by Count Vitaliano Borromeo when he fled Genoa on the false charge of murdering his wife. The room where Napoleon had slept during his Italian campaign of 1797 was left untouched, but the other principal reception rooms were embellished with works of Titian, Van Dyke, Leonardo, and Guido Reni, sent up for the occasion from the Borromeo Palace in Milan.

The meals would be served in the Room of the Medals. The sculptured wooden medals depicted various episodes in the life of St. Charles Borromeo.

These were perhaps the only memorials to humility and the spiritual life in the Room of the Medals. Prince Borromeo wished to do honor to the occasion. His staff would be in costume. The sixteen footmen who served the assembled statesmen would wear the liveries of Cardinal Edward, last of the five Borromeo cardinals.

Prudent provisions were made for security. Mussolini was accompanied by his personal bodyguard who slept in the theater.

Mussolini arrived first. In the afternoon his trimotor seaplane landed beside the palace and soon above it flew his personal flag, the lictor's emblem embroidered in gold against a dark blue ground, and fringed in gold.[21] The French delegates, Prime Minister Pierre Etienne Flandin and Foreign Minister Pierre Laval, arrived that evening. On the morrow, April 11, the British delegation arrived. It was headed by Prime Minister Ramsay MacDonald, in rapidly failing health, here to attend his last international conference. He was accompanied by Sir John Simon. Anthony Eden had been unable to come. He had suffered a mild heart attack en route home to London from Moscow. In his place came Sir Robert Vansittart, thereby breaking the ancient tradition that the Foreign Secretary and the Permanent Undersecretary ought never to leave England at the same time.[22]

These were scenes of paradoxical grandeur and glory for the three once passionate and youthful Socialists, Benito Mussolini, Pierre Laval, and Ramsay MacDonald. The flag of the Italian Head of State which flew over Prince Borromeo's palace was also the flag of the blacksmith's son who had been in his youth a casual laborer, a tramp, a deserter, a panhandler in Swiss streets, who had slept in packing crates and warmed himself in the public lavatory, who had served time in the jails of three countries as a vagabond, an agitator, and an enemy of the state. Here was Pierre Laval, the boy-of-all-work at his father's inn, the rabble rouser, the rebel, who cheek by jowl with the midwife, the three franc dentist, and the pawnbroker whose white tie he borrowed, proclaimed himself the brother of manual laborers, the manual lawyer. Here, too, was James Ramsay MacDonald, the illegitimate son of a poverty-stricken Scottish croft, the apprentice clerk and union organizer who had nearly starved in his first years in London, subsisting on hot water and oatmeal sent from home. He had, like Mussolini, bitterly opposed the 1914 war while Laval was in 1914 one of two French deputies on Carnet B, the special list of subversives liable to arrest on the outbreak of war.

Far from having remolded the states against which they had once so ardently rebelled in the image of their youthful enthusiasms, they had adapted to the exigencies of power. They had come together to consider what concert of declaration or action might arrest the swelling power of Germany and of Adolf Hitler.

Hitler, too, had known hunger and privation. He had been a tramp, a day laborer, a denizen of flophouses, a sworn enemy of the state. What distinguished Adolf Hitler from Benito Mussolini, Pierre Laval, and Ramsay MacDonald was that he had never shared the generous impulses of their youths.

The Experts

On April 11, 1935 while the heads of state were meeting in the Borromeo Palace, Geoffrey Thompson discussed Abyssinia with Signor Vitetti and Signor Guarnaschelli. In a way, these talks were a continuation of the discussion Vitetti had initiated in London in January.

Thompson noted British discomfort at the widespread rumors of an Italian military movement against Abyssinia in October when the rains stopped. He hoped there was no truth in them. Guarnaschelli said he did not know the Duce's mind; certainly he was seriously concerned with the situation and the possibility of an offensive could not be dismissed. He held little hope for conciliation.

He put Italy's case in the most ingratiating manner. Compare, he urged Thompson, Abyssinia, a fourteenth-century empire, with its slavery, cruelty, and xenophobia, its resources undeveloped, with the enlightened and humane development being carried out in the British colonies and mandates.

Thompson stated bluntly that Italy would get no cooperation from Britain in any attack on Abyssinia. To the contrary, beyond the cost in blood and money, there would be a heavy cost in Anglo-Italian relations. There was a very vocal and humanitarian element in our public opinion, he said, and they would not conceal their feelings.

The same element, Guarnaschelli replied, had opposed Japan's policy in Manchuria but they had not prevented the eventual recognition by His Majesty's Government of the state of Manchukuo. He added that the Abyssinian question *might* be discussed at Stresa.[23]

The lengthy talks the next day covered all aspects of the Abyssinian issue. The Italians reiterated their complaints—even Germany was now demanding colonial rewards while Italy had been unjustly deprived of the fruits of victory. Thompson again warned of the consequences of an Italian campaign in Abyssinia and especially the repercussions in Europe. He did not attempt, he said, to answer their arguments, only to deliver a message. They arrived at a joint recommendation. Britain would make available to Italy the report of the Anglo-Abyssinian commission. Britain would remain faithful to the 1906 treaty and seek no economic advantage or rights which would adversely affect the status quo established by the treaty.[24]

The Conference

The British delegates had been amply warned of Italian preparations in Africa. On April 11, the opening day of the conference, Sir Sidney Barton, the British Ambassador at Addis Ababa, wired Simon at Stresa a complete description of the Italian efforts:

> Quite definitely you can expect war in October, do not be gulled by what you read in the papers. As soon as the rains are over they are going to advance. I do not see how Abyssinians are going to stop them as they are wonderfully well-equipped and have besides all the new troops 25,000 Somalis.

But normal courtesies were exchanged between the prospective adversaries. Sir Sidney had dined on two occasions with Major Cimmaruta who had been the Italian commander at Wal Wal. The two empire builders appreciated each other. The Major was, Sir Sidney said, "a very decent chap." Cimmaruta, in turn, showed Mussolini's telegram of congratulations and told how he had been promoted in the field. He then returned to Wal Wal.[25]

Britain and France assumed familiar postures as the conference opened. MacDonald stated that Britain would remain a loyal partner in the League and would cooperate with France and Italy to make the League supreme "as the moral authority in Europe."

M. Flandin did not dwell on moral considerations. What struck France, he said, in connection with the recent treaty violations was the need to devise machinery which would operate automatically in order to prevent further violations. This had been the French position from the birth of the League.

When the Central European pact was discussed, Simon related Hitler's opinion that Austria would inevitably join the German Reich. He did not need to shake the tree, MacDonald added; the fruit would fall into his hand when it was ripe.

The day that fruit fell, Mussolini observed darkly Germany would have 80 million inhabitants.[26]

Mussolini was curious. He asked Simon if Hitler had really claimed air parity with Britain. He had, Simon replied, without elaborating. He added that an air convention would clearly be useful. Laval was ready with French proposals designed to meet a German attack on Britain, or France, or Italy. He added that the French delegation also had proposals as to the Eastern European pact, the Central European pact, and the League of Nations. It was necessary to produce tangible results at Stresa, not a vague communiqué.

He went to the heart of the matter. France had appealed to the League based on the German actions of March 9 and March 16. If there were another treaty violation, what would Britain, France and Italy do?[27]

MacDonald agreed that the issue could be discussed but "there might well be points which British public opinion would be unable to accept" and which would require further study. Laval persisted. He offered a draft resolution on treaty violations for the League Council to adopt.[28]

Simon backpedaled with dexterity. The dream of an agreement with Germany had survived his frigid reception by the Führer. Ought not, he asked, Germany be consulted first? MacDonald thought that at an appropriate time efforts should be made to get Germany to understand the gravity of the situation.[29] This implied a belief that the Führer lacked such understanding.

At the second session, Laval again went to the heart of the issue. The French draft resolutions contained proposals for economic sanctions. The League Council had to act, he said, "otherwise the Council would make itself ridiculous."[30]

Economic sanctions were stern stuff for Simon. His lawyerly reflexes reacted. If a person were the subject of an accusation, he said, it was usual to communicate the accusation to that person and give him the opportunity to state his defense. Simon's stance was grounded in English common law; Hitler's in German interests. MacDonald seconded his Foreign Secretary. They ought, he opined, to bring Germany before the bar of all decent opinion in Europe, nay the world.[31] This was too much for Flandin. The time was long past, he said, for moral sanctions. France would never agree that the unilateral repudiation or treaties could not be prevented.[32]

He went on to say:

If they did not draw the necessary consequences from the violation that had occurred, the position would be intolerable. Let there be no delusion; violations in the past had succeeded so well that there would be more in the future.[33]

Flandin came to the point. If Germany remilitarized the Rhineland,

France would forthwith invoke Locarno. The proposed economic sanctions were designed to avoid such an eventuality. MacDonald asked for time to consider the French draft.

When they reconvened, MacDonald reported that the prospect for British collaboration in economic and financial sanctions was not encouraging. "Would it not be possible," he asked, "to make some declaration as to the seriousness of the situation, without actually establishing a committee (as the French proposed) as to economic and financial action?"

This was the British theme throughout the conference. Instead of concrete action, could there not be a declaration of concern? Mussolini had been unaccustomedly silent, the attentive observer of the Franco-British dialogue. He now said he agreed with the French delegation.

MacDonald and Simon knew they were in deep water. Summoning up his fading facilities, MacDonald put the question direct to Flandin. If the Council passed the French resolution and Germany committed another violation the next day, what would France do?

Flandin did not hesitate. He would ask his Government to mobilize the French army.[34]

Mussolini remembered his pact with France. If anything, he said, the French resolution was too moderate.[35]

MacDonald and Simon now recalled something else—the assurances they had given Parliament that no commitments would be undertaken at Stresa. It was impossible, MacDonald said, for him and Simon to return and report that they had committed the British Government to action anywhere in the world.

Flandin held firm. Once again he stated what to him was painfully obvious. The peace of Europe was at stake, there would be irreparable damage to that peace unless Stresa made it clear that violations like that of March 16 would not be passed over without action. He then expressed a thought that gave him comfort. In any event, France had a guaranty greater than the Covenant. That guaranty was Locarno.[36] Did MacDonald and Simon think in that moment of the British cabinet's resolution of January 14—that the Rhineland was not a vital British interest?

MacDonald returned to the task of adding large quantities of water to the thin soup of commitment. Could not instead, he plaintively inquired, a resolution be drafted which said that they would not be indifferent to further violations which endangered the peace of Europe and that they agreed to call a meeting of the League Council to deliberate on what should be done.

He now spoke the plain truth. "What he was trying to do," he said, "was to find a way of declaring that they could not be indifferent to violations without at the same time entering into the definite commitments which had been included in the French draft."[37]

Still struggling to escape from the nets which France cast time and again, Simon opened the fourth session with a reminder of the assurance he had given to the House of Commons that Britain would enter no new engagements at Stresa.[38] Pierre Laval displayed his legal talents. He would have no trouble in the House of Commons, he said, reconciling that assurance with the French draft resolution. Simon recognized a skillful advocate when he saw one. He would try, he said, to join in the French draft, but some amendments might be necessary.[39]

An important point was now clarified. If Germany were not prepared to enter into an Eastern European pact, would she object to bilateral arrangements for mutual assistance there? Simon said that he had received assurances from the German Foreign Minister that Germany would not object.[40]

Laval plunged into this opening. France now had the latitude, he observed, to proceed with a bilateral Franco-Soviet pact of mutual assistance. This was a point pregnant for the future. The main lines of the pact had not yet been fixed, but he would keep Britain and Italy fully informed.[41] Here was another omen.

Simon urged that any Franco-Soviet pact be constructed within the framework of the League of Nations because he said, of the attitude of British public opinion.[42]

When the Central European pact was again discussed, Mussolini took the lead. *Anschluss* would not only be a direct threat to Italy, but an indirect danger to everybody. He detailed the consequences. Something must be done for Austria, he said. He would propose a resolution reaffirming the declarations of February and September last.[43]

The Stresa meeting ought to do better than that, Laval said. He preferred an agreement to a resolution. This naturally evoked the rejoinder from Simon, that Britain's relation to the issue was not the same as that of the continental states. Britain could support a pact, but could not contract into it. Britain would be in the position of a state, that blessed and approved without being committed further.[44]

France now presented a plan for an air pact. Simon again tested

French will. Was France prepared to come to the aid of Italy? Laval's answer was a single word—Yes.[45]

Simon looked wistfully to Germany. Instead of bilateral pacts, perhaps it would be wise to get all of the Locarno powers, including Germany to agree to a draft treaty.[46] Laval thought otherwise. He favored bilateral pacts which had meaning. After Mussolini had given challenging and detailed estimates of German air strength, Laval observed that the best thing for all of them to do was to build as many airplanes as possible, and of the best quality.[47]

The wheel turned round once more. Was German rearmament a fait accompli, Laval inquired rhetorically? The answer was obvious. This gave him the opportunity to sum up. France wanted to create a chain of peace, he said, and that chain went from Paris to Rome. It would be completed with a Soviet agreement. Germany could then no longer impose her will.[48]

After a discussion concerning rearmament of Austria, Hungary, and Bulgaria, Laval again raised the issue of the demilitarized zone. He submitted France's memorandum detailing German military activity there.[49] We may very soon be faced, it said, with the fait accompli of reoccupation.[50]

MacDonald's misty mind harked back to the defunct Disarmament Conference. Could not something favorable be said about the Conference?[51] Mussolini declared the Conference hopeless. Perhaps, Simon said, they might declare that Hitler's March strokes had gravely prejudiced the prospect of an arms agreement and that a report in that sense should be transmitted to the President of the Disarmament Conference.[52]

Pierre Laval poured on this suggestion the ice water of Gallic realism. There were circumstances, he offered, in which it was wise to say nothing at all for the sake of dignity.[53]

It was Mussolini who next raised the issue of the demilitarized zone. The British delegates were prepared, faithful to the Cabinet's instructions. They proposed a simple reaffirmation of Locarno, omitting any mention of specific cases. This evoked French gratitude. It would have a profound effect, Laval said, on the French people.[54]

The deliberations were over. Flandin once more said how much France would appreciate the reaffirmation of Locarno.[55]

What had the Conference wrought? The vigorous leadership of Mussolini and the firm determination of France to arrive at concrete courses of action to face up to the German threat contrasted to the British horror of any commitment and Britain's yearning for some kind of arrangement with Germany. The clarity, the logic, the pertinacity, and the force of the Franco-Italian position had been met by British vacillations, hesitancies, and obfuscations. In the end, Britain demonstrated that by her own reluctance to act, she could forestall meaningful action by others.

This was illustrated by the Joint Resolutions of the Conference. They affirmed that the three Powers had agreed on a common line of conduct to be pursued at the meeting of the League Council. They confirmed their view that negotiations should be pursued for the development of security in Eastern Europe. They reaffirmed the Anglo-French-Italian declarations of September 27, 1934 and February 17, 1935 concerning the independence and integrity of Austria and recommended a conference to discuss a Central European pact. They agreed to continue discussions of an air pact and any related bilateral agreements.

How did they respond to Germany's unilateral violations of Treaty? They "regretfully recognized" the German action, which had invalidated the assumptions upon which disarmament efforts had been based. This led to a modest conclusion:

> The Representatives of the three Powers nevertheless reaffirmed their earnest desire to sustain peace by establishing a sense of security and declare for themselves that they remained anxious to join in every practical effort for promoting international agreement on the limitation of armaments.[56]

This clause spoke in the voice of Ramsay MacDonald and not Benito Mussolini or Pierre Laval. Vansittart called it an agreement "with dentures, not teeth."[57]

In a separate declaration, Britain and Italy reaffirmed their Locarno obligations. There had been no discussions of concrete cases. The plan of evasion foreseen by the British Cabinet had succeeded.

The climax of the work of the Conference was its final declaration:

> The three Powers, the object of whose policy is the collective maintenance of peace within the framework of the League of Nations, found themselves in complete agreement in opposing by all practicable means, any unilateral repudiation of treaties which may endanger the peace of Europe, and will act in close or cordial collaboration for this purpose.[58]

The hopes of Signor Guarnaschelli had not been fulfilled. It was notable that the conferees, who gave extended attention to Memel, never mentioned Abyssinia at Stresa. Flandin recalled the discussion of the final draft of the declaration:

> The final draft, when it came up for discussion, reviewed the various outstanding problems in Europe—*but did not make the reference to Africa* which, presumably, Mussolini was awaiting. When he came to the phrase 'after having reviewed the various outstanding international problems' he paused for a moment and said, 'Shouldn't we add *in Europe?*' This was a clear invitation to the British delegates to refer to Abyssinia. But neither MacDonald nor John Simon blinked. *Laval and I, and presumably Mussolini, got the impression that the British Government had given its implied consent to Italy's Abyssinian ambitions.*[59]

Vansittart summarized the same moment:

> We wanted to 'strengthen peace' generally. That would make a *finale*, but Mussolini interpolated 'in Europe.' Since we could not even keep it there, we could hardly cavil at the limitation; but some took him to intend a free hand in Africa.[60]

This was the view Mussolini took. He chided Grandi, his Ambassador in London and expert in British policy: "You said they would say Yes on Austria and No on Abyssinia. Instead they said No on Austria and Yes on Abyssinia."[61]

Why had Britain so carefully evaded the issue? Anthony Eden had advised Simon to confront Mussolini on Abyssinia.[62] Sir Eric Drummond had made the same recommendation, adding that Simon should start the conference with a warning.

But Vansittart had disagreed:

> Knowing the fellow's [Mussolini's] antipathy to Ramsay and John, I felt that by such a course we should never sit down at all. We should not save Abyssinia by immediate quarrel, and should certainly lose Austria if we broke up abortively. I told Eric that I thought a better tactic might be to land Mussolini first and lecture him later. Get an agreement, I suggested, make it look valuable if we can—and there is the rub—then tell him that all will go for nothing if he embroils himself for nothing.[63]

Perhaps the last word was spoken by Anthony Eden when he said that at times diplomacy must decide what to act upon and what to sweep under the rug.[64]

But the matter went far beyond the issue of Abyssinia. Georges Bonnet depicted MacDonald and Simon as cold and reserved. "Their one steady intention was to keep clear of the hornet's nest of Central Europe."[65]

Vansittart agreed and gave the reason:

> The Italians were out to save Europe, the French to secure eastern Europe, but the British people cared for none of these things.

The problem for the British delegates was twofold: how far could they go, backed by inadequate armed forces. To this Vansittart replied:

> The answer was always the same: no more than the electorate would allow, and it would not allow enough to keep up an anti-German front.[66]

The modest achievements of Stresa, and the League Council action that followed marked the height of Franco-Italian-British cooperation on the continent of Europe. There was much talk of the Stresa Front.

Germany was unimpressed. The British Ambassador informed Simon that the German press regarded the Stresa conference with quiet satisfaction. There had been protests, but no action.[67] Lord Cecil was not satisfied at all. To him Stresa was an "alliance," a special arrangement outside the League of Nations from which Germany had been excluded.[68]

The League Council Resolves

The next act in the Stresa scenario was played out at Geneva where the Council of the League of Nations met to consider the French resolution on economic and financial sanctions.

France reviewed its security proposals, starting in 1919. The resolution stated the duty of all states to observe treaty obligations; citing Germany's Treaty violations, it declared Germany had failed in the duty of all members of the international community to respect the undertakings which they have contracted. This was mild language indeed.

The resolution then called for a committee to propose means to make the Covenant more effective, and economic and financial measures to be applied against treaty breakers.[69]

France had finally succeeded in bringing to Geneva the concept, however mild, of economic and financial sanctions.

No state other than France, Italy, and Britain could be found to present the resolution when the meeting opened on April 16, 1935. Germany was too strong and too close to many of the Council members. The three proponents offered their own resolution.

The smaller nations of the Council had misgivings over the resolution and the unusual procedure. Clearly there was much they did not know about the meeting at Stresa; clearly they were being asked to endorse the decision of the three Powers.

The Soviet delegate, Maxim Litvinov, inquired especially why the resolution, like the five final Stresa declarations, spoke only of treaties affecting Europe. Was it meant to exclude other areas?[70]

Simon wanted no broadening of what had been so arduously extracted from him. With some heat he ascribed the limiting words to the limited content of the Stresa conference. It had concerned itself with European problems; hence the resolution.[71]

But why, some delegates wondered, did the meeting not consider Abyssinia? The answer was that on April 10, Italy had informed Abyssinia that it would proceed to conciliation under the 1928 Treaty, named two members of the conciliation commission and agreed upon terms of reference, to all of which Haile Selassie had agreed.[72]

The Council had therefore excluded Abyssinia from the agenda of the extraordinary session on the dual grounds that it was clearly on the May agenda and that the parties had agreed on conciliation.[73]

Denmark abstained from the vote on the resolution. Germany's immediate neighbor, she had lost Schleswig to a Prussian attack in 1864. Germany was, of course, absent. The required unanimous vote was obtained; the resolution was adopted.[74]

Germany duly protested the resolution. What was clearly seen in Germany was that once again declarations had been made, once again resolutions had been passed, and once again no meaningful action had been taken. Unilateral treaty denunciation was proving to be a profitable, and not even a risky, business.

Added to the Stresa Declarations, the resolution of the League Council did offer a basis for the organization of European security but only if the states of Europe could remain of the same mind and could also translate declarations and resolutions into reality.

This was not easy. Italy had followed up willingness to arbitrate the

Abyssinian issue by staking out the position that the location of Wal Wal relative to the frontier was irrelevant to the arbitration. That Wal Wal was Abyssinian territory was the basis of the Abyssinian case. Haile Selassie, incensed, thought he had been tricked.

Simon suggested an abbreviated time schedule for the arbitration so the May meeting of the League would know if further action were needed. The Emperor promptly agreed. This incensed Mussolini who thought the British were trying to trick him.[75] The tensions of Abyssinia were placing early and increasing strains on the Stresa Front.

The Voice of the Public

If Lord Cecil disliked the Stresa method and its results, he would have been well satisfied, had he been privy to the proceedings, with one particular aspect. The British delegates in conference, and British diplomats in dealing with their foreign colleagues, made it clear that the limits of British policy were set by public opinion. That there was a large, vocal, and active public opinion was constantly on their minds.

It could hardly have been otherwise. By brilliant organization and publicity, and the incessant labours of his half million volunteers, the Peace Ballot was producing extraordinary results.

In March and April, the large cities began to report, Manchester and Birmingham. In April, Huddersfield reported a 69 percent poll. The Huddersfield committee was widely representative. It included a canon of the Church of England, a schoolmaster, a trade union official, a railway employee, a bank clerk, weavers, social workers, and an education expert. The spirit of the team that produced the result was exemplified by the comment of one of them: "Our only regret," he said, "is that we did not know one another sooner."[76]

Wales gave a fervent response to the Peace Ballot, with many communities recording votes of 80 percent of the electorate and higher. Only in April did the early London returns start to flow in. To the 2 million votes received in March, April added 2.8 million. By May 2, 7,290,895 Britons had cast their ballots. From the beginning, the votes hardly varied. They showed a consistent 97 percent of the voters supporting continued British membership in the League of Nations; and over 90 percent supporting all-round disarmament by international agreement, the abolition of the private manufacture of arms, and economic sanctions.[77] These were results which the elected representa-

tives of the people were not likely to ignore. A storm of immense
proportions was impending on the horizon and how to ride it out, or
even take advantage of it, was the normal concern of prudent politicians, policymakers, and the executants of those policies.

The Duce Reaches Out

Mussolini had said of his Abyssinian plans that he had calculated
well, he had reflected well, and he had weighed everything. He left
Stresa thinking that British silence implied consent. He was not content to leave it at that. He wanted more concrete assurances that Britain would not stand in his way. He could see no good reason why she
should and many excellent reasons why she should stand aside.

He sent his Ambassador, Grandi, to see Vansittart on April 30,
1935. They respected and dealt honestly with each other. Grandi knew
Vansittart shared Mussolini's fear of Germany and thought Austria
was more critical than Abyssinia.

What Grandi gave Vansittart was a dress rehearsal of his presentation to Simon. It was an appeal to the British Government to adopt a
more sympathetic and helpful attitude to Italy's Abyssinian problem,
combined with assurances that British interests would be protected.

Vansittart issued a blunt warning. If Italy invaded Abyssinia, there
would be an outcry in the press and Parliament and this would, in turn,
provoke Italian replies. This would be tragic in a moment when Britain and Italy should be working to carry out the Stresa resolutions in
the interest of peace.[78]

On the same day Signor Fracassi called on Geoffrey Thompson
with the same mission. Contrary to Simon's suggestions at the meeting of the League Council, Italy did not want any time limits or pressure on the conciliation process.

Thompson told Fracassi that Abyssinia's willingness to accept any
arbitral award had gotten a favorable response. But, he said, there was
another element to take into account:

[I]n any event, his Majesty's Government certainly could not ignore the
views entertained on the subject by public opinion in the country. People
of humanitarian motives were doubtless troublesome; the fact remained,
however, that there was a strong humanitarian streak in our people, and
their spokesmen would make themselves heard. Already the Secretary of
State had been called on to answer four questions in Parliament about the

Italo-Ethiopean dispute. The reactions of our public opinion to Italian policy and the effect on Anglo-Italian relations which might possibly be caused in Italy by public criticism in this country, was one of our preoccupations in this whole question.

Signor Fracassi replied that if further incidents occurred, Italy might be compelled to put the Abyssinians down, if necessary to march to Addis Ababa. What would be the attitude of Great Britain then? This was clearly, said Thompson, a question for the Foreign Secretary. He added that he didn't think a march on Addis Ababa would be easy.[79]

Grandi in turn conveyed the Duce's message to Simon. Abyssinia was a cancer that had to be cut out. Italy could take no other course. What, Simon asked, did Italy want? New territory and uniting Eritrea and Italian Somaliland Grandi replied.

Britain wanted to be friendly and helpful, Simon said. But he could not restrain British public opinion which was sure to be highly aroused. In short, the responsibility lay with Italy. He warned that Italy's Abyssinian policy could adversely affect all Italy had hoped to accomplish at Stresa with Italy spending in Africa the energies that were needed in Europe.

Simon concluded by asking Grandi how he could answer the questions that were bound to be raised in Parliament. This is hardly what Grandi had come to hear. Nor did it respond to his urgent message.[80]

Ramsay MacDonald and Simon could have issued a stern warning to Mussolini at Stresa against Abyssinian aggression. They chose silence. Once again, Simon had the opportunity to warn Mussolini in unmistakable terms. He did not choose to take that opportunity. He had been invited, on repeated occasions, to come to terms with Italy. He had declined to pursue that course. *Popolo d'Italia* had warned on the eve of Stresa that irresolution could be dangerous. Simon chose irresolution.

Eden was shocked and perturbed. He was recuperating from his heart attack when he received Simon's account of his meeting with Grandi. Eden had no confidence that the Foreign Secretary's rather oblique warning would produce a change of heart:

> Once again we were resting our case on the effect of Italian action on British opinion. No firm indication was given of how his Majesty's Government would have to react against Italian aggression in Abyssinia. . . . I wanted to preserve the Stresa Front, but with the best will in the world, I did not see how this could be done if Italy launched herself upon the

conquest of Abyssinia. Grandi was the most astute and experienced of ambassadors and probably realized the dangers to his country of the Abyssinian adventure.

Eden, continuing, reached the heart of the matter:

[B]ut the only conclusion he could draw from his exchange with the Foreign Secretary was that we were troubled and uncertain in our course.

Eden recorded his judgment:

Even from his [Simon's] own account, nothing like stiff enough. Italy's request was a diplomatically phrased demand for a free hand in Abyssinia. This should have been strenuously resisted, emphasis laid on our support of the League, etc. It is useless to ask Musso how he thinks that Simon can answer questions on the subject in the House.[81]

Mussolini had no doubts. He had given Britain every possible warning, every opportunity to react. In an interview in September, he told the *Morning Post* that after Stresa, he had invited Britain to open friendly talks on Abyssinia; "Even that overture led to inconclusive conversations."

Britain had not said yes. More significant to Mussolini, she had not said no—after having been given every opportunity. On this basis, Mussolini was ready to go forward.

One clear warning had been given to Mussolini—British policy would be shaped by British public opinion. This was a warning Mussolini chose to ignore.

15

Arms Control—1935

"Tactless rather than faithless we asked for trouble."

—Sir Robert Vansittart[1]

Voting for Peace

When the British Cabinet prepared for the Stresa Conference, considerations of public opinion were an important influence on policy. At the conference, the British delegates time and again pointed out that public opinion prescribed the limits of British commitments.

Never before had British statesmen been so exposed to and so moved by public opinion. It spoke to them in a volume and with an authority they had never known. Lord Cecil was orchestrating an overwhelming demonstration of public concern for foreign policy issues.

The votes tell the story: from the 5 million votes cast by April 5, the totals swelled in a majestic progression.

Week after week the responses hardly varied. Ninety-seven percent voted Yes to Britain's continuing role in the League of Nations; 92 percent favored disarmament by international agreement; 85 percent favored the abolition of naval and military aircraft; 93 percent voted in favor of the prohibition of the private manufacture of arms; and 94 percent for economic sanctions against an aggressor. Military sanctions were another thing; 74 percent of the recorded Yes and No votes endorsed military sanctions, but there was a large abstaining vote.[2]

Lord Cecil was not hesitant to take advantage of the expression of opinion he had created. At the opening session of the Royal Commission on the Private Manufacture and Trading in Arms on May 1, 1935 he was the first witness.

Proudly he stated that up to the past week, 6,964,000 had voted in the Peace Ballot. By a tally of 6,500,000 to 49,000, they had voted to prohibit the manufacture and sale of arms for profit.

He was pleased to note in his testimony that one effect of the Peace Ballot had been to increase membership in the League of Nations Union. His recommendation to the Royal Commission was sweeping: the total abolition of the private manufacture and trade in weapons. If only Britain would take a strong lead, he said, he was confident of agreement. Never had the opportunity been so good as at the present.[3]

Laval and Soviets

While the British public voted and the British Parliament debated, Pierre Laval went purposefully about his task of containing Germany. On May 2, 1935 in Paris he signed the Franco-Soviet Treaty of Mutual Assistance.

The treaty was not a simple reciprocal engagement by each party to aid the other party under attack. At Stresa, Simon had insisted that a Franco-Soviet pact be drafted within the framework of the League of Nations. Two concerns moved the British public. The first was not to extend British commitments under Locarno. The second was more recent: a fervent interest in the League of Nations.

This made for a complicated treaty. In essence, the treaty spoke in terms of violations of the Covenant and of mutual assistance through the enforcement of the Covenant.[4]

This meant that any obligation or request for mutual assistance under the treaty would be thoroughly enmeshed in the complexities and procrastination of the League of Nations. That was not the way the Soviets had wanted it. But that was what Laval offered. His first concern was Britain. The term of the treaty was five years.

The protocol attached to the treaty spoke to another British concern. It stated that the treaty could not bind any state to obligations contrary to its existing treaty obligations. This was a direct reference to Locarno.

Indeed, the very day the treaty was signed, Simon assured the House of Commons that in the event of a German-Soviet conflict, and French assistance to the Soviets, Britain would incur no obligation whatsoever under Locarno. No new commitments remained the British watchword.

The protocol also stated that if the League Council should fail to act after such action had been requested under the Treaty, the obligation of mutual assistance would come into play. Hitler carefully noted this clause. He would use it skillfully.

A final note in the protocol recalled that there had been proposals for an East European Pact open to all nations in the area and for a related Franco-Soviet-German treaty. This had not been achieved, but the present treaty was designed to be compatible with the larger framework, as well as the procedures of the League of Nations. These provisions were meant to assure Germany that the Pact, to which she could adhere, was not specifically directed against her.[5]

Laval visited Moscow from May 13 to May 15, 1935. The communiqué issued after the visit lauded the new treaty, and declared the will of the parties to safeguard peace, while continuing to pursue regional pacts. From these no nation was excluded; the sincere collaboration of all states was welcome. This was another message of reassurance to Germany.

Laval solved a practical problem at the same time. The French Communist Party had stridently opposed the army law extending the term of service to two years.

This was another occasion where blunt talk produced results. Stalin told Laval: "I can't talk in diplomatic language; I'm not a diplomat." The erstwhile manual lawyer shot back: "All right, you'll get it straight."

How could Stalin pretend, he asked, that he had nothing to do with the Comintern and the French Communist Party? Let him give the word and the French Communists would cease to oppose military preparations that supported the new Treaty. Stalin promptly agreed. The communiqué read:

> M. Stalin understands and fully approves of the policy of national defense carried out by France in order to maintain her armed strength at the level required for her security.[6]

The message was swiftly received and clearly understood by the French Communist Party.

Laval's other problem was Italy and her Abyssinian ambitions. Italy had managed to lengthen the conciliation and arbitration process without meaningful progress. The real progress had been in Italy's open and widely advertised military preparations. Were it to persist in a war of conquest in Abyssinia, Italy would be on a collision course with the League of Nations and the League's supporters. First and foremost among these was Britain where, by June 1, more than 10 million Britons had cast their votes in the Peace Ballot. Of these, 97 percent gave their enthusiastic support to the League of Nations as, in Lord Cecil's words, the cardinal point of British policy.

Anglo-Saxon Attitudes

Ramsay MacDonald reported to the House of Commons on May 2, 1935 on the proceedings at Stresa and Geneva and the then pending Franco-Soviet Pact. Circumstances, he said, had changed since the London Declaration of February calling for a General Settlement in Europe but this still remained the objective of British policy. The participation of Germany was needed and would be welcome.

A future naval agreement between Britain and Germany had been suggested to Sir John Simon during his visit to Berlin. That suggestion, the Prime Minister said, had been accepted and such talks would take place, notwithstanding the ominous German announcement of a new submarine program. To this report, MacDonald added an assurance: not only the United States and Japan but also France and Italy would be informed of what took place "because we have nothing to hide and no intention of making any secret or private agreements."

MacDonald now addressed the German air threat. Baldwin had stated in November, 1934 that Britain would in no circumstances accept a position of inferiority to Germany in the air. Germany now claimed air parity. The government stood on Baldwin's declaration and would take all necessary steps to implement it.[7]

There were predictable responses. George Lansbury counseled prayer and the abolition of aerial warfare. Sir Herbert Samuel concurred that Britain's conscience was uneasy over the wrongs done to Germany. He deprecated the balance of power and declared that all sections of the House were devotedly attached to the collective system. Winston Churchill was sure his warnings had not been heeded and that enough had not been done. The Foreign Secretary assured the House that the Franco-Soviet Pact meant no added British commitment under Locarno. Clement Attlee again announced that only the surrender of national sovereignty would gain anything like a peaceful world.[8] Since he did not advise how to induce Herr Hitler to join in this act of self-abnegation, his contribution lacked practical merit.

In the House of Lords on May 7, 1935, Lord Dickenson offered a

motion regretting the resolution condemning Germany adopted by the
League of Nations Council. He called for negotiations acceptable to
the German people which would assure permanent peace in Europe.
Had Germany been treated as generously at Versailles as the Boers
had been at Vereeniging, he said, Hitler would still be painting sign-
boards in Vienna.

To Lord Mottistone the League's resolution was all an anti-German
stunt and shocking at that. He had always found the Germans decent,
friendly people.

Lord Cecil responded with a withering appraisal of Nazi policies.
His devotion to the collective system had in no way affected his analysis of the facts. Lord Lothian pointed to a practical concern that arose
from the Geneva resolution. The French had incorporated provisions
for sanctions under the Covenant. Would these not spring obligations
in the event of a breach of the Covenant anywhere? This would mean
an express undertaking to uphold the status quo under the threat of
war.[9]

The motion was in the end withdrawn but not before illuminating
the emotional and practical considerations that lay behind British policy.
It was becoming clear that the cause of collective security was gaining
new prominence, a new constituency, and enhanced influence. It was
not a member of the Opposition but Anthony Eden who on May 16,
1935 told the East Fulham Conservative and Unionist Association that
isolation was dead and buried. The balance of power, he said, was no
solution. All that remained was collective security as embodied in the
League of Nations. Instead of talking about new commitments, Britain
should emphasize its will to carry out those that had already undertaken under the Covenant. The knowledge of that determination, Eden
thought, would be the best deterrent to an aggressor.[10]

At the Crossroads

Lord Lothian's concern over the application of sanctions under the
Covenant and Anthony Eden's devotion to collective security under
the Covenant were diametrically opposed views. This divergence now
became the immediate problem for British foreign policy to resolve.

Sir John Simon recognized the conflict. Britain had no quarrel with
any legitimate Italian interest, he wrote to the British Ambassador in
Paris. But if Italy were to go to war in Abyssinia, a grave situation

would be created for France and England, for the League of Nations and for European security. For these reasons, Britain would do all in its power to give Italy an increasing role in the economic development of Abyssinia.[11]

Simon prepared a memorandum for the Cabinet on which he detailed the events since Wal Wal. His conclusion was stark:

> We now have the clearest indication from the Italian Government that they contemplate military operations on an extended scale against Abyssinia as soon as climatic conditions permit and Italian preparations are complete. As the rainy season is understood to end in September, it is probable that the advance will take place in that month or in October; there is a possibility of aerial action before that date.

He was especially clear as to the consequences:

> In the light of the foregoing it will be clear that His Majesty's Government are in this matter likely to be faced with an exceedingly difficult decision. If they support against Italy a practical application of the League principles, their action is bound greatly to compromise Anglo-Italian relations and perhaps even to break the close association at present existing between France, Italy, and the United Kingdom. Indeed Italy's reaction in Signor Mussolini's present mood is incalculable; the possibility of Italy retorting by leaving the League must not be overlooked. In any event, the European situation would be most seriously affected, and it would in fact, be hard to imagine a state of affairs which would be more welcome to Germany.

To break up the Stresa front, to undo the patient work of Laval's diplomacy, to turn Italy, the defender of Austria, into Germany's ally, were the potential consequences of a League policy:

> On the other hand, if the United Kingdom acquiesce in what would be a misuse of the League machinery by acting in a manner acceptable to Italy, but certainly unjust towards Ethiopia, His Majesty's Government will undoubtedly lay themselves open to grave public criticism.

As is so often the case with lawyers, Simon's brilliance was critical and analytical, not creative or imaginative. He offered the Cabinet no solution. He had spoken frankly to the Italian Ambassador in London:

> warning him not only of the harmful effect Italy's becoming entangled in Abyssinia would exert upon the European question, but also of the grave

danger to Anglo-Italian relations of the very strong views undoubtedly held, and certain to be expressed, by British public opinion should Italy embark on an attack upon Ethiopia.

There was no reason to suppose, he candidly added, that this friendly warning had exerted any restraining influence on Rome.[12]

The issue was as clear in Geneva where Joseph Avenol, Secretary General of the League of Nations, wrote to Rene Massigli at the Quai d'Orsay that a conflict between Italy and Abyssinia would be marvelously efficacious to dissolve the Stresa Front.[13]

The French Ambassador in London told Laval of the efforts of the German General Staff to continue exchanges of officers and technical information with Italy, which had begun a year and a half before and which were undoubtedly directed against France. Italy now had declined, for technical reasons, to go beyond an exchange of letters. The German General Staff knew perfectly well, the Ambassador advised, that "today Italy is ranged with joy at the side of France."[14]

The British and French Governments agreed to make joint representations to Italy of the dangers involved and the benefits of a solution acceptable to both parties. Italian disregard of the Covenant, the Kellogg-Briand Pact, and the 1906 Treaty would, Simon wired Drummond in Rome on May 14, 1935, produce results in press, Parliament, and public opinion which would be as deplorable as they would be inevitable:

> You will also appreciate the possible bearing on such a situation of the resolution recently agreed to at Geneva in regard to the repudiation of treaties, and the effect on the whole impression of solidarity happily created at Stresa.[15]

As so often happened, the *Times* had published reports of the proposed Anglo-French representations to Italy before they were made. Mussolini responded in the manner which would mark much of his conduct in the whole Abyssinian affair. As a veteran journalist, he would not let press reports shape his policy.

He acted promptly, making his response before he had ever received the diplomatic visit. He went public. He made his reply not to the British and French diplomats, but to the Italian Senate, a thoroughly captive audience.

He was firm. There had been no such representations, which would, he said, have been unacceptable. Only Italy could judge her necessities in Africa; no one else could tell her what preparations and precautions were sufficient. He would far rather be reproached for having erred on the side of excess than deficiency where Italian lives and colonies were at stake.

At the same time he answered those whose concern was that an Italian presence in Europe was indispensable. "It is just in order to be tranquilly present in Europe," he said, "that we intend to feel ourselves thoroughly safe in Africa."

Italy would keep 800,000–900,000 men under arms—perfectly trained, he boasted, of superb morale and equipped with the most modern weapons.

These forces would, he said, enable Italy to continue a policy of willing, frank, and complete collaboration with all the European powers, great and small, far and near, to maintain the balance of power and the understandings "without which the world and our continent would go adrift."[16]

Mussolini now announced that Italy had appointed two members to the Italo-Abyssinian Conciliation Commission. Mussolini, who had added the words "in Europe" to the Stresa resolution, thus proclaimed his readiness to pursue European security. The price he named was Abyssinia; but even here, he kept open the door of the conciliation process. This, in turn, would enable him to claim, at the May meeting of the League of Nations Council that the matter, being under conciliation, ought not to find a place on the Council's agenda. Whatever the issue, he perceived the value of always retaining a vigorous initiative.

The Cabinet reviewed Simon's gloomy memorandum on May 15, 1935. His colleagues were no more imaginative in creating a course of action than Simon had himself been. They limited themselves to instructing Anthony Eden that the British Government could not accept, at the meeting of the League Council, any procedure which would put the Abyssinian matter over until September. Beyond that, Eden was to act at his own discretion.[17]

The Cabinet met two days later without accomplishing anything further. They heard from the Ambassador in Rome, Sir Eric Drummond. He thought there was little chance of a settlement. Soon it would be necessary to pressure the Emperor of Abyssinia to afford worthwhile economic incentives to Italy. If that failed, the world was in for trouble; for Drummond was certain that Mussolini would not give way to League pressure.

Was there any understanding, Drummond was asked, between France and Italy over Abyssinia? He thought not. When Laval had made his agreement with Italy, "he had said definitely that the free hand only affected economic questions and must not be construed as affecting the territorial position." Laval, Drummond added, had called on him in Rome to emphasize that the concessions were economic only.[18]

In default of policy resolutions, the Cabinet recorded sentiments. It attached great value to Italian friendship and hoped Britain could discharge its duty as a member of the League Council without offending Italy or impairing Anglo-Italian relations.

The Cabinet was gratified by the appointment of the Italian conciliators:

"Signor Mussolini will be aware of the deep feeling that is entertained in the United Kingdom in support of promoting the peaceful solution of international disputes by or under the League of Nations."

Here was recognition of the immense wave of support for the League of Nations and its procedures which the Peace Ballot had brought forth. This was a statement of fact. What is more dramatic is the sentence immediately following:

This is the avowed policy of His Majesty's Government from which they cannot depart.

The hesitancies and reticences of the past, the fear of commitments and especially of any automatic operation of the Covenant which had been the refuge of British statesmen since Versailles were fading before the voice and the will of the British people.

The conclusions of May 15 were reaffirmed. The League could not disassociate itself from the Abyssinian issue until September. Some means was needed for the League to maintain contact with the issue while conciliation proceeded. To further this, Eden was sent forth with his vague brief.

At the same time, Drummond was instructed personally to discuss the matter with Mussolini, both to emphasize its seriousness and to probe for a mutually acceptable understanding.[19]

Nowhere was the danger seen more clearly than in Berlin. The British Ambassador there wired to the Foreign Secretary on May 20:

I fear, therefore, that if we oppose Italy too strongly we may find Herr Hitler posing as Signor Mussolini's best friend with the possible risk of an Italo-German understanding concluded behind our backs.

This, Vansittart noted was a very real danger, particularly in the next two years.[20]

When Anthony Eden dined with Italy's representative to the League of Nations, Baron Aloisi, on May 20, 1935, the difficulty of his task was made clear. What was at stake, Aloisi said, was the whole prestige of the Fascist regime. He could hardly expect Mussolini to spend 600 million lire only to change his mind at the request of the League of Nations.

No, Italy was committed. It had been unfortunate that the matter had not been cleared up at Stresa. Mussolini wanted to save the League's face, too, but only if he could achieve his goal.

Eden made the same case to Aloisi that Sir John Simon had made to Grandi. The British Government was not free to act as it saw fit. Eden wrote,

> I viewed the future with the utmost concern if [the] Italian government were really engaged in a policy of military aggression in Abyssinia. British public opinion was really stirred upon this matter and would become more so. It was not only members of the League of Nations Union who felt keenly but also people of the Right usually very friendly to Italy like Sir A. Chamberlain and Mr. Churchill who deplored as much as we did the trend of Italian policy in Africa.

Italy, Eden said, was indispensable to peace in Europe. Were she to persist in her Abyssinian policy, Eden did not see how a breach between Italy and Britain could be avoided.

Aloisi promised to do his best. They discussed techniques to keep the League in touch with the situation although this was precisely what Mussolini wished to avoid.[21]

Laval arrived in Geneva on the following day. He shared Eden's concern. Eden asked him about his January conversation with Mussolini.

At no time, Laval said, had he given encouragement to an Italian military campaign in Abyssinia. "You have strong hands," he had warned Mussolini by way of emphasizing that Italy must confine itself to economic objectives.

Eden and Laval agreed that the Abyssinian problem could place their governments in a difficult if not impossible situation. They agreed to keep in continuous consultation and, more important, to act together.[22]

On the following day, Sir Eric Drummond called on Mussolini, who liked neither Abyssinia's appointment of an American and a Frenchmen, rather than Abyssinians, to the Conciliation Commission,

nor the suggestion that the League retain some competence and jurisdiction over the problem.

Drummond again pleaded the impact of British public opinion:

> There was no doubt that the theory of collective security had made great
> progress. I thought that it was now very widely accepted. This theory was,
> however, based on the League of Nations, and I believed that the League
> had seldom had so much support in England as it had today.

Britain, he said, did not act out of sympathy for Abyssinia or concern for British interests there but in order to maintain the prestige and
effectiveness of the League to which "not only the government, but
public opinion as a whole attached the greatest importance."

Drummond laid his cards on the table. If the British Government
had to choose between its old friendship with Italy and support of the
League:

> I thought I ought to tell him frankly that in my view (and I was not
> influenced because I had been Secretary General of the League) public
> opinion in England might well feel bound to support the League as against
> Italy.

He hoped that this would not occur. Drummond had made a profound distinction. He did not cite his Government as the decisive force
in supporting a League policy, but public opinion. Here was a clear
recognition that the Government, in his opinion, would not act contrary to public opinion. This, indeed, had been precisely Lord Cecil's
objective in framing the Peace Ballot though he could never have
dreamed that a confrontation between Italy and Abyssinia would prove
a decisive test of the power of public opinion.

Mussolini met frankness with frankness. The situation had become
intolerable. Were Italy to be engaged in Europe, he had no doubt the
Abyssinians would attack. To Sir Eric's suggestion of economic concessions, Mussolini replied that months ago they might have sufficed.
That time had passed. If he had to go to war, he would.

This was appalling. It could destroy not only the League, but
Locarno, Drummond said.

Mussolini was consistent. Collective security should be confined to
Europe, he said, just as he had emphasized at Stresa. If he must leave
the League he would; and once he left he would never return.

But, Mussolini observed, perhaps the impact on Italo- British relations would be transitory. He followed the British press closely. Certainly there would be an outcry, particularly from pacifists and old ladies, but it would pass.

Could anything be done, Drummond asked? Mussolini replied that Abyssinia would be a hard nut to crack; he would be happy to obtain his aims by other means. Perhaps, he suggested, the Emperor might yield if Britain and France so advised him. Why not a protectorate such as France had laboriously acquired in Morocco and Britain in Egypt?

This was Mussolini in the summer of 1935—aware of the consequences, weighing risks and rewards, but determined to exert his will. He knew his actions could seriously weaken the League, and affect Italian relations with Britain. But that was how things were, and he could not change. To Drummond it seemed that Mussolini was controlled by rather than controlling his destiny—a man driven by fate.[23]

Hitler Plays a Hand

To the confrontation among the three members of the Stresa Front who had pronounced unacceptable the unilateral revocation of treaties, and who had sponsored the resolution of the League Council to the same effect, there was no keener observer than Adolf Hitler.

Unlike Mussolini, who had traveled widely, even if at first as a vagabond, Hitler's only experience outside Germany and Austria had been on the battlefields of Flanders. He spoke only German; Mussolini prided himself that he could conduct diplomacy in German, had a reasonable command of French and English, and was a voracious consumer of the foreign press. Hitler's self-education was, to say the least, uneven and tended to concentrate on German and military history.

For all this, Hitler possessed an extraordinary ability to divine the thoughts and emotions of the public and the statesmen of Europe. To reverse the condemnation of German rearmament, to blunt the development of British air power, to hearten the supporters of pacifism and disarmament—outside Germany to be sure—by portraying Germany as a rational and constructive supporter of peace, to drive a wedge between Britain and France on the one hand and Britain and Italy on the other, to beckon seductively to Italy as an ally rather than as the keystone of an anti-German alliance—these were enchanting possibilities which could pay huge dividends.

In his address to the Reichstag on May 21, 1935[24] Hitler paid tribute to Woodrow Wilson's vision of collective security. He associated himself with the Wilsonian ideals of universal justice, equality, disarmament, and security. Germany had welcomed these and had been cruelly deceived, especially by the failure of the victors at Versailles to carry out their duty to disarm. To support his case he cited eminent witnesses—Lord Cecil, Arthur Henderson, Paul-Boncour, and Aristide Briand.

The consequence of this enforced inequality, Hitler said, was that Germany must reject the Geneva resolution of April 17, 1935. Germany could not return to the League of Nations until real legal equality—the abolition of the military clauses of Versailles—was established. Hitler knew, he said, that war was futile; the blood shed in Europe over the past three hundred years had produced no result proportional to the cost. He had no ambition forcibly to amalgamate aliens into the German Reich for the subjugation and domination of alien peoples could only weaken Germany.

Most people, of course, had never read in *Mein Kampf* Hitler's vision of the German sword preceding the German plow in the vast reaches of the East, where future generations of racially pure Germans would reap the harvest fertilized by the blood of conquerors. And it was open to those who had read it to conclude that the lonely and absurd streetcorner orator of the 1920s had ripened into the responsible, if somewhat eccentric, statesman of today.

Hitler reassured the world that the future could be different:

> Once in possession of absolute equality of rights Germany will never refuse to participate in those efforts which are intended to serve the cause of human peace, progress and economic welfare.[25]

Hitler had assurances for all. To France he offered friendship. The issue of Alsace Lorraine had been settled; Germany had no territorial ambitions in France. To Italy he announced that Germany had no desire to interfere in the internal affairs of Austria, to annex Austria, or to conclude an *Anschluss*. He regretted that Austrian tensions had disturbed good relations with Italy with whom otherwise Germany had no conflict of interests.

Britain's chief concerns were the threats from the air and on the seas. Germany, Hitler said, was ready to supplement Locarno with an air pact. Germany, recognizing Britain's maritime supremacy and the unique needs of the British Empire at sea, would limit her navy to 35 percent of the Royal Navy, a figure Hitler said which would be 15 percent less than the French navy.

Nor was this all. Germany was prepared to conclude nonaggression pacts with all her neighbors. What Germany could not do was enter a multilateral Eastern pact because it might lead to completely unforeseeable consequences and because of the great gulf between Germany and the Soviet Union. In this respect, the Franco-Soviet pact was a throwback to the old system of military alliances. It introduced, Hitler noted, an element of legal insecurity into the Locarno pact.

Locarno, he said, was the most valuable treaty of mutal assistance of them all. Germany would scrupulously maintain it, specifically including the provisions for the demilitarization of the Rhineland, hard as they were. Indeed, Hitler's Germany would scrupulously maintain any treaty voluntarily signed, even before the Nazis took power.

Germany was willing at all times to pursue peace on a collective basis, including arms limitation at a disarmament conference. The goals might be the abolition of poison gas and aerial bombing, limitations on heavy weapons, including artillery and tanks, and the size and armament of warships.

Finally, Germany would be glad to enter international agreements preventing outside interference in the affairs of national states.

The existence of German military forces, Hitler argued, had filled a dangerous vacuum. It was a contribution to the cause of peace. Let effective arms limitation commence and progress.

"We believe," Hitler pronounced,

> that if the peoples of the world can agree to destroy all their gas, inflammatory, and explosive bombs, this would be a more useful undertaking than using them to destroy one another.[26]

Hitler had chosen to speak not only when Britain was placing obstacles in the path of Mussolini's ambitions, but on the day preceding a debate on air rearmament in the House of Commons.

Hitler's speech, the *Times* said the next day, was reasonable, straightforward, and comprehensive:

> No one who reads it with an impartial mind can doubt that the points of policy laid down by HERR HITLER may fairly constitute the bases of a complete settlement with Germany.

It was to be hoped, the *Times* editorialized, that Hitler's speech "will be taken everywhere as a sincere and well-considered utterance meaning precisely what it says."[27] But there was no reason, the *Times* added, why Britain should cease to pursue air parity at present while negotiating agreements for the future.

This was a point on which Baldwin, speaking for the Government remained firm. He reviewed the deficiencies of the years of hope for disarmament and the obligation, which no responsible Government could neglect, of repairing those deficiencies. Yet he sounded a new note. Arms were needed, not only for the defense of the nation, but also to fulfill British obligations under the Covenant of the League of Nations. Arms would not only encourage the friends of peace, but also deter a nation tempted to disregard its solemn undertakings under the Covenant and the Kellogg-Briand pact.

Baldwin now made a celebrated admission. He had said last November that Britain was superior to Germany in the air and would remain so. He had been wrong, completely wrong in his estimate of the future. Britain now must base her policy on Germany's revelations. Production facilities and labor must be equal to the demand.

But he closed with a reference to Hitler's speech: "I look for light wherever I can find it," he concluded, "I believe there was some light in the speech that was made last night." Here was a combination of resolution and hope which carried the House.

Churchill warned against the delusion that any new and hopeful situation had arisen as a result of Hitler's speech. Germany was incomparably stronger in the air; new German naval construction would qualitatively outweigh a part of British numerical superiority; Britain was entering a dark and dangerous valley. But even Churchill dared to hope that the march through the valley could end in a blessed agreement for which no exertion should be spared.[28]

Labour leaders who reviewed Hitler's speech called for the suspension of British rearmament pending renewal of the Disarmament Conference. In the House of Lords on May 22, Lord Hutchinson said that Hitler meant to do away with the bombing of cities, women, and children, and called for agreement with him.[29] Herbert Morrison warned the Government not to miss the boat; Sir Bolton Eyres-Monsell, First Lord of the Admiralty thought Germany prepared to negotiate and abide by arms limitation treaties and the rules of submarine warfare.[30]

Attlee's reply to Baldwin on May 21 was significant because it enshrined the thoughts and hopes of all those earnest and concerned Britons, of whatever party or class, who were devoted to peace and collective security:

> As a party we do not stand for unilateral disarmament. . . . We stand for collective security through the League of Nations. We reject the use of force as an instrument of national policy. We stand for the reduction of armaments and pooled security. . . . We have stated that this country must be prepared to make its contribution to collective security. Our policy is not one of seeking security through rearmament but through disarmament. Our aim is the reduction of armaments, and the complete abolition of national armaments and the creation of an international police force under the League.[31]

These were words for Hitler to ponder as he proceeded day and night to rearm Germany. Mussolini could consider Baldwin's references to the power of arms to deter would-be Covenant breakers, as he directed Italian moves at the meeting of the Council of the League then in session at Geneva.

A Temporary Compromise

When Anthony Eden read Drummond's report of his meeting with Mussolini, he was concerned lest silence should make Britain Italy's accessory. Mussolini should be warned, he advised, that Britain could not condone a breach of the Covenant or the treaties. All this made Eden's position more difficult and unless some agreed resolution were reached, the issue would be plainly before the Council.

That evening, May 22, Eden met with Laval who agreed to produce a compromise proposal and did. It fixed a date for the conclusion of conciliation and a meeting of the Council if there had been no result. All incidents since Wal Wal could be covered; and the parties would agree not to resort to force during the proceedings. Most important, from the Italian point of view, no rapporteur would be appointed. The only connection of the League would be the continual surveillance by the Secretary General of the proceedings and such reports to members of the Council as he saw fit.

Eden agreed, but warned he would be attacked in Britain for any solution outside the League. Aloisi was pessimistic; he would nonetheless transmit the proposals to Rome. Laval was frank. He wanted, he said, not to offend Italian susceptibilities but at the same time he had to be aware of the general sentiment of the Council.[32]

Laval had every intention to resolve the conflict. The French chargé d'affaires in Berlin again reminded him in a lengthy dispatch how much Germany hoped that the Abyssinian conflict would both cause a falling out among the Stresa partners and embarrass and devalue the League of Nations, especially if Italy were to leave.[33]

The Italian delegation returned the next day with counter proposals. If they were not satisfactory—they omitted any assurance not to resort to force—at least this was better than Mussolini's intransigence. Eden insisted the agreement must cover all incidents, contain a fixed time limit and an undertaking not to resort to force. When Aloisi reported to him on Mussolini's meeting with Drummond, an account not differing materially from Drummond's own, Eden clearly warned him that Britain could not condone, much less support, breaches of the Covenant, the Kellogg-Briand pact and the Tripartite Treaty. Aloisi understood and said he would do his best to help.[34]

After midnight, Massigli heard from Aloisi that Mussolini might accept a compromise. He would agree to consider all incidents under a fixed time limit. He would not undertake to refrain from the use of force. In any event, the parties were to meet on the morrow hoping to find a way to bridge the gap.[35]

The next day, Eden argued tenaciously for the engagement not to use force. Here was clearly the sticking point. Laval suggested that the resolution contain a reference to Article 5 of the 1928 Treaty which contained this express engagement. This did not satisfy Eden who wanted the text of the Article contained in the proposed resolution. Once more Laval found an ingenious solution. The final agreement would contain only the reference to the 1928 Treaty; but the president of the League Council would read Article 5 at the opening of his presentation.[36]

This did not resolve any fundamental issue. But it did produce a resolution which the League Council duly adopted on May 24, 1935. It agreed that the conciliation procedure should comprehend all issues since Wal Wal; that the members of the commission nominated by Abyssinia were acceptable to Italy; that August 25 be fixed as the final date of the conciliation process. In the meantime, the Secretary General of the League would keep members of the Council informed. The second resolution referred to the obligations of the parties under Article 5 of the 1928 Treaty and further provided, in the absence of agreement by July 25, for the choice of a fifth arbitrator. The Council would reconvene to examine the situation if by August 25 no result had been obtained.[37]

Mussolini had tried to exclude the League and the League Council from the Abyssinian issue and process. Not only did the League Council retain cognizance of the issue, but a fixed date had been set by which the issue, if not resolved, would revert to the League. Here was another pattern. Hitler had made a clean break with the League. Mussolini had not. This was an important difference. One day soon, the issues would be framed, not as England and France vs. Italy, but as the League of Nations vs. Italy.

For the moment, the crisis had been postponed. Aloisi had played an important part. He had understood the urgency of the issue and had not hesitated to take a strong stand before an imperious master.

For the rest, the result had been achieved by a combination of firmness and flexibility. The firmness had been Eden's, the flexibility Laval's. Their approaches had different sources. Eden was more devoted to principle, Laval to results. In the end, ingenuity and flexibility achieved what firmness alone could not. Laval knew as well as Eden that the basic problem remained unresolved. He could well have concluded from this experience that some day, somehow, a solution could be found, so long as the parties kept talking and addressing their mutual interests.

On May 25, 1935, the day after the League Council's resolution, Mussolini faced his Chamber of Deputies. He reviewed the Franco-Italian accords, the improvement of relations with France and the optimism caused by the Anglo-French declaration of February. Stresa had been positive because, in the face of urgent problems, the three Western powers had achieved solidarity.

Hitler's speech he barely acknowledged. It should be studied, he said, and neither accepted nor rejected wholesale. Austrian independence remained vital. This was the issue, he said significantly, that compromised relations with Germany. But it was not exclusively an Italian concern. In any case, Italy would never be so concerned with a single problem as to limit her responsibilities and freedom of action elsewhere.

The Abyssinian threat was real. There should be no undue illusions about the outcome of negotiations. Mussolini made it clear that he would judge European states by their attitude toward the Abyssinian issue. "Thus," he concluded,

> nobody should hope to make out of Abyssinia a pistol which is to be pointed continuously against us and which in case of European trouble should make our position in East Africa untenable. Let everyone clearly grasp that when the safety of our territories and of the lives of our soldiers is at stake we are ready to assume all, even the supreme responsibilities.[38]

Vansittart asked himself which was more important—Austria or Abyssinia. His answer was always Austria. Mussolini had stated that he would judge European powers by their attitude toward Abyssinia. The implication was clear that in the end he would chose Abyssinia over Austria.

Not long after, Laval was called upon to accept heavier burdens. The Flandin Government fell on May 30, 1935, precipitated by a financial crisis and a run on the franc. The Chamber would accord to neither Flandin nor his short-serving successor, Bouisson, the emergency powers they asked.

On June 7, 1935, Laval became Prime Minister. He had formed his government, he said in his ministerial declaration, to combat speculation and to defend the franc. He spoke in modest and practical terms. The budget deficit could not go on: "You don't have to be an expert on finance," he told the French people in a broadcast several days later," to realize that if you want to spend more than you have, you soon end up bankrupt."[39]

The decree powers were granted and Laval used them to reduce central and local government expenditures, increase income taxes, and reduce government controlled prices of rents, mortgages, bread, coal, gas and electricity. Further decrees were designed to stimulate economic activity including public works programs.

All this had to be done in an increasingly fragmented and bitter political atmosphere. The parties of the left, the Socialists and Communists, were moving closer together; the Popular Front was forming. On the right, the Croix de Feu was only chief among veterans and paramilitary organizations whose oratory, programs, and sympathy with Mussolini raised suspicions of Fascism. The conditions for a confrontation, always present since the riots of February, 1934, seemed immensely to have increased.

Amidst all this, Pierre Laval explained another reason for the need to defuse the crisis. A prolongation, he said, of the ministerial crisis would put in danger forty months of difficult and delicate foreign policy initiatives. As Prime Minister, Laval retained the Ministry of Foreign Affairs, to which, however, he was no longer at liberty to give his undivided attention.[40]

Sir Samuel Hoare

A change of government took place in Britain, too. Ramsay MacDonald's health had long been failing. On June 7, 1935, he was succeeded as Prime Minister by Stanley Baldwin, becoming in turn Baldwin's successor as Lord President of the Council. MacDonald's appointment was largely symbolic and he died not long after. The new alignment represented what had been the reality of MacDonald's last years as Prime Minister; the moving force of the administration had been Baldwin.

Sir John Simon left the Foreign Office for the Home Office. For the post of Foreign Minister, Baldwin gave serious consideration to the Conservative Party's rising star and preeminent champion of the League of Nations, Anthony Eden. Eden was forthright. He sought out Baldwin and told him he would understand if he were passed over because of his youth. In that case, he would prefer not to remain in the Foreign Office as a subordinate.

Back from Geneva in late May, Eden received congratulations on his appointment as Foreign Secretary. They proved premature. Baldwin told Eden: "Sam is to go to the Foreign Office and I want you to stay on and help him there."

Sam was Sir Samuel Hoare. The help Baldwin suggested was Eden's appointment as Minister for League of Nations Affairs. But, Eden protested, foreign affairs are League of Nations affairs and League affairs are foreign affairs. How could they be separated?

Baldwin was persuasive. He urged Eden to talk it over with Hoare. "After all," he said "it isn't everyone who has the chance to be in the Cabinet before he is thirty-eight."[41]

Hoare understood Eden's difficulty but urged him to accept. They could view the arrangement as temporary. Eden, the good soldier, accepted, but unhappily. In a critical time, the Foreign Office would not speak with a single voice.

Hoare's ancestors had been Quakers. He thought that important.

They had been bankers. He thought that important, too. The more they had become bankers, the less they remained Quakers and Hoare was born into wealth and prominence. He did well at Harrow and Oxford, married an earl's daughter, followed his father into the House of Commons, then succeeded to the family title. In the 1920s, he was Air Minister. As Secretary of State for India he had successfully performed immensely complex labors in steering the Government of India Act through Parliament. He would have preferred to become Viceroy of India, but Baldwin, urged by Neville Chamberlain and Geoffry Dawson of the *Times*, prevailed upon him to become Foreign Secretary.

His Quaker ancestors had been men of peace. His banker ancestors were cautious. They avoided risk and adventure. "Instinctively," Hoare said,

> he [the banker] detests the alarms and excursions that deflect the even tenor of his business and, when disputes arise, prefers to see them settled by mutual compromise, rather than by recourse to courts of law.[42]

Hoare had a keen mind. His industry and ability were not in doubt. But the strain of his work on the India bill had left him exhausted and ill, more in need of rest than an arduous new task.

The impression he made on his contemporaries was uniform. Vansittart sketched him briefly and colorfully:

> He was prim and precise, an accurate though not severe tennis player— that was symbolic—and brilliant on skates—that wrecked him in *The Comédie Humaine*.[43]

Why the last should be true is hard to say. Surely nimbleness and a keen sense of balance are valuable properties in a Foreign Secretary, as is the ability, under stress, to cut accurate figures gracefully.

But the impression of primness and preciseness rang true and Lord Birkenhead's celebrated observation that he seemed to be "the last of a long line of maiden aunts" was widely appreciated.[44]

Sir Samuel Hoare was not given the benefit of a period of orientation and adaptation as Foreign Secretary, nor the time to contemplate problems and solutions. Immediately upon his appointment he found on his desk a nearly completed naval agreement between Britain and Germany.

The Anglo-German Naval Agreement

An Anglo-German naval agreement had been discussed when Simon and Eden visited Hitler in Berlin in March. It had been in the air ever since and was a prominent feature of Hitler's May 21 speech.

Britain knew that Hitler, in addition to his army and air force, was rebuilding the German fleet. In April it was learned that Germany had placed orders for twelve submarines, strictly forbidden by the Versailles Treaty.[45]

On May 29, 1935, Britain was disconcerted to learn of a naval construction program far larger than previously suggested. Perhaps this was done to give Germany an ampler supply of bargaining chips in the forthcoming negotiations.[46]

But it was Hitler's favorable reference to an air pact that appealed most to Britain. The offer might not be sincere, Sir Herbert Samuel said in Parliament on June 1, 1935, but Britain should lose no time in testing Hitler's sincerity and advancing the pact. This was what the public wanted, and the public had recently given a remarkable demonstration of its views, Samuel said, citing the Peace Ballot. There had never been such an expression of public opinion. The second question—are you in favor of an all-round reduction of armaments by international agreement?—had gained an affirmative response of 8,326,000, more than with one exception had ever voted for a single party in a national election, Samuel told Parliament.

The same theme was taken up by Mr. Bernays. There had been a remarkable change, he said, in the attitude of the House to collective security. There were practically no isolationists left. Even Mr. Churchill had been making speeches on the grandeur of the peace system at Geneva which would qualify him to be a vice president of the League of Nations Union. This was an invitation which Mr. Bernays slyly hoped would be extended.[47]

The German delegation, headed by Joachim von Ribbentrop in his capacity as Special Reich Commissioner for Disarmament, arrived in London on June 3. Ribbentrop's first move was to confer with the then Foreign Secretary, Simon, and plead the need to keep the talks secret from other governments. When Simon blandly said no course should be foreclosed except as the parties agreed, Ribbentrop moved in for the close.

"Then you agree in principle with what I have suggested?" he inquired. Simon retreated. It would require consideration.[48]

The British clearly foresaw the issue of the meeting. Germany would demand a ratio of 35 percent of the overall tonnage of the British fleet. Britain wanted to be more precise, more limiting, seeking instead agreement on specific building programs for specific vessels.

In opening the first session on June 4, Simon praised Hitler's understanding of British naval needs and his desire for friendly relations. The thrust of Hitler's speech of May 21 had been greatly appreciated by the British Government and public opinion. The subject at hand was technical and complicated and could perhaps best begin by consultations among the respective naval experts.

Ribbentrop struck hard and fast. In accepting the 35 percent ratio, he said, Germany was forever excluding Britain as a future enemy. Under its clear instructions, the German delegation could only commence discussions if at the outset Britain recognized the 35 percent ratio as "fixed and unalterable."

This was not negotiation. It was an ultimatum. Simon icily thanked Ribbentrop for his statement. He pointed out that he was trying to achieve an all-round naval agreement and that in any case a simple ratio left many important questions unanswered.

Ribbentrop did not budge: "The conversations would not be possible unless the 35 percent ratio was accepted. This was not a demand but a final decision, not liable to alteration."[49]

Simon pleaded an engagement with the Prime Minister and abruptly left. The British experts valiantly argued the case for a more comprehensive approach. Ribbentrop hardened. He would be glad to hear explanations, he said, but only after the principle of the ratio had been accepted. He then restated his earlier concern that no communication should be made to other countries. The British finally agreed that only after the conclusion of talks would the other naval powers be informed and then in a guarded communication.

When the British tried to reopen the principal issue, they were solidly rebuffed. It would be wrong, Ribbentrop responded, to think that the 35 percent ratio could be a matter of give and take. After making a serious decision, Hitler would not change is mind by one inch.[50]

The parties, Simon absent, returned to the conference table the same afternoon. Ribbentrop stood firm. Moreover, he greatly regretted any need to inform other naval powers. Britain and Germany were two sovereign nations. Why could they not arrange their decision and communicate the results? Were the other powers to be consulted, he greatly feared a chance of agreement might be lost forever.[51]

At the third meeting on June 5, the British experts put their case that other existing naval treaties were involved in the issue of ratios; that the necessary limitations could only be arrived at by specific programs. Ribbentrop was unmoved.

He was precise in his terminology. Could not Britain give a clear and formal recognition to the decision taken by Hitler in establishing the 35 percent ratio? This was, again, not negotiation, but surrender pure and simple.

Again, the British sparred for time. Political changes, the pending reconstruction of the government would complicate matters. The temptation was enormous to seize Hitler's offer and freeze the German navy vis-à-vis Britain. The perils were equally obvious. Ribbentrop was gracious. He would not press for too early a reply.[52]

The British representatives now reported to their Government. Germany would agree, even if France increased its navy and Britain did not, to maintain the Anglo-German ratio. In a future international naval treaty Germany would abide by the Anglo-German ratio.

The question of the other naval powers was clearly bothersome. But the British representatives concluded that it was in Britain's interest to accept Hitler's offer; if not, it would be withdrawn. There being nothing then to limit German construction, Britain might soon regret its action:

This German offer is of such outstanding importance that it would be a mistake to withhold acceptance merely on the ground that other Powers might feel some temporary annoyance at our action.[53]

To this, the Naval Staff added that Germany would accept no other agreement and that adequate margins of safety were provided. The Naval Staff now ventured far afield. In the matter of submarines it observed:

In the present mood of Germany, it seems probable that the surest way to persuade them to be moderate in their actual performance is to grant them every consideration in theory. In fact, they are more likely to build up to submarine parity if we object to their theoretical right to do so, than if we agree that they have a moral justification.[54]

This was a mixture of psychology and morality not likely to commend itself to clear French minds. But the experts and the Naval Staff had been persuasive. When the conferees met again on June 6, Simon sealed British acceptance. The Government, he said, had considered the issue carefully. They recognized its historic importance. As a result, Britain intended to recognize the Reich Chancellor's decision and to agree to a permanent ratio of 35:100 between the German and British fleets.

This was done business. It would be necessary, Simon added, to inform the other naval powers of the decision, offering them the opportunity to make any observations. Ribbentrop demurred. It was unclear to him whether the communication to other naval powers was a tacit admission of their right to object, or was it merely a courtesy.

It was indeed, Simon said a matter of courtesy and fairness. But the language meant that Britain had *decided*. The communication was to inform of this decision.

The discussion of details that followed was not difficult. Even there, Ribbentrop suggested, it might be better to preserve them as a private document.[55]

So it was done. Instead of preliminary negotiations, Hitler's intransigence had forced a commitment. Inherent in that commitment was the plain denunciation and abrogation of the naval clauses of Versailles.

Only now, on June 7, did Britain communicate, in like terms, to the United States, France, Italy, and Japan describing the German demand and the British government's decision to accept it. This was framed as a contribution to future security of all countries. Before a formal reply, observations were sought. Meanwhile, Britain advised the matter should be kept secret.[56]

The Germans still worried that closure was less than firm. At the fifth meeting on June 7, they discussed the possibility of press leaks. Again, the British representatives said the communication to the other naval powers was a courtesy: "They merely wished to give the other governments a chance of making their observations. The British government had already informed the Powers of their decision."

There were elaborate courtesies before the adjournment. The British negotiators characterized the discussions as frank and friendly. No bargaining had been attempted nor would it be. The initial British hesitation had only been a question of method and a desire not to hurt the susceptibilities of the other powers. They would resume discussions after the holiday.[57]

The concern for the susceptibilities of others did not achieve the desired results in France as the British ambassador soon learned. He now addressed Sir Samuel Hoare, the new Foreign Secretary. Laval, he said, had been continuously absorbed for the week in domestic crises and then, good politician that he was, was attending the funeral of a colleague in the provinces.

But Sir George Clerk, the British Ambassador, reported that he had conferred with Alexis Léger, Secretary General of the Foreign Ministry. Léger had been blunt. Stresa had been torn to ribbons. He saw no sincerity in Hitler's speech, only the desire to drive a wedge between Britain and France. To judge by the British communication of June 7, Hitler was succeeding. Clearly he wanted to address British concerns at sea and in the air, and to separate those issues from land armaments which most concerned France. The French public would see itself sacrificed to British interests. What Germany was doing was sowing dissension among the Western powers. She would use Abyssinia to her advantage, to weaken Mussolini's resistance to German designs on Austria.[58]

Léger warned that the French reply would not be favorable. The French press expressed Léger's concerns; here was another blow at Versailles, this time by Britain. Not only did Britain disinterest itself in issues vital to France-land armaments, the Central and Eastern European pacts—but by concluding separate bilateral agreements with Germany, Britain had deprived France and others of leverage in these other matters. This was far from the General Settlement, in which all issues were related, which France and Britain had proclaimed as their goal in their Declaration of February 3, 1935.[59]

It now fell to Hoare to deal with France. He tried to persuade the French Ambassador in London how advantageous the agreement was, not only for Britain but for France and Italy. He emphasized another factor—the state of British public opinion:

> If we did not make the Agreement, or even if we delayed it, British public opinion being almost unanimously in favor of it, will react violently against France with a result that Anglo-French relations will be very gravely damaged.

Hoare was not without resources. He would send Anthony Eden to Paris to explain the whole thing to Laval. At the same time, they might discuss the air pact and Abyssinia.[60]

The Italians replied first. They were not impressed. Italy thought

German naval armaments should be considered in relation to the arms of other states, discussions in which Italy would be glad to participate and contribute.[61]

Clerk saw Laval on June 17, 1935. Laval preferred to reserve judgment until he had studied the matter more deeply. The French reply would be ready the following day. Laval expressed French regrets. He was direct. Not much seemed left of the declaration of February 3.

Clerk now pleaded British public opinion and British sincerity in dealing with France. He observed that for once Laval was moved from his usual serenity.[62]

On the same day, Laval asked Clerk to come to the Quai d'Orsay to receive personally the document by which France would reply to the British communication. What concerned him was the *conclusion* of a naval agreement independent of all other issues. To the plea of public opinion Laval replied that in dealing with the British he had always tried to see every question from their as well as his own point of view. But he had his own public opinion to confront and he had no alternatives.[63]

The British and German delegates met on June 18, 1935. Hoare headed the British delegation, there to reap what Simon had sown. Amid mutual congratulations, Hoare observed that the agreement would facilitate a general naval limitation agreement. The procedure, he admitted, had been unusual. The agreement would be published in the press the next day. The notes were signed.[64]

It was only on the following day that the French note was received in London. It expressed serious reservations and stated that the Treaty would affect not only naval matters. There were the London Declaration, Stresa, the April resolution of the League Council to consider. It pointed out that Britain, France, and Italy had agreed to act together in the matter of German rearmament, not by individual agreements, especially concerning revisions of Versailles. One could hardly accede, one by one, to German demands. What, it asked, would Germany do in respect of air and land armaments? For the neighbors of Germany, all these issues were one.

France declared that it would have to look to its own interests so far as the French navy was concerned. Additions or reconstruction might be required, depending on the German program. There would be naval implications in the Baltic where Germany had so far declined to enter into negotiations for an Eastern European pact of mutual assistance.[65]

Simon and Hoare had not misinterpreted British public opinion. The naval agreement was greeted rapturously by the press, left, right, and center.[66] The *Times* conceded that what had been started as preliminary negotiations had rather surprisingly produced a definitive agreement. It conceded, too, that it gave Germany the dangerous right to build submarines, that it infringed Versailles, and in a masterpiece of understatement, that the agreement "was not wholly congenial to French susceptibilities." Nevertheless, it lauded the result and looked forward to the conclusion of an air pact.[67]

Berlin was thrilled. Hitler said it was the happiest day of his life. To Germany it appeared a recognition of the injustices of Versailles and Germany's right to equality. More than that, in recognizing Britain's paramount interests at sea, it was also seen to carry an implicit recognition of German interests on the continent. And finally, it was a triumphant vindication of Hitler's diplomatic method, his system of bilateral agreements.[68]

Italy was stunned and disappointed. The agreement had dealt a blow to Stresa. Britain had betrayed Italy. The agreement would lead to increased armaments. Worst of all, it appeared in Rome that the Franco-Italian rapprochement had led Britain back into its traditional policy of the balance of power on the continent and to closer ties with Germany.[69]

The most poignant reaction was in Paris where the British Ambassador called upon Laval and Léger. As they saw it, France was asked to adapt to a naval situation which she had had no voice in creating. Moreover, the chances of an overall agreement on arms had been severely prejudiced.

It was just as if, they said, France had made a separate agreement with Germany as to air forces without consulting Britain. Indeed, when Laval had met Goering in Cracow in May, Goering had suggested a Franco-German agreement whereby their armies could dominate Europe. Laval had replied that he could never conclude a separate agreement that diminished rather than enhanced general security.

Now, the London Declaration had been destroyed of which unity had been the great value. Clerk sympathized with Laval, a man, he said, whose instinct was to reach agreement wherever he could find it.

The British statesmen had emphasized the pressure of public opinion. But Laval, too, was having problems in his Cabinet and in a

Chamber far more deeply and passionately divided than the House of Commons.

Plainly, the Ambassador reported, Laval felt he had been let down. He concluded his dispatch:

> While both M. Laval and M. Léger made no attempt to conceal their feelings, neither showed any tendency to recriminate, but rather a desire to make the best of what they consider a bad job.[70]

Vansittart did his best to mollify the French. He told Corbin on June 19 that the British government could not resist the force of public opinion, that Britain would not allow Germany to drive a wedge between it and France, and that, in any case, the agreement was beneficial to France. British diplomats were at an obvious disadvantage in attempting to elucidate French interests to the French.

The agreement, Vansittart said, did not for one moment imply a breaking of the Stresa front. The problem of Abyssinia made it all the more important for Britain and France to march in step. A sensitive diplomat may have foreseen in this comment an early British appeal for French help.[71]

Hoare ably defended the naval agreement in Parliament on July 11, 1935 but he had not persuaded his friends and he had delighted his enemies. Truly it had been Hitler's happiest day. The French government and the French public were deeply disturbed both by the agreement itself and the way in which France had been treated. There was a sense of betrayal at a critical moment when trust and confidence would be most needed.

To France, Britain had abandoned Versailles. To Italy, Britain had abandoned Stresa. To both, Britain appeared unreliable, and to Latin minds, her policy was neither logical nor wise.

The problems remained—Germany, Austria, Abyssinia—and the Anglo-German Naval Agreement had infinitely complicated efforts to resolve any of them.

16

The Triumph of the Peace Ballot

"In effect the Prime Minister was confessing himself to be a captive of Lord Cecil's bow and spear. He found himself constrained to pay heed to the voice of eleven and a half million electors whose vote might turn the scale when next Mr. Baldwin's Government appealed to the Country. . . . The effect of the Peace Ballot upon the policy of Mr. Baldwin's Government was, indeed, profound and enduring."
—Arnold J. Toynbee[1]

A Compromise Offer

The May 24 resolution of the League Council setting a schedule for the conciliation process between Italy and Abyssinia was only a temporary measure. Something had to be done and Sir Eric Drummond outlined the problem for Sir John Simon on June 1.[2]

His interview with Mussolini had given Drummond a clear picture. Mussolini was not about to give up his Abyssinian ambitions. He looked for a substantial result. But, Drummond advised, the League might well not survive an outright annexation, or even a protectorate. The alternative was some kind of compromise. It might be argued that this was blackmail, Italy obtaining by threat of force what she could never gain in a true negotiation. When Drummond added that the idea would undoubtedly be highly repugnant, he was underestimating the response of Lord Cecil and his followers. He concluded starkly:

There are, however, some situations in which one is only offered a choice of two evils, one greater and one less.

He put his finger directly on the greater evil—Germany. Hitler said only one issue divided Italy and Germany. Mussolini said he would judge other nations by their attitude to Abyssinia. Were the League to thwart Mussolini's ambitions, nothing would be more natural for Italy and Germany than to join hands. "All that is required," Drummond advised, "is a deal over Austria."

Would it not be logical, then, Drummond asked, whether overtly or covertly, to help Italy to obtain satisfaction? Mussolini was himself awaiting some move from his "friends," that is to say, Britain and France.

Drummond issued a warning that would be repeated by others. If Britain and France were not ready to coerce Italy in Abyssinia, they ought to let Abyssinia know lest they arouse false hopes of help that would never come. Here was the naked issue—what, in the last resort, would Britain and France do? Whatever that might be, Drummond counseled first consulting the French to determine how far the two nations would satisfy Mussolini.

Vansittart agreed. He did not mince words: "The position," he wrote on June 8, 1935,

> is as plain as a pikestaff. Italy will have to be bought off—let us use and face ugly words—in some form or other, or Abyssinia will eventually perish. That might in itself matter less, if it did not mean that the League would also perish (and that Italy would simultaneously perform *another* volte-face into the arms of Germany, a combination of haute politique and haute cocotterie that we can ill afford just now.)[3]

If the price were all of Abyssinia, it would be impossibly high. It would, Vansittart thought, cause a disastrous explosion that would wreck the League, which was one thing, and very possibly the British Government, which was quite another. For Britain was on the eve of an election.

This was a critical consideration. The Government had been reconstituted but its statutory term would end in 1936. In the forthcoming national election, Abyssinia would be an issue.

Here was a problem indeed. Col. Clifford had proceeded into the Ogaden escorted by the Abyssinian levies, and the Somaliland Camel Corps, not solely to mark the boundary between Abyssinia and Britain Somaliland. There had been talk, and it had upset the Italians, of the trade to Abyssinia of a seaport on the Red Sea for portions of the

Ogaden which would interpose the British as a buffer between Abyssinia and Italian Somaliland.

Vansittart now reduced this to a concrete proposal. To protect the League and the Government, Britain would have to pay a price. Let Britain provide compensation to Abyssinia, by way of a Red Sea port, in exchange for such concessions, territorial and otherwise as Italy might expect. This would save something.

> I should like to see the question of Somaliland considered at least, while we can still get something for less than nothing. If this cock won't fight, let someone else produce another that will. But whence? Failing these, we may prepare for a horrid autumn—and beyond.[4]

Vansittart got his wish. He met with Hoare and Eden over the weekend of June 16, 1935. They proposed to offer to Abyssinia the port of Zeila in British Somaliland. Abyssinia would in turn cede to Italy territory in the Ogaden. This was the earlier British plan with Italy substituted as beneficiary.

They consulted Drummond in Rome who was hopeful. Mussolini might not like to see an Abyssinian port on the Red Sea, but the territorial and mineral resources of the Ogaden might tempt him.[5] Vansittart prepared Hoare for the Cabinet meeting of June 19. The prospects were gloomy—an early move forward by Italy, which would leave the League and turn to Germany, thereby shattering both the League and the Stresa front:

> That alone would be bad enough. There is worse. All this would happen on the eve of the General Election—one of the most important in the nation's history—and the consequences might well be catastrophic to His Majesty's Government. They would be assailed on both sides and would lose a great body of support whether they took action against Italy or whether they did not.

There were two methods of preventing the crisis of Italian aggression. One was to mobilize world opinion against Italy. The other was to offer concrete inducements. Vansittart thought public opinion could not be relied upon. Lord Cecil would hardly agree. The Abyssinian drama would be a confrontation between these two points of view. The Zeila proposal was a minimum; but it offered a chance. If the Cabinet approved, Eden would bear it to Rome. It would, of course, Vansittart noted, be essential to keep the French informed. They had their own considerable interests at stake in Djibuti, French Somaliland, Abyssinia's sole outlet to the sea. But, Vansittart continued, it would pay them to go along—by saving the Franco-Italian agreement, the League and Stresa.[6]

To all this, the Cabinet on June 19, 1935 agreed on condition that the cession of British territory should be part of a complete settlement that would rule out any possibility of war. The Italian response was prompt. On June 20, Drummond wired that Mussolini would be delighted to receive Eden—under cover of discussions of a naval agreement and an air pact.[7]

Drummond alerted Hoare to a potential problem. Mussolini might well complain that since January all his approaches to the British Government had been rebuffed or ignored. This had been, in Vansittart's opinion, neither wise nor courteous. They should have been given the classic explanation for delay which Hoare now suggested—a committee had been appointed to study the matter and report.[8]

On June 18, 1935, the Maffey Committee to submitted its report.[9]

The Maffey Report

The report had, of course, originated in the visit in January of Signor Vitetti to the Foreign Office to explore the development of British and Italian interests in Abyssinia in a "mutually harmonious manner."

The Committee took a realistic stance. It assumed that Italy would absorb Abyssinia in whole or in part. What would be the impact on British interests?

To answer this question, the Committee defined British interests as local and immediate. It did not attempt to answer the question of how such Italian action would affect the League of Nations or the European situation. Those were matters of high policy beyond the Commission's competence. It did not attempt to pass judgment on the moral issues involved in breaches of international agreements or outright aggression.

What the Commission did was to produce a concise and informative report on Abyssinia, its geography, people, economy, and history. It noted that Abyssinian foreign trade was negligible, confined mostly to coffee, hides and skins, and beeswax. Trade with Britain was more negligible still amounting in 1934 to British exports to Abyssinia of less than £50,000 and imports of some £125,000. There was no sizeable British population or enterprise in the country—indeed, the only substantial foreign enterprise was the French built and owned Djibuti Railway.

Of the population of 7.5 million, about a third were estimated to be of the true Amhara, or Abyssinian ruling race, a Christian people. These inhabited the central plateau north of Addis Ababa. The remainder were Gallas, Somalis, Danakils, either pagan or Mohammedan, whose allegiance to the Abyssinian Emperor was dubious.

Italy would surely claim, the report noted, that Abyssinia was an anachronism, a savage country lacking an effective central government, its borders in continuing turmoil, unable or unwilling to control widespread slavery, a country in which the ruling Amharas oppressed and persecuted the outlying subject races they had conquered in the years since Adowa.

But Sir John Maffey, the honorary Pathan, the champion of the native peoples, was generous in his assessment:

> The Empress died in 1929 and Ras Tafari became Emperor. Since the war the internal condition of Ethiopia has slowly improved. There has been, in recent years, no revolt serious enough to menace the stability of the regime. The Emperor has endeavored to make his authority effective over the local chiefs and in the outlying districts, particularly by the provision of better communications; there has been a sincere, though unhappily only partially successful, attempt to improve frontier administration, to eradicate slavery, brigandage and other abuses. Cruelty, crudity, and confusion can still be found in Ethiopia. Ethiopian pride, suspicion, intolerance, and indolence make reform slow and difficult; but it does not appear reasonable or just to write off the Ethiopian Empire as irremediably barbarous and uncivilized without any hope of eventual reform.[10]

The report concluded, first that Italy would indeed attempt to obtain control over Abyssinia. There were, it further concluded, no vital British interests in Abyssinia that would be adversely affected by an Italian conquest. There would be advantages (more secure borders) and disadvantages (in trade), but no balance one way or the other. From the military standpoint, an independent Abyssinia might be preferable, but any threat to British interests was entirely remote. Britain should, of course, in any train of events protect its position at Lake Tana and the sources of the Nile. The veteran proconsul also recommended that steps be taken to protect the grazing rights of the "British" tribesmen in British Somaliland. Perhaps there could even be advantageous frontier adjustments.

This was a lucid and professional document that did credit to the Colonial Office and its chief. He clearly saw the three different levels of the problem and confined his attention to the area of his expertise and his department's competence—the local level. The next level was Europe and the likely impact of Abyssinia on European security. This was the prime concern of Mussolini as it was of Pierre Laval and Sir Robert Vansittart who exercised increasing influence on the new Foreign Secretary. Beyond this were the international concepts of collective security, the League of Nations, and international morality. These were the banners that Lord Cecil held aloft and behind him marched the millions who had cast their votes in the Peace Ballot. They were joined by those others who loved peace, hated war and armaments, who sought security not in rearmament but in disarmament, who were concerned over German grievances and French arms. Such people tended to reject evil absolutely, even though it might be the lesser evil, and instinctively to grasp the solution consistent with their views of morality, without deep consideration of the practical consequences.

Anthony Eden's Journey

Anthony Eden had not become Foreign Secretary, but he could hardly complain that he had been relegated to menial tasks. Immediately upon the conclusion of the Anglo-German Naval Agreement, he was sent on the road as a salesman. He was first to sell the French the naval pact. Presumably having accomplished this, he was then to sell Mussolini the Zeila compromise.

His task may have been complicated by his increasingly intimate identification with the collective system. He had given the system a ringing endorsement on May 16, 1935 in his speech to the East and West Fulham Conservative and Unionist Association, concluding that

> There was much talk these days of new commitments. A great part of the fears expressed on this account were superfluous. What was really important was not that this country should shoulder new commitments but that it should emphasize its determination to fulfill those obligations it had already undertaken. In the last resort, the authority of a collective system must flow from the overwhelming potential force it was able to array against the aggressor. Clearly the efficacy of such a deterrent must depend upon the known determination of the parties to fulfill their obligations.[11]

Mussolini's was first and last a journalist. An avid reader of the foreign press, he might have registered these sentiments in appraising his forthcoming visitor.

But when in Parliament on June 7, 1935, Clement Attlee asked for a plain statement of Britain's intention to uphold the League, and even to close the Suez Canal to Italian traffic, Eden's reply was in a milder vein. Italy had agreed to conciliation, he said, and the Government hoped for a solution which would square with the Covenant, the Kellogg-Briand Pact and the 1928 Italo-Abyssinian Treaty. This was different from a straight policy of upholding the Covenant and between these two policies the British Government would oscillate for the next six months.[12]

Eden's mission to Paris was to convince Laval and the French government not only of the wisdom of the Naval Agreement, but also of British good faith. His prospects were not enhanced by a decision he had taken before his arrival. The announced purpose of his continuing journey to Rome was to discuss air and land armaments with the Duce. Eden did not in his talks with Laval mention the Zeila proposal, in which French interests were directly concerned, and which was the real purpose of his journey.

When Anthony Eden, the beau ideal of the idealists, sat down at a Paris conference table to protest British good faith to Pierre Laval, who was widely regarded as a devious fellow, it was Eden who was at the same time concealing cards and spades in his well-tailored sleeve. What he did not know was that Corbin, French Ambassador in London, had learned of the Zeila offer from confidential sources and had informed Laval.[13]

At their meeting on June 21, 1935, Laval went straight to the point. The French Government and the French public were thoroughly upset by a Naval Agreement which did not even mention Versailles. It was not only a revocation of that Treaty, and a repudiation of the Declaration of February 3, but it had broken the Stresa front into pieces.

The whole point in Laval's view was to secure a general agreement. He wanted peace with Germany but only if Germany would make peace with everyone else. This, he thought, was just what the separate Anglo-German agreement encouraged Germany not to do. France would never, in dealing with Germany, act without fully informing and consulting Britain.

Eden valiantly argued that the offer was one no British Government could refuse. He urged Laval to send French naval experts to London to participate in technical discussions. Laval resolutely declined this effort to associate France with the Agreement. If the British Government had to look to public opinion, so did he.

Would Britain now proceed on an air pact separate from limitations on land armaments the French asked? And would there be bilateral pacts to enforce an air pact? As the French saw it, an air pact must be part of a General Settlement involving land armaments, Austria, Eastern Europe, and Germany's return to the League. This was, after all, no more than they had said on February 3, and there must be supporting bilateral agreements to make an air pact effective.[14]

This was more than Eden had bargained for and he obtained an adjournment to consult his Government to which, that evening, he wired his impressions. The meeting had been difficult. Laval was clearly troubled, less buoyant than he had ever been. "None the less," he concluded, "Monsieur Laval is himself not unduly disposed to cry over spilt milk. He is however determined to preserve what is left of February 3."[15]

When Eden arrived in Rome on June 23, he was disconcerted to learn that the Zeila offer had been leaked to the press. The French would know of Eden's duplicity and Mussolini would understand that the carefully constructed cover of his meeting with Eden had been penetrated.[16]

Eden met with Mussolini June 24. Mussolini was realistic. He thought the Naval Agreement had been a great success for Germany. It was now a fait accompli. Still, the same result could have been obtained in consultation with Italy and France. Mussolini's own priorities were, in order: an air pact, a Central European pact and an Eastern pact. When the discussion of European issues had been completed, Eden turned to the real subject. His Majesty's Government, he said, were irrevocably committed to the League of Nations on which their foreign policy was founded. On this subject there was no real division in the British public. It was for these reasons that Britain was anxious to find a solution to the Abyssinian crisis. Eden then unveiled the Zeila plan.

Mussolini responded promptly and in the sense foreseen by Drummond. There were grave objections. The proposal would strengthen Abyssinia by giving her a seaport through which she could import arms. It would be a victory for Abyssinia and for Britain as Abyssinia's protector. No, the plan was positively dangerous. Mussolini now proceeded to lay his cards on the table. He would reciprocate, he said, the sincerity underlying the British offer by detailing his objectives which would no longer be a matter of speculation.

He would be content with those outlying parts of Abyssinia which were not inhabited by Abyssinians and which Abyssinia had conquered in the past fifty years. He made a circular gesture to indicate these outlying territories. The central plateau would remain under Abyssinian sovereignty, though there would be Italian control.

If Abyssinia would not come to terms, if Italy had to fight, then, with a sweeping gesture, Mussolini indicated that Italy would take all. He had sent 150,000 men to Africa. He would send 500,000 more, if necessary.

Eden could have taken note of Mussolini's position and retired to consider it and what advantage could be derived from it. He could, like Laval, have seen it as a basis for negotiation, an invitation to further discussion, and the continuing search for mutual advantage. He did not. If Italy were to take the law in its own hands, he lectured, and if the League were destroyed, the British people would deeply resent it; relations between the two nations would suffer the gravest injury.

Mussolini said that he understood British public opinion. He had no desire to leave the League. But if given no choice, he would. Laval in Rome, he said, had given him a free hand. "Economically," Eden interjected. Perhaps as far as the written instruments were concerned, Mussolini replied, but comparing all that Italy had given to France's modest concessions—a few palm trees, a strip of desert without even sheep—it must be clear that France had disinterested herself.

Eden recalled Laval's warning: "Vous avez de mains forts." "At this," Eden reported, "Signor Mussolini flung himself back in his chair with a gesture of incredulous astonishment."

The tone of the conversation was friendly, Eden reported. But like Drummond earlier, he observed that Mussolini was quiet. There was no bluster. He appeared resigned. "There was a gloomy fatality about his temper which I fear it may be beyond power of reasoning to modify," was Eden's concluding observation.[17]

Eden met Mussolini again in the late afternoon and conveyed his government's regrets that the proposal had not succeeded. It now seemed to him impossible for Britain to be of any help.

Mussolini confirmed his stance of the day before. He indicated on the map Italy's demands—those territories surrounding what he viewed as Abyssinia proper—Tigre, Amhara, Gojjam, and Shoa. Eden again declined to pursue the possibilities inherent in this approach. Instead he told Mussolini that a war to acquire the territories he desired would violate the Covenant and the 1906 Treaty. If there had to be such a war, Mussolini said, he would wipe Abyssinia from the map. Eden hoped Mussolini would not be deluded as to British public opinion. "Public opinion in England," he said, "took its stand on this question upon the League of Nations."

This was neither a negotiation, nor an exchange of views, but a statement of positions. Eden talked of the League and Mussolini talked of the need to settle the Abyssinian question. There was no more to be done or said.[18]

An embarrassed Eden now had to face Pierre Laval on his home-ward journey. They met on June 27. To Laval the Zeila offer was a trick which would have forced France to make Djibuti a free port adversely affecting the railway which paid most of the expenses of French Somaliland and he said so. Eden's account does not indicate his response. He then told Laval of his meeting with Mussolini.

Laval had, as usual, a practical suggestion. Had they thought of a protectorate? In this way, the Emperor could maintain his throne and his sovereignty against the rases. Now that Laval knew the full extent of Italian demands, he thought it worth trying.

They talked of Laval's January discussions with Mussolini. If Mussolini thought France had given him a free hand, this might be true, but it all depended on what use he made of it. He only gave up, Laval said, what France had a right to give up. He had agreed not to obstruct. Curiously, the French documents do not cover this meeting.

Eden now said that Britain had done all it could. It was time for France to come forward. Perhaps Laval could sound out Mussolini and let him know how gravely he was concerned.[19]

There was little discussion this time about the Naval Agreement. François-Poncet had met Hitler the day before. Hitler's assurances could only have aroused Laval's suspicions. He certainly had not tried, Hitler had said, by the Naval Agreement to separate Britain and France. "No idea," he said, "could be further from my mind."[20]

Laval had asked Eden on his outward journey if Britain would proceed on an air pact separate from an agreement on land armaments, and Eden had referred the inquiry to London. London, always asking clarity of France, replied to Eden's inquiry with equivocation. Eden was to note the French desire for all-round agreement, being careful at the same time not to say or imply that all agreements must be simultaneously concluded.[21]

Eden nonetheless stated Britain's willingness to proceed only on an all-round basis, but Laval soon probed the hesitancies and the ambiguities of British policy. Why had Britain changed its mind so soon? This was not what the February 3 Declaration said. In the end, they understood that they did not agree. While Eden continued to protest British devotion to the February Declaration, the disparity between British words and British acts was clear to Laval.[22]

Anthony Eden's journey had not been a success. He had hardly improved British standing in France and had raised grave doubts as to British fidelity to a common Franco-British-Italian front against Germany. More than that, his confrontation with Mussolini had clearly advanced the Abyssinian crisis to the point of no return—the explosion capable of wrecking the League and the Stresa front.

Under such circumstances, the French valued more than ever their relationship with Italy. Military and air conversations had been proceeding steadily. The Italians took the laboring oar. Marshal Badoglio and General Gamelin drafted joint military plans. Was France ready to sign, Badoglio asked? Gamelin replied that he could only initial agreed plans; the final decision was political, for his Government to decide. He talked of the different cases—*Anschluss* and the Rhineland.

Badoglio first and then Mussolini took pains to assure Gamelin that Italian involvement in East Africa would in no way weaken Italy in Europe, and it was Mussolini who distinctly specified the Brenner.[23]

There was little question of the correspondence of French and Italian interests. France understood Italy's ambitions in Abyssinia. Both, however, agreed that their chief concern and primary interest lay in Europe in the person of Adolf Hitler and the Nazi state. They saw no particular difficulty in pursuing these interests simultaneously.

Britain was proceeding on a different basis. The British representatives at Stresa, and Eden in conference with Laval and then Mussolini, had not grounded British policy on strictly British interests. The Maffey report had clearly laid down that, at least in Africa, British interests were unlikely to be affected by an Italian conquest of Abyssinia.

Instead Britain was basing its stand on the League and the Covenant. The stated reason was that public opinion demanded this and that no British Government could withstand the force of this opinion.

This was remarkable for at least two reasons. From the League's inception, France had sought the automatic application of sanctions, an immediate response to any breach of the Covenant. France had never succeeded. The idea struck horror in the hearts and minds of postwar British statesmen. They were haunted by a perennial fear of being catapulted into commitments where Britain had no interest and where the reward was totally incommensurate to the risk. As in so many other things, the shadow of 1914 hung over British statesmen who reflected on how and why Britain had been precipitated into the maelstrom.

MacDonald and Simon had gone to Stresa under the express under-taking to enter no new commitments. No commitment was the British watchword in Central and Eastern Europe. The primary question raised in Britain concerning the Franco-Soviet Pact was whether it in any way increased British commitments. Locarno itself caused concern enough as A.J. Boorman had found in the Ilford poll.

At Stresa, the French plan for automatic sanctions had shocked and dismayed Britain, and its representatives fought a vigorous rear-guard action to substitute vagueness and good will for clarity and precision.

Now, in June, the British Government, faced with Mussolini's plans and demands, took its stand on the Covenant. It was now France which wanted to examine the matter and seek some solution which might render unnecessary the strict application of the Covenant. These were positions Britain and France would maintain as Mussolini stood firm and as the two nations were called upon to take their stands as the leaders and champions of the League of Nations.

The second remarkable feature of the crisis was the engine that had brought about this enormous and simultaneous change of fronts. On Friday, June 27, Lord Cecil announced the final results of the Peace Ballot to a mass meeting at Albert Hall.

The Final Results

Lord Cecil's penchant for public relations was as evident at the close of the Peace Ballot as it had been in the inception. The army of 500,000 volunteers had done its work. The vote totals, regularly an-nounced, were approaching 10 million at the end of May.

A great meeting was scheduled for June 27 at the Albert Hall at which the final tally would be announced. This would be, *Headway* predicted: "the last incident of a gallant story." "The meeting," *Head-*

*wa*y continued, "will enjoy the thrill of learning a secret. Is the Ballot's grand total ten million?"[24]

Lord Cecil was joined on the platform by the Archbishop of Canterbury and other dignitaries. There were ringing cheers when he announced the final total of 11,626,765 votes. He summarized the results. There had been immense affirmative majorities for every question except 5b, the issue of military sanctions against an aggressor. This affirmative vote was still a majority, but there were large negative votes and abstentions.

The returns had varied from 12 percent to 82 percent of the electorate, but since the responses to the individual questions had been so uniform, Lord Cecil considered them representative.

He was practical as usual. The Ballot, he said, was not an end, only a beginning:

> Governments come and go. But as long as the people stand for support of the League, that must be the national policy. Foreigners know that well enough, and I hope that the results of the Ballot will show that, whatever a few noisy newspapers may say, the world can safely rely on British support for the collective system. And there is another thing which Continental Governments would do well to notice. If they want British friendship, they also must regulate their foreign policy by the principle of the League.[25]

There was work to be done. The government must acknowledge the Ballot. A deputation headed by Lord Cecil would attend to this. It would represent all those who had worked so hard for the Cause, the churches, the women's organizations, the peace societies, and the trade unions.

Every member of Parliament, Cecil advised, should be personally approached in his constituency and told how his electors had voted. But the Ballot had little to do with "the ordinary claptrap" of party politics. Lord Cecil was contemptuous of power politics—the jackboot, the mailed fist, the shining armor, the half-clever diplomatic tricks. Of all these, he said, the British public was sick. There must be an appeal to world opinion so that war might be prevented by the action of the whole civilized community.

Lord Cecil pleaded for disarmament, the abolition of aerial bombing, and the private manufacture of sale of arms. His final words were blunt:

It [the Ballot] is a solemn declaration by a free and educated people of their will on vital issues on which they feel with passionate intensity. It is for those who represent them in Parliament and the Cabinet to carry those wishes into effect; and in that connection I hope that Members, Ministers and Candidates as well will not be allowed to forget that a General Election is near at hand.

The Archbishop of Canterbury told the audience that the Ballot had been a ringing declaration of faith in the League of Nations. Beyond the issue of policy was something greater still. The Ballot was "a great revelation of the ideals which were cherished by the great mass of people in this country. It was a great thing when in any country a great body of citizens recorded their convictions in a great ideal and their determination that it should ultimately prevail."[26]

This outlook accorded perfectly with Lord Cecil's. Church and state were of equal interest and importance to him. In the *Official History of the Peace Ballot*, which was promptly issued in June, he had viewed the League of Nations as "in the direct line of Christian progress" and nothing could be for him more beautiful or more meaningful than the union of the practical and the ideal.

The impact of the Peace Ballot was direct and forceful. The day after the announcement, the *Spectator* endorsed Lord Cecil's claim:

The verdict is decisive and impressive. . . . Henceforward there can be no reasonable doubt about the convictions of the mass of people of this country; no Government will dare flout public opinion by slighting the League, or by refraining from efforts to secure agreed disarmament and collective sanctions against peace breakers.[27]

When the new Prime Minister made a major policy address on June 30, 1935, his principal topics were domestic. Stanley Baldwin had been a businessman before he entered politics. He prided himself on his insularity. It was only with difficulty that he briefly turned his attention to foreign affairs:

I want to say a word about the recent naval agreement with Germany, and I want to preface my observations by saying that we shall continue in the future as we have done in the past, to follow unswervingly the paths of peace and reconciliation in Europe and everywhere else. The Covenant of the League of Nations is the sheet anchor of British policy. There is no need for me to affirm to you our intention to fulfill our obligations under the Treaty of Locarno. The objects set out in the London Declaration of

February 3 remain our programme and it is our earnest hope that the whole of that programme may be realized.

He then defended the Naval Agreement. There were those, he said, who had impugned German motives, who had said that you could not trust the Germans. This was painful.

"When you are trying to negotiate limitation of armaments or disarmament, what can you do if you do not trust? You revert straight to the law of the jungle and no progress is possible. [The] Germans and ourselves entered into this, in my belief with, equally honorable motives, and I rejoice to think that they as well as ourselves are in favor of the complete abolition of the submarine."[28]

Lord Cecil's Day of Triumph

On July 23, 1935 the Prime Minister received Lord Cecil's deputation. The attendance of the Foreign Minister and the Minister for League of Nations Affairs emphasized the importance of the occasion. On his side, Lord Cecil was accompanied by the Dean of Chichester, representing the churches, and Miss K.D. Courtenay representing the women's organizations.

Lord Cecil was not apt to be unduly impressed by the ministers of state. He had himself grown up in intimate contact with the Prime Minister; he had aspired to be Foreign Secretary, and had discharged the duties of that office; he was a founder and perhaps the greatest champion of the League of Nations. Rather, he might have viewed the occasion in quite another light. Here, in the persons of the Dean of Chichester, Miss Courtenay and most of all himself, was the voice of the public conveying not so much its opinion as its mandate to the Ministers.

He reported the results of the Peace Ballot. Especially in humble homes he said, the voters had shown an eagerness to vote and an intelligent appreciation of the issues. He emphasized the nonpolitical nature of the Ballot, the object of which had been "to show support for a vigorous and successful Peace policy through the League of Nations, and it had no other object."[30]

The Dean of Chichester, in describing the wholehearted support of the churches, stressed the happy coincidence that the plain teachings of Christianity could inform and support the policy of the Government.

Miss Courtenay said that women's organizations had furnished more than half of the 500,000 volunteers. Women liked the Peace Ballot because it was democratic, nonpartisan, and most of all, because it was practical and definite and not simply a sentimental appeal for peace.

The Prime Minister paid tribute to Lord Cecil. His response was direct and to the point:

> The deputation will be aware that the foreign policy of his Majesty's Government is founded upon the League of Nations. This has been many times made plain, not only by my own declarations and those of by colleagues, but also by the actions of his Majesty's Government at Geneva, where upon repeated occasions we have taken the lead in endeavoring to secure the settlement of international disputes by peaceful means in accordance with terms of the Covenant. . . .
>
> I am glad to know that I correctly interpret your sentiments when I say that the object of the Ballot was by no means to criticize the Government, even though some may have endeavored to use the movement for this purpose, but rather to show the Government that we had a large volume of public opinion behind us in the efforts which we are today making to maintain the authority of the League of Nations. We value this support. We are living in a period of very disturbed international relations, and I am glad of this opportunity to assure the deputation that the Government intend to persist in the policy they have hitherto pursued, and that the League of Nations remains, as I said in a speech in Yorkshire, 'The sheet anchor of British policy!'[30]

The British delegation at Stresa had shrunk in horror from the French suggestion of economic sanctions against Covenant breakers and this was consistent with the long tradition of British policy. Now British statesmen were emphasizing the devotion of the British public to the League of Nations. This is what Anthony Eden had told Pierre Laval and Benito Mussolini. This is what the Prime Minister had proclaimed in Yorkshire on June 30.

Now in direct response to Lord Cecil and his deputation representing the $11\frac{1}{2}$ million Peace Balloters, who had voted 97 percent in favor of the League of Nations, Baldwin categorically affirmed that British foreign policy was and would be based on the Covenant and the League of Nations. Nor could the timing have been more fortuitous. He made this declaration in the face of an international crisis in which one of the greatest League powers was clearly preparing to embark upon a deliberate campaign of aggression against one of its poorest, weakest, and most backward members.

Baldwin's response revealed, Professor Toynbee afterwards wrote, with his accustomed verve, "the almost ludicrously frank precipitancy with which the leading members of the United Kingdom Government now changed their tune."[31]

Indeed, Toynbee observed,

> In effect the Prime Minister was confessing himself to be a captive of Lord Cecil's bow and spear. He found himself constrained to pay heed to the voice of eleven and a half million electors whose vote might turn the scale when next Mr. Baldwin's Government appealed to the Country. . . . The effect of the Peace Ballot upon the policy of Mr. Baldwin's Government was, indeed, profound and enduring.[32]

How profound and enduring would be revealed again and again in the major events of the months to come, exercising in the end a decisive influence on the fate of Europe and of the world.

In this supreme moment, Lord Cecil could reflect upon his objectives in promoting the Peace Ballot.

One stated object had been to influence peace movements in other countries. Another had been to educate the British public, "to place before the public the real issue—namely what exactly is involved in Great Britain being a member of the League of Nations?"

But the first and foremost object had been to assure the British Government that the British people overwhelmingly approved the collective system and believed that the support and extension of the League of Nations should be a cardinal point of foreign policy. The results, Lord Cecil said, had far exceeded the most sanguine expectation.[33]

If the British people took the lead, if they spoke decisively, Lord Cecil was convinced the world would follow and the Covenant would be vindicated.

We can, in the moment of the Prime Minister's response to the deputation, imagine the scope of Lord Cecil's triumph. The League of Nations had failed in Manchuria and was fast losing confidence and support. The Disarmament Conference had collapsed. Europe was re-arming at an accelerating pace. Democracy in most of Europe had given way to dictatorship and monstrous tyrannies which gloried in hatred, repression, militarism, and aggression and which were not only firmly entrenched but seemed to have generated the enthusiastic approval of their citizens.

What was left of the hopes and goals of 1918—a world made safe for democracy, a world of freedom and justice, a world of peace after a war to end war, a world in which an international community, in the form of the League of Nations, would by peaceful means resolve the disputes of nations in a way that the balance of power and terror never had and never could?

Lord Cecil's faith had never wavered. His vision remained intact. He had carried on the fight whatever the odds. With immense courage and unflagging energy, he had melded imagination and a flair for public relations with a solid and practical talent for organization.

He could have carried on his campaign in the upper reaches of the British Establishment, where he had lived and worked all his life, where his access was hereditary and intimate. He could have proceeded in Parliament where he had served so long in both Houses and through the political system.

Lord Cecil had a grander vision. He would go directly to the British people in whom his confidence was unwavering. He would appeal to their sound practical judgment and at the same time to their ideals, which, Lord Cecil never doubted, were his own. He chose to operate, not through peers and parliamentarians, through politicians and civil servants, generals and admirals, but instead, in a glorious moment, he confronted them all with the will of the people.

No longer could the Government claim that the British people were uninterested in the League of Nations and unwilling to play a part in collective security. The British people believed in the League as mankind's best hope and Lord Cecil could point to the specific responses of the Peace Ballot to sustain this point.

The tumult and shouting which had accompanied Woodrow Wilson's journeys to Europe had long since faded. The dying President had implored Lord Cecil to carry on. Wilson was forgotten, but Lord Cecil remembered. Briand had said there would be no war as long as he lived; but he had died in 1932. Streseman, too, was gone, predicting on his deathbed that his country would wage a second Punic War.

At seventy, Lord Cecil was a relic of these other times. He was entitled to an honorable retirement from the responsibilities and the cares of public service. This had never occurred to him. He had indeed carried on, with matchless spirit and ability and he had compelled an uncertain and wavering government firmly to adopt his policy (insofar as they could understand it)—or at least for the moment to say they did.

If the Peace Ballot had been a triumph of inspiration and organization, there was one respect in which it owed its ultimate impact to fate. The Ilford Poll had taken place, the National Declaration Committee had been formed, the machinery put in place, and the first ballots returned in November 1934, before the shots were fired at the water holes of Wal Wal that precipitated the Abyssinian crisis.

Lord Cecil could never have imagined in the beginnings of the Peace Ballot that the campaign would march, step by step, with a growing public interest in the colorful and compelling drama of Abyssinia. Nor could he have foreseen that when the day came to confront the Prime Minister with the triumphant results, the African drama would have presented itself to a fascinated world as a direct confrontation between a would-be aggressor and the authority, the effectiveness, and indeed the very survival of the League of Nations.

What Did It Mean?

One of the objects of the Peace Ballot had been to educate the British people as to the meaning of being a member of the League of Nations. What, then, did it mean?

The British government may have been the captive of Lord Cecil's bow and spear; and the Prime Minister may have declared that the League of Nations was the sheet anchor of British policy. But, how would the Peace Ballot guide the policy of the British Government in confronting the hard practical choices of an international crisis?

To Lord Cecil, the answers were clear. The British public had been thoughtful. They had not voted in ignorance or carelessness. Indeed, the Ballot had showed the competence of the man in the street to deal with the complexities of international affairs. They now knew what it meant to be a member of the League of Nations—to pursue peace through collective means.

But the questions that the Peace Ballot propounded were less simple than they seemed, and the responses, overwhelming though the majorities may have been, took on a Delphic quality.

To the first question, 96 percent responded that Britain should remain a member of the League of Nations. But the League was an organization, not a policy. Membership in the League did not absolve the British government of the responsibility to formulate and carry out a policy. The League had no executive, no military force, though the

French had wanted it that way. Beyond debates and resolutions, it could function in the last resort only through the direct action of its members. Of these, Britain was incomparably the leader. The League would look to Britain for its policy and the force to back that policy.

British policy had heretofore been based on British interests. What would happen in the event British interests did not coincide with, indeed actively opposed the interests of a majority of the League? What were the obligations of membership? Was Britain obliged to take part in every world conflict, large or small, no matter how remote from British territory or British interests? Was Britain's obligation separate, or was it joint and several, depending upon the actions of others? And what must Britain do if others failed or refused to take effective action? Membership in the League was one thing, but how to make the League an effective instrument of policy was something else.

The second question was: Are you in favor of an all-round reduction of armaments by international agreement?

The 90.6 percent affirmative vote showed how deeply disarmament was wanted. This was an admirable sentiment. But it did not tally with reality. However much Hitler spoke of peace, Germany was proceeding to build a mighty army, an air force, and now a navy up to her shipbuilding capacity. Mussolini talked of nine million bayonets and prepared for war.

However desirable disarmament might be, there was no all-round agreement in sight and no serious movement toward such an agreement. The true question then became: How would Britain respond to the triple threat of a mighty air power within striking distance of its shores, a reborn German army, and an Italy prepared to take up arms in violation of the Covenant? To this question the Peace Ballot offered little help and no comfort. Here was an instructive example. Membership in the League was not enough. The League had neither the means nor the will to compel disarmament.

The third question exhibited the same defects: Are you in favor of the all-round abolition of national military and naval air craft by international agreement? The answer—85.2 percent affirmative, was not an adequate reply to the new Luftwaffe. If there were no such agreement, however ardently sought, what was the responsibility and what would be the policy of the British government? Here again, the voices of eleven and a half million voters did not offer much practical advice.

The fourth question was: Should the manufacture and sale of armaments for private profit be prohibited by international agreement? Krupp was subject to no such agreement and the support of arms manufacturers was a crucial ingredient in Hitler's success.

If it were in fact necessary for Britain to rearm, because all efforts at internationally agreed upon arms limitation had failed, the question was where efficient capacity existed rather than whether that capacity was in public or private hands. Once the British Government adopted a policy of rearmament, a unilateral decision to abstain from the private production of arms was as irresponsible as it was illogical.

There were graver difficulties with Questions 5a and 5b. 11,090,387 voters favored British membership in the League of Nations. In response to Question 5a, only 10,027,628 agreed that, if one nation insisted upon attacking another, the other nations should combine to stop it by economic and nonmilitary measures. A million voters, apparently, would not back the Covenant with economic sanctions. Only 6,784,368 believed, in the event of such an attack, that the other nations should combine to stop it, if necessary, by military measures. 2,351,981 disagreed. The affirmative vote tallied 74.2 percent of the combined Yes and No votes; but, significantly, only 58.7 percent of the total vote counting the abstentions.

This indicated that some 41 percent of the voters were of the opinion that the Covenant should be enforced either without economic sanctions or by economic sanctions alone. Moreover by their unwillingness to countenance military sanctions, they were expressing the opinion, whether or not they realized it, that economic sanctions could be effectively applied without the risk of war. This would be much debated, but in the event neither the military staffs nor the Cabinet accepted this viewpoint.

There was a more serious question for the Government to ponder. In a free and open society, liberally endowed with mass communications, could a war be sustained by the approval of less than 60 percent of the electorate? From 1914 to 1918 Britain had experienced its first people's war. The next war would be total war. Could total war be effectively waged by half the people?

To Lord Cecil the answers were clear enough:

The Ballot is over. More than eleven millions of our fellow-countrymen have declared their opinions on the broad issues of Peace and Disarmament through the League of Nations, and on the subsidiary points by the questions put to them. Their answer has been plain and decisive.[34]

What of the substantial minorities who favored neither the abolition of air warfare nor military sanctions? "I cannot help feeling," was Lord Cecil's analysis,

> that the hesitation on both points is largely due to misunderstanding. No doubt there is a certain school of opinion worthy of the utmost respect who conscientiously object to the use of force for any purpose whatsoever, even to protect the weak from oppression by the strong. But their numbers would scarcely account for the size of the minority on Question 5b and would certainly not explain at all those who voted (in Question 3) against the suppression of air warfare. In each case the explanation of the greater part of these negative votes is more likely to have been a misapprehension of the argument on the opposite side.[35]

Another explanation could be offered, especially with regard to Question 5b. Perhaps the negative voters were simply voting for peace. After all, this was the Peace Ballot, and it had been presented to the public under the dramatic question: "Shall it be War or Peace?" If Lord Cecil explained the vote as a misunderstanding of some of the issues, a critic of the Peace Ballot could complain, as many did, that there was ample room for misunderstanding of the rest.

On one point there was neither cavil nor criticism. Polling was in its crude beginnings and the questions could be questioned, but it was accepted that the proponents of the Peace Ballot had been scrupulously honest in their procedures, and that it had been a fair and impartial test of public opinion. At no point was the integrity of the Peace Ballot impugned and this was a tribute to the character and reputation of Lord Cecil and his associates.

The most apt criticism of the Peace Ballot lies not in the questions it asked, but in precisely the questions it failed to ask.

What, indeed, should Britain do if the other countries refused to disarm? And if Britain had to rearm, where would she find the production capacity if the private purveyors were eschewed? What should Britain do if, instead of agreeing to abolish military aviation, her potential foes built mighty aerial fleets capable of devastating the British Isles? And finally, in the case of aggression, what should and could Britain do if others did not join in economic sanctions, or if economic sanctions proved ineffective? This left the military option. But other countries might be unwilling or unable to join in military sanctions against an aggressor. Against a major power, the Swiss navy and the Danish army were unlikely to be effective.

The United States and Japan were leading naval powers but they were not members of the League. In the event that the sole effective naval force was the Royal Navy, was Britain obliged singlehanded to enforce the Covenant, with only British lives and British money at risk?

But, and this was the ultimate question, whose interests were at stake? In the event that Britain had no direct, material interest in the dispute, in the event that by reason of geography or economics it was remote and irrelevant to British interests, was Britain nevertheless compelled to take the lead in enforcing the Covenant?

More excruciating still was to frame a British policy in the case where not only the breach of the Covenant affected no material British interest but where its enforcement was capable of doing grave harm. This was the specter that haunted Vansittart, Hoare, and Baldwin in the summer of 1935. The Maffey Commission had dispassionately analyzed the specific case of the Italian conquest of Abyssinia. It had concluded that no direct British interest would be affected and that it was from this perspective a matter of indifference whether Abyssinia was conquered or independent. Yet the same statesmen knew that to oppose, and indeed ultimately make war on Italy would shatter the front against Germany, do irreparable damage to the Franco-Italian relationship, and most probably drive Italy directly into the waiting arms of Germany. This would in turn mean the probable falling of the Central European dominos, Austria, no longer protected by Mussolini, Czechoslovakia, encircled if Austria fell, and thence Poland. In that case, France, isolated, bereft of its Eastern European allies who had fallen into the German orbit, could only await the hour of the German onslaught. But the Peace Ballot did not address this issue.

How did the Peace Ballot instruct the British government in the matter of British commitments? It ignored them. The Ilford Poll had specifically inquired of the voters if they approved Britain's Locarno commitment to go to the aid of France or Germany if either were attacked. The answer was a firm and unequivocal negative by a vote of 18,498 to 5,898, a negative majority of 75.6 percent.

With the greatest deliberation, this question had been dropped from the Peace Ballot and replaced with the inquiries of 5a and 5b concerning economic and military sanctions. The conversion of the negative majority in Ilford to the positive majorities for questions 5a and 5b brilliantly illuminates the central difference.

The Peace Ballot was stated in terms of abstractions, principles, and propositions with which it would be difficult to disagree. This was not surprising. In its inception, the Covenant contained the work of many intellectuals. The League had a devoted following in the intellectual community where matters of principle often take precedence over the sordid and undisciplined realities of hard cases. The Peace Ballot was, moreover, a statement, the Archbishop of Canterbury had said, of the ideals of the country. No element of society had been more fervent in its support than the churches. Lord Cecil had never hidden his profound belief that the Peace Ballot enshrined basic principles of morality. It was in this sense that many electors may have cast their ballots—in favor not only of peace, but in defense of the Christian ethic. Whoever made morality the litmus test of foreign policy was usually to be found in the ranks of the supporters of the League and the Covenant.

In July 1935, statements of principle, however clear or however profound, could not solve the international crisis facing the British Government. It had to confront the immediate hard issues of today and tomorrow. The Peace Ballot had not absolved the British Government of the responsibility to weigh and protect British interests.

Lord Cecil's argument was direct. The greatest British interest lay in the enforcement of the Covenant. If this were done, the effectiveness of the League would be confirmed and enhanced and true collective security would be established. He rejected the test of direct British interests, because this would inevitably result in a relapse to the balance of power.

Here again the issues were practical and unlikely to be resolved by questions of principle. Could Britain coerce Italy into compliance with the Covenant, and, if she tried, would France follow? If she succeeded, (and the costs and losses of the effort had be reckoned) could Britain coerce the inevitable combination of the defeated Italy and Germany? Was there another, more acceptable solution?

These were the problems confronting the British Government. But the Peace Ballot was there, an enormous presence, popularly supposed to give a clear concise direction, a force which no Government could oppose and hope to survive. It was left to the Government, therefore, to read the results, interpret them as best it could and apply that reading to the case at hand.

How to reconcile and harmonize the answers, especially the response to 5b? As the summer wore on and the crisis developed, there were many who concluded that the people indeed had spoken and what they had mandated, in the face of aggression, was enforcement of the Covenant by all means short of war.

Quo Vadis?

If it was a day of triumph for Lord Cecil and for the Peace Ballot, it was a day, too, which would deeply affect the fate of vast multitudes who had never heard of the Peace Ballot.

These were the boys and young men who were or would soon be of military age upon whom the burdens of any war would fall. They were the citizens of great capitals and historic cities over whom lay the dark clouds of aerial devastation. They were the inhabitants of the ancient centers of Jewish life and learning across Central and Eastern Europe for whom there would be no place in Adolf Hitler's Reich. Africa might be remote and America disinterested but this day would cast a long shadow over them.

The British public's attention was now fastened upon an absorbing spectacle. Here was a colorful, compelling villain in the character of Benito Mussolini and an exotic hero in the person of Haile Selassie, King of Kings, Conquering Lion of Judah, who was not merely royal, but who claimed hereditary connections with King Solomon and the Queen of Sheba. Here, too, was a classic confrontation between a bully and an underdog. Underdogs enjoyed warm sympathy in Britain so long as they did not thwart British arms or British interests.

But, of course, the drama was more complex, as were the principal actors.

Mussolini saw earlier and more clearly than almost anyone else the fatal threat of Nazi Germany. He was determined to gain an empire, or at least the semblance of one, in Abyssinia. To his clear Latin mind, there was no incompatibility between this goal and the defense of Europe against Hitler because it was self-evident to him that no interest of his would-be allies, France and Britain, was threatened or even affected in Abyssinia, whereas those very interests were vitally engaged in Europe of which an independent Austria was the linchpin. It was difficult for him to understand that his friends, or at least the greatest of them, Britain, might not see things that way. But he would go forward, as Drummond had perceived, a streak of fatalism rising to the surface, more controlled by than controlling his fate.

Across the Brenner and Austria Adolf Hitler fixed his cobra stare on his Austrian homeland, destined on page one of *Mein Kampf* to become a cornerstone of a Greater Germany. He looked, with rapt interest, across Austria to Italy, the necessary ally, the indispensable partner with whom he would be prepared to go to war.

Hitler knew when to give smooth assurances and when to act swiftly and decisively. He also knew when to watch and wait and let events run their course, a bystander to controversies from which, whoever might be the loser, he would emerge the winner. All of this was part of the program he pursued with all the force of his determined will. The *sine qua non* of that program was arms for Germany and the redemption of German soil, of which there was no component more critical to both Germany and France than the Rhineland.

No one had to instruct Pierre Laval in these matters. He stood in the direct line of French policy at and since Versailles, the defense of France against the continuing threat of Germany, now materialized into Nazi Germany. In terms of demographics and economics, France was far outweighed by Germany. To his task Pierre Laval would bring his acute intelligence; the serenity that Torres had noted, and a self-confidence that his rise from the mail cart to the Elysee Palace did much to justify. To these he added patience and above all an acute realism that would pursue the ultimate goals by whatever supple devices were at hand, focusing on ends, open to means. And his end was never in doubt—the life and happiness of France.

Stanley Baldwin and Sir Samuel Hoare were equally devoted to the defense of the life and liberty of the British people. But they could not pursue these goals by any means. Baldwin was, as Toynbee had aptly said, the captive to Lord Cecil's bow and spear; and the means which the British Government had been instructed by its people to employ in facing the impending crisis were the Covenant and the League of Nations, the sheet anchor, as Stanley Baldwin had promised, of British Policy.

A gigantic wave of public opinion had confirmed British devotion to the League of Nations. Thus, it came about, in the summer of 1935, that the Abyssinian drama took center stage. Austria receded. Hitler carefully abstained from further threats while the Duce looked south and east to Africa.

Austria was critical to the fate of Europe. Here, British interests were directly involved and yet, by the conjunction of the Peace Ballot and the Abyssinian crisis, it was the League and the defense of the League that became the fulcrum upon which British policy would balance. The issue was framed by the Peace Ballot, not by any analysis of British interests.

This confirmed the dramatic change in British attitudes toward enforcement of the Covenant. Britain, long diffident or indifferent, was now committed to the defense of the Covenant while France withdrew to sit in judgment on the case.

All this Lord Cecil had accomplished. He had set out to instruct the Government as to the extent of public support for the League and collective security. By the juncture of events, he had now forced the Government, confronted by crisis, to deal with that crisis on the basis of his own terms of reference. But Lord Cecil did not relax. He knew that it might be necessary to hold the Government to its task. The membership of the League of Nations Union, swelled by the success of the Peace Ballot, would be a useful enforcement tool. The ultimate arbiter would, of course, be the electorate, in the General Election that was soon to follow.

One thing was clear. There was an explosive compound here. If Mussolini's African ambitions were modest compared to the Führer's grandiose visions, they were quite capable of wrecking the combination which could restrain and check those visions and the forces gathering to make them a reality. Whether British public opinion, which Lord Cecil had so successfully aroused and cultivated, would prove an irresistible force; whether Mussolini, in his thrust for African glory, would prove to be an immovable object must soon be known. Stresa had been bright with promise and with flowers, orange blossoms and azaleas, when Mussolini convened Britain and France there in April to address, and what is and more, to contain, the menace of Hitler's Germany. The climax would soon come and the fate of the world of 1935 would be told before spring came round again once more.

Notes

Abbreviations used in these notes:

CAB: British Cabinet Minutes
DBFP: Documents on British Foreign Policy
DDF: Documents Diplomatiques Francais
DGFP: Documents on German Foreign Policy
DIA: Documents on International Affairs
MG: *Manchester Guardian*
MK: *Mein Kampf*
NYT: *New York Times*
SIA: *Survey of International Affairs*
Times: *London Times*

Chapter 1: A Noble Idea, A Noble Lord

1. Lord Robert Cecil, *A Great Experiment*, 189.
2. Dame Adelaide Livingston, *The Peace Ballot, An Official History*, 7.
3. Livingston, 7.
4. Lord Robert Cecil, *All the Way*, 142.
5. Cecil, *All the Way*, 239.
6. The Cecil family history and anecdotes are taken from Kenneth Rose, *The Later Cecils*, Specific references are made to specific citations.
7. Wilson to Cecil, *All the Way*, 148.
8. Cecil, *All the Way*, 162.
9. Cecil, *All the Way*, 189, 197.
10. Cecil, *All the Way*, 226.
11. Rose, 159.
12. Cecil, *All the Way*, 17–18.
13. Cecil, *All the Way*, 72.
14. Cecil, *All the Way*, 22, 46.
15. Rose, 180.
16. Rose, 171.
17. Rose, 130.
18. Rose, 47.
19. Cecil, *All the Way*, 146.

20. Cecil, *All the Way*, 191.
21. Cecil, *All the Way*, 144.
22. Rose, 164.
23. Daniel P. Waley, *British Public Opinion in the Abyssinian War*, 91 et seq.
24. Livingston, 8–9.
25. Livingston, 9–10.
26. Livingston, 10.
27. Livingston, 10.
28. Livingston, 11.

Chapter 2: A Separate Peace

1. Thomas A. Bailey, *Woodrow Wilson and the Lost Peace*, cited at Louis R. Yates, *United States and French Security*, 20.
2. Cecil, *All the Way*, 141–2.
3. Francis P. Walters, *A History of the League of Nations*, 20.
4. Walbers, 20 Walters
5. Ferdinand Czernin, *Versailles, 1919*, 6.
6. Czernin, 31–2.
7. Georges Clemenceau, *Grandeur and Misery of Victory*, 119.
8. Minutes of Supreme War Council Meeting, November 1, 1919, cited at Czernin, 33–4.
9. Ministere des Affaires Etrangeres, Documents Relatifs aux negotiations concernant Les Guaranties de Securite Contre Agression de L'Allemagne, 7–14, appendix B, Yates.
9a. E.H. Carr, *The Twenty Years Crisis*, 8.
10. Harold Nicholson, *Peacemaking 1919*, 38.
11. Robin Renwick, *Economic Sanctions*, 9.
12. Woodrow Wilson, Address at the Sorbonne, 21 December 1919, cited in Robert H. Ferrell, *Woodrow Wilson and World War I*, 165.
13. Cecil, *A Great Experiment*, 64.
14. Clemenceau, 162.
15. Clemenceau, 167.
16. Clemenceau, 173.
17. Nicholson, 41–2.
18. Czernin, 139–63.
19. Note 9 supra.
20. Clemenceau, 147–8.
21. Walter Langsam, *Documents and Readings on the History of Europe since 1918*, 51.
22. Langsam, 49.
23. Langsam, 50–1.
24. Yates, 45.
25. Czernin, 108.

26. Senator G.M. Hitchcock to Wilson, 4 March 1919; Czernin, 108.
27. Taft to Wilson, 18 March 1919; Czernin, 109.
28. Czernin, 110.
29. Edwin M. House, Diary, 16 March 1919, 18 March 1919, cited at Czernin, 114–5.
30. Woodrow Wilson, *Public Papers, War and Peace*, vol. 1, 444, cited at Czernin 108.
31. David Lloyd George, *Memoirs*, 188, cited at Czernin, 245.
32. Andre Tardieu, *The Truth About the Treaty*, 172, cited at Czernin, 248.
33. Yates, 147.
34. Yates, 47–8.
35. Czernin, 250–1.
36. Ministere des Affaires Etrangeres, Document no. 4; Yates, Appendix F.
37. Yates, 56.
38. Yates, 58.
39. Yates, 60.
40. The American Treaty, Congressional Record, 66th Congress, 1st Session, vol. 58, part 4, 3310–11; Yates, Appendix H; The British Treaty, British Foreign and State Papers, 1919, 601–2; Yates, Appendix H.
41. Department of State, *The Treaty of Versailles and After*, 159.
42. Clemenceau, 247.
43. Yates, 113.
44. Congessional Record, 66th Congress, 2nd Session, 4599, cited at Czernin, 404–6.
45. *Treaty of Versailles*, 14; Ferrell, 176.
46. Ferrell, 176–7.
47. Cecil, *All the Way*, 177.
48. *Treaty of Versailles*, 14; Ferrell, 177.
49. Ferrell, 176.
50. Ferrell, 177.
51. Statutes at Large of the United States, vol. 42, part 2, 1939–45; Yates, Appendix I.
52. Paul Mantoux, *Paris Peace Conference, 1919: Proceedings of the Council of Four*, cited at Anthony Adamthwaite, *The Lost Peace*, 24–30.
53. Clemenceau, 247.

Chapter 3: Collective Security

1. Lord Robert Cecil, *The League of Nations, Its Moral Basis*, 12.
2. Livingston, 6–7.
3. E.H. Carr, *International Relations Between the Two World Wars*, 28.
4. Walters, 148.
5. Carr, 28–9; Walters, 258–9.
6. Cecil, *A Great Experiment*, 125.
7. Gilbert Murray, *The Ordeal of this Generation*, 91, 113.

348   The Avoidable War

8. Clemenceau, 310.
9. G.M. Young, *Stanley Baldwin*, 61.
10. Hansard, 14 July 1924.
11. Clemenceau, 331.
12. Cecil, *All the Way*, 187.
13. Sir Robert Vansittart, *The Mist Procession*, 503.
14. Memorandum from General Stulpnagel, 6 March 1926, cited at Adamthwaite, *The Lost Peace*, 79.
15. Vansittart, *Procession*, 379.
16. Murray 134.
17. Hansard, 23 March 1926.

Chapter 4: Mussolini

1. Luigi Sterzo, *Italy and Fascisimo*, 121–2.
2. Ivone Kirkpatrick, *Mussolini*, 243.
3. Kirkpatrick, 242–3.
4. Denis Mack Smith, *Mussolini*, 46.
5. Smith, 100.
6. R.W. Seton-Watson, *Britain and the Dictators*, 160.
7. Kirkpatrick, 240.
8. Kirkpatrick, 240.
9. The summary of Mussolini's life is adapted from Smith, 1–10.
10. Basic biographical information for this section is taken from Smith, 13–32.
11. Kirkpatrick, 83–4.
12. Smith, 32–3.
13. Kirkpatrick, 80.
14. Smith, 35–6; Kirkpatrick, 83–4.
15. Kirkpatrick, 80.
16. Kirkpatrick, 85–6.
17. Kirkpatrick, 87.
18. Kirkpatrick, 99–100.
19. Smith, 44.
20. Kirkpatrick, 105–10.
21. Smith, 46, 48.
22. Kirkpatrick, 123–4.
23. Kirkpatrick, 128–9.
24. Kirkpatrick, 134.
25. Smith, 51; Kirkpatrick, 135.
26. Smith 52–4.
27. Smith, 54.
28. Smith, 54.
29. Smith, 54–5.
30. Smith, 56.

31. Smith, 63.
32. Smith, 58.
33. Smith, 69.
34. Smith, 74–5.
35. Smith, 75.
36. Smith, 78–86.
37. Smith, 100–3; Kirkpatrick, 240.
38. Kirkpatrick, 239–40.
39. Kirkpatrick, 248.
40. Kirkpatrick, 265.
41. Kirkpatrick, 281.
42. Kirkpatrick, 156.
43. Smith 126.
44. Smith, 33.
45. Kirkpatrick, 168.
46. Kirkpatrick, 158.
47. Gaetano Salvemini, *Prelude to World War II*, 46.
48. Kirkpatrick, 187.
49. Salvemini, 155.
50. Smith, 106.
51. Smith, 107.
52. Kirkpatrick, 245.
53. Kirkpatrick, 271.
54. Smith, 188.

Chapter 5: Anglo-Saxon Attitudes

1. Nevile Henderson, *Failure of a Mission*, 23.
2. George Lansbury, *My Pilgrimage for Peace*, 24.
3. Lansbury, 107–8.
4. Vansittart, *Procession*, 231.
5. Vansittart, *Procession*, 369.
6. Cecil, *All the Way*, 183.
7. Covenant of the League of Nations, Article 8; Walters, 48.
8. David Lloyd George, *The Truth About Reparations*, cited at Corelli Barnett, *The Collapse of British Power*, 393.
9. Vansittart, *Procession*, 341.
10. Arnold J. Toynbee, *Survey of International Affairs*, 1935, vol. 2, 19.
11. Winston S. Churchill, *The Gathering Storm*, 40.
12. Young, 107.
13. Keith Middlemas and John Barnes, *Baldwin, a Biography*, 735.
14. Anthony Eden, *Facing the Dictators*, 19.
15. 2 *SIA*, 1935, 19.
16. Lansbury, 8.
17. Beverly Nichols, *Cry Havoc*, 63.

18. Nichols, 63.
19. Nichols, 66.
20. Nichols, 66.
21. Nichols, 84–5.
22. 2 *SIA*, 1935, 17–18.
23. 2 *SIA*, 1935, 18.
24. Elaine Windrich, *British Labour's Foreign Policy*, 24.
25. Windrich, 24.
26. Nichols, 267–72.
27. Nichols, 26.
28. Nichols, 273.
29. Young, 176.
30. Windrich, 24.
31. Carr, *Crisis*, 30.
32. Livingston, 60.
33. CAB 32/2, E-A, cited at Barnett, 241.
34. Murray, 100.
35. Murray, 109.
36. *Headway*, November 1930, 215.
37. Donald S. Birn, *The League of Nations Union*, 24.
38. Birn, 36.
39. Birn, 65.
40. Cecil to Murray, 2 September 1927; Birn 68.
41. Birn, 90.
42. Cecil to Murray, 16 November 1926; Birn 64.
43. Birn, 125–6.
44. Birn, 131–2.
45. Birn, 135–7.
46. Birn, 136.
47. Birn, 138–40.
48. Birn, 139–40.
49. Birn, 124, 134.
50. Barnett, 290.
51. Barnett, 291.
52. CAB 29/128, 22 March 1930, cited at Barnett, 293.
53. Vansittart, *Procession*, 397.
54. Vansittart, *Procession*, 404.
55. Vansittart, Procession, [PAGE?].
56. Lord Norwich, *Old Men Forget*, 146.
57. Sir James Headlam-Morley, *Studies on Diplomatic History*, 182–4, cited at Hajo Holborn, *The Political Collapse of Europe*, 128–9.
    House of Common Debates, June 24, 1931, Co. 936 cited at Holborn, *Political Collapse*, 133.

Chapter 6: Adolf Hitler

1. Adolf Hitler, *Mein Kampf*, 177.
2. *MK*, 201–2.
3. *MK*, 204.
4. *MK*, 204–6.
5. The summary of Hitler's early life is taken from Alan Bullock, *Hitler, A Study on Tyranny*, 23–31.
6. Bullock, 32–3.
7. *MK*, 21.
8. *MK*, 21–2.
9. *MK*, 25.
10. *MK*, 35–6.
11. *MK*, 36.
12. *MK*, 22.
13. *MK*, 23.
14. *MK*, 34.
15. *MK*, 51–65, 65–91.
16. *MK*, 77.
17. *MK*, 61–5.
18. *MK*, 123.
19. Bullock, 47.
20. Bullock, 48–9.
21. *MK*, 161.
22. *MK*, 163–4.
23. Bullock, 51.
24. Bullock, 51–2.
25. Bullock, 51–4.
26. *MK*, 163.
27. *MK*, 198.
28. Bullock, 61.
29. Bullock, 61–3.
30. *MK*, 208.
31. *MK*, 208–10.
32. *MK*, 215–16.
33. *MK*, 218–19.
34. *MK*, 220–2.
35. *MK*, 222–3.
36. *MK*, 224.
37. *MK*, 355.
38. *MK*, 355.
39. *MK*, 358.
40. *MK*, 366.
41. *MK*, 369.
42. *MK*, 369.
43. Joachim Remak, *The Nazi Years*, 27–30.

44. *MK*, 350.
45. Bullock, 92.
46. Bullock, 96–7.
47. Bullock, 100–4.
48. Bullock, 108.
49. Bullock, 109.
50. Bullock, 110–13.
51. Bullock, 117.
52. *MK*, 3.
53. Reserved.
54. Reserved.
55. *MK*, 151.
56. *MK*, 383.
57. *MK*, 384.
58. *MK*, 214.
59. *MK*, 688.
60. *MK*, 286.
61. *MK*, 65.
62. *MK*, 132.
63. *MK*, 289.
64. *MK*, 29.
65. *MK*, 30.
66. *MK*, 29.
67. *MK*, 30.
68. Walter C. Langer, *The Mind of Adolf Hitler*, 190.
69. *MK*, 255.
70. *MK*, 405.
71. *MK*, 96.
72. *MK*, 327.
73. *MK*, 379.
74. *MK*, 131–2.
75. *MK*, 137–9.
76. *MK*, 138.
77. *MK*, 139.
78. *MK*, 140.
79. *MK*, 79.
80. *MK*, 652.
81. *MK*, 654.
82. *MK*, 609–10.
83. *MK*, 619.
84. *MK*, 666.
85. *MK*, 613–21.
86. *MK*, 675.
87. *MK*, 681.
88. *MK*, 26–30.
89. *MK*, 627.

90. *MK*, 138.
91. *MK*, 134.
92. *MK*, 135.
93. *MK*, 632.
94. *MK*, 399.
95. *MK*, 171.
96. *MK*, 170.
97. *MK*, 170.
98. *MK*, 180.
99. *MK*, 180.
100. *MK*, 231.
101. *MK*, 485.
102. *MK*, 103.
103. *MK*, 107.
104. *MK*, 470.
105. *MK*, 107.
106. *MK*, 44.
107. *MK*, 42.
108. *MK*, 42.
109. *MK*, 118.
110. *MK*, 103.
111. Remak, 26.
112. *MK*, 381.
113. *MK*, 113.
114. *MK*, 449.
115. *MK*, 450.
116. *MK*, 532.
117. *MK*, 91.
118. *MK*, 58.
119. *MK*, 456.
120. *MK*, 679.
121. Bullock, 144.
122. Bullock, 161.
123. Bullock, 169.
124. Bullock, 124.
125. Bullock, 192–4.
126. Bullock, 196–9.
127. Bullock, 198.
128. Bullock, 109.

Chapter 7: Arms Control—1932

1. *Times*, 3 February 1932.
2. *Times*, 3 February 1932.
3. *Times*, 5 February 1932.

4. *Times*, 3 February 1932.
5. *Times*, 4 February 1932.
6. *Times*, 8 February 1932.
7. Carr, *International Relations*, 163.
8. Carr, *International Relations*, 164.
9. Carr, *International Relations*, 164–7.
10. Carr, *International Relations*, 167.
11. *SIA*, 1932, 196.
12. *SIA*, 1932, 200.
13. *Times*, 9 February 1932.
14. *SIA*, 1932, 201–3.
15. *SIA*, 1932, 204.
16. *SIA*, 1932, 204.
17. *SIA*, 1932, 205.
18. *SIA*, 1932, 215.
19. *SIA*, 1932, 227.
20. *SIA*, 1932, 229.
21. *SIA*, 1932, 232.
22. Carr, *International Relations*, 167.
23. Carr, *International Relations*, 167–9.
24. Bullock, 201.
25. Bullock, 201–2.
26. Churchill, 73.
27. Bullock, 208–9.
28. Bullock, 209.
29. Bullock, 210–11.
30. Bullock, 214.
31. Bullock, 216–17.
32. *SIA*, 1932, 239.
33. *SIA*, 1932, 242.
34. Carr, *International Relations*, 147.
35. Maurice Baumont, *The Origins of the Second World War*, 37.
36. *SIA*, 1932, 249.
37. *SIA*, 1932, 254.
38. *SIA*, 1932, 255.
39. Baumont, 28.
40. Carr, 169.
41. Middlemas and Barnes, 735.
42. Middlemas and Barnes, 735.
43. Middlemas and Barnes, 736.
44. Bullock, 230.
45. Bullock, 233.
46. Bullock, 233–4.
47. Bullock, 236.
48. *SIA*, 1932, 287.
49. *SIA*, 1932, 28.

Chapter 8: The German Challenge

1. Bullock, 315.
2. Bullock, 244.
3. Bullock, 247.
4. *SIA,* 1933, 142; Bullock 250.
5. DGFP, C-I, 37.
6. David Irving, *The War Path*, 30.
7. Irving, 30.
8. Gerhard L. Weinberg, *The Foreign Policy of Hitler's Germany*, 36.
9. Bullock, 257–8.
10. Bullock, 258.
11. Bullock, 259.
12. Bullock, 263.
13. Bullock, 264.
14. Bullock, 265.
15. Remak, 52–3.
16. Bullock, 266.
17. Bullock, 270.
18. Bullock, 271.
19. Bullock, 272.
20. Bullock, 272–3.
21. Remak, 54.
22. Bullock, 284.
23. Remak, 56.
24. Norman H. Baynes, *The Speeches of Adolf Hitler*, vol. I, 289.
25. Baynes, I, 287.
26. Eden, 62.
27. Bullock, 299.
28. Bullock, 301–5.
29. Bullock, 304–5.
30. Baynes, I, 321–2.
31. Bullock, 309.
32. Bullock, 310.
33. *SIA,* 1933, 232.
34. David Carlton, *Anthony Eden*, 135.
35. *SIA,* 1933, 226, 251–7.
36. Carlton, 39.
37. Churchill, 75.
38. *SIA,* 1933, 267.
39. Baynes, III, 1041–58.
40. Baynes, III, 1047.
41. Baynes, III, 1057.
42. Baynes, III, 1056–7.
43. *SIA,* 1933, 295–6; E.M. Robertson, *Hitler's Pre-War Policy and Military Plans, 1933–1939*, 22.

44. *SIA,* 1933, 302–5.
45. Telegram from von Neurath to president of the Disarmament Conference, 14 October 1933, *Documents on International Affairs, 1933,* 285.
46. Proclamation of the German Government, DIA, 1933, 286; *SIA,* 1933, 311.
47. Baynes, III, 1089.
48. Baynes, III, 1090.
49. Adolf Hitler Proclamation, 14 October 1933; DIA, 1933, 287.
50. Baynes, III, 1099.
51. Baynes, III, 1107.
52. Baynes, III, 1107.
53. Baynes, III, 1110–15.
54. Baynes, III, 1109–10.
55. Baynes, III, 1116.
56. Baynes, III, 1141.
57. Baynes, III, 1137.
58. Bullock, 324.
59. *SIA,* 1933, 316.
60. Memorandum of German Government to French Ambassador in Berlin, 18 December 1933; DIA, 1933, 328–32.
61. Memorandum of French Ambassador to German Chancellor, 1 January 1934; DIA, 1933, 332–8.
62. *SIA,* 1934, 386.
63. Baynes, III, 1162, 1163, 1169.
64. Memorandum of the United Kingdom on Disarmament, DIA, 1933, 360–72.
65. Eden, 64.
66. Eden, 62–5.
67. Eden, 76–9.
68. Eden, 82–3.
69. Memorandum to the United Kingdom from the French Ambassador, 19 March 1934; DIA, 1933, 375–80.
70. Seton Watson, 221.
71. Statement of views by the German Government on the United Kingdom Memorandum, DIA, 1933, 384.
72. Baumont, 78.
73. Gordon A. Craig and Felix Gilbert, *The Diplomats, 1919–1939,* vol. 2, 342.
74. Cecil, *Experiment,* 242.
75. Baynes, III, 1163.
76. Baynes, III, 1172.
77. Baynes, III, 1173.
78. *SIA,* 1934, 428.
79. Denis Mack Smith, *Mussolini's Roman Empire,* 48–9.
80. *SIA,* 1933, 209–20.
81. *SIA,* 1934, 439.

82. *SIA*, 1934, 447.
83. Weinberg, 94.
84. *SIA*, 1934, 450.
85. *SIA*, 1934, 452.
86. *SIA*, 1934, 454–5.
87. *SIA*, 1934, 462.
88. *SIA*, 1934, 455; DIA, 1933, 394.
89. *SIA*, 1934, 499; DIA, 1933, 396.
90. Salvemini, 148.
91. Smith, *Mussolini*, 184–5.
92. Smith, *Mussolini's Roman Empire*, 53–4; *SIA*, 1934, 468.
93. *SIA*, 1934, 471–80.
94. *SIA*, 1934, 475.
95. Salvemini, 162.
96. *SIA*, 1934, 479.
97. *SIA*, 1934, 480.
98. *SIA*, 1934, 485.
99. Salvemini, 162.

Chapter 9: France and the German Challenge

1. Salvemini, 149.
2. Claude Paillat, *La Guerre a l'Horizon, 1930–38*, 145–9.
3. Clemenceau, 280–1.
4. Carlton, 51.
5. Cecil, *Experiment*, 255.
6. Baumont, 84.
7. *SIA*, 1934, 387.
8. Sir Robert Vansittart, *Lessons of My Life*, 8.
9. DIA, 1933, 381–3.
10. *SIA*, 1934, 383.
11. *SIA*, 1934, 384.
12. *SIA*, 1934, 347.
13. *SIA*, 1934, 347.
14. *SIA*, 1934, 387–8.
15. *SIA*, 1935, 65–6.
16. *SIA*, 1935, 67–71; Baumont 94–5, Robertson, 46.
17. Baumont, 95.
18. *SIA*, 1934, 401–2.
19. Baumont, 97–101.
20. Paillat, 406–15, *Times*, 10 October 1934.
21. Geoffrey Warner, *Pierre Laval and the Eclipse of France*, 1–2.
22. Henry Torres, *Pierre Laval*, 12–13; Warner, 2.
23. Warner, 2–3.
24. Warner, 3.

25. Torres, 14.
26. Torres, 14–15.
27. Warner, 4.
28. Torres, 12.
29. Warner, 4.
30. Torres, 18–19.
31. Torres, 20.
32. Torres, 21–2.
33. Torres, 23.
34. Warner, 16.
35. Warner, 17.
36. Warner, 17.
37. Warner, 18.
38. Torres, 62.
39. Warner, 20–1.
40. Warner, 20.
41. Salvemini, 212.
42. Torres, 90.
43. Guy Bechtel, *Laval, 20 Ans Apres*, 117–18.
44. Bechtel, 116.
45. Warner, 22.
46. Warner, 25.
47. Warner, 25.
48. Andre Francois-Poncet, *The Fateful Years*, 6.
49. Warner, 60.
50. Warner, 60–5.
51. DIA, 1934, 84–5.

Chapter 10: Britain and the German Challenge

1. DBFP 2d, no. 241.
2. *Dictionary of National Biography*, 1941–50, 744–5.
3. DBFP 2d, IV, no. 243.
4. DBFP 2d, IV, no. 258.
5. DBFP 2d, IV, no. 265.
6. DBFP 2d, IV, no. 268.
7. DBFP 2d, V, no. 36.
8. DBFP 2d, V, no. 223.
9. DBFP 2d, V, no. 229.
10. DBFP 2d, V, no. 127.
11. Ian Colvin, *None So Blind*, 19–20.
12. Vansittart, *Procession*, 474; Colvin, 335.
13. Colvin, 345.
14. Vansittart, *Procession*, 479–80.
15. Cecil, *All The Way*, 246–7.

16. Thomas Jones, *A Diary with Letters*, 109, 114.
17. *SIA,* 1934, 338.
18. DBFP 2d, VI, no. 195.
19. DBFP 2d, VI, no. 241.
20. DBFP 2d, VI, no. 241.
21. DBFP 2d, VI, no. 313.
22. CAB 23/78 10(34).
23. DBFP 2d, VI, no. 363.
24. DBFP 2d, VI Appendix III, Memorandum by Sir R. Vansittart on the Future of Germany.
25. Ibid.
26. Churchill, 101–2.
27. CAB 23/86 41(34).
28. DBFP 2d, XII, no. 136.
29. Sir Robert Boothby, *Recollections of a Rebel*, 118.
30. Martin Gilbert, *Plough My Own Furrow*, 351 cited at Barnett, 420.
31. Barnett, 389.
32. *The History of the Times, Part II, 1921–1948*, 734.
33. *Times*, 2 July 1934.
34. Malcolm Muggeridge, *Things Past*, 224.
35. Gilbert, 354–5.
36. Lansbury, 118.
37. J.R.M. Butler, *Lord Lothian*, 206.
38. A.L. Rowse, *Appeasement*, 7.
39. Jones, 95–6.
40. Henderson, 27.
41. Lansbury, 245.
42. Lansbury, 244.
43. Jones, 233.
44. A.A. Milne, *Peace with Honour*, 152.
45. Milne, 202.
46. Milne, 152.
47. Claude Cockburn, *The Devil's Decade*, 119.
48. Vansittart, *Procession*, 474.
49. Milne, 97.
50. Philip Gibbs, *Across the Frontiers*, 241.
51. William McElwee, *Britain's Locust Years*, cited at Birkenhead, 342.
52. *Report of the Thirty-Third Annual Conference of the Labour Party*, 1933, 186–92, cited at Windrich, 117–18.
53. *Times*, 13 December 1933.
54. *Times*, 13 December 1933.
55. Labour Party, *For Socialism and Peace*, 8–15, cited at Windrich, 119–20
56. Windrich, 119–20.
57. Windrich, 120.
58. Rowse, 23.

59. W. Arnold-Forster in Leonard Woolf, *The Intelligent Man's Guide to Peace*, 455.
60. *Times*, 16 October 1933.
61. *Times*, 25 October 1933.
62. *Times*, 27 October 1933.
63. *Times*, 24 October 1933.
64. Middlemas and Barnes, 745.
65. *Times*, 27 October 1933.
66. *Times*, 25 October 1933.
67. *Times*, 27 October 1933.
68. Middlemas and Barnes, 735.
69. Middlemas and Barnes, 738.
70. Middlemas and Barnes, 741–2.
71. *Times*, 3 November 1933.
72. *Times*, 9 November 1933.
73. *Times*, 22 November 1933.
74. *Times*, 23 November 1933.
75. *Times*, 30 November 1933.
76. *Times*, 10 February 1934.
77. *Times*, 17 February 1934.
78. *Times*, 20 February 1934, 21 February 1934.
79. Middlemas and Barnes, 746.
80. *Times*, 8 November 1933.
81. *Times*, 30 November 1933.
82. *Times*, 30 November 1933.
83. *Times*, 30 November 1933.
84. *Times*, 22 December 1933.
85. *Times*, 7 February 1934.
86. *Times*, 8 February 1934.
87. *Times*, 8 February 1934.
88. *Times*, 8 February 1934.
89. DIA, 1933, 394.
90. CAB 16/109 DRC 14.
91. *Times*, 9 November 1933.
92. *Times*, 9 November 1933.
93. *Times*, 9 November 1933.
94. *Times*, 21 April 1934.
95. *Times*, 25 April 1934.
96. *Times*, 10 May 1934, 11 May 1934.
97. *Times*, 10 May 1934, 11 May 1934.
98. *Times*, 10 May 1934, 11 May 1934.
99. *Times*, 10 May 1934, 11 May 1934.
100. *Times*, 10 May 1934, 11 May 1934.
101. Middlemas and Barnes, 770.
102. Middlemas and Barnes, 774–5.
103. *Times*, 30 July 1934.

104. *Times*, 30 July 1934.
105. *Times*, 30 July 1934.
106. *Times*, 30 July 1934.
107. *Times*, 30 July 1934.
108. *Times*, 25 October 1934.
109. CAB 23/80 41(34), Barnett 413.
110. *Times*, 30 November 1934.
111. *Times*, 29 November 1934.
112. *Times*, 29 November 1934.
113. *Times*, 29 November 1934.
114. *Times*, 30 November 1934.
115. DBFP 2d, XII, no. 235.
116. Vansittart, *Procession*, 444.
117. Vansittart, *Procession*, 445.

Chapter 11: Voting for Peace

1. *Headway*, November 1934, 204.
2. Birn, 93.
3. Headway, July 1933, 138.
4. *Headway*, August 1934, 158.
5. *Headway*, March 1933, iii.
6. *Headway*, May 1933, iii, November 1933, 226
7. *Headway*, August 1933, 167.
8. *Headway*, September 1933, 188.
9. *Headway*, August 1933, 167.
10. *Headway*, November 1933, 226.
11. *Headway*, August 1933, 167.
12. *Headway*, May 1933, iii.
13. *Headway*, June 1934, 119.
14. *Headway*, March 1934, 54.
15. *Headway*, June 1934, 119.
16. *Headway*, March 1934, 54.
17. *Headway*, October 1934, 198.
18. *Headway*, October 1934, 198.
19. *Headway*, August 1934, 158.
20. *Headway*, July 1934, 138.
21. *Headway*, April 1934, 80.
22. *Headway*, July 1934, 118.
23. Livingston, 8–9.
23. Livingston, 9–10.
25. Livingston, 60.
26. Livingston, 6.
27. Livingston, 6.
28. Livingston, 6.

29. Livingston, 59.
30. *Headway*, April 1933, 75.
31. Livingston, 60.
32. Livingston, 60.
33. *Headway*, August 1934, 160, November 1934, 213.
34. *Headway*, September 1934, 168.
35. *Headway*, November 1934, 204.
36. Adamthwaite, *Lost Peace*, 151–2.
37. Adamthwaite, *Lost Peace*, 153–4.
38. Livingston, 26–7.
39. Livingston, 27.
40. Livingston, 25.
41. Livingston, 25.
42. Livingston, 29–31.
43. Livingston, 26.
44. Livingston, 28.
45. Livingston, 20.
46. Livingston, 20.
47 Livingston, 21.
48 Livingston, 29.
49. Livingston, 22.
50. Livingston, 31–2.
51. Livingston, 13.
52. Livingston, 23–6.
53. Livingston, 25.
54. Livingston, 59.
55. Livingston, 7.
56. Cecil, *All the Way*, 206.
57. Livingston, 10.
58. *Headway*, November 1933, 220.
59. Livingston, 14.
60. Livingston, 29–30.
61. Livingston, 30–1.
62. Livingston, 31.
63. Livingston, 31.
64. Livingston, 61.
65. Vansittart, *Procession*, 503–4.
66. *Public Opinion Quarterly*, I, 3758.
67. Lord Norwich, 182.
68. Neville Thompson, *The Anti-Appeasers*, 71–2.
69. *Headway*, November 1933, 213.
70. Livingston, 12.
71. Livingston, 21.
72. Livingston, 22.
73. Livingston, 21.
74. Livingston, 22.

75. Livingston, 21.
76. Livingston, 14.
77. Livingston, 15.

Chapter 12: An Abyssinian Incident

1. League of Nations, *Official Journal*, 1926, 1517.
2. George W. Baer, *The Coming of the Italo-Ethiopean Way*, 46.
3. Baer, *Coming*, 50.
4. Baer, *Coming*, 51–2.
5. Baer, *Coming*, 45–7.
6. Baer, *Coming*, 47.
7. Baer, *Coming*, 48.
8. Baer, *Coming*, 49.
9. Baer, *Coming*, 48–9.
10 Baer, *Coming*, 50.
11. Baer, *Coming*, 52.
12. Baer, *Coming*, 53.
13. Baer, *Coming*, 53.
14. Baer, *Coming*, 54.
15. Baer, *Coming*, 54.
16. Baer, *Coming*, 54.
17. Baer, *Coming*, 54.
18. Baer, *Coming*, 54.
19. Salvemini, 172.
20. Anthony Mockler, *Haile Selassie's War*, 150.
21. Frank Hardie, *The Abyssinian Crisis*, 11.
22. Hardie, 12, 17.
23. Mockler, xxxix-xxxxii.
24. Baer, *Coming*, 6–7.
25. Baer, *Coming*, 7.
26. Walters, 258.
27. Baer, *Coming*, 9–11; Walters, 258.
28. Mockler, 3–4.
29. Baer, *Coming*, 15–18; Zilliacus, *Mirror of the Past.*
30. Baer, *Coming*, 16.
31. Baer, *Coming*, 17; League of Nations, *Official Journal*, 1926, 1517.
32. Baer, *Coming*, 19–20.
33. Salvemini, 153.
34. Mockler, 9–12.
35. Mockler, 12–13.
36. Mockler, 16.
37. Hardie, 15; CAB 24/256; CP 161.
38. Mockler, 14.
39. *NYT*, 30 September 1934.

40. Baer, *Coming*, 41–2.
41. Baer, *Coming*, 43; *NYT*, 30 September 1934.
42. Baer, *Coming*, 38.
43. Baer, *Coming*, 56–7.
44. Baer, *Coming*, 57.
45. Bear, *Coming*, 57.
46. G. Rochat, "Militari e politici nella preparazione della campagna d'Etiopia, 1932–9," no. 29, cited at Adamthwaite *Lost Peace*, 164–6
47. Mussolini, "La Dottrina del fascismo", *Enciclopedia Italiana di scienza, lettere ed arte*, XIV, 846–51, cited at Baer, *Coming*, 30.
48. *Times*, 19 March 1934; 2 *SIA*, 1935, 23.
49. Adamthwaite, *Lost Peace*, 166.
50. Interview, *Le Petit Journal*, 27 September 1935 cited at Hardie, 33
51. Livingston, 16.
52. Livingston, 16.

Chapter 13: A Double Challenge

1. Jones, 144.
2. Baumont, 78.
3. Warner, 65–6.
4. 2 *SIA*, 1935, 138.
5. 1 DIA, 1935, 15.
6. 1 *SIA*, 1935, 17.
7. Warner, 67.
8. Baer, *Coming*, 74.
9. 1 DIA, 1935, 23.
10. Warner, 70–1.
11. Torres, 134.
12. Torres, 134; Paillat, 221; Warner, 71.
13. Baer, *Coming*, 84; Baumont, 106.
14. *Le Proces du Marechal Petain*, 184, cited at Salvemini, 176.
15. Warner, 79.
16. Baumont, 107.
17. Vansittart, *Lessons*, 39.
18. Craig and Gilbert, 385.
19. 1 *SIA*, 1935, 10–9.
20. L.B. Namier, *Europe in Decay*, 16.
21. Infra, 948–51.
22. 2 DIA, 1935, 13–14.
23. DBFP 2nd, XIV, nos. 1 and 2.
24. DBFP 2d, XIV, no. 56.
25. DBFP 2d, XIV, no. 104.
26. DBFP 2d, XIV, no. 111.
27 DBFP 2d, XIV, no. 143.

28. 2 DIA, 1935, 14–15.
29. DBFP 2d, XIV, no. 141.
30. DBFP 2d, XIV, no. 145.
31. DBFP 2d, XIV, Appendix II, the Maffey Report.
32. *Dictionary of National Biography, 1961–70*, 713.
33. DBFP 2d, XIV, no. 145, fn. 25.
34. Geoffrey Thompson, *Front Line Diplomat*, 95.
35. *Times*, 17 December 1934.
36. Smith, 194; *Mussolini's Roman Empire*, 90–5.
37. Baer, *Coming*, 93; *Morning Post*, 17 September 1935.
38. CAB 23/81 2(35).
39. CAB 23/81 3(35).
40. CAB 23/81 CP 6(35).
41. DGFP, C-III, 873–6, cited at Robertson, 54.
42. DGFP, C-III, 798–9, 873–6, cited at Robertson.
43. Butler, Lord Lothian.
44. 1 DIA, 1935, 25–7.
45. Jones, 153.
46. 1 DIA, 1935, 31.
47. Cecil, *Experiment*, 255.
48. Windrich, 125–6.
49. 1 DIA, 1935, 35–6.
50. Livingston, 20.
51. *Headway*, November 1934, 204.
52. *Headway*, October 1934, 204.
53. Livingston, 16.
54. Livingston, 20.
55. Livingston, 20.
56. Livingston, 23.
57. Livingston, 21.
58. Livingston, 21.
59. Livingston, 22.
60. *Headway*, September 1934, 169.
61. *Headway*, September 1934, 169.
62. *Headway*, September 1934, 169.
63. Waley, 21.
64. Livingston, 24.
65. DBFP 2d, XV, no. 404.
66. 1 DIA, 1935, 38–47, Cmd 4827.
67. 1 DIA, 1935, 41.
68. 1 DIA, 1935, 45.
69. 1 DIA, 1935, 47.
70. Baumont, 118–19.
71. *Times*, 9 March 1935.
72. *Times*, 11 March 1935.
73. *Times*, 11 March 1935.

74. *Times*, 12 March 1935.
75. *Times*, 12 March 1935.
76. *Times*, 12 March 1935.
77. *Times*, 12 March 1935.
78. *Times*, 12 March 1935.
79. *Times*, 12 March 1935.
80. *Times*, 12 March 1935.
81. *Times*, 12 March 1935.
82. *Times*, 12 March 1935.
83. *Times*, 12 March 1935.
84. *Times*, 12 March 1935.
85. *Times*, 13 March 1935.
86. *Times*, 14 March 1935.
87. *Times*, 13 March 1935.
88. *Times*, 15 March 1935.
89. Paillat, 204–7.
90. *Times*, 18 March 1935.
91. 1 DIA, 1935, 58–64.
92. Waley, 27.
93. *Times*, 18 March 1935.
94. *Times*, 18 March 1935.
95. *Times*, 18 March 1935.
96. DBFP 2d, XII, no. 579.
97. DBFP 2d, XII, no. 581.
98. DBFP 2d, XII, no. 587.
99. DBFP 2d, XII, no. 590.
100. Eden, 129.
101. 1 DIA, 1935, 64–6.
102. DBFP 2d, XII, no. 603.
103. DBFP 2d, XII, no. 604.
104. *Times*, 25 March 1935.
105. *Times*, 21 March 1935.
106. *Times*, 20 March 1935.
107. *Times*, 20 March 1935.
108. *Times*, 22 March 1935.
109. DBFP 2d, XII, no. 621.
110. DBFP 2d, XII, no. 634.
111. DBFP 2d, XII, no. 642, 644.
112. Eden, 132; DBFP 2d, XII, no. 641.
113. Eden, 133.
114. CP 69(35), 2.
115. CP 69(35), 7.
116. CP 69(35), 9.
117. CP 69(35), 19.
118. CP 69(35), 20.
119. Eden, 139.

120. CP 69(35), 20–3.
121. CP 69(35), 27–8.
122. CP 69(35), 29.
123. CP 69(35).
124. CP 69(35).
125. CP 69(35).
126. CP 69(35), 38.
127. Eden, 145.
128. Eden, 156.
129. Eden, 160–1.
130. Eden, 167.
131. Eden, 172–4.
132. *Times*, 27 March 1935.
133. 2 DIA, 1935, 17–18.
134. 2 DIA, 1935, 19.
135. Mussolini, *Omnia Opera*, XXVII, 276–7, cited at Baer, *Coming*, 114.
136. Baer, *Coming*, 116–17.

Chapter 14: Stresa

1. Eden, 181.
2. DBFP 2d, XIV, no. 207.
3. DBFP 2d, XII, no. 707.
4. DBFP 2d, XII, no. 681.
5. DBFP 2d, XII, no. 702.
6. DBFP 2d, XIV, no. 216.
7. DBFP 2d, XIV, no. 218.
8. DBFP 2d, XIV, no. 225.
9. 2 DIA, 1935, 20–1.
10. DDF 1st, X, no. 23.
11. Eden, 180.
12. DDF 1st, X, no. 67.
13. DBFP 2d, XII, no. 697.
14. DDF 1st, X, no. 101.
15. DDF 1st, X, no. 103.
16. DDF 1st, X, no. 112.
17. DDF 1st, X, no. 128.
18. DBFP, XIV, no. 175.
19. CAB 23/81 21(35).
20. *Times*, 11 April 1935.
21. *Times*, 10 April, 11 April 1935.
22. Vansittart, *Procession*, 516.
23. DBFP 2d, XIV, no. 230.
24. DBFP 2d, XIV, no. 231, 232.
25. DBFP 2d, XIV, no. 229.

26. DBFP 2d, XII, no. 722, Notes on the Stresa Conference, 862–918.
27. DBFP 2d, XII, 867–8.
28. DBFP 2d, XII, 871, 872.
29. DBFP 2d, XII, 873.
30. DBFP 2d, XII, 874.
31. DBFP 2d, XII, 875–6.
32. DBFP 2d, XII, 876.
33. DBFP 2d, XII, 876–7.
34. DBFP 2d, XII, 880.
35. DBFP 2d, XII, 880.
36. DBFP 2d, XII, 881.
37. DBFP 2d, XII, 881.
38. DBFP 2d, XII, 883.
39. DBFP 2d, XII, 883–4.
40. DBFP 2d, XII, 885.
41. DBFP 2d, XII, 885.
42. DBFP 2d, XII, 885.
43. DBFP 2d, XII, 886.
44. DBFP 2d, XII, 887–8.
45. DBFP 2d, XII, 889.
46. DBFP 2d, XII, 889.
47. DBFP 2d, XII, 904.
48. DBFP 2d, XII, 891.
49. DBFP 2d, XII, 899.
50. DBFP 2d, XII, 901.
51. DBFP 2d, XII, 905.
52. DBFP 2d, XII, 905.
53. DBFP 2d, XII, 905.
54. DBFP 2d, XII, 909.
55. DBFP 2d, XII, 912.
56. 1 DIA, 1935, 80–82.
57. Vansittart, *Procession*, 519.
58. 1 DIA, 1935, 82.
59. P.-E. Flandin, *Politique Francaise*, cited at Georges Bonnet, *Quai d'Orsay*, 121.
60. Vansittart, *Procession*, 520.
61. Kirkpatrick, 293.
62. Eden, 179.
63. Vansittart, *Procession*, 520.
64. Eden, 181.
65. Bonnet, 120.
66. Vansittart, *Procession*, 519.
67. DBFP, 2d, XIV, no. 724.
68. Cowling, 80.
69. 1 DIA, 1935, 98–9.
70. 1 DIA, 1935, 114.

71. 1 DIA, 1935, 114–5.
72. DBFP 2d, XIV, no. 234.
73. DBFP 2d, XIV, no. 239.
74. *Times*, 18 April 1935.
75. DBFP 2d, XIV, 238.
76. Livingston, 22.
77. Livingston, 40.
78. DBFP 2d, XIV, no. 241.
79. DBFP 2d, XIV, no. 242.
80. DBFP 2d, XIV, no. 244.
81. Eden, 204.

Chapter 15: Arms Control—1935

1. Vansittart, *Procession*, 527.
2. Livingston, 40.
3. *Times*, 2 May 1935.
4. 1 DIA, 1935, 116–18.
5. 1 DIA, 1935, 118–19.
6. Warner, 81.
7. *Times*, 3 May 1935.
8. *Times*, 3 May 1935.
9. *Times*, 9 May 1935.
10. *Times*, 17 May 1935.
11. DBFP 2d, XIV, no. 250.
12. DBFP 2d, XIV, no. 253.
13. DDF 1st, X, no. 349.
14. DDF 1st, X, no. 353.
15. DBFP 2d, XIV, no. 259.
16. *Times*, 15 May 1935.
17. CAB 23/81 27(35).
18. CAB 23/81 28(35), Annex II.
19. CAB 23/81 28(35).
20. DBFP 2d, XIV, no. 276.
21. DBFP 2d, XIV, no. 278.
22. Eden, 209.
23. DBFP 2d, XIV, no. 281.
24. Baynes II, 1218–47.
25. Baynes III, 1229.
26. Baynes III, 1246.
27. *Times*, 22 May 1935.
28. *Times*, 23 May 1935.
29. Salvemini, 221.
30. 1 *SIA*, 1935, 183.
31. Churchill, 124.

32. DDF 1st, X, no. 442.
33. DDF 1st, X, no. 445.
34. DBFP 2d, XIV, no. 287, 288.
35. DBFP 2d, XIV, no. 289.
36. DDF 1st, X, no. 452.
37. DDF 1st, X, no. 451.
38. *Times*, 27 May 1935.
39. Warner, 90.
40. *Times*, 8 June 1935.
41. Eden, 217–18.
42. Viscount Templewood (Sir Samuel Hoare), *The Unbroken Thread*, 14.
43. Vansittart, *Procession*, 522.
44. Barnett, 357.
45. DBFP 2d, XIII, no. 129.
46. DBFP 2d, XIII, no. 271.
47. *Times*, 1 June 1935.
48. DBFP 2d, XIII, no. 281.
49. DBFP 2d, XIII, no. 289.
50. DBFP 2d, XIII, no. 289.
51. DBFP 2d, XIII, no. 290.
52. DBFP 2d, XIII, no. 304.
53. DBFP 2d, XIII, no. 305.
54. DBFP 2d, XIII, Annex to no. 305.
55. DBFP 2d, XIII, no. 311.
56. DBFP 2d, XIII, nos. 315, 317.
57. DBFP 2d, XIII, no. 318.
58. DBFP 2d, XIII, no. 335.
59. DBFP 2d, XIII, no. 338.
60. DBFP 2d, XIII, no. 339.
61. DBFP 2d, XIII, no. 340.
62. DBFP 2d, XIII, no. 343.
63. DBFP 2d, XIII, no. 345.
64. DBFP 2d, XIII, no. 348.
65. DBFP 2d, XIII, no. 352; DDF 1st, XI, no. 83.
66. "Cato," *Guilty Men*, 40.
67. *Times*, 19 June 1935.
68. DBFP 2d, XIII, no. 351.
69. *Times*, 20 June 1935.
70. DBFP 2d, XIII, no. 353.
71. DBFP 2d, XIII, no. 357.
72. Churchill, 141–2.

Chapter 16: The Triumph of the Peace Ballot

1. 2 *SIA,* 1936, 53.
2. DBFP 2d, XIV, no. 296.
3. DBFP 2d, XIV, no. 301.
4. DBFP 2d, XIV, no. 301.
5. DBFP 2d, XIV, no. 312.
6. DBFP 2d, XIV, no. 308.
7. DBFP 2d, XIV, no. 316.
8. DBFP 2d, XIV, no. 318.
9. DBFP 2d, XIV, no. 313, Appendix II.
10. DBFP 2d, XIV, 752.
11. 1 *SIA,* 1935, 170–1.
12. *Times*, 8 June 1935.
13. DDF 1st, XI, no. 106.
14. DBFP 2d, XIII, no. 363.
15. DBFP 2d, XIII, no. 362.
16. DBFP 2d, XIV, no. 324.
17. DBFP 2d, XIV, no. 320, XIIII, no. 377.
18. DBFP 2d, XIV, no. 325.
19. DBFP 2d, XIV, no. 327.
20. DDF 1st, XI, no. 379.
21. DBFP 2d, XIII, no. 379.
22. DBFP 2d, XIII, no. 384.
23. DDF 1st, XI, no. 179.
24. *Headway*, June 1935, 105.
25. *Headway*, July 1935, 130.
26. *Times*, 28 June 1935.
27. Spectator, 28 June 1935.
28. *Times*, 1 July 1935.
29. *Times*, 24 July 1935.
30. *Times*, 24 July 1935.
31. 2 *SIA,* 1935, 51–2.
32. 2 *SIA,* 1935, 53.
33. Livingston, 60.
34. Livingston, 59.
35. Livingston, 63–4.

Bibliography

Documents

Documents on British Foreign Policy, 1919–1939, Ser. 2, vols. I-XVI, edited by W.N. Medlicott, Douglas Dakin, and M.E. Lambert. Her Majesty's Stationery Office, London: 1947– (cited as DBFP).

Documents Diplomatiques Francais, 1932–1939, Ser. 1, vols I-XIII Ser. 2, vols I-II, edited by Maurice Baumont and Pierre Renouvin. Paris: Imprimerie National, 1963–1966 (cited as DDF).

Documents on German Foreign Policy, 1918–1945, Ser. C, vols I-V, edited by Margaret Lambert et al. Department of State. Washington, D.C.: 1962 (cited as DGFP).

Documents on International Affairs, 1933, 1934, 1935, 1936, edited by Steven Heald. Oxford University Press. Public Record Office, London: Cabinet Documents.

The Treaty of Versailles and After. Department of State. Washington, D.C.: 1947.

Adamthwaite, Anthony. *The Lost Peace.* New York: St. Martin's Press, 1981.

———. *The Making of the Second World War.* London: George Allen &Unwin, 1977.

Baynes, Norman H. *The Speeches of Adolf Hitler,* 3 vols., London: Oxford University Press, 1942.

Langsam, Walter. *Documents and Readings in the History of Europe Since 1918.* Philadelphia and New York: Lippincott, 1951.

Remak, Joachim. *The Nazi Years.* Englewood Cliffs, N.J.: Prentice-Hall, 1969.

General

Avon, Earl of (Anthony Eden). *The Eden Memoirs, Facing the Dictators.* London: Cassell, 1962.

Baer, George W. *The Coming of the Italo-Ethiopian War.* Cambridge, Mass.: Harvard University Press, 1967.

———. *Test Case.* Stanford, Cal.: Hoover Institution Press, 1976.

Barnett, Corelli. *The Collapse of British Power.* New York: William Morrow, 1972.

Baumont, Maurice. *The Origins of the Second World War.* New Haven, Conn.: Yale University Press, 1978.

Bechtel, Guy. *Laval vignt ans apres.* Paris: Laffont, 1963.

Birkenhead, Earl of. *Halifax.* Boston: Houghton Mifflin, 1966.

Birn, Donald S. *The League of Nations Union.* Oxford: Clarendon Press, 1981.

Bloch, Marc. *Strange Defeat.* New York: W.W. Norton, 1968.

Bonnet, Georges. *Quai D'Orsay.* Isle of Man: Times Press and Anthony Gibbs & Phillips, 1965.

Boothby, Lord (Sir Robert Boothby). *Boothby, Recollections of a Rebel.* London: Hutchinson, 1978.

Bullock, Alan. *Hitler, A Study in Tyranny.* New York: Harper & Row, 1962.

Butler, Harold. *The Lost Peace.* New York: Harcourt Brace, 1942.

Butler, J.R.M. *Lord Lothian.* London: Macmillan, 1960.

Carlton, David. *Anthony Eden.* London: Allen Lane, 1981.

Carr, E.H. *International Relations Between the Wars, 1919–1939.* Harper Torchbooks, New York: Harper & Row, 1966.

————. *The Twenty Years' Crisis, 1919–1939.* Harper Torchbooks, New York: Harper & Row, 1964.

Carr, William. *Arms, Autarky and Aggression.* New York: W.W. Norton, 1973.

"Cato." *Guilty Men.* New York: Frederick A. Stokes, 1940.

Cecil of Chelwood, Viscount (Lord Robert Cecil). *All the Way.* London: Hodder & Stoughton, 1949.

————. *A Great Experiment.* New York: Oxford University Press, 1941.

Churchill, Winston S. *The Second World War, The Gathering Storm.* Boston: Houghton Mifflin, 1948.

————. *The River War.* New York: Award Books, 1964.

Clemenceau, Georges. *Grandeur and Misery of Victory.* New York: Harcourt Brace, 1930.

Cockburn, Claud. *The Devil's Decade.* New York: Mason & Lipscomb,1973.

Colvin, Ian. *None So Blind.* New York: Harcourt, Brace & World, 1965.

Coote, Colin and Batchelor, Denzil. *Winston S. Churchill's Maxims and Reflections*, Boston: Houghton Mifflin, 1949.

Cowling, Maurice. *The Impact of Hitler, British Politics and British Policy, 1933–1940.* Chicago: University of Chicago Press, 1977.

Craig, Gordon A. and Felix Gilbert. *The Diplomats, 1919–1939,* vol. 2. New York: Atheneum, 1977.

Czernin, Ferdinand. *Versailles, 1919.* New York: Capricorn Books, 1965.

Del Boca, Angelo. *The Ethiopian War.* Chicago: University of Chicago Press, 1969.

Dictionary of National Biography. Oxford: Oxford University Press.

Dreifort, John E. *Yvon Delbos at the Quai D'Orsay.* Lawrence: University of Kansas Press, 1973.

Dugan, James and Lawrence LaFore. *Days of Emperor and Clown.* Garden City, N.Y.: Doubleday, 1973.

Emmerson, James T. *The Rhineland Crisis.* Ames: Iowa State University Press, 1977.

Epstein, Leon D. *British Politics and the Suez Crisis.* Urbana: University of Illinois Press, 1964.

Feiling, Keith. *The Life of Neville Chamberlain.* London: Macmillan, 1947.

Ferrell, Robert H. *Woodrow Wilson and World War I.* New York: Harper & Row, 1985.

Francois-Poncet, Andre. *The Fateful Years.* New York: Harcourt Brace, 1949.

Furnia, Arthur H. *The Diplomacy of Appeasement.* Washington, D.C.: University Press of Washington, D.C., 1960.

Gallo, Max. *L'Affaire d'Ethiopie.* Paris: Editions du Centurion, 1967.

Gathorne-Hardy, Geoffrey M. *A Short History of International Affairs, 1920 to 1938,* London: Oxford University Press, 1938.

Gatzke, Hans W. *European Diplomacy Between Two Wars.* Chicago: Quadrangle Books, 1972.

George, Margaret. *The Warped Vision, British Foreign Policy, 1933–1939.* Pittsburgh, Pa.: University of Pittsburgh Press, 1965.

Gibbs, Sir Philip. *Across the Frontiers.* New York: Doubleday Doran, 1938.

Gilbert, Martin. *Plow My Own Furrow.* London: Longmans, 1965.

———. *Winston Churchill, 1922–1939,* vol. 5. Boston: Houghton Mifflin, 1977.

———. *The Roots of Appeasement.* New York: New American Library, 1970.

Gilbert, Martin and Richard Gott. *The Appeasers.* Boston: Houghton Mifflin, 1963.

Graves, Robert and Alan Hodge. *The Long Weekend.* New York: W.W. Norton, 1963.

Haines, C. Grove and Ross J.S. Hoffman. *The Origins and Background of the Second World War.* New York: Oxford University Press, 1947.

Halifax, Lord. *Fullness of Days.* New York: Dodd Mead, 1957.

Hardie, Frank. *The Abyssinian Crisis.* Hamden, Conn.: Archon Books, 1974.

Harris, Kenneth. *Attlee.* New York: W.W. Norton, 1982.

Havighurst, Alfred H. *Britain in Transition.* Chicago: University of Chicago Press, 1979.

Henderson, Sir Nevile. *Failure of a Mission.* New York: G.P. Putnam, 1940.

Hitler, Adolf. *Hitler's Secret Book.* New York: Grove Press, 1961.

———. *Mein Kampf.* Boston: Houghton Mifflin, 1943.

Holborn, Hajo. *The Political Collapse of Europe.* New York: Alfred A. Knopf, 1962.

Irving, David. *The War Path.* New York: Viking, 1978.

James, Robert Rhodes. *Anthony Eden, A Biography.* New York: McGraw Hill, 1987.

———. *Winston Churchill, His Complete Speeches, 1897–1963.* New York: Chelsea Books, 1983.

———. *Memoirs of a Conservative.* New York: Macmillan, 1970.

Jones, Thomas. *A Diary with Letters.* London: Oxford University Press, 1954.

Kapuscinski, Ryszard. *The Emperor.* New York: Harcourt Brace Jovanovich, 1978.

LaFore, Lawrence. *The End of Glory*. Philadelphia and New York: Lippincott, 1970.

Lange, Walter C. *The Mind of Adolf Hitler*. New York and London: Basic Books, 1972.

Lansbury, George. *My Pilgrimage for Peace*. New York: Henry Holt,1938.

Laurens, F.D. *France and the Italo-Ethiopian Crisis, 1935–1936*. The Hague and Paris: Mouton, 1967.

Laval, Pierre. *The Diary of Pierre Laval*. New York: Charles Scribners, 1948.

Le proces Laval. Paris: Albin Michel, 1946.

Lawford, Valentine. *Bound for Diplomacy*. Boston: Little Brown, 1963.

Livingston, Dame Adelaide. *The Peace Ballot, An Official History*. London: Gollancz, 1935.

Manchester, William. *The Last Lion, Alone, 1932–1940*. Boston: Little Brown, 1988.

Marwick, Arthur. *Clifford Allen, Open Conspirator*. Edinburgh: Olwer and Boyd, 1964.

Macmillan, Harold. *Winds of Change, 1914–1939*. New York: Harper University Press, 1989.

Medlicott, W.N. *British Foreign Policy Since Versailles*. London: Methuen, 1940.

Meehan, E.G. *The British Left Wing and Foreign Policy*. New Brunswick, N.J.: Rutgers University Press, 1960.

Middlemas, Keith and John Barnes. *Baldwin, A Biography*. New York: Macmillan, 1969.

Milne, A.A. *Peace with Honour*. New York: E.P. Dutton, 1934.

Mockler, Anthony. *Haile Selassie's War*. New York: Random House, 1984.

Mowat, Charles L. *Britain Between the Wars, 1918–1940*. London: Methuen, 1955.

Muggeridge, Malcolm. *Things Past*. New York: William Morrow, 1979.

Murray, Gilbert. *The Ordeal of This Generation*. London: Allen & Unwin, 1929.

Mussolini, Benito. *My Autobiography*. New York: Charles Scribners, 1928.

Namier, Sir L.B. *Europe in Decay*. London: Macmillan, 1950.

Nichols, Beverley. *Cry Havoc*. New York: Doubleday Doran, 1933.

———. *News of England*. New York: Doubleday Doran, 1938.

Nicholson, Harold. *Diaries and Letters, 1930–1939*. New York: Atheneum, 1966.

———. *Peacemaking, 1919*. Universal Library Edition, New York: Grosset & Dunlap, 1965.

Nobel Lectures. *Peace, 1926–1950*. Amsterdam: Elsevier, 1972.

Northedge, F.S. *The Troubled Giant*. London: G. Bell, 1966.

Norwich, Earl of (Alfred Duff Cooper). *Old Men Forget*. New York: E.P. Dutton, 1954.

Paillat, Claude. *La Guerre A L'Horizon*. Paris: Laffont, 1981.

Papen, Franz von. *Memoirs*. London: Andre Deutsch, 1952.

Peterson, Sir Maurice. *Both Sides of the Curtain*. London: Constable, 1950.

Remak, Joachim. *The Origins of the Second World War.* Englewood Cliffs, N.J.: Prentice-Hall, 1976.
Renwick, Robin. *Economic Sanctions.* Cambridge: Center for International Affairs, 1981.
Reynaud, Paul. *In the Thick of the Fight.* New York: Simon & Schuster, 1955.
Robertson, E.M. *Hitler's Prewar Policy and Military Plans.* New York: The Citadel Press, 1967.
Rose, Kenneth. *The Later Cecils.* London: Weidenfeld & Nicholson, 1975.
Roskill, Stephen. *Hankey, Man of Secrets,* vol. III. London: Collins, 1974.
Rowse, A.L. *Appeasement.* New York: W.W. Norton, 1963.
Salvemini, Gaetano. *Prelude to World War II.* London: Gollancz, 1953.
Schmidt, Paul. *Hitler's Interpreter.* New York: Macmillan, 1951.
Scott, William Evans. *Alliance Against Hitler, the Origins of the Franco-Soviet Pact.* Durham, N.C.: Duke University Press, 1962.
Seton-Watson, R.W. *Britain and the Dictators.* New York: Macmillan, 1938.
Shirer, William. *The Collapse of the Third Republic.* New York: Simon & Schuster, 1969.
Simon, Viscount (Sir John Simon). *Retrospect.* London: Hutchinson, 1952.
Simon, Yves. *The Road to Vichy, 1918–1938.* New York: Sheed & Ward, 1942.
Smith, Denis Mack. *Mussolini, A Biography.* Vintage Books Edition, New York: Random House, 1983.
———. *Mussolini's Roman Empire.* New York: Viking, 1976.
Spencer, John H. *Ethiopia At Bay.* Algomac, Mich.: Reference Publications, 1984.
Swinton, Earl of (Phillip Cunliffe-Lister). *Sixty Years of Power.* London: Hutchinson, 1966.
Tabouis, Genevieve. *They Called Me Cassandra.* New York: Scribners, 1942.
Taylor, A.J.P. *English History, 1914–1945.* London: Oxford University Press, 1965.
———. *The Origins of the Second World War.* New York: Fawcett Premier, 1961.
Templewood, Viscount (Sir Samuel Hoare). *Nine Troubled Years.* London: Collins, 1954.
———. *The Unbroken Thread.* New York: Alfred A. Knopf, 1950.
Thompson, Geoffrey. *Front Line Diplomat.* London: Hutchinson, 1959.
Thompson, Neville. *The Anti-Appearers.* Oxford: Clarendon Press, 1971.
Torres, Henri. *Pierre Laval.* London: Gollancz, 1941.
Toynbee, Arnold. *Acquaintances.* New York: Oxford University Press, 1967.
———. *Experiences.* New York and London: Oxford University Press, 1969.
———. *Survey of International Affairs.* 1932, 1933, 1934, 1935, 1936. London: Oxford University Press.
Toynbee, Arnold and G.M. Urban. *Toynbee on Toynbee.* New York: Oxford University Press, 1974.
Vansittart, Lord (Sir Robert Vansittart). *Lessons of My Life.* New York: Alfred A. Knopf, 1943.

————. *The Mist Procession.* London: Hutchinson, 1958.

Villari, Luigi. *Italian Foreign Policy Under Mussolini.* New York: Devin-Adair, 1956.

Voigt, F.A. *Unto Caesar.* New York: G.P. Putnam, 1938.

Waley, Daniel P. *British Public Opinion and the Abyssinian War.* London: Maurice Temple Smith, 1975.

Walters, F.P. *A History of the League of Nations.* London:Oxford University Press, 1952.

Warner, Geoffrey. *Pierre Laval and the Eclipse of France.* New York: Macmillan, 1968.

Watt, D.C. "The Anglo-German Naval Agreement of 1935, An Interim Assessment." *Journal of Modern History,* June, 1956.

————. "The Secret Laval-Mussolini Agreement of 1935 on Ethiopia." *The Middle East Journal,* Winter, 1961.

Weinberg, Gerald. *The Foreign Policy of Hitler's Germany.* Chicago: University of Chicago Press, 1970.

Wilson, Duncan. *Leonard Woolf, A Political Biography.* New York: St. Martin's Press, 1978.

Williams, Frances. *A Prime Minister Remembers.* London: Heineman, 1961.

Windrich, Elaine. *British Labour's Foreign Policy.* Stanford, Cal.: Stanford University Press, 1952.

Wiskeman, Elizabeth. *Europe of the Dictators.* New York: Harper & Row, 1966.

Wolfers, Arnold. *Britain and France Between Two Wars.* New York: W.W. Norton, 1966.

Woolf, Leonard. *The Intelligent Man's Guide to Peace.* London: Gollancz, 1933.

Yates, Louis R. *United States and French Security.* New York: Twayne Publications, 1957.

Young, G.M. *Stanley Baldwin.* London: Rupert Hart-Davis, 1952.

Index

Abyssinia. *See* Italo-Abyssinian relations
Acland, Sir Francis, 166, 167
Allen, Clifford, 46, 150, 152, 236, 252, 256
Aloisi, Baron, 138, 229, 296, 302–3
Amery, Leopold, 245
Angell, Sir Norman, 49, 187, 188–89
Anglo-German relations
  British politics, 141–42
  and Disarmament Conference, 109–10, 114–15, 117
  government response to, 159–72
    British elections, 160–62
    economic sanctions, 166–67
    to German rearmament, 160–71
  knowledge of, 142–49
    concentration camps, 143
    Eastern Europe, 145–46
    German elections, 143
    German rearmament, 143–45, 146–49
  Naval Agreement, 290, 308–15
    and France, 310–11, 311–15, 322–24, 326–27
    and Italy, 312–13, 314
  public response to, 149–59
    apathy, 155–56
    to British policy, 152–53
    disarmament, 150
    to French policy, 151–52
    Hitler support, 150–51
    Labour Party, 156–59
    pacifism, 153–55
Archbishop of Canterbury, 58, 85, 95, 187, 222, 329, 330
Archbishop of York, 86, 95, 187, 188, 222
  Anglo-German Naval Agreement
    and France, 310–11, 311–15, 322–

24, 326–27
  and Germany, 290, 308–15
  and Great Britain, 290, 308–15, 322–24, 326–27
  and Italy, 312–13, 314
and France
  economics of, 305
  Franco-Soviet Treaty of Mutual Assistance, 288–89
  and Italo-Abyssinian relations, 289–90, 302–5, 317–20
  politics of, 305–6
and Germany, 298–302
  air force, 290
and Great Britain
  and Italo-Abyssinian relations, 291–98, 302–5, 317–22
  politics of, 306–7
Italo-Abyssinian relations
  and France, 289–90, 302–5, 317–20
  and Great Britain, 291–98, 302–5, 317–22
  and League of Nations, 288–89, 290–91, 295–96
  Maffey report, 320–22, 339
  and Peace Ballot, 287–88, 308
  and public opinion, 287, 314
  Zeila proposal, 319–20, 322–25, 326
Attlee, Clement, 163, 165, 243, 244, 250, 290, 301–2, 323
Austria, 16, 17, 46
  and Adolf Hitler, 69, 71, 75, 117–19, 120–23, 342–43
  and Peace Ballot, 339
Avenol, Joseph, 229, 293

Badoglio, Pietro, 213, 327
Balabanoff, Angelica, 36
Baldwin, Stanley, 10, 48, 306

and Anglo-German relations, 141–42,
    159, 160–61, 163, 164, 165–
    66, 167, 168, 170
and armaments, 96, 290, 301, 302
British White Paper, 243, 244
German reparations, 29
Peace Ballot, 193, 330–31, 332–33,
    342
and Rhineland, 235
war attitude, 50
Balfour, Arthur, 10
Baratieri, Oreste, 207
Barrymore, Ethel, 188
Barrymore, John, 188
Barthou, Louis, 115, 126–32
    and Eastern Security Pact, 128–31
    and Italy, 130–31
    and Soviet Union, 128–30
    and Yugoslavia, 130–32
Barton, Sir Sydney, 229, 230, 274
Baumont, Maurice, 127
Bavaria, 69
Beaverbrook, Lord, 198
Belgium, 4, 30
Benes, Eduard, 138, 146, 259
Bentham, Jeremy, 53
Blomberg, General von, 100, 107, 248
Blood Purge, 148, 150–51
Blum, Leon, 247
BonarLaw, Andrew, 48
Bonnet, Georges, 281
Boorman, A. J., 7–9
    Ilford Poll, 8–9
Boothby, Sir Robert, 149
Borromeo, Vitaliano, 271
Brown, Joe E., 188
Brüning, Chancellor, 83–84, 91, 93–94,
    118
Buck, Pearl, 188
Butler, Nicholas Murray, 42, 188

Canada, 1, 27–28
Capitalism, 47
Cazalet, Captain, 166
Cecil, Lord Robert, 7, 15
    and armaments, 47, 88, 91, 287–88
    background of, 9–13
    British White Paper, 242, 246
    and Christianity, 11
    Disarmament Conference, 87, 88
    Ilford ballot, 9, 191

League of Nations, 9, 10–11, 13, 27,
    28, 56–58, 190, 238
    Covenant, 19, 20
    on Louis Barthou, 127
    National Declaration Committee, 13
    Peace Ballot, 13–14, 55, 57, 58, 115–
        16, 173–82, 185, 186, 189,
        193–94, 218, 232, 239, 283,
        287–88, 328–35, 337–38, 340,
        343
    Treaty of Locarno, 30
    Treaty of Mutual Assistance, 30, 86–
        87
Cecil, William, 9
Chamberlain, Neville, 48, 167, 307
Chamberlain, Sir Austen
    British White Paper, 245
    Peace Ballot, 197
    Treaty of Locarno, 30
Chautemps, Camille, Prime Minister, 125
Christianity, 11, 85–86
    and Peace Ballot, 180
Churchill, Winston
    on Abyssinia, 216–17
    and Anglo-German relations, 162,
        164, 165, 168–69, 170
    and armaments, 60, 93, 96, 162, 252–
        53, 290, 301
    Blood Purge, 148
    MacDonald Plan, 110
    and war avoidance, 5
    on World War I, 49–50
Ciano, Galeazzo, 42
Cimmaruta, Captain, 204, 274
Claussat, Dr., 133, 134
Clemenceau, Georges
    Fourteen Points Program, 16, 18–19
    German reparations, 29
    League of Nations Covenant, 19
    Treaty of Guaranty, 21–22, 25, 221
    Treaty of Locarno, 30
Clerk, Sir George, 312–13, 314
Clifford, E. H. M., 201–2, 203, 204, 229,
    318–19
    Stresa Conference, 263, 265
Colson, Everett, 212
Communism, 72, 84, 102–3
Cooper, Duff, 197
Courtenay, K. D., 331–32
Cripps, Sir Stafford, 158, 166, 246, 250
Culles, Winifred, 187

Cummings, Homer, 188
Curzon, Lord, 22, 55
Czechoslovakia, 16, 46

Daladier, Edouard, Prime Minister, 125
Delafield, E. M., 187
Davies, Lord, 187
Davis, Norman, 97
Dawes, Charles Gates, 29
Dawson, Geoffrey, 150, 159, 307
de Bono, General Emilio, 213, 260
de Chambrun, Charles, 267
de Gaulle, Charles, 247
d'Esperey, Franchet, 211
Dickenson, Lord, 290–91
Dingman, Mary, 87
Disarmament Conference (1932)
    assessment of, 97–98, 116, 119
    and France, 89–90, 92, 94–95, 98,
        109–10, 112–16
    and Germany, 90–92, 94–96, 97, 98,
        108–17
        Anglo-German relations, 109–10,
            114–15, 117
        Franco-German relations, 109–10,
            112–16
        and League of Nations, 112–13
        MacDonald Plan, 110–12
        and Poland, 114
        withdrawal of, 8, 112–13
    and Great Britain, 86, 90, 91, 94, 109–
        10, 114–15, 117
    and Ilford Poll, 8
    and international events
        German elections, 93–94, 96–97
        Manchuria invasion, 88–89, 92–93,
            96, 98
    and Lord Robert Cecil, 87, 88
    opening of, 85–88
    party positions, 89–92
    and reparations, 94–95, 98
    and Rhineland demilitarization, 98
    and United States, 90, 94
Dollfuss, Engelbert
    assassination of, 122, 148, 167, 213
    Italian support of, 120–21
    and Social Democratic Party, 120–21
Doumergue, Gaston, 115, 126, 132, 133,
    137
Drummond, Sir Eric, 229, 253, 263, 280
    and Italian relations, 293, 294, 295,

        296–98, 302–3, 317–20
    Peace Ballot, 317–18

Eastern Security Pact, 128–31, 138, 255
Economics
    capitalism, 47
    and France, 305
    and Germany, 3
        and Adolf Hitler, 67–68, 84, 101
        and Great Britain, 47–48
Economic sanctions
    and France
        Stresa Conference, 267, 275, 281–82
    and Great Britain, 166–67
        Stresa Conference, 276
    and League of Nations, 27–28
Eden, Anthony, 48, 306
    Anglo-German Naval Agreement, 308,
        322–28
    and armaments, 106–7, 291
    British White Paper, 241, 246
    and Eastern Europe, 138, 255
    and Italian relations, 285–86, 294,
        295–296, 302–4
    League of Nations, 32
    on Louis Barthou, 127
    Peace Ballot, 196
    Rhineland, 254, 258
    Stresa Conference, 263, 272, 280
    war attitude, 50, 109–10, 114–15
Elections
    Germany, 93–94, 96–97, 102–3, 143
    Great Britain, 160–62
    Peace Ballot organization, 182–86
Elliot, Canon Thompson, 194
Enabling Act, 103–4
Eyres-Monsell, Sir Bolton, 301

Facta, Luigi, 39
Farley, James A., 188
Fascism, 33, 34, 38–41
    and Italo-Abyssinian relations, 216–18
Feder, Gottfried, 66
Ferber, Edna, 188
Fisher, H. A. L., 187
Flandin, Pierre-Etienne, 115, 227–28,
    233, 305
    British White Paper, 247
    Stresa Conference, 271, 274, 275–76,
        280
Foch, Marshal, 17, 19

Fosdick, Reverend Harry Emerson, 188
Four Power Pact, 119–20
Fourteen Points Program, 15–16, 17–18
Fracassi, Signor, 264–65, 284–85
France
    and Adolf Hitler, 76, 109–10, 112–16
    and arms control (1935)
        Anglo-German Naval Agreement,
            310–11, 311–15, 322–24, 326–
            27
        and economics, 305
        Franco-Soviet Treaty of Mutual
            Assistance, 288–89
        Italo-Abyssinian relations, 289–90,
            302–5
        and politics, 305–6
    and Disarmament Conference, 89–90,
        92, 94–95, 98, 109–10, 112–16
    dominions of, 1
    Four Power Pact, 119–20
    and Italo-Abyssinian relations, 208,
        317–20
    arms control (1935), 289–90, 302–5
    Franco-Italian alliance, 221–28
    French military build-up, 242, 247–
        48
    General Settlement, 237–39
    and German threat, 217–21, 222–
        23, 225
    and Italian threat, 220
    Lake Tana dam, 210
    national security, 1–3
    dissolution of, 3–6
    and reparations, 16, 29, 32
    and Stresa Conference
        and Anglo-German alliance, 266
        economic sanctions, 267, 275, 281–
            82
        German rearmament, 266–67, 274–
            75, 277–78, 279
        Rhineland demilitarization, 266–67,
            275–76, 278
    Three Power Declaration, 121
    and Treaty of Guaranty, 22, 25
    and Treaty of Locarno, 2, 30
    and Treaty of Versailles
        military protection, 2
        Rhineland demilitarization, 2, 4–5
Franco-German relations
    British perspective of, 127–28, 130

Disarmament Conference, 109–10,
    112–16
Eastern Security Pact, 128–31
Four Power Pact, 119–20
French politics, 125–26
and Italy, 130–31
and Louis Barthou, 126–32
and Pierre Laval, 132–39
Rhineland demilitarization
    and Disarmament Conference, 98
    German reoccupation, 4–5, 32
    and peace efforts, 16, 17, 21–22, 25
    and Stresa Conference, 266–67,
        275–76, 278
    and Versailles Treaty, 2, 4–5
and Soviet Union, 128–30, 138–139
and Yugoslavia, 130–32, 138
Francois-Poncet, Andre, 137, 256, 266,
    326

Gable, Clark, 188
Gabreishu, Fitaurari, 207
Gamelin, General, 327
General Act for the Pacific Settlement of
    International Disputes, 31
General Settlement, 237–39
Geneva Act, 55
Geneva Protocol, 30, 55, 87
German Worker's Party, 66
Germany. See also Anglo-German
        relations; Franco-German
        relations; Hitler, Adolf
    air force, 2, 4, 290
    and arms control (1935), 298–302
        Anglo-German Naval Agreement,
            290, 308–15
    army, 2, 4
    and Disarmament Conference, 90–92,
        94–96, 97, 98, 108–17
    and France, 109–10, 112–16
    and Great Britain, 109–10, 114–15,
        117
    and League of Nations, 112–13
    MacDonald Plan, 110–12
    and Poland, 114
    withdrawal from, 8, 112–13
    economics, 3
    and Adolf Hitler, 67–68, 84, 101
    elections, 93–94, 96–97, 102–3, 143
    Four Power Pact, 119–20

and Italo-Abyssinian relations
British alliance, 250–59
rearmament, 213, 215, 217–20,
241–42, 243–45, 248–59
threat to France, 217–21, 222–23,
225
threat to Great Britain, 217–21, 231,
233–37, 241–42
navy, 4, 5
Anglo-German Naval Agreement,
290, 308–15
High Seas Fleet, 2, 17
rearmament of, 31–32, 77–78, 100–
101
and Disarmament Conference, 108–
17
and Italo-Abyssinian relations, 213,
215, 217–20, 241–42, 243–45,
248–59
and Stresa Conference, 264, 266–
67, 274–75, 277–78, 279
and reparations, 16, 29, 32
Rome-Berlin Axis, 5
and Treaty of Guaranty, 21–22, 25
and Treaty of Locarno, 2, 30
and Treaty of Versailles
military restrictions, 2
Rhineland demilitarization, 2, 4–5
Ghandi, Mahatma, 53
Gibbs, Phillip, 156
Goering, Hermann, 69, 102–103, 107,
243, 314
Gould, Mrs. Ayrton, 242–43
Grandi, Dino, 60, 231, 280, 284, 285–86
Graves, Robert, 48
Grayson, Admiral Cary T., 24
Great Britain
and Adolf Hitler, 76, 109–10, 114–15,
117
and arms control (1935)
Anglo-German Naval Agreement,
290, 308–15, 322–24, 326–27
British politics, 306–7
German air force, 290
Italo-Abyssinian relations, 291–98,
302–5
and Disarmament Conference, 86, 90,
91, 94, 109–10, 114–15, 117
dominions of, 1
Four Power Pact, 119–20
and Italo-Abyssinian relations

arms control (1935), 291–98, 302–5
British expansion, 212
British military build-up, 242–47
British non-commitment, 229–32
compromise between, 317–20, 324–
26
French military build-up, 242, 247–
48
General Settlement, 237–39
German alliance, 250–59
and German threat, 217–21, 231,
233–37, 241–42
and Italian threat, 220
Lake Tana dam, 210
Maffey report, 320–22, 339
Wal Wal incident, 202–5
White Paper, 241–48
national security, 1–3
dissolution of, 3–6
peace efforts, 15, 17, 21–22, 25
Royal Navy, 2, 17
and Stresa Conference
Abyssinia, 268, 273, 280, 284–86
British non-commitment, 276–77,
278–79, 328
economic sanctions, 276
German alliance, 268–70
German rearmament, 274–75, 279
Rhineland demilitarization, 270
Three Power Declaration, 121
and Treaty of Guaranty, 22, 25
and Treaty of Locarno, 2, 30
Great Britain, postwar attitudes
armaments, 47
capitalism, 47
economics, 47–48
and France, 47
future war prospect, 49–52
and Germany
blame on, 45
sympathy for, 46
human loss, 48–49
Marxism, 47
nationalism, 47
peace efforts, 53–60
and Labour Party, 53, 54, 59
and League of Nations, 54–56
and League of Nations Union, 56–
58
and Socialism, 54
reparations, 45–46

Green, James, 88
Guarnaschelli, Signor, 273, 280

Haldane, J. B. S., 187
Hammerstein-Equord, General von, 100
Hankey, Sir Maurice, 165, 167, 181
Hardwicke, Sir Cedric, 187
Hart, B. H. Liddell, 146
Hayes, Cardinal, 188
Headlam-Morley, Sir James, 60
Henderson, Arthur, 48, 59, 111, 116,
    160, 187
Henderson, Sir Nevile, 45, 153
Herriot, Edouard, 115, 129
Hess, Rudolf, 70, 81
High Seas Fleet, 2, 17
Hindenburg, Oskar, 99
Hindenburg, Paul von, 3, 83–84, 94, 96–
    97, 99–100
  and elections, 93
Hitler, Adolf, 3–4
  and Austria, 69, 71, 75, 117–19, 120–
    23, 342–43
  background of
    education, 62–63
    military service, 64–65
  and Bavaria, 69
  and Benito Mussolini, 117–23
    attitude toward, 77
    Four Power Pact, 119–20
    Three Power Declaration, 121
  and Disarmament Conference, 108–17
    and France, 109–10, 112–16
    and Great Britain, 109–10, 114–15,
      117
    and League of Nations, 112–13
    MacDonald Plan, 110–12
    and Poland, 114
    withdrawal from, 8, 112–13
  foreign policy of, 74–78
    methodology for, 78–83
    and France, 76, 109–10, 112–16
    and Great Britain, 76, 109–10, 114–
      15, 117
  ideology of
    centralized power, 68
    Communism, 72, 84, 102–3
    economics, 67–68, 84, 101
    Jews, 64, 67
    media, 68
    Mein Kampf, 68, 71–72, 74, 81–82

    nationalism, 61, 64
    natural law, 73–74
    race, 71–72
    social programs, 68
    war, 61–62
  and Italy, 77, 117–23
    as ally, 4, 5
  and Marxism, 73
  oratory of, 80
  political ascent, 83–84
    Chancellor appointment, 99–100
  political consolidation, 102–8
    Enabling Act, 103–4
    Law Against the Formation of New
      Parties, 104–5
    Law Concerning the Head of the
      German State, 108
    SA forces, 106–7
    and Socialism, 105–6
  political introduction, 65–67
    German Worker's Party, 66
    National Socialist Worker's Party,
      67
  and propaganda, 78–79
  and rearmament, 4, 77–78, 100–101
    and Disarmament Conference, 108–
      17
  and Rhineland reoccupation, 4–5, 32
Hoare, Sir Samuel, 306–7, 312–15, 342
Hobbs, Jack, 187
Holmes, Reverend John Haynes, 188
Hoover, Herbert, 188
  and armaments, 94, 95
Hutchinson, Lord, 301
Ilford Poll, 8–9, 190–91

Inskip, Sir Thomas, 187
Italo-Abyssinian relations
  Abyssinian governance, 206–7, 208–9,
    211, 212, 213
  Abyssinian history, 205–7
  arms control (1935)
    and France, 289–90, 302–5
    and Great Britain, 291–98, 302–5
  and Fascism, 216–18
  and France, 208, 317–20
    arms control (1935), 289–90, 302–5
    Franco-Italian alliance, 221–28
    General Settlement, 237–39
    German threat to, 217–21, 222–23,
      225

Italian threat to, 220
Lake Tana dam, 210
military build-up, 242, 247–48
German-British alliance, 250–59
German rearmament, 213, 215, 217–
20, 241–42, 243–45, 248–59
German threat
to France, 217–21, 222–23, 225
to Great Britain, 217–21, 231, 233–
37, 241–42
and Great Britain
arms control (1935), 291–98, 302–5
British expansion, 212
compromise of, 317–20, 324–26
French military build-up, 242, 247–
48
General Settlement, 237–39
German alliance with, 250–59
German threat to, 217–21, 231,
233–37, 241–42
Italian threat to, 220
Lake Tana dam, 210
Maffey report, 320–22, 339
military build-up, 242–47
non-commitment of, 229–32
Stresa Conference, 268, 273, 280,
284–86
Wal Wal incident, 202–5
White Paper, 241–48
and League of Nations, 209, 210, 214–
15, 231–32, 259–61
and Peace Ballot, 232, 239–41, 242
and Stresa Conference, 264–65, 273,
280, 282–83, 284–86
and Great Britain, 268, 273, 280,
284–86
Treaty of Friendship, 210–11, 212–13
Treaty of Ucciali, 206–7
Wal Wal incident, 202–5, 214–15
war preparation, 213–16
Italy. *See also* Mussolini, Benito
and Adolf Hitler, 4, 5, 77, 117–23
and Anglo-German Naval Agreement,
312–13, 314
Four Power Pact, 119–20
and Franco-German relations, 130–31
as German ally, 4, 5
Rome-Berlin Axis, 5
and Stresa Conference
Abyssinia, 264–65, 273, 280, 282–
83, 284–86

Anglo-German alliance, 263
German rearmament, 264, 274–75,
277–78, 279
Three Power Declaration, 121
and Treaty of Locarno, 2, 30

Japan
Manchuria invasion, 3, 8, 88–89, 92–
93, 96, 98
Pearl Harbor, 3
Jews, 64, 67
John IV, 206
Jones, Bobby, 188
Jones, Thomas, 146, 153, 219

Kaas, Monsignor, 102, 104
Kahr, Gustav von, 69–70
Kiddermaster, Sir H. Baxter, 211
Kellogg-Briand Pact (1927), 31, 109
Kennedy, Margaret, 187
Kerr, Phillip, 46
Keyes, Admiral Sir Roger, 162
Keynes, John Maynard, 18, 46
King Alexander, 131–32, 138, 222
King George V, 42, 45, 210
King Ludwig III, 65
King Solomon, 205, 341
King Victor Emmanuel III, 224
Knight, Dame Laura, 187

Labour Party
postwar attitudes, 53, 54, 59
response to Germany, 156–59
LaFollette, Robert, 188
LaGuardia, Fiorello, 188
Lake Tana dam, 210
Lambton, Lady Eleanor, 11
Lansbury, George, 46, 152–53, 160
armaments, 253, 290
war attitude, 51
Laval, Pierre, 115
Anglo-German Naval Agreement,
312–15, 323–27
background on, 132–37
Franco-German relations, 220–21,
250–51, 342
Franco-Italian relations, 222–230, 233,
259, 292, 296, 302–6
Franco-Soviet relations, 138–39, 288–
90
Stresa Conference, 253, 266–67, 271,
274–279

and Yugoslavia, 138
Law Against the Formation of New
    Parties, 104–5
Law Concerning the Head of the German
    State, 108
League of Nations
    arms control (1935), 288–89, 290–91,
        295–96
    and Canada, 27–28
    Covenant of, 3, 17, 18, 19–20
    Disarmament Conference, 112–13
    and France, 28–29
    and Great Britain, 29
    Ilford Poll, 7–8
    and international objectives, 27–28
    and Italo-Abyssinian relations, 209,
        210, 214–15, 231–32, 259–61
    and Italy, 28
    and Lord Robert Cecil, 9, 10–11, 13,
        27, 28, 56–58, 190, 238
    Peace Ballot, 13, 58, 173–78, 180
    and postwar British attitudes, 54–58
    and reparations, 29
    and sanctions, 27–28
    and Soviet Union, 128–30
    spirit of, 32
    Stresa Conference, 281–83
    Treaty of Locarno, 30
    Union of, 7, 13, 56–58, 173–78, 180
Leger, Alexis, 227, 312
Lenin, Vladimir, 128
Lindsay, A. D., 187
Little Entente, 128, 138, 166, 214, 222–23
Litvinov, Maxim, 129, 138, 282
Lloyd George, Dame Margaret, 175
Lloyd George, David
    and armaments, 47
    British war aims, 15
    German reparations, 29
    and Rhineland, 17, 21
    Treaty of Guaranty, 21
Lodge, Henry Cabot, 22–23, 24, 25
Lothian, Lord, 46, 153, 252, 291
Lowell, Abbott Lawrence, 188
Lausanne Conference on Reparations,
    94–95
Ludendorff, Erich Friedrich Wilhelm,
    69–70
Ludwig, Emil, 41
Lytton, Lord, 89, 196
Lytton Commission, 93, 96, 98

Macaulay, Rose, 187
MacDonald, Ramsay, 306
    and Anglo-German relations, 141–42,
        159
    and armaments, 290
    German reparations, 29
    and Italian relations, 285
    Stresa Conference, 271–72, 274–276,
        278, 279, 281, 328
    war attitude, 59
MacDonald Plan, 110–12
Mackensen, Field Marshal von, 248
Maffey, Sir John, 211, 212, 231, 321
    Stresa Conference, 265
Maffey report, 320–22, 339
Malleson, Miles, 187
Manchuria invasion (1931–1932), 3, 8,
    88–89, 92–93, 96, 98
Marxism, 47, 73
Massigli, Rene, 293
Matteotti, Giacomo, 40
Maurice, Emil, 70
Media, 68
Mein Kampf (Hitler), 68, 71–72, 74, 81–
    82
Menelik, 206–7, 208
Menelik II, 10
Milne, A. A., 154–55, 156, 187
Mitchell, Margaret, 188
Morrison, Herbert, 250, 301
Mottistone, Lord, 291
Muggeridge, Malcolm, 151–52
Murray, Gilbert, 28, 32, 55–56, 57, 110
Mussolini, Benito. See also Italo-
    Abyssinian relations; Italy
    and Adolf Hitler, 4, 117–23
        attitude toward, 77
        Four Power Pact, 119–20
        Three Power Declaration, 121
    background of, 35–36, 42
    and Fascism, 33, 34, 38–41, 216–18
    political evolution of, 36–43
        dictatorship, 40–43
        Fascism, 38–41
        Socialism, 36–38, 39, 40–41
    and Treaty of Locarno, 33–34
    war attitude, 50–51

Nagurski, Bronko, 188
Napier, Sir Robert, 206, 210
Nationalism

and Adolf Hitler, 61, 64
and Great Britain, 47
National Socialist Worker's Party, 67,
    102–3
Natural law, 73–74
Neurath, Baron von, 120, 255
Nichols, Beverly, 51–52, 53
Nicholson, Harold, 18–19, 197
Night of the Long Knives, 107
Noel-Baker, Phillip, 9
Norris, George W., 188

O'Keefe, Georgia, 188
Optional Clause, 55

Pacifism, 153–55
Palmerston, Lord, 206
Papen, Franz von, 3, 97
    Chancellorship of, 94, 99–100
    resignation of, 96
    as Vienna ambassador, 122–23
Paris Pact, 109
Peace Ballot (1934). *See also* Cecil, Lord
    Robert
    and arms control (1935), 287–88, 308
    and Christianity, 180
    election organization, 182–86
    endorsement, 186–89
    future effects, 341–43
    and Italo-Abyssinian relations, 232,
        239–41, 242
    and League of Nations Union, 13, 58,
        173–78, 180
    opponents, 196–98
    and public opinion, 179, 186
    questions of, 13–14, 178, 189–95,
        335–41
    and Stresa Conference, 283–84
    vote counting, 195–96
    vote returns, 198–99, 281, 335–41
Peace efforts, post World War I. *See also*
        Arms control (1935); Disarma-
        ment Conference (1932);
        Stresa Conference (1935)
    France, 16–17, 18–19
        and reparations, 16
        Rhineland demilitarization, 16, 17,
            21–22, 25
        Treaty of Guaranty, 22, 25
    Germany, 16
        Rhineland demilitarization, 16, 17,
            21–22

Treaty of Guaranty, 21–22, 25
    Great Britain, 15, 17, 21–22
        Treaty of Guaranty, 22, 25
    Italy, 17
    League of Nations Covenant, 17, 18,
        19–20
    Treaty of Guaranty, 21–25
        and France, 22, 25
        and Germany, 21–22, 25
        and Great Britain, 22, 25
        and United States, 21–25
    United States
        Fourteen Points Program, 15–16,
            17–18, 25
        Treaty of Guaranty, 21–25
Peale, Reverend Norman Vincent, 188
Pearl Harbor, 3
Phipps, Sir Eric, 141, 146–47, 149
Poland, 16, 114
Ponsonby, Lord, 158
Poor Prisoners Defense Act (1903), 12
Price, G. Ward, 113
Propaganda, 78–79
Public opinion, 9, 179, 186
    and arms control (1935), 287, 314
    and Stresa Conference, 283–84, 286
Pu Yi, Henry, 93

Queen Elizabeth, 9
Queen of Sheba, 205, 341
Queen Victoria, 9
Queen Zauditu, 208, 211

Race, 71–72
Ras Hailu, 209
Ras Makonnen, 207, 208
Ras Mangushu, 207
Ras Mikail, 207, 211
Ras Seyoum, 209
Ras Tafari, 208–11
Ras Wule, 207, 211
Rava, Maurizio, 204
Remarque, Erich Maria, 48–49
Reparations, 16, 29, 32, 45–46
    and Disarmament Conference, 94–95,
        98
Reynaud, Paul, 247
Rhineland, demilitarization of
    German reoccupation, 4–5, 32
    and peace efforts, 16, 17, 21–22, 25
    Disarmament Conference, 98

Versailles Treaty, 2, 4–5
and Stresa Conference
British issues, 270
French issues, 266–67, 275–76, 278
Ribbentrop, Joachim von, 308–11
Rigott, Reverend W. Chanter, 86
Rochester, Lord, 187
Rockefeller, John D., 45
Roehm, Ernst, 68, 106, 107
Rome-Berlin Axis, 5
Roosevelt, Theodore, 110–11
Rowse, A. L., 153, 159
Royal Navy, 2, 17
Royden, Maude, 247
Rumbold, Sir Horace, 142–45, 146, 147, 150
Ruth, Babe, 188

Salandra, Antonio, 39–40
Salter, Sir Arthur, 187
Samantar, Omar, 202–3, 214
Samuel, Sir Herbert, 164–65, 187, 244–45, 290, 308
Sanctions. See Economic sanctions
Sandys, Duncan, 243, 247
Sarfati, Margarita, 36, 42
Sassoon, Siegfried, 48
Schleicher, Kurt von3
Chancellorship of, 97, 99
and Hitler's power, 93, 107
Schuschnigg, Kurt, 123
Selassie, Haile
Italo-Abyssinian relations and, 201, 202, 204, 205, 211, 212, 213, 214, 223, 229, 282, 341
Selborne, Lord, 56
Shearer, Norma, 188
Sheppard, Reverend Dick, 154, 171–72, 187
Sheriff, R. C., 48
Shiferra, Fitaurari, 203, 204
Simon, Kathleen, 209
Simon, Sir John, 306
Anglo-German Naval Agreement, 308–9, 311, 313, 314
Anglo-German relations, 169, 170–71, 241, 250–51, 254–55, 256
and armaments, 90, 257–58, 290
Eastern Security Pact, 129–30
Italo-Abyssinian relations, 231, 284, 285, 291–94

Locarno Treaty, 234
MacDonald Plan, 112
Peace Ballot, 317
Stresa Conference, 253, 263, 266, 270, 272, 274–278, 280–81, 282, 283, 328
Simpson, Major, 211
Socialism
and Adolf Hitler, 105–6
and Benito Mussolini, 36–38, 39, 40–41
and postwar British attitudes, 54
Social programs, 68
Soviet Union, 3
and Franco-German relations, 138–139
and League of Nations, 128–30
Franco-Soviet Treaty of Mutual Assistance, 288–89
and Stresa Conference, 277
Stalin, Joseph, 128–29, 258, 289
Stavisky, Serge, 125
Stimson, Henry L., 188
Strasser, Gregor, 107
Stresa Conference (1935)
arrangements for, 270–72
British issues
Abyssinia, 268, 273, 280, 284–86
economic sanctions, 276
German alliance, 268–70
German rearmament, 274–75, 279
non-commitment, 276–77, 278–79, 328
Rhineland demilitarization, 270
French issues
Anglo-German alliance, 266
economic sanctions, 267, 275, 281–82
German rearmament, 266–67, 274–75, 277–78, 279
Rhineland demilitarization, 266–67, 275–76, 278
German reaction to, 281, 282
Italian issues
Abyssinia, 264–65, 273, 280, 282–83, 284–86
Anglo-German alliance, 263
German rearmament, 264, 274–75, 277–78, 279
League of Nations resolutions, 281–83
and Peace Ballot, 283–84
and public opinion, 283–84, 286

and Soviet Union, 277
Stuelpnagel, General, 31
Sueter, Rear Admiral Sir Murray, 162–
    63
Summerskill, Edith, 169
Suvich, Fulvio, 250, 254
Symes, Sir Stewart, 211

Tardieu, Andre, 115, 125, 136
Temperly, Brigadier, 145, 149, 150
Theodore II, 206
Thomas, J. A., 187
Thompson, Geoffrey, 264–65, 273, 284–
    85
Three Power Declaration, 121
Thyssen, Fritz, 84
Tiedge, Ernst, 105
Tilden, Bill, 188
Torres, Henri, 137
Toscanini, Arturo, 39
Toynbee, Arnold J.
    on Abyssinia, 207
    on Anglo-German relations, 146
    on Louis Barthou, 127–28, 131
    on Peace Ballot, 333
    on World War I, 49, 52
Treaty of Friendship, 210–11, 212–13
Treaty of Guaranty, 21–25
    and France, 22, 25
    and Germany, 21–22, 25
    and Great Britain, 22, 25
    and United States, 21–25
Treaty of Locarno, 2, 30
Treaty of Mutual Assistance, 30, 86–87
Treaty of Rome, 38
Treaty of Ucciali, 206–7
Treaty of Versailles, 1–2
    French military protection, 2
    German military restrictions, 2
    Rhineland demilitarization, 2, 4–5

United States
    and Disarmament Conference, 90, 94
    and Fourteen Points Program, 15–16,
        17–18, 25

and Treaty of Guaranty, 21–25

Vansittart, Sir Robert, 47, 48
    and Anglo-German relations, 145–46,
        147–48, 150, 165, 171–72,
        231, 315
    and armaments, 287
    and Franco-Italian relations, 227, 231,
        284, 296, 315, 318–19
    on Louis Barthou, 128
    Naval Treaty, 59
    Peace Ballot, 196–97, 318
    Rhineland occupation, 32
    Stresa Conference, 265, 268–70, 272,
        279, 280, 281
    Treaty of Locarno, 30
Vaughan-Morgan, Sir Kenyon, 160
Vitetti, Leonardo, 230–31, 264–65, 273,
    320

Wakefield, W. W., 187
Waldron, W. J., 160
Waldthaussen, Baron von, 211–12
Wal Wal incident, 202–5, 214–15
Weatherhead, Reverend Leslie, 86
Wheeler-Bennett, Sir John, 150
Wilbur, Ray Lyman, 188
Wilkinson, Ellen, 152
Wilmot, J. C., 160, 161, 163
Wilson, Woodrow, 9
    Fourteen Points Program, 15–16, 17–
        18, 113
    League of Nations Covenant, 19–20
    and Rhineland, 17, 21–22
    Treaty of Guaranty, 22–25
Wise, Rabbi Stephen S., 188
World War I, 1–2, 7. See also Peace
    efforts, post World War I
World War II, 5–6
Wynyard, Diana, 187

Young, G. M., 29
Yugoslavia, 130–32, 138

Zeila proposal, 319–20, 322–25, 326